南开哲学百年文萃（1919—2022）

南开大学中外文明交叉科学中心资助出版

总主编　翟锦程

通变古今　融汇中外

（科学技术哲学卷）

贾向桐　主编

南开大学出版社

天　津

图书在版编目(CIP)数据

通变古今 融汇中外.科学技术哲学卷 / 贾向桐主编.—天津:南开大学出版社,2023.3(2023.9 重印)
(南开哲学百年文萃:1919—2022 / 翟锦程总主编)
ISBN 978-7-310-06391-8

Ⅰ.①通… Ⅱ.①贾… Ⅲ.①技术哲学－文集 Ⅳ.①B－53②N02－53

中国国家版本馆 CIP 数据核字(2023)第 002227 号

通变古今 融汇中外(科学技术哲学卷)
TONGBIAN GUJIN RONGHUI ZHONGWAI(KEXUE JISHU ZHEXUE JUAN)

南开大学出版社出版发行
出版人:陈　敬
地址:天津市南开区卫津路 94 号　　邮政编码:300071
营销部电话:(022)23508339　营销部传真:(022)23508542
https://nkup.nankai.edu.cn

天津创先河普业印刷有限公司印刷　全国各地新华书店经销
2023 年 3 月第 1 版　　2023 年 9 月第 2 次印刷
230×170 毫米　16 开本　19 印张　2 插页　311 千字
定价:99.00 元

如遇图书印装质量问题,请与本社营销部联系调换,电话:(022)23508339

出版说明

一、2022 年是南开哲学学科建立 103 年，建系 100 周年，哲学院（系）重建 60 周年。为全面展现南开哲学百年来的发展进程和历史底蕴，特编选出版"南开哲学百年文萃（1919—2022）"。

二、本文萃的编选范围是自 1919 年南开大学设立哲学门以来，在南开哲学学科任教教师所发表的代表性论文，并按现行一级学科的分类标准，分马克思主义哲学、中国哲学、外国哲学、逻辑学、伦理学、美学、宗教学、科学技术哲学八个专集编辑出版。

三、本文萃编务组通过各种方式比较全面地汇集了在南开哲学学科任教的教师名单，但由于 1952 年以来的历史档案和线索不甚完整，难免有所遗漏。如有此情况，专此致歉。

四、本文萃列入南开大学中外文明交叉科学中心 2022 年度支持计划。

五、本文萃在编辑过程中，得到校内外各界人士的全力支持，在此一并致谢。

六、本文萃所收录文章由于时间跨度大、发表于不同刊物以及原出版物辨识困难等原因，难免有文字错误及体例格式不统一等问题，敬请读者谅解。

南开大学哲学院

2022 年 10 月

前 言

近代以来，科学技术成为人类社会关注的一个重要议题，而哲学作为时代精神的精华，亦将其视为最关键的研究内容之一。特别是 20 世纪的五四运动以来，"德先生""赛先生"在我国逐步深入人心，在对自然科学的推崇和普及之外的深入反思也随之变得重要。在此境况下，科学与技术哲学的理论与现实意义同样是极为特殊的，是具有非常重要意义的。南开大学在立校之初就明确强调文以治国、理以强国、商以富国的公能教育理念，赋予科学教育救亡兴国的重任。但科学教育并不单纯就是对科学知识、科学理论或方法的灌输，南开教育很早就认识到要对自然科学本身进行全面的认识和反思，恰如张伯苓老校长所说的"不重玄想而重观察，不重讲解而重实验"；科学教育同时也意味着对科学自身的再思考和再教育。可以说，这种通识性的、文理兼容的科学教育理念逐渐形成了南开教育与学术研究的一大传统，为南开哲学的科学技术哲学发展奠定了基石和良好氛围，也为我们的相关研究指明了基本的方向和目标。

当然，对科学（技术）的反思不仅仅只是哲学的专利，许多其他学科也同样在做一些相关的研究工作，例如社会学、历史学、人类学乃至政治学、管理学等等也都深深牵涉到对自然科学本身的一系列理论思考。但相较而言，哲学对自然科学的反思无疑是最具代表性和一般性的，其透彻性的理性审视构成人们对科学基本理解的必要条件，也成为贯穿诸多学科实现跨越对话的基础。也正是在此意义上，科学技术哲学逐渐聚拢了一系列以自然科学本身为研究对象的学科，它们共同形成了广泛意义的科学技术哲学，应该说，较之于其母学科哲学，科学技术哲学具有更明显的跨学科特色。鉴于此，就有必要作一追问：何为科学技术哲学？对此，学界一直难以给出一个统一的、没有争议的回答，约翰·洛西颇有代表性地写道："不幸的是，哲学家和科学家并没有对科学哲学的本质达成一致意见。即使是专业的科学哲学家也经常对其学科的议题充满争议。"①

但这一点并不影响科学技术哲学本身的发展，它作为一个学科的历史和发展脉络还是非常清晰明确的，而且相关议题仍有着相对稳定的问题域，更为主要的是，这些研究均将视野置于对科学技术本性的追寻上，这些内容共同构成科学技术哲学的不可或缺的组成部分。在这里，我们不再专门为科学技术哲学给出一个明确的定义或概念，而是将其理解为一个历史性、发展性的社会文化现象，在动态的描述中通过几个视角或维度来展现它的本来面貌。

科学作为人类认识世界最成功有效的经典认知模式，早已经深入人心，所以人们在理解或界定科学的时候，"知识"或"认识"是第一个能够想到的。科学是对外部世界客观性的描述，是"反映自然、社会、思维等的客观规律的分科的知识体系"，"通过对事实、物理世界的观察和检验获得的，关于自然和社会规律的系统化知识"。②认识论是科学技术哲学研究最基本的探究进路，20世纪逻辑实证主义以来的标准科学哲学奠定了这一研究方式的主要范式。在科学认识论方面，我们选取的论文主要是从宏观整体的知识属性问题出发，结合科学理论的结构、科学定律属性以及科学模型等层面分析科学知识与认知方面的基本问题。其中，李建珊教授在《科学认识论的若干问题》中着眼于科学认识论的三个关键问题，即认识客体与仪器的属性以及主客体发生的同时性问题，主张要以科学活动为基础，从认识能动性和创造性相统一的机制进行探究才能揭示出科学认识的意义与价值。李祖扬教授的论文《经验定律的形成过程和发现模式——科学规律形成的认识论问题探讨之一》以经验定律的一般逻辑程序为起点，具体分析了经验定律的形成过程，进而总结出经验定律三种基本的发现模式并将其与理性和非理性思维实现了统一。阿基·莱蒂宁教授以虚拟关联词为对象，在《虚拟主张的三种类型》一文中详细分析了虚拟主张的基本模式以及其各种形下归因的是否确定性问题，而"各种类型的主张可以通过确定其潜在的'归因'来识别"。

科学与技术作为一种现实的社会活动这一观点已为人们所普遍认同，"科学是一项社会性的事业。那么看起来，为了理解这一事实我们需要转向

---

① John Losee. A Historical Introduction to the Philosophy of Science. Oxford University Press, 2001, p. 1.

② 可参见《现代汉语词典》商务印书馆 2020 年版，第 735 页；Oxford advanced learner's English-chinese dictionary, p. 1342。

的是社会学，对人类社会结构的一般性研究"①。应该说，从社会维度进行分析和研究也是实现对科学技术哲学反思的必要角度，而且，这一维度的研究自20世纪历史主义兴起以后影响越来越大，特别是在科学社会学和科学知识社会学发展起来之后，情况更是如此。这也是本书取材的重要视角，刘珺珺教授的论文《科学社会学的研究传统和现状》早在20世纪80年代就系统梳理了科学社会学的历史、研究传统、现状、基本进路和主张等重要问题，并对这些基本内容作了深入的剖析和整理。张俊心教授在《科学学理论发展与学科建设的紧迫问题》一文中结合我国的元科学研究状况，对科学学学科的定位和基本问题进行了系统分析，这些研究对20世纪八九十年代这门新兴学科的发展和建设具有一定的借鉴意义。柯礼文教授的《关于两类技术社会学》着眼于对技术问题的社会研究，特别是在广义技术社会学和狭义社会学相比较的语境下，提出了社会技术的集合理论，强调了"社会建构主义纲领可以继续采用，但要扩展视角——应以社会技术集合而不是技术作为未来社会的考察主体"的基本主张。牛叔成教授在《试论科学技术革命与社会革命的关系》的论文中，把科学技术革命和社会革命问题作了对照分析和比较，以马克思对科学技术生产力关系的论述为基础强调二者之间的"并行不悖，相互促进"关系。

科学技术哲学的研究是将科学技术置于具体社会环境之中进行的，而且科学不仅仅只是一种知识或认识形态，作为一种社会文化现象，对其历史、思想文化和价值的研究同样至关重要。宋斌在《近代科学革命时期基督教与科学的相互作用——以麦尔赛纳为例》中以迪昂研究为起点，重点探讨了亚里士多德自然哲学以及基督教的自然秩序思想的关系，并以自然主义兴起与机械论自然观的出现为标志展示了科学革命的内在根源。

科学技术哲学的议题是具有时代性的，伴随着自然科学以及哲学本身的发展，其自身总会演化出新的研究问题和方向，这亦是科学技术哲学能够保持鲜活生命活力的重要原因。在这方面，我们选择了数学哲学、社会科学哲学、人工智能哲学以及当代新先验论进路的发展等几个方面的论文，以便从多个不同视角透视科学技术哲学的当代发展情况。其中，任晓明教授等的《自我升级智能体的逻辑与认知问题》以人工智能的自我升级智能

---

① Peter Godfrey-Smith. Theory and Reality: an Introduction to the Philosophy of Science. The University of Chicago Press, 2003, p. 122.

体模型为研究对象，重点考察了其创生思想的演进、意义与风险以及破解困境等基本问题，提出了"从互斥到互补，进而达到融通的新境界。"佛兰西斯科·迪·爱奥里奥的《方法论个体主义、结构限制和社会复杂性》在比较方法论个体主义以及整体主义进路的基础上，从复杂的自组织系统视角提出了一种复杂的方法论个体主义主张，这一见解是"非还原的方法论个体主义的一个特定变种，它有助于将这种特定变种同还原论的个体主义和其他非还原论的方法论个体主义变种区分开来"。王琦的《波爱修斯的知识划分及后世影响》以波爱修斯对物理学、数学和神学知识的划分为思考起点，对照七艺的标准原则解析了波爱修斯在古典与中世纪转变过程中的特殊地位与意义。贾向桐的《论当代科学哲学动态先验论路径的实用主义阐释及其超越的可能性》在比较自然主义和先验论科学哲学路径过程中，主张借鉴实用主义来为动态先验论的探究方向辩护，并进而认为科学实践哲学可以提供这种结合的基础。胡瑞斌的《重复计算的方法论问题与意义》以重复计算问题为研究对象，进而解析了其背后存在的方法论问题与意义，"在最大化对数据利用程度方面，重复计算具有极大的优势。"麦基教授的《模型及其真实性所在》系统讨论了科学模型与真理性的关系问题，他认为可以通过功能分解的方法揭示科学模型孤立化表征的内在意义与价值。

　　试图用一本论文集来展现近几十年南开科学技术哲学的发展是难以完成的任务，我们在此过程中也只能做到以小见大，而管中窥豹的遗憾不可避免。但是，我们还是希望通过这一很小的"管孔"最大限度使得读者能够了解科学技术哲学，也为推动科学技术哲学做一点力所能及的工作。为此，在论文的选择和收集过程中，我们把文章的时代性和主题性作为重要的指向标准，特别强调了这些论文在当时相关研究领域的影响力和特色，同时也兼顾论文主题本身的意义和价值，并在此基础上努力折射和反映科学技术哲学研究的时代面貌。

目　录

科学社会学的研究传统和现状

刘珺珺[*]

　　早在 20 世纪 30 年代，年轻的社会学家默顿写下了著名的《十七世纪英国的科学技术与社会》（以下简称《十七世纪》），开始了对科学的社会研究。但是，科学这种社会现象并没有吸引很多社会学家的注意，直到 20 世纪的六七十年代，才出现了更多的有影响的成果，科学社会学终于发展成为可以和其他学科并列的社会学分支学科。不仅如此，在以科学为研究对象的诸学科中，科学社会学因为具有自己独特的研究角度和研究方法，作出了科学的历史研究或科学的哲学研究没有也不可能作出的贡献，成为和科学史、科学哲学并列的重要学科，并且给予这两个学科以重要的影响。科学社会学还赢得了从事实际研究的自然科学家或社会科学家的重视。默顿的著作被广泛引用，[①]他对于科学的社会学研究的成果，被誉为基本正确的论述。[②]

　　科学社会学虽然取得了这样重要的成就，产生了比较重要的影响，但是，关于科学社会学的研究对象，科学社会学形成过程中不同流派与研究路线，却存在着不同的理解与认识。例如，斯托勒在关于科学社会学的形成与发展的论述中，以主要的笔墨说明默顿所代表的发展路线，同时还提到了独立发展的本·戴维的路线、普赖斯的路线和库恩的路线，并且指出

---

　　* 刘珺珺，曾任南开大学哲学院科技哲学教研室教授，主要研究方向为科学哲学与科学社会学研究。

　　① E. Garfield. Citation Measures of the Influence of R. K. Merton. In *Science and Social Structure: A Festschrift for R. K. Merton*. Translations of the Nes York Academy of Sciences, Vol.2, No. 39, 1980, pp.61-74.

　　② E. Magr. *The Growth of Biological Thought*. The Belknap Press of Harvard University Press, 1982, p. 830.

了美国以外的其他学者的工作。①又如，克兰在《无形学院》一书的第一章中，从研究途径和方法的角度，提出了研究科学与其他社会体制关系的路线、研究科学的内部社会结构的路线、研究科学知识发展的路线和研究科学家文献引用关系的路线等。②和任何一个学科的情况一样，这种理解和说明上的分歧并不影响这个学科的存在与发展。每个有见解的学者可以根据自己对于这个学科的来龙去脉的认识，确定自己的研究重点和方向，把这个学科的研究推向前进。

笔者对于这个问题的思考最早开始于有人根据斯托勒的分析提出了"科学社会学的四大流派"。笔者认为，本·戴维、普赖斯、库恩是有很大影响的作者，但是，在科学社会学领域中，他们并没有形成可以和默顿学派相匹比的科学社会学的学派（准确地说，普赖斯开创的是科学计量学研究，库恩的影响在于科学哲学的历史学派）；相反地，他们的学术成果为专业社会学家所吸收，纳入了这条发展路线。英国社会学家马尔凯（M. Mulkay）就把普赖斯和默顿联系在一起，称之为 20 世纪六七十年代发展成熟的科学社会学的代表。③笔者认为，纵观科学社会学领域的发展，可以清楚地看到这个领域中的两种研究传统及其相互交错和彼此渗透，正是这样，才形成了科学社会学（sociology of science）学科和更为广泛的科学的社会研究（social studies of science）。本文就将根据这样的认识，说明科学社会学的历史与现状。

（1）科学社会学的研究，或者说科学的社会研究从一开始就存在着两种研究传统，这就是以默顿为代表的研究传统和以贝尔纳为代表的研究传统。本·戴维曾经以"科学社会学民族传统的出现"为题把前一种传统称为美国的传统，后一种传统称为英国的传统。他着重指出，以英国为代表的研究传统是在大学的社会学系中展开的，是专业社会学家所从事的工作；以英国为代表的研究传统，则是跨系、跨学科的研究，跨系、跨学科的计划（program），并不限于专业社会学家的工作。④笔者认为，本·戴维的分

① N. W. Storer. *Introduction, in Robert Merton: Sociology of Science*. The University of Chicago Press, 1973, pp.xv-xxx, p. xxx.

② 黛安娜·克兰：《无形学院》，华夏出版社，1988 年，第 3-4 页。

③ K. D. Knorr-Cetina, M. Mulkag. *Science Observed*. Preface. Sage Publications, 1983, pp.115-120.

④ J. Ben-David. Emergence of National Traditions in the Sociology of Science. In J. Castoned.: *Sociology of Science*. Jorsey-Bass Press, 1978, p. 197-200.

析是具有重要意义的。他在这里把两种传统的要点明确地指了出来，这就是专业社会学家所代表的社会学研究传统，以及非专业社会学的、各个学科学者从多角度研究科学的传统。笔者本人试图以狭义的科学社会学来说明前一种传统；而以广义的科学社会学来称呼后一种传统，也就是以广义的科学社会学来概括科学的社会研究。

（2）专业科学社会学的研究传统，是使这个学科具有确定面貌的基础。这个传统所确立的研究路线，在广泛的研究课题中确定了自己的主攻方向，从社会中的科学，转移到了科学体制中的人际互动与交流、科学家的行为规范，科学内部的社会结构与社会分层等问题。科学社会学选择了其他学科（如，科学史或科学哲学）所没有也不能顾及的方面，运用社会学的一般理论和由此引出的假设，进行经验性的研究。在科学社会学的历史发展中，在广泛吸收社会学领域以外的成果的基础上，使用了诸如"引证分析""内容分析""集体传记研究"等方法，形成了诸如"科学共同体""无形学院"以及"马太效应"等概念或经验描述规律，作出了学术界公认的成就。可以说，如果没有专业社会学家对科学的研究，就不会有科学社会学这个具有确定内容的学科，就不存在从社会学角度研究科学这个领域。

（3）但是，追溯历史，我们看到了发展的另一个方面，这就是科学社会学家的专门研究完全离不开对科学的广泛研究，专业的科学社会学研究，是以对科学的广泛研究作为产生的必要前提和新发展的必要条件的；没有这一条广泛的研究路线及其成果，很难设想专业科学社会学的形成与发展。默顿的《十七世纪》一书，今日被誉为科学社会学的奠基性文件，但是人们知道，这部著作是以科学史家的研究成果为出现的前提的。默顿的《十七世纪》中所引用的经验研究的资料来源有英国皇家学会的《哲学会刊》和德国达姆施达特的《科学技术史手册》这类科学史的工具书籍；默顿的全部研究工作是在哈佛科学史家萨顿的研究室中完成的；《十七世纪》是首先发表在科学史杂志 *ISIS* 的专刊 *OSIRIS* 上的。《十七世纪》这部著作被作者默顿称为"历史的科学社会学"，被科学史家称为"科学史研究的默顿纲领"，也就是科学社会史的研究纲领。可见，科学的社会学研究与科学的历史学研究关系之密切。

（4）科学社会学在其进一步发展成熟时期的情况进一步说明了专业科学社会学的研究离不开对科学的广泛研究，社会学家的工作离不开许许多多社会学以外的专家的工作。就以"科学共同体"这个重要的科学社会学概念来说，它并不是社会学家单独创造的产物。它是在 20 世纪三四十年代的英国的科学家之间的论战当中出现的。当时，波朗依和左派科学家贝尔纳持有不同的观点，他反对贝尔纳所推崇的以苏联为代表的科学事业的计划性观点，强调科学的自主发展。20 世纪 40 年代初，波朗依发表了《科学的自治》一文阐述他的思想，在文中首先使用了"科学共同体"这个表达科学家主体意识的概念。他认为，科学家按专业形成为不同的集团，总和而为科学共同体；科学借助于传统、通过自己的传统形成自己的标准；科学（纯粹科学）的发展是自主的，是献身于某种信念的人的共同体的自然法则。[①]科学共同体的概念的重要发展是和科学史家库恩的范式理论分不开的，是库恩把科学范式的更迭和科学共同体也就是科学家人群的活动联系在一起。科学共同体这个概念为广大的社会学家所沿用，以此标识从事科学活动的人员，标示不以地缘关系而以科学学科为基础、以科学交流为媒介而形成的人群。科学共同体概念很好地概括了科学家之间的人际互动行为，社会学家可以通过多种方法对科学家的交流活动进行经验研究与描述。在一个时期，在科学社会学领域出现了研究科学共同体的许多成果，因而有人认为，在一定意义上可以把科学社会学称为科学家共同体的社会学。与科学共同体概念紧密相关的"无形学院"概念也是如此，它的首次引入是科学史家兼科学计量学家普赖斯的工作。[②]

（5）科学社会学在方法上的发展与成熟也有赖于相关研究方法的引入和采用。普赖斯的《小科学、大科学》一书，奠定了以数量描述科学的基础，这种数量研究的方法，提供了科学社会学所需要的经验描述的工具，有人把普赖斯与默顿并列誉为"标志科学社会学发展成熟的代表人物"的原因正在于此。科学社会学在发展成熟期的另一项得心应手的工具是《科学引文索引》（SCI），由于这种工具的出现，科学社会学才得以完成大量的经验研究。人们知道，《科学引文索引》杂志的出现，并不是社会学家的工作，它也不是为着社会学家的。SCI 是科学情报学的成果，是为着科学家快速检索的需要而诞生的，但对科学社会学的发展提供了很好的工具。[③]

（6）从以上可见，科学的广泛研究（包括科学的历史学研究、科学的

① M. Polanyi. *The Logic of Liberty*. University of Chicago Press, 1951, pp.49-67.

② D. J. S. Price, *Little Science, Big Science*. Columbia University Press, 1963, pp.84-85.

③ R. Merton, J. Gaston ed. *The Sociology of Science in Europe*. South Illinois University Press, 1977, p. 52, p. 245.

哲学研究、科学的计量学研究、科学的情报学研究等等）这条路线，不断以自己的多种多样的研究成果滋育着科学社会学家的专门研究，而科学社会学家又以自己本学科的专门研究把这些学科所提供的东西凝固化、规范化，纳入自己的发展、形成自己的成果，形成科学的社会研究中最有学科依据的东西。在笔者看来，这种汇合表明科学社会学的凝聚力量。科学情报学家——SCI 的创办人加菲尔德曾说，普赖斯从历史学转向了图书目录学，默顿从社会学转向图书目录之山而找到了金子，他自己正好相反，从图书目录学家变成了历史学家和社会量度学家。[①]专业的科学社会学是发展的中坚，影响着宽泛的科学的社会研究。

（7）就这两种研究传统发展的现状来说，尽管专业的科学社会学家以自己坚实的研究确立了科学社会学这个学科；但是以默顿为代表的路线或范式、专业的科学社会学研究是一种狭义的科学社会学。这条路线虽然在它的高峰时期出现了令人瞩目的成果，但在目前的进一步发展中似乎有某种"枯竭"之感。在 1978 年，斯托勒就已经指出，默顿的范式问世以来，科学社会学已经发展到了库恩所指出的常规科学的阶段，默顿本人的和许多人的著作不过是对于已有范式中已经说明了的或者模糊的问题的说明，指出"科学社会学已经成熟到这样的地步，许多研究只不过是'解难题'而已"[②]。目前，具有创造力的研究所见不多；大约某些有研究能力的科学社会学家已经被吸引到社会学研究的其他路线。

（8）现在，应该说，广义的科学社会学研究，即科学的社会研究，也是美国的研究现实。在美国，目前盛行"科学、技术与社会"这种广泛的研究课题，这以麻省理工学院为典型代表，许多技术类的学院以至于某些大学都有类似于"科学、技术与社会"这样的课程计划，有的还设置相应的学位，即使在设立了社会学系、有受过专门社会学训练的大学，也注重这种宽泛的科学的社会研究，以各种课题吸引着社会学以及社会学以外的专业人员和学生。美国的 4S 学会（society for social studies of science）的活动也充分说明了这个问题，提交这个学会的 1987 年年会的各类文章大约有 120 多篇，共分二十多个分组会进行讨论，我们仅从这些分组会的名称就可以看出研究兴趣分布的广泛性：科学技术的财产、权力和意识形态，

---

① E. Garfield. *Essays of an Information Scientist*, Vol.I, p. 158.

② N. W. Storer. *Introduction*, in *Robert Merton*: *Sociology of Science*. The University of Chicago Press, 1973, pp.xv-xxx, p. xxx.

科学中的写作、引证和出版，科学研究工作的样式，医药和医学知识的社会研究，科学流动和技术革新，风险、接受和技术变化，科学的哲学社会学研究（philosophical social studies of science），科学与技术的关系（在学术、工业和军事中的），人工智能领域的社会关系，科学领域的社会结构，技术设计的社会学，科学技术中的利益磋商和争论，数量科学研究，科学政策展望，科学共同体中的社会组织和社会变迁，对科学进行研究中的比较方法和历史方法，修辞学家和科学修辞，科学实践和科学知识，科学与技术的政治维度，科学、技术、研发和政策展望，科学的社会心理学研究，等等。①

从以上的题目可见，科学的社会研究，是一个包容甚广的研究传统。这个研究传统虽然开始于贝尔纳所在的英国，但是在美国同样存在着，无论是本·戴维的、普赖斯的，还是库恩的、加菲尔德的研究传统，甚至是默顿的研究传统都可以容纳在这个传统之内。这是一个开放的、有多种发展可能的研究传统。

（9）目前，在默顿以外的科学社会学研究传统中，出现了许多论文和著作，在这些分散的、多角度、多方位、多课题的研究中，有一批作者的研究逐步形成了共同的研究对象和相互接近的研究方法，在某种程度上形成了科学社会学中的新范式或新流派，这就是新的科学知识社会学以及随之出现的技术社会学。

（10）新的科学知识社会学是 20 世纪 70 年代末 80 年代初，首先在英国出现的新流派。这个流派的代表人物认为，以默顿为代表的科学社会学并没有研究科学的最重要的内容——科学知识，因而不是真正的科学社会学，不过是科学家的社会学、科学职业的社会学。②这个学派的代表人物自称，他们是在库恩的哲学思想影响下，在批判了传统的实证主义科学观之后，研究科学知识的相对性和社会内容的学派。③显然，这个学派的出现与哲学有紧密的关系，关于这一点，本·戴维曾经指出：这个学派是在"反实证主义"哲学（马克思主义、现象主义、社会学中的人类学方法）兴起和科学哲学中相对主义、建构主义影响之下产生的。他并且指出，这个

---

① *Science and Technology Studies*, 1987, Vol.5, No. 2.

② M. Mulkay. Sociology in the West. In *Current Sociology*, 1980, Vol.28, No. 3, pp.1-184.

③ M. Mulkay. *Science and Sociology of Knowledge*. George Allen d Unwin Ltd, 1979.

学派是和迪尔凯姆和曼海姆的知识社会学传统相联系的。[①]

（11）科学知识社会学的代表人物有马尔凯、巴恩斯（B. Barnes)、埃奇（D. O. Edge）、布鲁尔（D. Bloor）、惠特利（R. Whitley）、柯林斯（H. M. Cllins）等人；其中爱丁堡大学的人数较多，形成了所谓的爱丁堡学派。科学知识社会学的代表人物并不仅仅局限在英国，法国哲学家布鲁诺·拉都尔（Bruno Latour）代表着另一种发展路线。这些人的工作在美国也都产生了影响。他们的研究都区别于默顿所代表的科学社会学，形成了科学知识社会学研究中的两大流派，即以英国为代表的传统的、宏观研究方法，研究科学知识产生发展的社会坏境条件及其与人的集团、人的社会利益的关系，有人称之为宏观定向相一致模式；以法国为代表的、从微观角度研究科学知识的建构过程的研究方法，有人称之为微观倾向发生学方法或建构主义纲领。[②]

（12）马尔凯是科学知识社会学中有影响的代表人物之一。他在 1972 年发表的《革新的社会过程》似乎是在默顿传统中的工作。1977 年他在默顿及加斯东主编的《欧洲的科学社会学》一书中撰写《英国的科学社会学》一文，文章最后说明了他本人以及其他英国学者与默顿学派的分歧，认为把库恩的著作作为科学社会学研究的出发点更加合适，因为这样就可以把科学的复杂文化和整个社会过程联系在一起，把科学社会学作为整个知识社会学的一个部分来发展。[③]

马尔凯在 1979 年发表了《科学和知识社会学》一书，全面阐述了他的观点。他认为，传统的实证哲学和知识社会学把自然科学知识与知识的其他形态区别开来，把自然科学知识排除在社会学分析之外是错误的。他援引了汉森、耐格尔、波普尔和费耶阿本德等哲学家的观点，认为这些哲学家的观点为自然科学知识的社会学研究留下了余地。他认为，科学知识社会学就是要考察科学内部的文化因素、对科学做文化的说明和解释。他同时认为，科学共同体内部的科学家行为，并不存在统一的规范；由于科学家具有不同的目标和利益，而有不同的规范，也就是在科学家中存在着不

---

① J. Ben-David. Sociology of Scientific Knowledge. In The *State of Knowledge*. Sage Publications, 1981, p. 44, p. 55.

② K. D. Knorr-Cetina, M. Mulkag. *Science Observed*. Sage Publications, 1983, pp.115-120.

③ R. Merton, J. Gaston ed. *The Sociology of Science in Europe*. South lllinois University Press, 1977, p. 52, p. 245.

同的专业意识形态，默顿所提出的科学家行为规范不过是这些意识形态中的一种叙述"词汇"。在这里，他提出了科学的社会修辞学（the social rhetoric of science）来概括这种现象。马尔凯主张用评价标准的"节目单"（evaluative repertoire）来代替默顿的科学家行为的社会规范，意在强调存在着不同的规范，表明文化背景所提供的全部可供选择的东西，指出这种东西表现为词汇和语言的形态。马尔凯认为，在科学知识形成过程中存在着"磋商"（negotiation）现象，不仅科学的社会规范可变，科学的认识与技术规范也是可变的。①

（13）巴恩斯和布鲁尔与马尔凯一样，是科学知识社会学中宏观研究路线的代表，他们又以强主题（strong thesis）或强纲领（strong program）的代表人物而著称。所谓强主题或强纲领，是继承知识社会学的传统，主张知识的各种形态（其中包括自然科学知识）都受到社会因素影响的观点。巴恩斯在他的《科学知识和社会学理论》（1974）一书中提出，知识是一种信念，这种信念并不是正确的，只不过是被接受了的；自然科学的知识也是如此。他认为，科学家的社会地位，他们所处的社会团体决定他们的思想。他认为，科学是亚文化的集合，作为一种文化现象，是和整个文化联系在一起的，依赖于整个文化资源，科学的变迁不是纯粹内部变化的结果。②他在《利益和知识增长》（1977）一书中，讨论了自然科学知识和社会集团的利益关系。他认为，利益影响着由现成文化资源形成的知识结构，应该从利益的角度说明知识怎样利用现成的文化资源而产生或维持的过程。③

布鲁尔在 1976 年发表了《知识和社会形象》一书，以"知识社会学中的强纲领"为标题，写下了该书的第一章，提出了社会学对知识的研究应该遵循原因、公正、对秩和反身四条原则。这就是：知识社会学注意研究原因，关心信念和知识所处的不同情况条件，关心社会的和其他形式的原因；公平地对待真和伪，理性和非理性，成功的和失败的，两方面都要求得到说明；说明方式是对称的；它的说明适合于社会学本身。他认为这四条原则组成了知识社会学的强纲领。这是强纲领之说法的由来。他在书中强调科学是社会的约定，认为，即使是数学也是社会的创造和社会的约定，

---

① M. Mulkay. *Science and Sociology of Knowledge*. George Allen and Unwin Ltd, 1979.

② B. Barnes. *Scientific Knowledge and Sociological Theory*. Routledge and Kegan Paul, 1974.

③ B. Barnes. *Interests and the Growth of Knowledge*. Routledge and Kegan Paul, 1977.

数学实际上也是某种关于社会的东西。他认为，数学也和道德具有多样性一样，并不是唯一的。他同时认为，数学中的证明过程实际上就是一个创造和磋商的过程。①

（14）法国哲学家拉都尔和英国社会学家乌尔加（W. Woolgar）在 1979年发表了《实验室生活》一书。这是拉都尔在美国加利福尼亚州萨尔克实验室进行了将近两年实地考察的结果；是拉都尔运用人类学方法，把实验室看作现代生活中的科学家"部落"活动的地区，采取不介入的原则，观察科学知识怎样在一个实验室中生产出来的报告。拉都尔本人由此得到了"人类学家"的称号。人类学家拉都尔和社会学家乌尔加的观察描述首先是关于实验室的。在实验室中，他们看到了机器、仪器的运转及显示，看到了实验技术人员的操作和记载，看到了博士们的阅读和写作论文。他们的观察结论是把实验室的活动归结为生产论文；把实验室看作由机器、仪器和实验技术人员综合在一起的装置组成，这些装置是进行文学标记（literary inscsiption）的装置；实验室不过是通过文学标记进行说服的组织。在进一步描述中，他们写道，实验室中的科学事实不是被发现出来，而是被制造出来的，科学研究的过程是因人而异的、是幻想的建造；科学过程的产物，只不过是从实验室中的装置得到的，或是在其他实验室产生的论文中存在的。拉都尔在实验室的观察中得出的另一方面的结论是，科学家活动的动机并不是默顿学派所说的得到承认或者奖励，而是得到信用（credit）。他认为，"信用"一词比"奖励"（reward）一词有更宽的含义，可以表示科学事实生产过程的总体经济模式。他认为，从这方面说，科学家的行为和资本投资者有惊人的相似，在科学活动中，可以用可信用性或借贷能力（credibility）的循环来说明，认为可信用性或借贷能力这个概念，可以使社会学家把外部因素和内部因素彼此联系起来。②拉都尔在 1987 年还有新著《行动中的科学》问世，把他的发现进一步理论化、系统化。③

（15）拉都尔所开始的对知识的生产过程进行研究的路线，在美国有谢廷娜（K. D. Knorr-Cetina）追随。她的《知识的制造》（1981）一书，系统阐述了科学知识社会学的微观建物主义的观点。④她的文章《科学工作的

---

① D. Bloor. *Knowledge and Social Imagery*. Routledge and Kegan Paul, 1976.

② B. Latour, W. Woolgar. *Laboratory Life*. Sage Publications, 1979.

③ B. Latour. *Science in Action*. Harvard University Press, 1987.

④ K. D. Knorr-Cetina. *The Manufacture of Knowledge*. Pergamon Press, 1981.

人种志研究：走向对科学的建物主义说明》（1983）则更加简洁地说明了这种观点，其要点是：科学现实是人工的、人为的；科学实验中的活动是决策-负荷的；实验室活动具有因地而异和偶然发生的特点；科学知识建物活动要求社会条件、具有社会内容。她说，体现在科学产物中的选择是和在一定时空中发生的磋商这种社会过程相联系的，并不是单个人的逻辑决定。①

（16）从以上几个代表人物的论述来看，科学知识社会学各种主张的目的都在于说明自然科学知识中的社会内容，在于要把科学的认识内容与社会内容结合起来。他们所提出的社会文化分析、利益原则、借贷能力循环、知识产生过程中的"磋商"等等，都致力于说明社会因素对于自然科学知识内容的渗透。从这点上说，他们完全继承了老的知识社会学的传统。新的科学知识社会学究竟前进了多少？从宏观的研究来看，似乎仍然是重复过去的理论框架或一般分析，并没有（大概也不可能）前进多少。微观的科学知识建构过程的研究，虽然在方法上有所进步，使用了人类学的、语言学分析等经验研究的方法；但是，使用这种方法进行研究的结果又在多大程度上说明了作者想要说明的问题（科学知识内容中的社会因素）？拉都尔把信贷能力循环纳入科学知识生产过程，但是这种循环仍然在认识的循坏之外。至于不断提及的"磋商"，如果有，一定是利益分歧的协商吗？是否也可以理解为认识差异的调整呢？

其实，科学知识社会学所作经验研究的目的是在于证明他们的哲学观点，这一点他们是直言不讳的。本·戴维关于这个问题的看法是值得思考的。他指出，哲学观点是并不需要经验证明的；科学知识社会学家的做法，恰恰堵塞了提出经验研究课题的道路。②

（17）科学知识社会学作为一种社会思潮，具有比较明显的反科学主义的性质。在拉都尔的《实验室生活》一书出版后，《科学》杂志上曾经发表一篇书评，认为这本书揭开了包裹在科学迷雾下的实验室的真实生活，说明科学也并不是神圣的殿堂。惠特利则指出，科学知识社会学的目的在于把科学这个黑箱变成半透明箱，拉都尔则以人类学家的笔记，把科学家这个奇怪团体的活动，像撕开吃人生番部落的秘密一样，揭露无遗。这本书

---

① K. D. Knorr-Cetina, M. Mulkag. *Science Observed*, Preface. Sage Publications, 1983, pp.115-120.

② J. Ben-David. Sociology of Scientific Knowledge. In *The State of Knowledge*. Sage Publications, 1981, p. 44, p. 55.

的读者可能都会感受到一股反对科学的阴冷气息。

埃奇曾经讨论过科学主义。他认为，在当代社会中，科学和科学家受到尊重，科学语言渗入日常生活，事物的进步被称为科学化，这些都是科学主义的表现。他认为，基于普遍接受的关于科学共同体的信念和实践的看法，推崇他们所提出的论据和他们所推行的实践，这种做法是科学主义；对于那些从前认为不可能应用科学的语言、方法、模型和比喻的领域实行"殖民地化"的企图，就是科学主义。[①]显然，他们的使命就是反对这种"殖民地化"的企图，就是反对科学主义。

（18）近几年来，科学社会学的学者们试图把他们认为已经成熟的科学知识社会学的研究路线用于研究技术，对技术进行社会学的分析。这种趋势是在 1982—1984 年间，在欧洲研究科学技术协会（European Association for the Studies of Science and Technology, EASST）所组织的会议上，首先由科学知识社会学家平奇（T. Pinch）和技术社会学家毕克尔（W. Bijker）所倡导而形成的。目前，这种研究吸引了一部分技术史家，形成了在荷兰特文特大学校园中定期举行的研讨会，研讨会的成果已经形成了论文集《技术的社会建构》（1987）。[②]在这本书中，不同作者通过对不同的技术、技术过程、技术体系以至与技术有关的事件的分析，阐发了若干共同的观点，其中最主要的就是认为，在纯粹技术和技术的政治、经济、社会诸因素之间并没有明确的区别与界限，这也就是说，以前认为是纯技术的过程，实际上紧密交织着政治、经济及社会的内容，因此，他们提出了"无缝的网"（seamless web）来描述这种现象。他们认为，在技术所涉及的自然因素和人的因素之间也不存在泾渭分明的界限；在任何技术领域中，不同的参加者，为发明家、科学家、设计人员和设计工程师、生产工程师、市场和销售人员、银行家及财政人员、律师、政治家、国家官员、消费者（个人、公司或政府机构）都聚集起来汇合于某个地点实现某种技术过程，交织成所谓"无缝的网"。在他们的讨论中，结合各自研究的技术对象或技术过程、技术体系，提出了不少的概念，但这些概念或说法尚未成为被普遍采用或普遍接受的东西。总之，这是一个很不成熟的领域，从现有的论文看，现在还没有明确的思想一致，当然也就没有清晰的研究路线的分野，一切

---

① I. Cameron, D. Edge. *Scientific Images and Their Sociol Uses*. Butter Worths, 1979, pp.3-4.

② W. E. Bijker, T. P. Hughes, T. J. Pinch. *The Social Construction of Technological Systems*. MIT Press, 1987.

都有待于进一步的发展。

讲到技术的社会学，不能不提到吉尔费兰（S. C. Gilfillan) 1935 年发表的《发明的社会学》这部先于默顿的《十七世纪》而问世的书籍，该书主要讨论了造船历史上的技术发明，也许可以视为技术社会学的开创性著作。值得注意的是这部书在最近又出了增订版。阅读这部不大为当今技术社会学家提到的著作，进行对比性思考，也许是有益的。

以上的说明，是个人的学习所得，并不是全面的综述。在几十年间，在科学社会学、科学知识社会学、技术社会学以及相关领域中的文献和著作，可以说是浩如烟海；在不受外界条件局限的情况下，一个人也是很难概括全面的。就说明而言，即使是笔者已经了解的某些研究课题及成果，也很难在行文中顾及。这大概只有由各种全面的或专题性的综述性研究的互相补充来解决了。

参考文献：

[1] E. Garfield: Citation Measures of the Influence of R. K. Merton, in *Science and Social Structure:A Festschrift for R. K. Merton*, pp.61-74. Translations of the Nes York Academy of Sciences, Vol.2.No.39, 1980.

[2] E. Magr: T*he Growth of Biological Thought*, p.830, The Belknap Press of Harvard University Press, 1982.

[3] N. W. Storer: *Introduction, in Robert Merton:Sociology of Science*, pp.xv-xxx, p.xxx, The University of Chicago Press, 1973

[4] 黛安娜·克兰：《无形学院》，3-4 页，华夏出版社，1988.

[5] K. D. Knorr-Cetina and M. Mulkag: *Science Observed*, pp.115-120, Sage Publications, 1983.

[6] J. Ben—David; *Emergence of National Traditions in the Sociology of Science*, in J. Castoned.: Sociology of science, pp.197-200, Jorsey-Bass Press, 1978.

[7] M. Polanyi: *The Logic of Liberty*, pp.49-67, University of Chicago Press, 1951.

[8] D. J. S. Price: *Little Science, Big Science*, pp.84-85, Columbia University Press, 1963.

［9］R. Merton and J. Gaston ed.: *The Sociology of Science in Europe*, p.52, p.245, South lllinois University Press, 1977.

［10］E. Garfield: *Essays of an Information Scientist*, Vol, I. p.158.

［11］*Science and Technology Studies*, Vol.5. No. 2 Summer, 1987.

［12］M. Mulkay: Sociology in the West, in *Current Sociology*, Vol.28. No. 3, Winter, 1980, pp.1-184

［13］M. Mulkay: *Science and Sociology of Knowledge*, George Allen and Unwin Ltd. 1979.

［14］J. Ben-David: *Sociology of Scientific Knowledge*, in p.44, p.55, in the *State of Knowledge* p.44, p.55, Sage Publications, 1981.

［15］B. Barnes: *Scientific Knowledge and Sociological Theory*, Routledge and Kegan Paul, 1974.

［16］B. Barnes: Interests and the Growth of Knowledge, Routledge and Kegan Paul, 1977.

［17］D. Bloor: *Knowledge and Social Imagery*, Routledge and Kegan Paul, 1976.

［18］B. Latour and W. Woolgar: *Laboratory Life*, Sage Publications, 1979.

［19］B. Latour: *Science in Action*, Harvard University Press, 1987.

［20］K. D. Knorr-Cetina: *The Manufacture of Knowledge*, Pergamon Press, 1981

［21］I. Cameron and D. Edge: *Scientific Images and Their Sociol Uses*, pp.3-4, Butter Worths, 1979.

［22］W. E. Bijker, T. P. Hughes and T. J. Pinch: *The Social Construction of Technological Systems*, The MIT Press, 1987.

（本文原载于《自然辩证法通讯》1989 年第 4 期）

科学学理论发展与学科建设的紧迫问题

张俊心*

科学学在中国经过了 70 年代的引进，80 年代的深入研究，进入 20 世纪 90 年代，对社会发挥着越来越大的作用。科学学在推进科技体制改革，促进企业技术进步，实行高技术产业革命，揭起科技兴市热潮等方面，呈现出一派兴旺发达的景象。然而，正是在这个时候，人们却感到了它在理论上的危机起伏：研究的问题十分庞杂；指导思想不明确；学术活动随着行政中心转；经验介绍和布置工作占据主导位置；学术交流和理论探讨日趋衰落；概念混乱和观念矛盾随处可见，人们开始怀疑科学学是不是一门严肃的科学学科，它有没有自身的理论体系，等等。

这不是一个小问题，如果这些问题得不到研究和解决，科学学的繁荣景象将像海市蜃楼一样随时会消失。本文主要将科学学理论发展中出现的一些理论问题明确地提出来，加以分析，希望抛砖引玉，引起人们对这些问题的重视并认真研究加以解决，将科学学理论向前推进一步。

一、科学学理论发展中的问题

1. 科学学的研究对象是什么

众所周知，一门科学能否成立，首先在于它有没有自身特有的研究对象，如果研究对象不是特有的，那么它与其他学科就难以划清界限，就难于成为一门与其他学科相区别的确定的学科。人们常说，科学学是以科学技术整体为对象的学科。这样虽然回答出了科学学的对象是科学技术整体，

---

* 张俊心，南开大学哲学系教授，研究方向为科学技术哲学。

但是还没有解决问题。因为这一对象并不是科学学所专有。以科学技术整体为对象的学科太多了，写出专著的就不下几十种，如科技史、科学哲学、科学经济学、科学社会学、科学心理学、科学情报学、科学逻辑学、科学预测学、科技管理学……可以说，有多少门人文科学，从它们出发来研究科学就会产生多少门以科学为对象的科学。这许多学科都是属于科学学吗？问题不那么简单。

目前学术界对这个问题有三种不同的认识。

一种认识认为，它们都是以科学为对象的学科，应当属于科学学。另一种认识认为，它们从某一科学的理论出发去研究科学，它们就应属于某门科学，如科学社会学，是由专业社会学家运用社会学的概念与方法，对科学研究的结果，就是社会学的分支学科。科学经济学是从经济学角度研究科学问题的一门新兴学科，它是一种部门经济学，等等。还有一种认识认为，像上述这些学科，都是科学与其他人文科学交叉而成的边缘学科，因而它们具有两方面的性质，既是科学学的分支学科，又是某种人文科学（如社会学的、经济学的、历史学的、哲学的）的分支学科。

这一问题在理论上争执起来就归结为一门学科的性质到底是由什么决定的，这在国内外普遍存在着两种观点：一是主张由对象决定，一是主张由方法决定。如果说由对象决定，那么就应当说出科学学的对象与某门人文科学的对象究竟有什么不同；如果说应由办法决定，那么就应该说出在研究同一对象时科学学有什么独特的研究方法。明确了这些问题，才能划分清楚这些以科学为对象的众多学科的归属，这个问题不解决，并且像某些人文科学学者所声称的那样，这些学科归属于它们，而不属于科学学，那么，科学学尽管热闹一番，将来岂不面临着竹篮打水一场空的危险？一个没有底的大口袋，装的东西虽多，到头来一个也没有留下，那是多么可悲的局面。

必须进一步确定科学学的对象和性质特点，界定科学学的分支学科与属于社会学的、经济学的、历史学的、哲学的……各人文科学的分支学科的区别和界限，才能使这些问题得到解决。

2. 科学学是自然科学的科学学，还是整个科学的科学学

人们在给科学学下定义时，说它是研究科学整体发展规律的理论，是整个科学的科学学。但是在论说中又声明其内容只限于自然科学（包含技术）的科学学。定义与内容自相矛盾。可是这一矛盾还很难解决，国际上

通用的是英语国家的"Science of Science"，就是自然科学的科学学，因为科学一词 Science 是指自然科学。但是，俄文 АЙКА 的科学概念则是指所有的科学，因而 АЙКА О ХАЙХ 就是所有科学的科学学。国际上也难于否定哪一个。撇开名词概念的纠缠，从科学学的实际内容来看，科学学的主要内容确实是从自然科学那里概括出来的；但是，科学学研究的深入发展，早已将研究锋芒深入到社会的政治、经济之中，特别是自然与社会交叉的学科领域、软科学领域，越来越成为科学学研究的主要内容。客观形势表明，把科学学理解为自然科学的科学学是不行的了。科学学家夏禹龙说："虽然在科学学主要创始人例如 J. D. 贝尔纳那里，科学学的研究对象并没有把社会科学排除在外，但是，在以后学科的发展中，科学学却几乎等同于自然科学学，社会科学学作为研究对象差不多已从研究者的视野里消失了。这是科学学发展史上一个耐人寻味的现象。"[1]我国最早倡导科学学的著名科学家钱学森也对这种状况不满意，他说，"科学学不能只是自然科学的科学学，科学学也是社会科学的科学学，而且也是技术科学和工程技术以及哲学的科学学"。一些学者针对自然科学的科学学的现状和不足，干脆另辟蹊径，提出研究《社会科学学》《技术学》以及《科学技术学》。我国还出版了农学学、医学学、数学学以至哲学学等方面的著作。学科发展的这种情况表明，既然各门科学、各类科学都有了自己的科学学，那么，没有一门能作为它们前提和基础的整个科学的科学学的存在能行吗？基于自然科学的科学学的现状，其能承担作为各种特殊科学学理论基础这一伟大的历史使命吗？人们提出要全方位地研究科学学[2]，和要研究广义的科学学，即包括自然、社会、工程技术科学在内的科学学[3]，正是在学科发展的这种情况下提出来的研究课题。这个课题反映科学学发展的历史使命和当前的紧迫要求。而且这也是从逻辑上进一步明确科学学对象的外延所必须解决的一个课题。

3. 科学学是一门学科，还是一类学科

许多学者在介绍科学学或是在科学学专著中都说科学学是一门新兴学科，然而，在谈科学学的具体内容时，却又列举出科学社会学、科学经济学、科学管理学等一系列的学科。这样给人的印象是，科学学并不是一门

① 夏禹龙：《社会科学学》，湖北人民出版社，1989 年，第 1 页。

② 夏禹龙．《社会科学学》，湖北人民出版社，1989 年，第 1 页。

③ 钱学森：《论系统工程》，湖南科学技术出版社，1982 年，第 191 页。

具有严密理论体系的学科，而是拼盘式的不成体系的学科。有人可能这样想：一门大的学科，其中包容许多小的学科，例如，普通生物学这一门学科，包容了动物学、植物学、微生物学、细胞学、组织学、胚胎学、解剖学、生理学、遗传学等等，有什么奇怪的呢？问题是，作为一门科学的普通生物学，并不是上述生物学分科的拼盘和罗列，它本身虽包容那些分科的内容，却是经过综合加工，以生命的本质特征为中心，描述了生命的存在形式和机能。相比之下，科学学却没有形成由基本概念把全部内容串联起来的严密的理论体系。

如果说，科学学是一类学科，即是以科学为对象的科学群，那么把它叫作科学学就不合适了，科学学毕竟是一门科学的名称。叫作科学的科学倒具有类科学的味道。但是，即使明确了科学的科学是一类以科学为对象的学科群，也不解决问题。因为一类科学必须有一门科学作为中心理论学科，才能使一类学科成为有内在联系的科学群。像系统科学那样，一大类系统科学必须有一门带有基础理论性的系统学才能把它联系起来。所以，科学学无论是一门科学，还是一类科学，都需要一门具有严密逻辑体系的能成为以科学为对象的科学群的基础理论学科，即科学学。但是，现在的科学学却起不了这种作用，需要人们去构建、改造并完善它。

4．理论科学学与应用科学学能构成统一体吗

从贝尔纳到现代的每本科学学著作都说科学学包括了理论科学学和应用科学学两部分，说它们成为科学学的完整的统一体。然而，这是可能的吗？

理论科学学是研究科技活动的规律性的，其特点是抽象性、单一性和真理性；而应用科学学则是应用科学学的规律去实现目的的学问，其特点是综合性、价值性和实践性。二者性质完全不同，为何能形成统一的学科？

理论科学学与应用科学学要作为一门学科的两部分是不行的，但是，把它们看作同一类群中的两门互相关联的学科，比如，一个是基础科学，一个是工程技术科学则是合乎逻辑的。

5．科学学的总论与分论的关系问题

科学学的著作常常采用总论和分论的结构形式来表述，认为总论是带共性的基础理论部分，分论则是一个个分支学科的内容。

科学学的结构形式这样来表述，除了有上述的基础理论与应用部分共处于统一体中的逻辑矛盾之外，还会带来一个概念上的混乱。因为学术界

一般把总论和绪论、导论一样地看待。它们不是对内容本身的表述，而是对全书内容为什么这样安排所作的说明，是属于元科学的性质。如今把总论当作了内容的基础理论部分，这也是分不清一门科学与一类科学的区别而造成的混乱。

二、对问题的初步分析

以上这些理论上的问题，在科学学的活动中越来越显得尖锐和突出，似乎动摇了科学学大厦的根基，若解决不好会使科学学大厦发生倾倒和崩溃。但若仔细分析一下，却发现问题不是这样的，而是科学学发展到一个新的历史阶段时必然产生的现象，是科学学的发展将跃上一个新台阶的前奏。

我们可用一段科学史作类比。近代自然科学在得到独立之后发展十分快速，各门科学分门别类、井井有条地搜集材料、从事经验研究，扩展学科领地。进入 19 世纪，蓬勃发展的经验科学产生了思想混乱和危机，人们滥用科学概念，比如，"力"和"能"这两个概念就曾使整个学术界纠缠不清。问题迫使人们去整理资料、分析概念，研究各门科学自身的理论系统，于是科学由经验科学研究阶段进入了理论化的发展阶段。一门门具有严密理论体系的现代科学就形成了。科学理论形成之后，科学的威力大大增强，于是科学的分化与综合、转移与应用发展形式加快了科学发展的速度，扩展了科学的社会功能，科学走上了新的发展道路。

目前科学学理论上的混乱状况，正是它由经验现象的研究阶段走向理论概括阶段的反映，它预示着科学学一个新的发展阶段即将到来。

科学学进入理论化阶段之后其最紧迫的任务是什么呢？

从当前的社会发展的实际形势来看，当然有许多任务，阐明和贯彻科学技术是第一生产力的问题，依靠科技进步繁荣经济的问题，推进科技管理体制的改革提高管理效能问题，展望世纪之交的科技与经济社会的协调发展问题，等等。但是笔者认为最关键的还是学科建设的问题，因为这些实用的研究课题，对科学学的要求越来越高，希望科学学在我国改革开放和现代化的建设中发挥越来越强的作用。但是科学学作为一门科学只有自身形成了严密的理论体系之后才能发挥学科的威力,充分显示自己的功能。

在本身的理论还处于混乱之中的时候，科学的作用毕竟是有限的。而加强科学学的学科建设，解决自身理论上的诸多问题，已成为科学学发展中刻不容缓的任务了。

那么，加强科学学学科建设，其具体任务是什么呢？归纳前述的几个问题到一点，就是要求科学学成为一门具有现代严密理论体系的学科。要研究如何使科学学成为具有严密理论体系的现代科学，就得对科学学进行元科学的研究，即阐明科学学的对象、性质特点，与其他相邻学科的界限和关系，提炼学科的基本概念和逻辑关系，构建逻辑严密的理论体系。元科学研究是任何科学进入理论化发展阶段必须进行的研究活动。只考虑经验的实用问题，不进行理论思维是不行的，那样对科学学的期望，往往会欲速而不达。

通过对科学学的元科学研究，抓住提炼基本概念、建立一门科学的体系结构、阐明一类科学的内在联系这三个关键环节，就会使科学学向理论化方向上飞跃一步。

以上拙见只是提出问题，并没有解决问题，目的在于抛砖引玉，引起人们的思考，求得对上述问题的多方面的研究和重视，以便最终解决问题。

（本文原载于《科学学研究》1993 年第 1 期）

关于两类技术社会学

柯礼文*

对于技术的社会研究必将随着社会主义市场经济的建立与发展而在我国受到高度关注，因为在市场经济条件下，技术的引进或创新，以及继而发生的一系列演化过程，都与多种多样的社会因素相关联。决定技术发展的速度、方向与规模，以及技术对于社会的作用的，不是像形形色色的技术决定论者所断言的那样是一群技术专家或决策官员，而是涉及广大的社会公众，取决于他们的利益与选择、价值取向与心理、习俗及文化背景等。技术与社会的这种多维度、多层次而又模糊不清的相关性，吸引着众多的研究工作者，导致近十几年来不仅在发达国家，而且也在许多发展中国家里，蓬勃地兴起这类探索工作。国内在此期间也出现很多成果，有的高校还建立了"技术与社会研究中心"这样的学术机构。

不论从历史或逻辑的角度看，与技术的社会研究关系最密切的当推科学的社会研究（简称"3S"），因而从这种相关性出发，比较便于说明前者的研究对象、学科从属关系等基本问题。

本文以文献分析为基础，先揭示技术的社会研究在 3S 中的地位，指出它已是一个独立的研究领域；继而提出有必要区分广义的和狭义的技术社会学及各自的特征；最后简述技术社会学理论的新进展。

需要申明的是，本文着眼于有关研究工作的进展和成果及个人的看法，而不是在于规定它们应该是什么样的。

---

* 柯礼文，南开大学哲学系教授，研究方向为科学技术哲学。

一、技术的社会研究在 3S 中的地位

不论在学术机构系列还是研究领域的称谓方面，技术的社会研究（SST）至今还"附"在 3S 中。[①]为搞清它在 3S 中的地位，笔者对 1988 年 11 月 16—19 日在阿姆斯特丹举行的，由美国 3S 学会和欧洲科学和技术研究协会（EASST）主办的联合讨论会上宣读的 163 篇论文提要[②]作了内容分类，见下表。

序号	论文主题	篇数	序号	论文主题	篇数
1	科学政策、科学与政治	18	12	科学史理论问题	1
2	科学动力学	4	13	科学计量学	4
3	科学与生产	3	14	科学技术与社会总论	2
4	科学共同体	2	15	科学技术教育	2
5	国际科学交流	1	16	科学技术情报学（包括引证分析）	8
6	科学学派	2	17	技术与社会总论	10
7	性别分析	6	18	技术的伦理学问盟	1
8	其他专业性科学社会学课题	57	19	技术研究组织	2
9	科学知识社会学	9	20	其他非专业性技术社会学课题	9
10	环境保护	3	21	建构主义理论、方法及评述	12
11	科学哲学流派	7			

分类根据国内外习惯尽量细分。对涉及多项主题者，将其归类于主要方面，不重复计数。各细目并非完全独立，如 4—7 号论文可分别纳入 8、9 号，17—19 号也可并入 20 号，这样做的目的在于显示 3 S 的多学科性。表中所称"专业性科学社会学"即狭义科学社会学。按论述对象，这些论文可分为 3 组。一是专论科学，二是兼及科学与技术，三是专论技术的。

---

① 以及在 STS 中。STS 在西方有两种含义：一是我国普遍认同的，即指"科学、技术与社会"；另一种意义是指"科学与技术研究"，有的高校设有这样的系。前者着重于政策实践，后者有较强的学术性。

② *Science, Technology, Human Values*, Vol.13, No, 1-2.

它们广泛地涉及科学技术与政治、经济、生产、教育、伦理、生态的关系，以及分别从哲学、历史学、情报学等角度，其中从社会学角度加以考察的占大多数。

还可以从权威的《社会学文摘》（*Sociological Abstract*）中说明技术社会学的地位。该文摘的"科学社会学"代号为 1700，它又细分为两个分支领域："科学社会学"（代号为 1734）和"技术社会学"（代号为 1772）。查阅了 1988 年、1989 年的《社会学文摘》后加以统计，此两年间科学社会学与技术社会学文摘篇数分别为 252 与 167。

上述情况表明，技术的社会研究或技术社会学在近 10 年里，已经成为一项独立的研究领域。它在 3S 中占据一定的、不容忽视的地位。实际上，在新近的著作中，学者们已经十分明确地指出了这一点。①

但从表中看出，占据最大部分比例的是科学社会学，共 117 篇，占 71%，其中专业性科学社会学又是主体。专论技术的 34 篇，占 21%。这说明科学社会学是 3S 的主旋律，而技术社会学尚处于较弱地位。虽然人们一般认为就社会的作用而言，技术的重要性至少不亚于科学，但学科的实际发展水平仍无情地决定于自己的历史。科学社会学作为一门独立的学科，在 20 世纪 60 年代初已经沿着四条主要研究路线蓬勃发展：一是普赖斯的科学产出计量研究；二是库恩建立在"常规科学""科学范式""科学革命"等概念基础上的历史分析；三是本·戴维在教育和其他社会建制范围内的职业动力学基础上对于科学发现的研究；四是哈格斯特隆关于科学家创造性、竞争和奖励等行为的经验研究。②而技术社会学则是借 70 年代以后科学社会学新方向——科学知识社会学兴起之风，在若干重要的经验研究基础上，于 80 年代中期才迈上社会学专业化的道路。

至于科学社会学和相关领域"技术的社会研究""技术与社会研究"以及"技术社会学"等的关系，我们已经可以借助于国内学者对科学社会学类似状况所提出的思路与解决方案，恰当地、类比地加以认识和处理。"广义的科学社会学是在一般意义下讨论科学与社会诸方面的关系……当西方社会，特别是在讲英语的国家，总称'对科学的社会研究'……从事这样

---

① Ronald N Giere. Science and Technology Studies. Prospects for an Enlightened Postmodern Synthesis. In *Science, Technology, Human*, 1993, Vol.18, No 1.

② Randall Collins. The Development of a Sociological Theory of Sciences A 50-Year Perspective. In *Science, Technology, Human*, 1988, Vol.13.

工作的不仅限于社会学家，也有政治学家、经济学家等。""狭义的科学社会学是由专业社会学家运用社会学的概念与方法，对科学进行研究的结果，正是由于这一类工作专门化的特点，科学社会学才真正发展为一个学科。"①

笔者的想法是，凡从不同视角考察技术与社会互动效应的，都属于技术社会学范畴。技术社会学可以区分为广义的和狭义的（或专业性的），两者的界限和关系与社会学中的相似。

二、广义的技术社会学

实际上加斯通在十几年前就已经提出广义技术社会学的设想。在评价他所收录文献的学科属性时，他指出，"这些文献从相当广义的社会学角度看，可以认为是技术社会学的"，"它们的作者大多是从事科学知识应用研究的科学家，没有探讨真正的技术社会学的应该谈到的那些问题。当代许多有关技术课题的研究都含有某些社会学内容，若认为它们代表技术社会学，那是根本错误的"。他还指出，技术的社会问题已从技术对社会的影响的角度作了阐述，至于社会对技术的影响，以及技术的社会因素，则未加强调。②这样，他基本上提出了广义技术社会学在研究者的专业训练、研究方向与内容三个方面的特征，即：从事这方面工作的主要不是社会学家；研究是多视角、宽泛的；在技术与社会互动模式中，着重于技术的社会影响，在西方，更着重于负面影响。这样的划分界线与上述本文欲依循的国内学者的思路基本一致。

从加斯通收录的文献单子中可以看出，他的议论是针对 20 世纪二三十年代至 70 年代末的研究实况而发的。事实上，广义技术社会学已有悠久的历史传统。在这方面，马克思主义经典作家已为我们确立了一系列基本理论观点与方法论原则。特别是对于英国工业革命的社会分析，已成为东西方马克思主义者分析总体技术的模式。此外，马克思还曾精辟地剖析了工业革命时期多门类技术相互影响所引起的一系列连锁式的技术变革反应。

① 刘珺珺：《科学社会学》，上海人民出版社，1990 年。

② Jerry Gaston. Research in the Sociology of Technology. In Paul T. Durbin ed.: *A Guide to the Culture of Science. Technology and Medicine*. Free Press, 1996.

在分析机器生产过程的形成时他提出："机器生产是在与它不相适应的物质基础上自然兴起的。""当大工业特有的生产资料即机器本身，还要依靠个人的力量和个人的技巧才能存在时，……大工业也就得不到充分的发展"。为了克服这一矛盾，"大工业必须掌握它特有的生产资料，即机器本身，必须用机器生产机器"。[1]苏联学者遵循这条路线，在 20 世纪 50—80 年代初相继问世的几部技术史著作中，普遍采纳这样的模式：技术的变革主要由社会经济基础决定；技术的社会作用表现在生产力和生产关系的变革两个方面。根据他们对政治经济学理论和技术本质（物质性）的解释进一步得出结论，技术的社会作用在不同社会制度下是根本不同的，技术发展的方向、速度与规模也因此而异，因此，这些著作的技术史分期与社会制度相一致，而且在 1962 年出版的《技术史》中，以十月革命作为世界技术通史的一个分期线。

除了上述以社会经济制度作为技术发展的社会解释因素，还有一种分析路线着眼于广泛的社会文化背景。在李约瑟博士卓越的中西科技对比研究中，曾以古代"自然法则"在两种不同社会里的确认度说明两种不同的科技发展道路。他说，西方文明中最古老的观念之一就是，正如人间的帝王立法者们制定了成文法规为人们所遵守那样，至高无上的、有理性的造物主这位神明也制定了一系列为矿物、晶体、植物、动物和在自己轨迹上运行的星辰所必须遵守的法则。而传统的中国学者不可能有这样的思路。中国古代道家虽思想深沉又富于灵感，但他们不相信理性和逻辑的力量，所以未能发展出任何类似于自然法则观念的东西。在尚未奠定牛顿的世界图景的基础以前，就探索一种爱因斯坦式的世界图景，沿这条路科学是不可能发展的。墨家并不比道家更接近于自然法则观念，法儒两家对人身以外的周围自然界不感兴趣。到近代，以人类理性为基础的世俗化自然法则和以数字表达的自然界的经验法则是平行发展的。[2]

以上列举了早期对技术的社会分析的两种理论框架，它们至今仍为研究者们所沿袭。

在当代，有两类工作组成广义技术社会学的主体。一是以技术自主性为认知基础，分别以技术乐观主义或悲观主义为表现形式的技术与社会分

---

① 马克思：《资本论》第 1 卷，人民出版社，1976 年，第 419-420 页。

② 李约瑟：《中国科学技术史》第 2 卷，科学出版社、上海古籍出版社，1990 年。

析，着重预测现代技术的社会后果。其中技术批判运动更是一股强大的舆论和社会力量。但在 3S 或 STS 学术会议或期刊上，甚少见到这类论文，这大概是由于它们的议题太广泛了。另一类就是本文表中 17—20 号诸文所包容的课题。这些论文把技术从科学中"取出"，专致于考察技术与社会诸方面的相互关系，是 STS 或 3S 中常见到的，但为期并不久远，因为这类期刊杂志创建至今不过十来年。《社会学文摘》也收集这样的论文。笔者认为，国内近些年来有关技术的研究，大致属于这一类。它们对于政府和社会公众来说有十分重要且现实的意义：在技术政策、经济与文化发展的战略决策方面，在对广大群众进行宣传与教育—舆论导向方面，都发挥着重大作用。它确实拥有巨大的社会动能，以致使人认为，它就是全部的技术社会学。但同样地，它具有上述广义科学社会学的那些特征。

三、狭义的（专业性的）技术社会学

F. 奥格本的《社会变命》（1922）和 S. 吉尔菲朗的《发明社会学》（1935）是社会学家对技术进行分析的早期成果。默顿的《十七世纪英国的科学、技术和社会》涉及某些技术门类发展的社会因素。总的说来这些社会学家的工作没有给出促成进一步研究的技术社会学理论范式，因而未能使它成为社会学的一门实体化分支。

与科学社会学所经历的过程相似，作为社会学分支学科的狭义的（专业性的）技术社会学，也必然是社会学家运用社会学概念和方法，对技术发展过程进行分析的结果。在它的成长过程中，必然会出现某种（或几种）理论框架，尤为重要的是，框架应包含本专业特异的可操作概念工具。

具备上述条件的工作起始于 1984 年的一次研究讨论班，结果提出三种对待技术的态度，或三种研究路线：技术的社会建构主义（英国的 T. Pinch，现任教于康奈尔大学；荷兰的 W. Bijker）；技术系统方法（美国的 T. P. Hughes）；操作子网络分析法（法国的 M. Callon, Bruno Latour, John Law）。三者既互有争辩，也部分地覆盖。由于理解的不同，目前国内外都有人径直地称它们是"技术的社会建构主义"。

上述成果可视为专业性技术社会学的雏子，其双亲是技术史（主要是美国学者的）和科学知识社会学（主要是欧洲学者的）。这种对技术的历史学与社会学结合研究当时被称为技术与社会的整合研究，近年来有人称其为"新"技术社会学，以与新科学社会学（科学知识社会学）相对应。

每一研究路线都以个案为基础，个案是运用社会学方法，对近现代重要技术事件的原始材料（专利、专利诉讼与法律裁定，原初的报道与评论，发明家日记与通信）加以发掘和认真整理分析后完成的，它们表明，事件的真实过程与传统技术史所述颇有出入。

理论所包含的主要概念是：相关社会群体，解释灵活性（建构主义）；退却突出部，激进与保守的发明，技术系统的动量（技术系统法）；操作子的异质性与异质工程（操作子网络分析法），以及共同使用的"技术与社会的无缝之网"。还有一些中程概念，如复杂性与简化（用以从大量材料中提取要点便于分析），战略研究点（确定研究工作的焦点），技术的社会建构（SCOT，用于技术人造物演化的描述性模式）与技术框架（用于技术人造物演化的分析性模式），它们具有可操作性。

相应成果的陆续问世迅速引起学术界的关注，论者们频繁地介绍、评述，本文表中第 21 号的 12 篇论文都涉及这类课题。

虽然已有一定的经验基础，但讨论班的辩论主要是纲领性的。作为一名新产儿，人们既抱希望，也提出质问。为此于 1987 年举办了第二次讨论班，总体上指出新的研究纲领肯定能产生丰硕的经验研究成果，并回答一些普遍关注的问题。[①]该讨论班及后几年的努力在于探索技术社会学的前景——"我们由此去向何处？"

需要回答的问题可归纳为：相对主义、灵活性、实践与理论问题。

当前技术的社会研究中经常提及相对主义因素的两方面问题：一是关于本体论相对主义，一是关于规范相对主义。但技术的社会研究中关于相对主义的拒斥主要是方法论方面的。柯林斯（Collins）曾指出，认识论或本体论的相对主义不能由经验研究加以证实或证伪。这样，技术的社会建构主义研究就不蕴含任何本体论意义。规范问题为罗素（Russell）所述[②]，系导源于这样的思想，即对方法论相对主义的拒斥意味着一种政策相对主义形式，例如关于技术的社会影响、技术变革引起的劳动力非熟练化，或

---

① W. E. Bijker, J. Law eds. *Constructing Stable technologies. Towards a theory of Sociotechnical Change*. MIT Press, 1992.

② S. Russell. The Social Construction of Artifacts: A Response to Pinch and Bijker. In *Social Studies of Science*, 1986, Vol.16. pp.331-346.

对技术的民主控制等问题的政策的相对主义。当伏尔泰宣称上帝是不存在的，因而使他受到一切规范和价值被腐蚀的谴责时，他曾回答道，上帝不存在并不意味着任何事情现在都是许可的。它只是意味着，由于与圣经所云不相同的理由，使有的事情不被许可。与此相似，根据技术的相对主义研究，有可能根据技术的选择作政策及伦理方面的辩论。

　　实践问题在荷兰有特殊意义。荷兰的 STS 主要不是起源于社会学、历史学或哲学流派分支。它主要发源于荷兰的"科学与社会"运动，后者起因于20世纪70年代初在大多数科技人员中确立的批判性 STS 纲领的建立。到 70 年代末，对于批判性 STS 与教学的进一步经验与理论基础的需要日益迫切。80 年代的科学与技术研究走了一段弯路，即致力于搜集材料以与政治、科学、技术界的权威人士抗争。当然也可以认为这是正常的迂回。如果这样，就无所谓实践问题了。如果有人仍受旧的科学、技术与社会研究观点的束缚，那么问题就变成这样：当前 STS 中的成果是否与科学和技术的民主控制相联系，或如有一人指责的那样，建构主义与政策制定不相干？[①]目前有人认为，技术决定论可以重新评估为有活力且成果丰硕的考察技术与社会互动的理论观点，只是需要一个模型，使技术的本质或内容能独立地形成最终的政治、经济与社会选择。建构主义者对此作出了明确的回答。技术决定论是一种可以随便玩弄的观点。如果它仍像现在那样流行，那么技术仍由自主性因素、内部动力所决定，并且是不可控的。这样的技术变革形象不可能刺激社会公众参与技术民主控制过程。如果科学事实是由自然支配的而不是由人所建构的，那么任何科学争论都会导致这样的结论，即一部分参与争辩的人是正确的而另一部分人则是错误的，或是"好人"反对"坏人"。相似地，如果技术发展的社会建构主义未被建立起来，不强调技术变革的可能性与强制性，那么大部分公众就会被扭转方向，并让技术不受控制。

　　但是，对所有质询的进一步辩解均有待于理论（灵活性是其中一个基本概念单元）的发展，本杰克（Bijker）对此迈出了重要的一步。[②]

----

① Ronald N Giere. Science and Technology Studies, Prospects for an Enlightened Postmodern Synthesis. In *Science, Technology, Human*, 1993, Vol 18.

② M. Callon. Some elements of a sociology of translation. In Law ed.: *Power, Action and Belief*. Routledge & Kegan Paul, 1986.

四、走向社会技术集合（Sociotechnical Ensembles）理论

理论问题从技术的历史社会学研究之初就被提到日程上来，某些批评者针对技术史状况曾经指出，虽然历史学家常打开技术的"黑箱"以考察技术的内容（技术的经济学和哲学研究不是这样），但他们几乎从不把该黑箱与其他案例研究加以对比，从而归纳出技术变革过程的普遍性解释。现在已经有了不断增加的经验材料，因此当务之急在于作出理论性概括。

本杰克分三个步骤加以处理。第一步，先运用自行车案例，把技术变革作为社会过程加以分析。关键性概念是相关社会群体和解释灵活性。为了在哲学水平上支持这样的分析，对称性原则起到重要作用。第二步，把酚醛树脂案例用于发展技术框架的理论概念。讨论关于技术变革的理论应当满足哪些要求，以及技术框架如何符合这些要求。第三步，把技术框架概念用于荧光灯案例，由此认为，对于技术人造物的原初定义已显得过于狭窄，因而建议以"社会技术集合"取代它作为分析单元。在哲学水平上，这意味着从以往的单纯对称性原则过渡到普遍对称性原则。兹分述如下。

（1）自行车演化表明，仅从人造物内在性质说明技术事件的过程和设计是不可能的。

19 世纪 70 年代英国的高轮自行车似乎是一项错误的专利：为什么制成如此笨重的结构而不采用达·芬奇时代就已经知道的链条、链轮、齿轮构成现代的低轮自行车呢？追踪不同相关社会群体赋予自行车的意义可以找到答案。对于妇女和中年男子来说，高轮车是危险的、无法使用的，并且在维多利亚时代，妇女骑这种车上街也惹人侧目。这类车应该在商业上失败。但正好相反，在几年内，它取得很大成功。存在着一个特定的相关社会群体：富裕和有勇气的青年男子。体格健壮的上层和中上阶层男子骑着高轮自行车吸引着海德公园里的女性。他们建构了"强壮男子自行车"。

以相关社会群体作为描述的起点，可以说明人造物的解释灵活性。后者是社会建构主义的核心和前提，它实际上适用于大多数当代技术史与技术的社会研究。解释灵活性概念是严格地与技术决定论相对立的。实际上，承认前者与拒斥后者是同义的。因此，该概念在技术的社会研究中的关键作用是：只有把技术看作非自主的，并且不是由纯内部动力学驱动的，才

可能对技术进行社会分析。

解释灵活性在对称原则方面找到了自己的哲学方法论基础。此原则是布鲁尔在 20 世纪 70 年代为科学的社会研究提出来的。他认为，为了分析科学的信念体系，科学知识社会学家们应该不偏袒体系的真与伪，对真与伪的断言应用同一概念工具作对称分析。平奇和毕克尔后来把此原则扩展于技术分析，指出对成功和不成功的机器要作对称分析。不能把投入使用的机器看作其成功的原因，而是被相关社会群体接受的结果，从中可以提取一般性模式来描述技术的发展。这种描述性模式应允许分析者进入各种个案研究的黑箱，但还应最后能走出黑箱，以与其他个案进行比较。这样，模式应在具体水平和横向对比分析之间保持精细的平衡。前述技术的社会建构（SCOT）模式经过实际研究，已能满足这样要求。

（2）运用 SCOT 描述赛璐珞和酚醛树脂发展的目的在于提出概念框架，以便对大量详尽资料进行概括。这样的概念框架应能表达三项特征：技术与社会之网的无缝特征；变革/连续维度；操作子/结构维度。

现代技术发展的特征已用无缝之网的比喻加以说明（Hughes 等人）。现代社会之网不是由性质截然不同的科学的、技术的、文化的和经济的等布片"缝制"而成，而是其折缝可看作由操作子或分析者组成。另一条表达同样含义的途径是观察工程师的行为：一位成功的工程师不是一位纯粹的技术巫师，他也是一位经济的、政治的和社会的巫师。一位典型的优秀技术专家是一位"异质工程师"。上述分析导致的结果是，技术变革理论概念必须满足异质操作子行为及无缝之网的要求。如果不是这样，传统的陈旧的二分法从描述模式的前门被撵出，又会从概括的后门窜入。因此，理论框架不得对特定范型的社会、技术或科学的特征作出任何预设的选定。

满足第二项特征的要求是，概念框架应能解释历史上的变革与连续性。此项要求的原始工作在 SCOT 描述性模式中是由稳定性和争论中止的概念提供的。稳定程度被作为相关社会群体对一件人造物的接受量度；对人造物所赋予的意义越是一致，稳定度就越高。争论中止与稳定是紧密联系的两项概念。起初，争论中止在科学知识社会学（SSK）中被引入用以表示科学共同体内部达成意见一致的科学争论的终止。SSK 的研究已经指出，一旦意见一致，科学断言的解释灵活性就不复存在。这样，建构主义的分析既着重于技术发展的偶然性（借助于展示一件人造物的解释灵活性），从而强调变革的可能性；也可以描述选择自由度由于争论中止和稳定过程而变得是有限度的。这项要求的实质是，把偶然的解释灵活性与强制的稳定性，或变革与持久性，间断与连续性结合在一起。解决这种任务的典型方式是给出静态的描述，然后加上时间维度，使得各项概念是内在的静态的。

至于操作子/结构维度特征，也蕴含于 SCOT 模式的相同方面中。展示人造物的解释灵活性就意味着任何事情都可能发生吗？人造物和相关社会群体的每种构型都可能随意建立或破坏吗？新人造物的产生以一种物质发明的不同设计路线，它们都没有尽头吗？当然不可能这样。正是在上述场合，概念的争论中止和稳定过程迈入新的阶段。SCOT 的第二步就是考察其中一种人造物是如何趋向稳定以及其他人造物是如何失去稳定和从历史上消失的。这样，未来技术发展的一个新的建构环境就产生了。因此，第三项要求应该是，把对技术发展的偶然性的理论分析与它的结构被强制化相结合，亦即把操作子战略与它们被束缚着的结构，或自由意志与"命运"相结合。

技术框架概念符合上述三项要求。第一，技术框架是异质的，并非特定地隶属于认知的或社会的范畴。在技术框架的组分中，有范例性人造物及文化价值、目标和科学理论、试验方案和固有的知识。第二，技术框架不是固定的实体，若干技术框架之间相互作用的特征使之成为一项内在动力学性质的概念。技术框架既非个体内在的，又非自然外在的，它涉及相关社会群体内个体的相互关系，因此需要通过相互作用被持续地维持着，其特征不是保持不变的。第三，技术框架提供了目标、思想及行为的工具。它既提供核心问题，又给出解决该问题的相关策略（如赛璐珞案例所述）。但同时，技术框架的建立将限制相关社会群体成员的自由度。结构是由相互关系创立的，它转而限制进一步的相互作用。在技术框架内，并非任何事情都是可能的（结构中心化），但所保留的可能性变得更为明晰，并已可适用于相关社会群体的全体成员（操作子中心化）。

（3）从荧光灯案例说起。荧光灯是 1938 年 4 月由通用电气公司为彩色照明推入市场。对它的建构主义分析的结果说明了它的解释灵活性：除了该公司的"彩色灯"，还有高效能灯（high efficiency lamp）可供相关的生产性社会群体使用，只是担心后者销路不畅并引起竞争。在一次通用电气公司上层经理人员与用户的会议上，争论中止。其结果是由第三种荧光灯——强照明灯（high intensity lamp）建构而成，它就是最终达到稳定化的荧光灯。但在 1939 年 4 月，这类灯尚没有在物质上可供利用的明确前景。

虽然与会者都赞同强照明灯，但当时在"技术上"还不可能。从中可以看到与此过程不可分割地存在着各种"其他的"因素——灯生产者与用户之间相互关系的重构，通用公司专利权的失效，以及 20 世纪 40 年代初美国的备战等。这样的社会学研究引导人们去探讨专利经济学、公司组织、国家的规章制度、发明经济学以及临战前的社会。实际上这要求分析者同意，在现代社会之网中，社会的与技术的因素之间的缝隙是不存在的，分析工作必须超越社会的与技术的因素之间的二分法。社会性关系只出现在社会学家的想象之中，而纯技术性关系则只出现在科学幻想小说里。技术是社会建构的，社会是技术建构的——一切稳定的集合既由技术的也由社会的因素相互联系在一起。过去曾经是"纯粹"性质的地方，现在都是异质的。社会上各阶级、职业团体、专业人员、公司、机器都由本质上相互联系的社会和技术手段被置于自己的位置。这种情景已超越讨论自行车案例时的描述：以总体对称原则取代对称原则，以社会技术集合取代技术人造物，并以前者为分析单元；最后，看来技术社会学将被迫进入一般社会学领域。

总体对称原则扩展了上述布鲁尔的对称原则。对称原则提倡的是，对真与伪的信念（在技术场合，是成功与失败的机器）要用相同的术语加以分析。卡隆（Callon）把这条原则扩展到另一水平以科学技术的建构为一方，以社会的建构为另一方，对于它们，都应在同一框架内加以分析。既不是技术还原论（把对社会的解释还原为技术的发展），也不是社会还原论（认为技术是由社会决定的），它们都不应成为技术与社会分析的基础。①默顿的工作就在于为在科学与其他社会建制之间求得对称，布鲁尔为把科学内容投入这样的分析，平奇和本杰克则为对称地对待科学与技术，并为把技术投入这样的分析而争辩。

至于还原论一词，它通常含有贬义，因而力图避免。但当社会的和技术的因素仍是两个世界时，实际存在着两种形式的还原论。技术还原论认为社会界的发展可用技术世界中发生的事件加以解释，从而形成技术决定论。社会还原论则暗示，技术世界完全由社会因素决定——科学知识社会学中的利益理论即为一例。如果以社会技术集合作为新的分析单元，两种

---

① M. Callon. Some elements of a sociology of translation. In Law ed.: *Power, Action and Belief.* Routledge & Kegan Paul, 1986, pp.196-233.

形式的还原论都可以避免。但是，如果还没有充分发展这一概念，那么某种形式的还原论还是必要的。没有某些形式的还原，研究工作将陷入杂乱无章的经验主义泥潭。目前许多工作就在于发现新的社会技术领域内的新的还原形式。

以上理论发展的最后结论是，社会建构主义纲领可以继续采用，但要扩展视角——应以社会技术集合而不是技术作为未来社会的考察主体；也要进一步深化，现在可以在过去十年经验研究的基础上对解释作进一步的深入化；还要加强与政治的联系，分析工作指向权力分配和社会的重新形成这样的议题。因此，最近这一时期技术社会学的理论主流也可称为"后建构主义"。

参考文献：

［1］Science, Technology, Human Values, Vol.13, No.1, 2.

［2］Ronald N Giere, Science and Technology Studies: Prospects for an Enlightened Postmodern Synt hesis, in Science, Technology, Human Values (Vol.18, No.1, 1993).

［3］Randall Collins, The Development of a Sociological Theory of Sciences: A 50-Year Perspective, in Science, Technology, Human Values (Vol.13，1988).

［4］刘珺珺：《科学社会学》，上海人民出版社，1990 年。

［5］Jerry Gaston, Research in the Sociology of Technology, in Paul T. Durbin (ed.): A Guide to the Culture of Science, Technology and Medicine.

［6］马克思：《资本论》第 1 卷，人民出版社，1976 年，第 419-420 页。

［7］李约瑟：《中国科学技术史》第 2 卷《科学思想史》，科学出版社，上海古籍出版社。

［8］W. E. Bijker, J. Law (eds.), Constructing Stable technologies:Towards a theory of Sociotechnical Change (Cambridge, MIT Press, 1992).

［9］S. Russell:The Social Construction of Artifacts: A Response to Pinch and Bijker, Social Studies of Science (Vol.16, 1986).

［10］W. E. Bijker, Do Not Despair: There is Life after Constructivism, in Science, Technology, Human Values (Vol.18, 1993).

[11]M. Callon, Some elements of a sociology of translation, in Law (ed.): 1 Power, Action and Belief, (London: Routledge & Kegan Paul, 1986).

（本文原载于《自然辩证法通讯》1994 年第 1 期。）

科学认识论的若干问题

李建珊*

我国马克思主义认识论的研究，长期以来受苏联教科书体系的影响很深。有些号称马克思主义认识论的著作也讲实践概念，也讲人的主观能动性，但对这些问题的论述均不占主要地位，甚至不难发现其中直观反映论的痕迹。一些人脱离现代各门类科学研究的成果谈哲学现代化，他们讲要发展认识论，却又排斥科学认识论。这种状况束缚着马克思主义哲学的发展。本文主要讨论目前科学认识论研究中三个有争议的问题：（1）认识客体是自在的，还是属人的；（2）主客体发生的同时性问题；（3）科学仪器是认识论客体吗？

一、认识客体是自在的，还是属人的？

科学认识活动是一种对象性的活动，这种活动的结构包括作为其两极的主体和客体，以及作为两极相互作用之中介的认识工具（科学语言、科学仪器、科学方法）。

正如"主体"和"客体"是认识论的基本概念一样，"科学认识主体"和与之相对的"科学认识客体"则是科学认识论中的基本概念。

所谓"科学认识主体"是指在科学认识活动中，具有一定的科学知识，以科学仪器和技术手段为工具，运用科学思维方法，并同科学认识客体建立了对象性关系的人。科学认识主体是有意识、能思维的社会存在物，是科学认识能力的活的载体，是科学认识活动能动的和主导的方面。这里所

---

* 李建珊，南开大学哲学院科技哲学教研室教授，主要研究方向为科学技术哲学与价值论。

说的科学认识能力其实就是马克思多次讲到的"人的本质力量"在科学活动中的具体表现。它包括主体选择并确定科学认识客体的能力，主体运用物质手段变革客体从而认识客体的能力，以及主体观念地掌握客体的能力。

如果说哲学家对"主体"的解释和规定存在分歧和差异，那么，哲学家们对"客体"的界定就有更大的分歧。在一定意义上讲，这几乎成了机械唯物论、形形色色的唯心论和马克思的辩证唯物论的重要分水岭之一。西方、苏联和我国科学认识论中不同流派的争论往往与此相关。

固然，"客体"一词是多义的，因此会有多种用法。但问题的关键是人们往往混淆本体论和认识论两个层次的问题，才使得对于客体的理解产生重大分歧。比如，有人用"客体"这个词来指称事物、物体、物质存在，总之是在"客观存在"的意义上理解"客体"这个概念的。根据这种理解，任何一个自然物在任何情况下都无条件地是客体；只要自然物一经产生，它就成为客体。于是，地球以及先于人类产生的动植物从它们生成时起就是客体，而不必管人类是否出现，也不必管人们是否开始把它们作为认识与实践的对象。在这种理解下的"客体"与主体无关，与主体的认识与实践无关，因此与认识论无关。这是对于"客体"的一种本体论理解。而与此不同的另外一种理解，则把客体看作主体的对立物，用"客体"一词指称主体活动的对象——认识对象或实践对象。后一种理解认为，"客体"不等同于物体、物质的东西，也不等同于"客观存在"。一个自然物在其没有进入认识过程的条件下不成其为认识对象，不能成为客体。在这种理解中，"客体"不仅必然与主体的认识有关，而且与主体是相互依存、相互规定的。在主体及其实践——认识活动产生之前，根本谈不上作为主体实践——认识对象的客体。因为自在之物没有与主体发生联系，因此不可能具有客体的品格。可见，这里所理解的"客体"，其规定性是认识论性质的；它以存在为基础，但比自在的存在有更高的层次。应该指出，客体尽管不等同于自在的存在，却可以由后者转化而来；而某个自在的存在所以能转化为主体有目的活动的对象——客体，是因为它同一定历史阶段中主体现实的需要、本性和本质力量相适应，即是说，它对主体的对象性活动具有意义。

在一般认识论中，我们把对主体的对象性活动具有现实意义从而被纳入主体对象性活动的结构，并同主体发生相互作用的客观事物，称为客体。而在科学认识论中，我们把在一定的社会史和认识史条件下进入人类科学认识范围、成为科学认识活动的对象并且同科学认识主体发生相互作用的那部分存在，称为科学认识客体。显然，客体是一个认识论的范畴，而不是本体论的范畴。认识论中的客体范畴不同于本体论中的物质、自然界、客观存在等范畴。同时，作为认识对象的客体，也不只包括物质存在，还包括精神性的存在。

马克思在《费尔巴哈论》中深刻批判了旧唯物主义或直观唯物主义。他指出，旧唯物主义的"主要缺点是：对事物、现实、感性，只是从客体的或直观的形式去理解，而不是把它们当作人的感性活动，当作实践去理解，不是从主观方面去理解"[①]。这里深刻批判了对于客体的直观的、本体论的理解。

我们以为，客体和客观存在两者的本质区别在于：如果说物质、自然界、客观存在等，不以任何主体的思维、意志和活动为转移而独立存在的话，那么，一般认识论和科学认识论中的客体恰恰同主体的思维、意志和活动相关联，同主体的现实需要、本性和本质力量相适应。我们否认两者的等同，而强调它们的区别，与承认客体的客观实在性丝毫不相悖。

实际上，不仅人类出现之前的纯粹独立自在的自然界不可能成为任何意义上的客体，而且在人类出现之后每个具体的历史时期，人类认识所及的永远只能限于自然界的一部分。除非有一个全知全能的主宰。在一定历史条件下，现实的科学认识客体，乃"是感觉之对象，是感性的对象"[②]，是科学认识主体直接或间接（通过仪器）感知到的、与主体有某种信息联系从而进入科学认识范围的那部分存在。

在科学认识客体的基本性质中最容易混淆的是它的客观性和属人性。

对于主体而言，科学认识客体的存在具有客观性，是它的基本属性。不论巨大的天体还是基本粒子，也不论原生生物还是复杂的人体，它们作为认识客体，都是客观存在着的具体物质形态，其运动规律均不以认识主体的意识为转移。即使是人工自然，它们一旦被创造出来，就是对象化了的客观存在，其存在和发展规律同样不依赖于研究者的意识。甚至人的精神活动及其成果，虽然本身具有精神属性，但一旦作为认识对象，就具有对象化的客观意义。

但是，科学认识客体更为本质的属性则是它的属人性。作为科学认识

---

① 《马克思恩格斯选集》第 1 卷，人民出版社，1995 年，第 16 页。
② 《马克思恩格斯全集》第 42 卷，人民出版社，1979 年，第 69 页。

主体对象性活动的客体的，只能是外部世界中同主体现实的需要、本性和本质力量相适应，因而对主体具有现实意义的那一部分存在。我们把科学认识客体对于主体在发现自然规律的活动中的现实需要和现实能力的依赖性这一特点，叫作客体的属人性。

马克思在《1844 年经济学哲学手稿》中指出："对象如何对他说来成为他的对象，这取决于对象的性质以及与之相适应的本质力量的性质；因为正是这种关系的规定性形成一种特殊的、现实的肯定方式。……从主体方面来看：只有音乐才能激起人的音乐感；对于没有音乐感的耳朵说来，最美的音乐也毫无意义，不是对象，因为我的对象只能是我的一种本质力量的确证，也就是说，它只能像我的本质力量作为一种主体能力自为地存在着那样对我存在，因而任何一个对象对我的意义（它只是对那个与之相适应的感觉来说才有意义）都以我的感觉所及的程度为限。"①这是对于客体的属人性的绝妙表述。

科学认识论的研究表明，科学认识客体从来是作为科学认识主体的科学家设定的。主体之所以选择、确定这一部分事物作为对象，与主体所代表的社会的、认识的、实践的需要有密切关系，同时与主体的本质力量密切相关。就物质的客体而言，虽然人类很早就能看到银河系的很多天体，但最先成为天文学家认识客体并成为人们重点观测与研究对象的，是与确定季节、农时及航海方位密切相关的少数天体；人类对地球上数以万计生物物种的认识几乎同整个文明史一样长久，但首先成为生命科学认识对象的，是与人类生产与生活直接相关的部分动植物与微生物。河外星系和众多的宇宙射线早在人类产生之前就存在，但直至 20 世纪才进入科学家的视野，成为科学认识客体。而在我们视野范围之外，如恩格斯所说："存在甚至完全是一个悬而未决的问题。"②

在认识论意义上，为什么说属人性是客体区别于客观存在的最本质的规定？第一，客体是人类活动和人类目的的结果。科学认识主体在认识自然的实践—认识关系中，总是首先把自然界的某些事物或过程设定为自己活动的对象即客体，以便达到主体的目的——发现该事物和过程的本质及规律性。于是，客体从产生开始就渗透着人的目的。第二，与日常认识活

---

① 《马克思恩格斯全集》第 42 卷，人民出版社，1979 年，第 125-126 页。
② 《马克思恩格斯选集》第 3 卷，人民出版社，1995 年，第 83 页。

动不同，科学认识活动是体现人类高度能动性的实践—认识活动，研究对象的设定不是随意的，而要根据社会发展和科学自身发展的需要，以及认识主体的认识能力和技术水平，选择那些最有可能产生预期认识成果的事物与过程，作为客体。第三，客体是通过理论渗透获得的。在科学认识活动中，自然界里的某种事物与过程之所以被发现，曾被解释为某种偶然的机遇，实际上是主体认识发展的必然。X 射线之所以和居里夫人及克鲁克斯擦肩而过，没有纳入他们的视野，而唯有伦琴抓住了它，是因为它和伦琴已有的经验、知识、理论相吻合。在理论的渗透下，X 射线进入科学认识领域，从自在的存在转化成为客体。

另外，同一客观事实被纳入不同的理论框架而变成不同的科学认识客体的情况，在科学认识史上比比皆是。就以石块下落来说，其视网膜映象从古到今无论对谁都是一样的，可是亚里士多德看到石块趋向它的自然位置；伽利略看到石块与天体一样作圆周运动；而牛顿看到石块在引力作用下直线下落；爱因斯坦看到石块在引力场中沿黎曼空间走最短路程。同理，在普利斯特列看到失去燃素的地方，拉瓦锡看到的却是氧气。

从认识论的角度讲，属人性是科学认识客体的最为重要的属性或规定性。没有这一属性，客体同自在的存在就没有了本质的区别。然而，人们往往因为局限于本体论的角度，仅仅强调客体的客观实在性而忽略其属人性，这是把认识论问题本体论化的表现。

二、关于主客体发生的同时性问题

科学认识论归根结底是研究"科学认识主体"和"科学认识客体"及两者关系的理论。在一定意义上可以说，主、客体关系问题是科学认识论的基本问题。

在认识论范围内讨论主体和客体的范畴时，往往遇到它同本体论中意识与物质这对范畴的关系问题。应当说，这是属于两个不同层次的问题。其中，意识和物质的关系更为基本，它是阐明认识论中主体和客体关系问题的本体论前提。只有在搞清意识和物质的关系的基础上，才能进一步搞清主体和客体的关系。但这是必要条件，不是充分条件。前者不能代替后者。

有一种看法认为，如果在认识论中谈主体和客体，就只能得出结论：

物质是客体，意识是主体；物质第一性，意识第二性，即客体在先，主体在后。这是把本体论和认识论这两个不同层次的问题混同了。实际上，在马克思主义哲学看来，这两个层次的问题既有联系，又有区别。所谓联系是指：客体首先应当是客观存在，而主体则包含主观意识。所谓区别是指：客体不等同于全部客观存在，只有成为人的认识与实践（变革）对象的客观实在才是客体；而主体也不仅仅具有意识的属性，它还具有社会属性、自然属性等等。同时，由物质第一性、意识第二性，不能一般地推出"客体在先，主体在后"。只有本体论才回答谁先谁后的问题，而认识论则已超出历史关系的范围。

从历史上不同哲学体系对主体和客体与意识和物质关系问题的解决中，我们发现了不同哲学体系之间错综复杂的关系，必须进行仔细的研究与理论上的分辨，否则会不自觉地把错误的概念当成正确的东西加以接受。这是造成上述理论混乱的思想根源。因此，必须注意：

第一，本体论上使用的"主体"一词，所涉及的是世界的本体，或某种派生物的本原，或某种现象、属性、状态、关系、变化、活动和过程的承担者。既然如此，在本体论意义上"严格说来，并没有什么主体和客体的区分与对立"[①]。

第二，直观唯物主义和辩证唯物主义在本体论上都认为世界的本体只有客观存在的物质实体；并都承认作为主体的人不等同于意识，人的物质实体性不亚于任何自然物。但在认识论上，前者只承认客体对主体的作用，主体只能被动地、消极地直观反映客体；而后者则承认主体在能动的实践—认识活动中对客体的巨大反作用。直观唯物主义在主客体关系问题上的失误就在于：他们没有从主体的能动的本质力量和实践活动方面去理解认识客体的规定性，没有看到正是由于主体能动的实践与认识活动才使自然界的事物由自在的东西转化为主体所认识的客体。

第三，唯心论和辩证唯物论在认识论上都承认客体是在活动中生成的，但其本体论前提则有天壤之别。如主客体含义，前者所称的"活动"是纯粹自我的意识活动，后者所指的"活动"则是具有物质性的实践—认识活动；前者所指的"生成"具有历史性的、派生的含义，后者所指的"生成"是共时的，即主客体同时发生。具体地说，唯心主义否认物质世界的本原

---

① 夏甄陶：《认识论引论》，人民出版社，1986年，第66页。

性，把某种精神的或观念的实体看作世界的本原。他们把这种实体当作绝对的主体，并从这种主体的活动即精神实体的活动中，引出主体和客体的关系以及客体的存在。客体被说成是主体活动的结果，是由主体本身生成的。唯心主义在主客体关系问题上的失误在于：（1）把客体看成是主体（精神实体）在纯粹自我的意识活动中创设和生成的；（2）同直观唯物论殊路同归的是，唯心论在主客体关系问题上也犯了混淆本体论和认识论两个不同层次问题的错误。而辩证唯物论认为，世界是统一的，世界的统一性在于它的物质性。认识论意义上的主体和客体范畴都属于统一的物质世界，是物质世界分化的结果。因此，不能把主体和客体这一对范畴同精神与物质的范畴等同起来。

在科学认识中，主体与客体是表示现实的认识关系的两极，二者互为前提、相互依存而不可分割。尽管主体和客体各自有自身的多种特性，但是对象性是它们共同具备的特性。人类的活动是一种对象性活动。毫不例外，科学认识活动也是人类的一种对象性活动。所谓对象性，是指主体、客体双方互以对方为自己的前提，从与对方的关系中获得自己的规定。在认识论意义上完全可以断定：没有无客体的主体，也没有无主体的客体。"去掉双方中的任何一方，都不能形成对象性活动的结构"。[1]

科学认识论的研究表明，认识论中的主、客体关系不仅仅是逻辑上（互为前提）的关系，而且是历史上（同时生成）的关系。马克思指出："只有当物按人的方式同人发生关系时，我才能在实践上按人的方式同物发生关系。"[2]从认识论角度讲，这正是认识活动中客体人化和主体对象化的过程。正是从这一时刻起，主体与客体同时生成。显然，在马克思上述思想中，已蕴涵了关于主客体同时性的思想。当天文学家将某一天文现象纳入自己的视野，作为其认识对象即客体时，同时就确立了科学家自身作为认识者的主体地位。

所谓"主客体的同时性"，其核心内容就是指认识主体和认识客体在历史上同时发生，并且同时并存。马克思在《〈政治经济学批判〉导言》中讨论人类的生产实践时指出："生产不仅为主体生产对象，而且也为对象生产

---

① 陈柏灵：《关于正确评价〈唯物主义与经验批判主义〉的若干问题》，《中国社会科学》，1989 年第 6 期，第 85—92 页。

②《马克思恩格斯全集》第 42 卷，人民出版社，1979 年，第 124 页。

主体。"①这不仅适用于一般实践—认识活动，而且适用于科学的实践—认识活动。人类学关于原始思维的研究以及自然科学中关于儿童心理学的研究成果，也证实了认识主体与客体在历史上同时发生的论断。

首先，关于人类认识史上主客体的同时发生。

人类认识史、思维史表明：在人类最初形成时，当他们第一次制造出工具，并用来作用于植物、动物、土地等自然界的一部分事物时，也就同时产生了主体和客体。但这只是一种事实上的主客体分化，而不是在意识中的主客体分化。换句话说，在原始人类的早期阶段，由于人类意识和自觉能动性的出现，使得原始社会在事实上已经同时分化出主体和客体，但是，主体还没有关于主客体分化的意识。法国人类学家、社会学家列维·布留尔（Lévy-Brühl, Lucién, 1857—1939）在其 20 世纪 20 年代有关原始人智力机能的著作《原始思维》中探讨了这一状况的诸方面表现。他发现：第一，原始人不能把自己同自然界分开来，具有拟人化的自然观，图腾崇拜就是这种自然观的表现；第二，原始人不能把自己同集体或社会区分开来，具有非个体的社会观，没有私有财产观念；第三，原始人不能把自己同自己的思维区分开来，具有"灵魂不死"的思维观。总之，原始人不能把自己同自然客体、社会客体和思维客体加以区分，因此处于主体和客体不分的状态。

只是在人作为主体同作为客体的外部对象发生相互作用的漫长的历史过程中，通过经验的长期积累，人类才初步具有了关于外部事物某些属性和规律的意识，掌握了外部事物的某些尺度；同时也初步具有了关于自己的需要、本性、力量和活动的自我意识。这是人把自己同外部对象加以区别的最初表现。随着人类实践的发展，人们产生了越来越多的关于外部对象的意识，同时，人们也在越来越广泛的范围内和越来越深刻的程度上把自己内在的尺度运用到对象上去，从而在认识和改造客体的同时，使自身的主体地位日益加强（至于从哲学史上把主体和客体作为认识论的范畴加以明确区分和深刻反思，是 17 世纪以来的事情②）。

其次，关于个体心理发展史上主客体的同时发生。

作为当代著名的心理学家、哲学家的皮亚杰（Jean Piaget, 1896—1980）

① 《马克思恩格斯选集》第 2 卷，人民出版社，1995 年，第 95 页。
② 邢贲思《中国大百科全书：哲学卷（II）》，中国大百科全书出版社，1987 年，第 240 页。

在《儿童心理学》和《发生认识论原理》等代表作中，通过对个体心理发展规律的探讨，第一次明确地提出了主客体发生的同时性问题。他的心理学研究表明，初生婴儿不分主体和客体，而是把两者融合在一起。由于儿童用自己的动作接触外界事物，使客体发生了移动或变化，这时婴儿才知道手是他自己身体的一部分，才开始区分自己和物体；大约四个半月的婴儿开始寻找他视野内看得到的客体，但还不能有效地寻找发生复杂位移的客体；直到将近周岁时，才能知道暂时"消失"了的客体的永久性，并设法找到这个客体。[①]

皮亚杰研究了儿童智力在各年龄段上的个体发生与发展，从认识的起源一直追踪到科学思维的发展。皮亚杰既反对"认识是主体求教于客体"的经验论，也反对"认识为主体的头脑所固有"的天赋论（或先验论），他从生物学和心理发生学的研究成果出发，指出："认识既不是起因于一个有自我意识的主体，也不是起因于业已形成的（从主体的角度来看）、会把自己烙印在主体之上的客体；认识起因于主客体之间的相互作用，这种作用发生在主体和客体之间的中途，因而同时既包含着主体又包含着客体……"这种作用使得主客体从完全未分化的状态而分化为认识论意义上的主体和客体，在这里，起中介作用的是活动本身[②]。皮亚杰强调认识起源于未分化的主客体的相互作用，强调主体的活动对于主体同客体的分化（同时发生）的决定作用，这样一来就克服了经验论和天赋论的片面性，这同马克思主义哲学强调实践在认识中的决定作用，强调人在认识中的主观能动性，是殊途同归的。

此外，皮亚杰还提出了"认识结构"的概念。他认为每一个智慧活动都含有一定的认识结构，这种结构的模式不是行为主义所提出的单向活动模式（刺激→反应，即 S→R），因为"一个刺激要引起某一特定反应，主体及其机体就必须有反应刺激的能力"[③]。所以他提出双向活动模式（刺激←→反应，即 S←→R 公式），以反对传统的单向活动模式。这一模式对于科学认识的发生同样适用。科学认识史表明，主体和客体产生和发展的同时性这一结论也适用于科学认识主体和客体的发生与发展。

然而，某些马克思主义哲学教科书硬把主客体的相互规定、互为依存

---

① 皮亚杰：《发生认识论原理》，商务印书馆，1981 年，第 12-13 页。
② 皮亚杰：《发生认识论原理》，商务印书馆，1981 年，第 21-22 页。
③ 皮亚杰：《发生认识论原理》，商务印书馆，1981 年，第 60 页。

的观点同主观唯心主义的本体论概念（如贝克莱"存在就是被感知"的思想）以及阿芬那留斯的"原则同格论"相提并论。认真研究一下认识论史，就会知道这种相提并论是不妥的，甚至是荒谬的。

为了澄清被一知半解的人们混淆了的概念，我们以为，必须要区分认识论意义上的主体与客体范畴同本体论意义上的思维与存在、精神与物质的范畴，这是截然不同的两类范畴。其中的关键是区分"客观实在"和"客体"这两个概念。必须明确，"客观实在"的概念包括不以人的意识为转移的一切存在着的事物，其对立面是意识；而"客体"的概念只是客观实在中的部分事物，它在社会发展的某个阶段上才成为人的实践和认识活动的对象，它的对立面不是意识，而是把客观存在的部分事物变为自己行为的客体的那个主体。

列宁曾经批评原则同格论的否定物（非我、环境）不依赖于意识（自我）而独立存在，而"把认识论建立在客体和人的感觉有不可分割的联系这一前提上"[①]。显然，列宁是在本体论领域讨论问题，因此这里的所谓"客体"显然应指"客观存在"。而他所强调的本体论前提问题，同马克思主义认识论以及科学认识论中所讨论的主客体相互依存、不可分割的问题应当说本质上是不矛盾的，因为这本来就是根本不同的两个层次的问题。

马克思主义认识论以及科学认识论中所讲的"主体"并不是人的意识，而是人本身和人类社会，它是自然界高级发展阶段分化出来的产物，这是不亚于动物、植物、矿物等自然事物的客观实在。马克思主义认识论及科学认识论中所讲的"客体"并不简单是自然界中的任何一个事物和对象，而仅仅是包括在人的活动范围之内的那部分事物和对象。就是说，只有客观事物同主体发生物质的、能量的和信息的联系和相互作用时，这个客观事物才具有客体的性质。因此，在认识论意义上，没有主体便没有客体，没有客体也不可能有主体；主体与客体同时生成、相互依赖、不可分割。

这样说丝毫不意味着否定或取代辩证唯物主义认识论的本体论前提。但我们更应当防止和避免用主客体问题的本体论分析代替或取消认识论的分析，防止和避免把本体论层次的问题同认识论层次的问题相混淆的错误。

总之，当我们肯定主体和客体之间相互依赖、不可分割和同时发生、同时并存的关系时，是严格地就认识论所涉及的事实来说的，具有确定的

①《列宁选集》第2卷，人民出版社，1995年，第69页。

认识论意义。不能从本体论意义上来理解这种关系，不能把这种关系本体论化。否则，其理论后果只能是：或者为了坚持主客体关系的唯物主义本体论前提而否定两者之间在认识论意义上同时发生、不可分割的关系，从而倒退到马克思、恩格斯以前的旧唯物主义即直观唯物主义；或者为了坚持主客体之间相互生成、彼此依赖的关系，而否定物质为本原、意识为派生这一唯物主义本体论前提，从而倒向唯心主义。二者必居其一。对于深受苏联教科书体系影响又缺少认真清理的我国理论界来说，前者至少在目前恐怕仍然是主要危险。

三、科学仪器的认识论属性问题

科学认识活动是有目的的对象性活动，在这种活动中，主体预期的目的是否能够实现，这在很大程度上取决于能否创造和使用适当的科学仪器以及科学方法。

在现代科学中，科学认识主体和科学认识客体之间的相互作用不是直接发生的。认识自然的主、客体直接相互作用模式早已过时，这种主客体的直接观照所产生的认识成果只能是常识，至多是自然哲学的猜测，而不可能是科学认识。而必须要借助理论思维指导下精心设计的仪器设备和程序，来分析和探测科学认识客体及其变化规律。科学仪器作为人的肉体认识器官（大脑、感官、效应器官）的体外延伸，是科学认识主体系统的重要组成部分，并标志着人类的新进化。

科学仪器，是人们为了克服人类认识器官（包括感官、效应器官和思维器官）的局限，从而审度自然，研究自然界各个领域中的具体现象、性质和规律时，创造和使用的专门物质技术手段。它作为科学认识主体系统中的一个不可缺少的要素，是在认识主体和客体之间建立信息联系、造成相互作用从而把握客体的实物形态的工具的总和。它包括对自然信息、经验资料等进行测量、记录、整理时所运用的一切工具和装置。

科学仪器主要有以下性质：第一，它是为实现科学认识目的而创造和使用的人工制造物。它是根据一定历史条件下科学研究的实际需要，利用客观物质的不同属性规律，而创造出来的一种物质技术手段。离开了认识目的，离开了主体的运用和操作，仪器就失去工具的意义。第二，仪器可克服人类认识器官的局限性，扩大接收、传递和加工信息的能力。它是人的肢体、感觉器官和大脑的延伸，或者说它是人的躯体之外的认识工具。第三，仪器是科学理论和方法的物化。马克思在论述机器和科学知识的关系时说道："自然界没有制造出任何机器，……它们是人类劳动的产物，……是人类的手创造出来的人类头脑的器官；是物化的知识力量。"①科学仪器不是现成的自然事物，也不是纯观念的东西。人们对科学仪器的设计、选材、制造和使用，取决于人们对自然物属性和规律的科学认识，以及利用自然物的方法。从这个意义上来说，科学仪器是科学理论和科学方法的物化。

那么，科学仪器属于认识客体还是认识主体？

国内有一种源于苏联哲学家 B. A. 什托夫的观点，认为，由于科学仪器是一种客观实在的事物，因此，属于认识客体。持有这种观点的人说：研究对象和包括科学仪器在内的实验手段"都包括在认识论客体的概念之中，因为它们是客观地存在着并且按照自然界的客观规律而运动的物质过程，不管它们是人造的还是大自然创造的"②。这个观点为了强调仪器及其运动规律的客观性，把实验手段和实验对象一同放在"认识论客体"的范畴中，而把"客观实在"概念同认识论的"客体"概念相混同。

我们认为，科学仪器根本不属于客体范畴。为什么呢？我们这样说，是因为在科学认识系统中，人们创造和使用的科学仪器是揭示自然事物本质和规律的武器，是被用来获取信息、传输信息、分析和整理信息的物质手段。因此，它是作为探索的工具而不是作为探索的目标（对象）而参与科学认识活动的，就是说，在科学研究活动中，科学仪器没有占据作为认识客体的科研对象的地位。仅仅在仪器研制活动这种特定的情况下，现有的、有待改进的仪器，才能作为探索的目标和改进的对象，因而才属于认识客体（实际上，在这种仪器研制活动中，用来测试、研究或改造待改进仪器的另外一些仪器，则充当了探索工具的角色）。正像龙头拐杖如果不是拿在老者或残疾人手中，而是作为健康人审美或改进的对象时，它就不再具有工具的资格，而转化成为审美客体或认识客体。

事实上，在科学研究过程中，探索的工具与探索的目标，科学认识的

① 《马克思恩格斯全集》第 46 卷下册，人民出版社，1979 年，第 219 页。

② 黄顺基：《自然辩证法教程》，中国人民大学出版社，1985 年，第 288 页。

物质手段与科学认识的对象，是既有联系又有根本区别的两种东西，它们具备各自特有的规定性。例如，医生使用听诊器、X 光透视仪时，并不会把这些器械当作自己所要治疗的病人；天文学家利用望远镜、航天仪时也没有忘记自己的研究对象是某个天体；物理学家利用电子显微镜、高能加速器时同样没有忘记自己的探索目标是微观粒子及其运动规律。这说明在具体的研究中，只有那些被设定为探索目标的事物及其规律才是现实的认识对象，才属于认识客体；至于作为探索工具的科学仪器，毕竟不能越俎代庖，充当科学研究的对象，因此，这时的仪器显然不属于认识客体。

认识论的一般原理告诉我们，认识客体并不简单是不依赖于意识而存在的客观实在，而是纳入了主体之认识的、实践的、变革的活动中的客观实在，是跟认识主体构成认识与被认识、改造与被改造的客观实在。可见，混淆"客观实在"和"客体"的概念是不合理的。科普宁指出：为了消除这种混淆的错误，"必须把'客观实在'和'客体'的概念分开"①。

那么，科学仪器是否属于认识主体呢？也不是。但它属于认识主体系统。为了说明这个问题，我们先得明确什么是认识主体和什么是认识主体系统。

所谓认识主体是指认识和实际行为的主体，指存在于一定社会关系中并从事认识与改造客观世界的人，即社会的、历史的人。而所谓认识主体系统是指以认识主体为中心，包括认识主体掌握的思想工具和物质工具在内的集合体。把这种关于认识主体和认识主体系统划分的思想应用于科学认识系统就可看到，认识主体系统是指以科学认识主体为中心，包括科学语言、科学方法和科学仪器在内的集合体。

按照上述对认识主体和认识主体系统的划分，我们可以说，无论是什么类型的科学仪器，都不可能完全代替科学劳动者而成为认识主体。这就是说，科学仪器不等同于认识主体。这种不等同性可以从许多方面加以说明。（1）从产生的方面来看，作为认识主体的人是处于一定的社会关系中的，它不仅是自然界长期演化的产物，而且是社会发展的产物，不仅具有自然属性，而且具有社会历史性；而科学仪器的产生和发展虽受社会因素的制约，但同社会上人与人之间关系的状况和变化没有直接的内在联系，它只具有自然属性，而没有社会属性。（2）从物质基础方面来看，作为认

---

① 科普宁：《马克思主义认识论导论》，求实出版社，1982 年，第 73 页。

识主体的人或人类，由生命物质组成，人脑更是建筑在高度发达的神经系统这种物质基础上的；而科学仪器没有丝毫活力，至今的一切科学仪器无论多么复杂、精密，全是由无机界的物质构成的。（3）从运动形式方面来看，作为认识主体的人的活动虽然也包括机械的、物理的和化学的过程，但主要的活动方式是生理—心理过程，它不仅具有包括数值计算、图像识别及形式逻辑、数理逻辑等技术性思维的能力，而且具有形象思维、概念思维以及诸如直觉、灵感等非逻辑的创造性思维能力；而科学仪器的活动方式始终没有超越无机物运动形式的类型，至多只能模拟低级的、技术性的思维活动。

概括起来，科学仪器与认识主体之间的最根本区别在于，科学仪器不具备人所特有的社会历史性和自觉能动性。

然而，科学仪器虽然不等同于认识主体，但从属于认识主体。我们这么说，是以科学仪器本身的规定性为依据的。科学仪器本来就是主体用来把自己的活动传导到认识客体并依照自己的目的作用于客体的中介物。形象地说，科学仪器是科学认识主体从实践上把握科学认识客体的"技术助手"。这是因为，在一般情况下，科学认识活动作为主体的一种对象性活动，不是主体直接作用于客体，而是让科学仪器起作用，通过主体对仪器的有目的的运用、操作、控制，使认识客体发生符合于目的的主观规定的变化。显然，在这里，科学仪器是科学认识主体各种认识器官的延伸、放大。当科学仪器跟人的体力和智力结合在一起后，就能成为一种认识和改造世界的非常活跃的因素。反之，科学仪器脱离了主体，就将失去它作为认识工具的概念的和职能的规定性。

玻尔作过一个比喻说：如果一个盲人把他的手杖紧握手中，"手杖就可以作为通过触觉摸索环境的手的一种延伸"；而如果放松手杖，"它就成为一种客体，它的存在通过触觉而为手所感知。因而就失去了它作为观察仪器的作用"。同样，科学仪器如果作为研制、改进或审美对象，它就是客体；但如果主体运用它作用于自然界的对象，它则是主体器官的延伸。同时，科学认识活动作为对象性活动，是有目的的活动。处于这个活动过程中的科学仪器不是一种孤立的单纯依靠自我规定的东西，它的规定性就是达到或实现主体目的的物质手段，因而与主体的目的联系在一起。但科学仪器并不会提出自己的目的，而只能蕴含着认识主体的目的。科学仪器如果不是为了满足认识主体的某种科研目的，是不会被创造出来的。仪器作为实现目的的手段只能是主体的手段，从来就没有，也永远不会有属于客体的手段。所以说，科学仪器从属于认识主体，并且是认识主体系统的要素之一。

笔者以为，科学认识论应当以科学认识活动为主线，阐明被以往认识论研究所忽视的、与反映世界过程密切联系的选择与创造过程的认识论机制；探讨人的"本质力量的性质"所决定的主体内在尺度和"对象的性质"所决定的客体尺度①之间在科学认识活动中相互接近和统一的途径等，以便从科学认识论角度验证马克思主义认识论的一般结论。为了实现哲学的现代化，必须结合当代科学发展的崭新成果来研究和阐述认识论问题，并且特别注意肃清苏联哲学教科书体系和直观唯物主义思想对马克思主义认识论研究的消极影响。

参考文献：

[1]马克思恩格斯选集：第 1 卷[M]．北京：人民出版社，1995.

[2]马克思恩格斯全集：第 42 卷[M]．北京：人民出版社，1979.

[3]马克思恩格斯选集：第 3 卷[M]．北京人民出版社，1995.

[4]夏甄陶．认识论引论[M]．北京：人民出版社，1986.

[5]陈柏灵．关于正确评价《唯物主义与经验批判主义》的若干问题[J]．北京：中国社会科学，1989（6）：85-92.

[6]马克思恩格斯选集：第 2 卷[M]．北京：人民出版社，1995.

[7]中国大百科全书：哲学卷（II）[Z]．北京：中国大百科全书出版社，1987.

[8]皮亚杰．发生认识论原理[M]．北京：商务印书馆，1981.

[9]列宁选集：第 2 卷[M]．北京：人民出版社，1995.

[10]马克思恩格斯全集：第 46 卷下册[M]．北京：人民出版社，1979.

[11]黄顺基．自然辩证法教程[M]．北京：中国人民大学出版社，1985.

[12]〔苏〕科普宁．马克思主义认识论导论[M]．北京：求实出版社，1982.

（本文原载于《文史哲》2005 年第 6 期）

---

① 《马克思恩格斯全集》第 42 卷，人民出版社，1979 年，第 97、125 页。

经验定律的形成过程和发现模式

——科学规律形成的认识论问题探讨之一

李祖扬[*]

经验定律是科学规律的重要组成部分，也是构成各门科学理论的基本知识要素之一。它和所有科学规律一样，以自然界的客观规律为其现实基础。所谓客观规律，就是隐藏在大量个别、偶然现象背后的客观事物的普遍必然联系和客观过程的普遍必然的发展趋势。而科学规律则是关于客观事物的某种普遍必然联系和客观过程的某种普遍必然发展趋势的判断，是主体对客观规律的能动反映。正如列宁所说："认识是人对自然界的反映。但是，这并不是简单的、直接的、完全的反映，而是一系列的抽象过程，即概念、规律等等的构成、形成过程，这些概念和规律等等有条件地、近似地把握着永恒运动着的发展着的自然界的普遍规律性。"[①]根据认识主体把握事物普遍联系的深度，通常把科学规律区分为两大层次：经验定律和理论定律。经验定律所陈述的是客观事物的表观的外部的普遍必然联系。而理论定律所陈述的则是客观事物的本质的内部的普遍必然联系。

在人类思想史上围绕科学规律的发现和形成曾经产生了一系列认识论问题，各种科学哲学流派提出了许多不同的见解和学说。我们认为，为了深入研究科学规律发现和形成的一般认识论问题，先要区分科学规律中的两种基本形态，分别加以考查。因为经验定律和理论定律的发现和形成，既有共同性，也有各自的特殊性。从一定的意义上说，经验定律的形成又

---

* 李祖扬，南开大学哲学院科技哲学教研室教授，主要研究方向为科学技术哲学。

① 列宁：《哲学笔记》，人民出版社，1974年，第194页。

是理论定律形成的前提和基础。本文主要围绕经验定律的形成过程和发现模式问题作一初步探讨。

一、关于科学规律发现的一般逻辑程序

一个诱人思考的问题是：是否存在一种普遍适用的固定的发现科学规律的逻辑程序？追寻发现的逻辑曾经是近代自然科学诞生以后一些科学哲学家梦寐以求的理想。例如归纳主义的创始人、英国哲学家弗·培根（F. Bacon，1561—1626）认为，可以按照一种严格的归纳程序去发现科学规律，使发现活动像用尺规作直线和圆一样的容易。他的追随者英国学者胡克（Robert Hooke，1635—1703）想创造一种用于科学发现的归纳逻辑机器——发明机器。而演绎主义者德国科学家和哲学家莱布尼兹（Leibniz，1646—1716）则主张通过演绎逻辑的符号化与演算化而建立一种科学发现的演绎逻辑机器。莱布尼兹设想的部分目标已通过建立数理逻辑而实现，而这种机器却不曾问世。

耐人寻味的是，归纳主义者和演绎主义者虽然在科学发现的具体逻辑程序上持不同见解，但是在坚信科学发现可以通过某种逻辑操作程序来实现这一点上却是一致的。不过，直到制成了人工智能机，他们的梦想还未能变成现实。

现代美国科学哲学家瓦托夫斯基（Wartofsky，1928—）对实现这一梦想的不可能性进行了论证。他指出，如果我们试图建立一个科学发现可以从中推出的理论，我们就会陷入一种两难的境地："或者理论是成功的，于是发现概念得以解释，亦即被还原地消除掉；或者理论是失败的，则发现仍然未得到解释。"[①]意思是如果一种理论对发现和发明的解释是成功的，它就可能把科学上的创造性思维还原为可演算的程序，这样科学的创造性也就随之消失；如果这种理论未能给出对发现和发明的圆满解释，那么它就是一种失败的理论。另一位奥裔美籍科学哲学家费耶阿本德（P. K. Feyerabend，1924—1994）从一般地反对方法的角度抨击了认为知识可以由预先定好的一系列固定的研究程序而获得的想法。他认为遵循任何一种

---

① 《科学发现的案例分析》英文版，第8页。

主要的方法都会抑制和妨碍科学家的创造力。"所有的方法论都有它们的局限性，留下的唯一'规则'是'怎么都行'。"①很显然，那些幻想存在发现的逻辑程序的学者，忽视了科学认识活动的创造性和多样性。

二、经验定律的形成过程

为了探讨上述问题，我们对一些典型的经验定律的发现和形成过程进行了历史的考察。这些定律涉及物理学、化学、生物学、天文学等不同学科。通过考察，我们看到几乎每个定律的发现和形成都有一部曲折和复杂的历史，都是多少代科学家艰苦探索的结晶。这些定律的发现过程绝不雷同，应用的思维方法也不完全一致，在发现定律的思维过程中确实不存在机械的固定的逻辑程序，但在定律的形成过程中却存在着基本相同的认识途径，大体经历以下五个主要阶段。

A. 提出科学问题　提出明确的科学问题是一切科学发现的先导，对于经验定律的发现亦不例外。在某一研究领域积累了一定数量的经验事实或具有某种理论知识后，人们往往提出寻求有关因素之间的稳定联系的问题，这类问题便会导致经验定律的发现。例如，人们在观察到大量自由落体现象后提出：在自由落体运动中，物体的重量与其运动速度的关系是怎样的？运动的时间和距离的关系又是怎样的？对这些定量关系的探索，导致自由落体定律的发现。当然，导致成功发现的科学问题必须具有正确性和成熟性。正确性是指该问题指出了正确的探索对象和解答域；成熟性是指该问题的解决已经具备了一定的科学知识前提和必要的物质技术条件。②

B. 搜集经验原据　为了解答前面所提出的科学问题，必须搜集一定的经验事实和数据，作为原始的经验根据，简称经验原据。虽然，获得经验原据的途径可能不同，有的是通过定律发现者自己设计实验，获得数据（如波义耳定律），有的是利用前人提供的观测数据（如开普勒行星定律）。但是，任何经验定律都必须建立在一定的原始经验事实之上，而不可能仅仅是抽象思维的产物。一般地说，"纯粹的逻辑思维不能给我们任何关于经验

① 费耶阿本德：《反对方法：无政府主义知识论纲要》，1975 年英文版，第 296 页。
② 参见李祖扬：《科学认识论简明教程》，南开大学出版社，1992 年，第一章第四节和第四章第五节。

世界的知识；一切关于实在的知识，都是从经验开始，又终结于经验。"[①]

在此需要指出，搜集经验原据的目的和作用，可能有两种情况：一种是为了从中探求规律性，以便提出定律的初始假设（如波义耳定律）；另一种是在有了初步的定律假设之后，为了检验这一假设的可靠性（如伽里略的自由落体定律）。因此就时间顺序而言，有的经验原据是在初始假设之前确立的，如后文所述的第二、三种定律发现模式；有的经验原据则是在初始假设之后确立的，如后文所述的第一种定律发现模式。

C. 形成定律假设　在经验定律形成的全过程中，提出定律的初始假设是关键性的一环。有关的经验材料和理论知识不会自动地导致新定律的发现。从既有的科学知识中得出新的科学定律是科学认识过程中质的飞跃，这一飞跃最突出地体现出认识主体的能动性和创造性。因此，尽管就一个定律的形成和确立而言，在实现这一飞跃前后还有赖于许多科学家的大量的先行的和后继的工作，但科学史的惯例是把科学定律的发现主要归功于定律假设的提出者。如在开普勒行星定律的形成过程中既有丹麦天文学家第谷搜集经验原据在前，又有牛顿以他的力学定律进行理论论证于后，但德国天文学家开普勒是定律假设的提出者，故推他为首功，定律也以他的名字命名。

D. 寻求经验判据　定律假设的提出虽以一定的科学事实作为其最初的经验基础，但和由其导出的科学定律相比，作为经验原据的科学事实在逻辑上总是很不充分的，必须寻求更多的经验判据，以弥补经验根据的不足。

经验判据和经验原据具有共同的本质属性：第一，它们都是从科学观察中直接获取的经验材料；第二，它们都是形成科学定律的经验基础。但在经验定律的形成过程中，它们又具有不同的认识功能：经验原据的作用在于为形成定律假设提供最初的经验材料；经验判据的作用则是在定律假设形成后，为它的真理性的判别及其进一步修正完善提供经验基础。就知识素质而言，由于研究工作的推移，研究条件和研究要求的提高，作为经验判据的经验材料和经验原据相比，不仅更具有普遍性和精确性，而且有时在同定律假设的逻辑关系上更具有直接性。例如伽里略自由落体定律的经验原据来自斜面实验的结果，但物体沿斜面运动只是近似于落体运动

---

① 《爱因斯坦文集》第 1 卷，商务印书馆，1977 年，第 313 页。

（二者均为匀加速运动，而斜面运动更为复杂），只有在真空条件下进行落体实验才能为该定律提供有直接确证价值的经验判据。

E. 寻求理论判据进行理论论证　一个经验定律在既有了经验原据，又有了比较丰富的经验判据之后，仍然不能确定它的真理性。第一，对于作为全称命题的定律而言，仅仅以若干单称或特称命题表述的经验事实（包括经验原据和经验判据）作为自己的依据，在逻辑上仍是不充分的。一个经验定律必须能够从某种理论前提中通过演绎推理推导出来，其可靠性才能获得充分的逻辑根据。第二，在经验定律仅仅具有经验根据时，它只是描述了事物是怎样运动的，而未能说明事物为何这样运动；只是描述了物质系统中存在何种联系，而未能说明何以存在这种联系；它虽然指出了客观过程发展的必然性，但仍是知其然而不知其所以然。显然，当人们只停留在对运动的描述上，而未能揭示出运动发生的机制和原因时，这种描述的可靠性就不能得到保证。上述两个理由表明，获得充分的理论判据，运用演绎推理进行圆满合理的理论论证，是确认经验定律的真理性的必不可少的环节。

一般地说，对经验定律的理论论证往往在形成定律假设的较长时间之后，即在以若干相关的经验定律为基础发现理论定律，并以若干理论定律为基本知识要素完成科学理论建构之时。只有在这时，经验定律才能得到圆满的理论论证，其真理性才能得到确认。例如，伽里略自由落体定律和开普勒行星定律的真理性的确认，有赖于在其后形成的牛顿力学的论证；波义耳定律、查理定律和盖-吕萨克定律的真理性的确认，有赖于在其后形成的气体分子运动论的论证等等。科学史还表明，只有在对经验定律作出深刻的理论说明的同时，人们才会真正明确这些定律的适用范围和精确表述。

通过以上考察可以看出，经验定律的形成有一个漫长的萌芽、发展和完善的过程。这一过程可以大体区分为提出问题和解决问题两大阶段，解决问题阶段包括发现过程和证明过程，而证明过程又包括经验证明和理论证明。

应当指出，科学认识活动既是认识现象，又是社会现象，它是二者的统一。到此为止，我们仅在确证经验定律的真理性的范围内讨论其形成问题。实际上，一项科学理论成果（包括科学定律）只有在其经过专业同行的评价，得到社会的普遍认同，从而被纳入人类科学知识的整个体系之内，成为其有机的组成部分之时，它才算真正得到确立。不过，科学理论成果的确立，涉及众多社会因素（如社会政治、经济状况、社会意识、社会心理、文化传统、科学规范等等）和更为复杂的环节，本文就不详加讨论了。

三、发现经验定律的几种模式

上面所述的五个阶段构成了经验定律形成的一般过程，而不同的经验定律在形成中又有千差万别的特点。我们能否从这千差万别中概括出几种主要的类型，提炼出科学规律发现的若干模式呢？

多年来，我国学者在这方面进行了有益的探索。有的学者通过分析科学发现的案例，总结出科学发现的若干模式[①]；有的学者根据一定标准，将科学发现区分为常规模式和非常规模式。[②]

我们在此选择一种新的研究角度。既然定律假设的提出是经验定律形成过程中的关键步骤，那么我们不妨根据定律假设形成方式来探索其发现模式的类型问题。而定律假设的形成方式主要取决于定律假设与经验原据的关系，取决于经验原据在定律假设形成中所起的作用。因此，我们把定律假设的形成方式，特别是它与经验原据的关系，作为划分科学定律发现模式的主要依据。

根据这一标准，可将经验定律的发现划分为三种基本模式。

第一种模式：理论推导型 在这种发现模式中，定律的发现者首先以既有的科学理论知识为基础推导出定律的初始假设，然后再进行观察实验，搜集有关的科学事实以检验初始假设的正确性。因此经验原据是在初始假设提出之后确立的。然而这并不意味着初始假定可以不依赖任何经验知识而得到，因为作为推论前提的理论知识仍是建立在一定的科学事实的基础之上的。我们把属于这种发现模式的经验定律的确立过程简化为下图1：

---

① 参见邱红宇主编：《成功之路——科学发现的模式》，人民出版社，1987年。

② 参见傅杰青编著：《生理学或医学诺贝尔奖八十年》，人民出版社，1987年，第二章第四节。

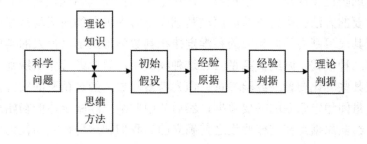

图 1

从已有的理论知识推出新的定律假设必须借助于一定的理论思维方法，这些思维方法的种类取决于理论原据和初始假设的内容以及二者之间的关系。根据提出初始假设时所采用的主要思维方法的种类，我们可将这种发现模式划分为两个亚类。

（1）演绎型　在此类型中既有的理论知识已经涵盖了初始假设所涉及的关系，因此研究者可以运用演绎推理把后者从前者中推导出来，然后通过科学观察检验初始假设的正确性。例如 1803 年英国科学家道尔顿提出原子学说后，又根据这一学说推论出倍比定律，当时他并未获得倍比定律的实验证据。1804 年他分析了甲烷和乙烯的组成，才使该定律得到初步验证。[①]

经典力学最早的经验定律之一——伽里略的自由落体定律，最初也是从已有的理论中推导出来的，与倍比定律不同的是，在推导过程中伽里略建立了一个关于落体运动的数学模型，作为推理的辅助工具。在得出定律假设之后，他才设计了斜面实验对定律假设作出初步的间接的经验证明。[②]

（2）类比型　这类定律是根据已有的理论知识（含科学定律），运用类比推理得出定律假设，然后通过实验观察证实其正确性。静电学中第一个定量的基本定律——库仑定律就是通过把电的作用力和万有引力相类比而形成的。[③]

---

①《化学发展简史》，科学出版社，1980 年，第 93-94 页；〔日〕原光雄著：《近代化学的奠基者》，科学出版社，1986 年，第 84-85 页。

②〔美〕M. W. 瓦托夫斯基著：《科学思想的概念基础——科学哲学导论》，求实出版社，1982 年，第 649-658 页。

③ 申先甲主编：《物理学史教程》，湖南教育出版社，1987 年，第 207-211 页。

借助类比发现新的科学规律，在科学认识活动包括现代科学研究中是一种重要的方法。类比方法的深刻基础在于客观世界物质运动规律的统一性，而其表现则为不同领域的科学定律在其数学形式上"惊人的类似"[①]。

第二种模式：归纳概括型　在这种模式中，研究者首先从纷乱的现象中选取某些变化要素（经验参量）作为考察对象，经过精密的实验，测得反映变量间稳定联系的必要数据，然后从中归纳出经验定律的初始形态。在此，经验原据是在定律假设之前确立的。我们把这种模式简化为图2：

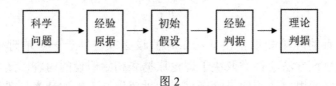

图 2

在从经验原据向初始假设的过渡中需要借助一定的理论思维方法，理论思维方法的类型取决于经验原据的性质和经验定律所表述的函数关系的性质以及它们二者间的关系。根据所用思维方法的不同，也可以将这种模式划分为两个亚类。

（1）归纳型　这类经验定律主要是运用归纳方法找出实验数据的共变关系（函数关系）而得出的。气体运动理论中的波义耳定律，电学中的欧姆定律，行星天文学中的波德定律都属于这种类型。这些定律主要运用了传统的归纳方法，同时在探求过程中还辅之以其他的思维方法，如分析、综合、类比等等。

（2）统计型　这类经验定律主要是运用数理统计方法，找出大量随机现象中的统计学规律，生物遗传学中的孟德尔遗传定律是这一类型的代表。

第三种模式：猜想逼近型　这种模式既不同于理论推导型，也不同于归纳概括型。它与理论推导型的不同在于，研究者在进行理论推导之前已掌握了经验原据。它与经验概括型的不同在于，它不是从经验原据中进行归纳概括得到某一定律假设，而是凭借直觉猜想提出一系列定律假设，而后再将假设和经验原据进行比较，根据其相符情况，对假设进行筛选、修正，使之逐渐达到和经验原据的统一，从而确立定律的初始形态。这种发现模式可简化为图3：

---

①《列宁选集》第2卷，人民出版社，1960年，第295页。

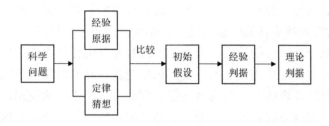

图 3

属于这种模式的典型案例有开普勒行星第一定律、开普勒行星第三定律、巴尔末氢原子光谱线公式等等。初看起来，把猜想作为一种科学研究方法似乎有悖于科学的严密性。实际上，在科学发现的初始阶段，由于当时所掌握材料的局限性，科学家有时不得不借助于直觉和猜想。杨振宁曾说过："在所有物理和数学的最前沿的研究工作，很大一部分力量要花在猜想上。在别的方面可能也是这样，不过我不太熟悉罢了。当然这并不是说可以乱猜，猜必须建筑在过去的一些知识上面，你过去的知识愈正确愈广泛，那么猜到正确答案的可能性愈大。"[1]苏联物理学家福克（B. A. Фок）也认为："伟大的，乃至于一般的科学发现，都不是按照逻辑的法则发现的，而都是猜测出来的，换句话说，大都是凭创造性的直觉得来的。"[2]福克对逻辑法则和猜测在科学发现中的作用的论述并不十分准确，但在肯定猜测的作用这一点上则表达了许多科学家的共识。

在西方近代科学诞生以后，先是弗·培根，接着又有赫舍尔（J. Herschel，1792—1871）和惠威尔（W. Whevell，1795—1866）主张把科学认识过程截然划分为发现和证明两个独立的阶段。以卡尔纳普（R. Carnap，1891—1970）为代表的逻辑实证主义者只关注证明问题，而把发现问题的研究摒除于科学哲学的视野之外，认为研究发现的任务应属于心理学。对科学史的考察表明，科学规律的形成过程内在地包含了发现和证明，发现和证明是完整的形成过程中不可分割的两个阶段。在科学发现过程中运用的思维方法和思维类型，既有逻辑思维方法，也有非逻辑的思维方法和思维类型——对问题答案的合理猜测、直觉判断和突发灵感等等。而且，实际上还不可避免地存在着某些与认识活动相关的非认知因素（需要、兴趣、意

---

[1] 张庆华等：《杨振宁讲演集》，南开大学出版社，1989 年，第 333 页。
[2] 王梓坤：《科学发现纵横谈》，上海人民出版社，1978 年，第 109 页。

志、情感、情绪、性格、气质等）对发现过程的影响。但在整个发现过程中，非逻辑思维和非认知因素只是主体思维活动中的特殊成分或作用因素，并不占据唯一或主导的地位。整个发现过程是在主体的逻辑思维支配下进行的，这一过程能够为主体的自觉意识所把握，在一般情况下主体能够用明确的语言清晰表达自己的思考过程。因此，科学规律的发现过程乃是一种包含不同思维方法和类型并受有关心理因素影响的创造性的理性思维活动。理性主义者把理性思维活动简单地等同于逻辑思维活动，完全否认非逻辑思维和非理性因素（或非认知因素）在科学发现中的作用。非理性主义者则走向另一极端，他们完全否定逻辑思维对科学认识的贡献，把科学认识活动中的非理性因素夸大到唯一或主导的地位。这两种观点都未能全面把握科学认识活动的实质，从而不能成为我们建构正确的科学认识论和方法论的理论基点。

（本文原载于《南开学报》1996 年第 4 期）

试论科学技术革命与社会革命的关系

牛叔成*

现在，世界上有两个巨大的潮流，一是科学技术革命的潮流，一是共产主义运动的潮流。这两个潮流的未来发展是什么关系？是共产主义运动为科学技术的革命所"融合"或代替，还是科学技术革命的最终结果会自然而然地导致共产主义？

当今世界两个潮流的关系问题，实际上就是关于科学技术革命同社会革命的关系问题。要回答这个问题，我觉得，应该从理论与实践的结合上对两个潮流及其相互关系作一些具体分析。

当今世界上确实客观地存在着科学技术革命和共产主义运动这两个巨大的潮流。1978 年 3 月 18 日，邓小平同志《在全国科学大会开幕式上的讲话》中就指出："现代科学技术正在经历着一场伟大的革命。近三十年来，现代科学技术不只是在个别的科学理论上、个别的生产技术上获得了发展，也不只是有了一般意义上的进步和改革，而是几乎各门科学技术领域都发生了深刻的变化，出现了新的飞跃，产生了并且正在继续产生一系列新兴的科学技术。"从 20 世纪中叶兴起的新的科学技术革命，目前正以激光、光导纤维、集成电路、电子计算机、超导技术、合成材料、生物工程、航天技术、海洋开发等一系列新技术和新兴工业为先导，迅猛地向前发展。而当代科学技术又以空前的规模和速度应用于生产，使社会物质生产的各个领域面貌日新。当代科学技术的革命是一个不以人们的意志为转移的世界性潮流，它既是人类文明发展的伟大成果，又是人类文明发展进入新阶段的重要标志。任何国家和民族要想使自己进入世界文明发展的前列，就必须适应这一世界性历史潮流，努力提高自己的科学技术水平。由

---

* 牛叔成，南开大学哲学系副教授，研究方向为科学技术哲学与科学史。

于历史的种种原因，我国现今的科学技术水平总的来说同世界先进水平相比还有着很大的差距，为了赶超世界先进的科学技术水平，就需要在坚持自力更生的基础上向外国学习，党的十一届三中全会所确定的关于改革、开放的总方针，就是我们党为适应当代科学技术革命的世界性潮流所作出的战略决策。

共产主义运动也是当代一种巨大的世界性潮流。所谓"共产主义"，其基本含义是指如下三个相互联系的内容：其一，是指共产主义的思想体系，它是反映社会发展普遍规律、揭示人类历史未来发展趋势的理论学说；其二，是指共产主义的运动，它是工人阶级和广大劳动群众在共产主义理论指导下自觉进行的革命实践活动；其三，是指共产主义的社会制度，它是物质和精神产品极大丰富，全体社会成员的文化素质、道德水准和自觉创造性空前提高，没有剥削和压迫，阶级和国家归于消亡的一种社会形态。这三项内容是有机的统一，其核心是消灭一切剥削制度，实现人类的彻底解放。自从《共产党宣言》问世一百多年来，共产主义以雷霆万钧之势磅礴于世界。共产主义作为一种思想体系，它以科学的世界观和全人类精神文明的伟大成果武装了世界亿万劳动群众，荡涤了一切剥削阶级的陈腐观念，成为当今世界上最有影响的精神力量；共产主义作为一种现实的社会运动，它以强大的物质力量冲垮了资本主义的世界体系，在剥削制度的链条上打开了一个个缺口，导致了一系列社会主义国家的建立和发展；共产主义作为一种社会制度或社会形态，已在一些社会主义国家里消灭了剥削阶级和剥削制度，广大人民群众成了国家和社会的主人，它的优越性已初步地显示出来，并现正经历着一个自我完善和发展的过程。一百多年来的历史发展深刻地表明，马克思主义指导下的共产主义运动已经成为一种不可阻挡的世界性潮流，它的存在和发展已经引起，并将继续引起人类社会发展的革命性变革。

关于科学技术革命同社会革命的关系问题，在马克思主义理论中早已作了明确的回答和解决。按照历史唯物主义的观点，人类社会的发展是一个自然历史过程，而推动人类社会发展的根本动力是社会基本矛盾。马克思在《〈政治经济学批判〉序言》中指出，"不是人们的意识决定人们的存在，相反，是人们的社会存在决定人们的意识。社会的物质生产力发展到一定阶段，便同它们一直在其中活动的现存生产关系……发生矛盾。于是这些关系便由生产力的发展形式变成生产力的桎梏。那时社会革命的时代就到来了。随着经济基础的变更，全部庞大的上层建筑也或慢或快地发生变革"①。马克思主义历来认为，科学技术是生产力。早在一百多年前马克思就说过：机器生产的发展要求自觉地应用自然科学，"生产力中也包括科学"②。正因为如此，科学技术的进步乃是推动人类历史向前发展的强大杠杆和动力，科学技术革命为社会关系的全面改造奠定坚实的基础，提供有利的客观条件；同样，社会关系即社会制度的变革也为科学技术的发展提供广阔的场所和前景。由此可见，科学技术革命同社会革命是并行不悖的，是相互促进的。

第二次世界大战以后，新的科学技术革命的兴起引起了社会生活的巨大变化，对现代社会的发展过程产生了重大影响。在新的科学技术革命的条件下，资本主义社会中的阶级关系和阶级斗争出现了新的特点。工业化和都市化的扩展使工人阶级的人数和力量空前增长，文化水平和觉悟程度有了很大提高，社会地位也有所改善。同时，在不改变生产资料私有制的前提下，资产阶级对经营管理形式和剥削方式也作了某些调整。当代资本主义国家的阶级斗争出现了复杂的情况，并在一定程度上有所缓和。此外，在新的科学技术革命的条件下，国家的社会管理、调节和组织的职能变得越来越突出，它往往在社会矛盾的激化过程中起着某种缓冲作用。在这种新情况下，社会革命也会相应地发生某些变化：其内容将变得更加复杂；其道路将更加曲折，并会经历较长的渐进过程；其形式必然更加多样。

那么，在资本主义社会中迅速兴起的科学技术革命的潮流能不能取代共产主义运动呢？答案是否定的。这是因为：

其一，就两种潮流的一般关系来说，科学技术革命和社会革命是两种不同性质的革命，其中任何一种革命都不能代替另一种革命。科学技术革命是人对自然界的革命，而社会革命则是人与人之间社会关系的革命。现代科学技术的发展会引起社会生活的巨大变化，会对社会的产业结构、阶级关系、劳动方式、思想观念、思维方式以及经济制度和政治制度等等产生重要影响，为社会的进步和人的解放提供现实的物质条件。但是，我们还应该看到，科学技术所发挥作用的方向及其社会后果的性质是由社会制度限定的，因而由科学技术的进步所导致的社会发展和人类的解放总是不

---

① 《马克思恩格斯选集》第 2 卷，人民出版社，1995 年，第 82-83 页。

② 《马克思恩格斯全集》第 46 卷下册，人民出版社，1979 年，第 84 页。

充分、不完全、不彻底的，这就是说，科学技术的进步并不是推动人类社会发展的唯一决定力量，并不能从根本上改变社会的性质和发展方向，社会关系上的矛盾或问题还须通过社会革命才能从根本上得到解决。

其二，就现代科学技术革命同资本主义社会基本矛盾的关系来说，现代科学技术的发展非但没有解决资本主义生产社会性同生产资料占有私人性的矛盾，没有从根本上动摇资本主义私有制，而且还加重对劳动人民剩余价值的剥削。众所周知，科学技术是由包括科学技术工作者在内的劳动者创造的，科学技术的发展理应造福于劳动人民。但是，在资本主义制度下，科学技术的发展却使劳动者倍受自然物的奴役和驱使，变成机器的奴隶。在资本主义条件下科学技术的发展所产生的这种"负的社会效应"，马克思曾经称之为"异化"现象，并对此作了深刻的揭露和批判。显然，科学技术社会效益的"正"或"负"、好或坏，并不完全取决于科学技术本身的发展状况和程度，而取决于社会制度的性质和它为哪个阶级服务。这也就是说，在资本主义制度下，科学技术不论发展到什么程度，它都无法从根本上解决资本主义社会的基本矛盾，因而也无法消除其自身的异化。

其三，就科学技术的发展来说，在资本主义制度下，不可能从根本上消除因科学技术的发展必然会引起的灾难性后果。大家知道，科学技术的发展带来有利于人类和社会发展的后果的同时，也可能带来十分严重的不良后果。20 世纪中叶以来，能源、原材料和粮食的短缺愈益严重，大工业（特别是化学工业和核工业）对大气、土壤和水源的污染日趋加剧，海洋生物和森林资源遭到逐步升级的狂捕滥伐，生态平衡受到毁灭性的破坏。这一切不仅严重地妨碍社会的进步，而且直接威胁着人类的生活。而这些"全球问题"之所以出现，固然有多方面的原因，但从根本上说则是资本主义发达国家利用科学技术的进步在世界范围内进行疯狂的资源掠夺所造成的结果。显然，在资本主义条件下，解决这些"全球问题"单凭发展科学技术是于事无补的，只有当科学技术完全掌握在人民的手中，才能从根本上消除因科学技术的发展而可能带来的不良后果，才能使科学技术真正成为造福人类的工具。

至于"科学技术的发展是否可以自然而然地导致共产主义"，我认为应作具体的分析。马克思主义是建立在 19 世纪自然科学三大发现和资本主义工业革命的基础上的，它的诞生和共产主义运动的兴起，是同科学技术的进步联系在一起的，科学技术革命和共产主义运动是相互制约、相互促进并彼此互为手段和目的的。一方面，科学技术革命为共产主义运动的进一步发展准备了雄厚的物质条件；另一方面，共产主义运动为不断提高科学技术的社会价值，消除科学技术异化开辟了最有效、最根本的途径。在当代，科学技术革命和共产主义运动在迅猛的发展进程中日益紧密地结合起来，逐步汇成不可抗拒的时代洪流，共同决定着社会发展的方向和人类历史的归宿。之所以如此，是因为科学技术革命和共产主义运动的发展在历史方向上是一致的，它们的社会意义都在于使整个社会得到革命性的改造，它们的终极价值都是使人类得到彻底的解放。因此，科学技术作为生产力，它的发展必然会导向共产主义。当然，就两大世界性潮流发展的具体过程而言，科学技术革命引起社会革命尚须其他诸多主客观条件，科学技术革命可以为共产主义运动的发展和共产主义的实现提供客观要求，奠定坚实的物质基础。但是，科学技术本身不能决定自身如何应用，科学技术发展不可能自发地或自然而然地导致共产主义。要想使科学技术成为促进社会进步、促进共产主义实现的巨大力量，从根本上说必须变革资本主义的社会制度。

（此文原载于《中国高校社会科学》1998 年第 1 期）

自我升级智能体的逻辑与认知问题

任晓明* 李 熙

在认知科学和哲学中，意识是最让人着迷又始终无法解释的问题。自我意识是我们再熟悉不过的了，但它又是最难以解释的。人工智能思想家通常用两种方式研究自我意识：其一是建立自我意识的计算机模型，这叫作"机器意识"；其二是用计算术语去分析自我意识，但不去模拟。[①]前者主要是人工智能技术专家的工作，他们通常只关注技术性问题而不讨论关于意识的哲学问题；后者主要是那些对人工智能有研究的哲学家感兴趣的，但他们在有关哲学问题上存在着巨大的分歧。例如，强人工智能系统会有自我意识吗？如果有，它指的是意向性还是感受质，或者什么别的属性？如此等等。这显然不是科学问题，而是人工智能中的哲学问题，是需要哲学家和科学家共同面对，通力合作而加以解决的问题。然而令人尴尬的是，人工智能研究近年来尽管取得了重大突破，但对强人工智能中涉及机器意识这类难题，哲学家和科学家要么避而不谈，要么泛泛而谈，机器意识的研究举步维艰。

幸运的是，一些机器意识研究成果正悄然改变着这个局面：关于机器意识的认知和哲学研究尽管面临巨大困难，但是自我升级智能体的理论成果有望打破困局，它能不能像图灵机的构建打破了人工智能研究的困局一样，人们正有所期待。自我升级（self-improvement）智能体，亦即自我改进智能体，是通用人工智能的一种理论模型。作为机器意识研究的成果，它试图为破解自我意识难题作出贡献。建立这种智能体的意义不仅仅在于它可以解决问题，而在于它与图灵机一样，可以为我们讨论自我意识的话

* 任晓明，南开大学哲学系教授，研究方向为科学技术哲学与逻辑学。
① 玛格丽特·博登：《AI：人工智能的本质与未来》，孙诗惠译，中国人民大学出版社，2017年，第145页。

题奠定一个程序的基础，或者一种科学验证的标准，从而使意识问题不再神秘。这是我们探讨自我升级智能体问题的一个动因。

以下探讨的主要问题有：第一，自我升级智能体在逻辑和哲学上有什么贡献？存在什么局限？第二，自我升级智能体的提出有什么认知意义和应用风险？第三，自我升级智能体能否具有自我意识？这种智能体在理论上的困局是什么？第四，破解自我升级智能体困局的出路何在？

一、自我创生思想的演进

自我升级智能体是一种关于自我意识的智能体。虽然这种思想在古希腊早已萌芽，但作为一种认知科学和人工智能理论是从冯·诺依曼（Von Neumann）开始的。冯·诺依曼第一次以数学的精确性和逻辑的严密性探讨了自创生系统。①

实现自我创生的前提是实现自我复制（self-producing）或自我生产。在冯·诺依曼看来，借助图灵程序来进行自动机的"自我复制"是不够的。因为图灵机输出的是一段带有 0 和 1 的纸带。而冯·诺依曼要构造的是这样的自动机：它的输出是另一自动机。

冯·诺依曼明确指出，借助构造的方法，即通过设计各种构造性的自动机，能够构造出自复制自动机。②这种自复制自动机不仅能够进行通用图灵机那种计算，而且能自我复制。但这种自动机离真正具有自我意识的智能体还有一定差距。

21 世纪初，斯蒂芬·沃尔夫勒姆（Stephen Wolfman）对冯·诺依曼的细胞自动机理论作了进一步阐述和改进。他指出，可以用简单的电脑程序来表达更一般的规律，在此基础上建立一种新的科学，启动另一场科学变革。③如果说冯·诺依曼主要从理论方面阐述自动机如何从简单规则和初

---

① autopoiesis（自创生）这个词意指自我生产或自我复制。生命系统是自创生的（autopoietic），它们将那些能够产生必要部件并能够持续发展的过程组织了起来。那些并不能自我产生或复制的系统被称为它生产的（allopoietic），例如，一条河流或者一块钻石。自我复制智能体、自我升级智能体都属于自创生系统。

② 参见 John Von Neumann. *Theoty of Self-Reproducing Automata*. University of Illinois Press, 1966.

③ Stephen Wolfman. *A New Kind of Science*. Wolfram Media. Inc., 2002, p. 1.

始条件进化到复杂系统，如何自我复制，那么可以说沃尔夫勒姆从技术细节方面更深入地探讨了自动机的自我复制功能，为自我升级智能体的建构奠定了基础。

受到细胞自动机研究的启发，认知科学中的生成主义者开展了对细胞自动机模型的研究。他们认为，在自治的复杂系统中，界定自治组织的关系不在于静态实体而在于过程，如细胞中的新陈代谢反应过程。这种自治系统的一个范例是活细胞。在一个活细胞中，其构成过程是化学的；其循环依赖性采取了自我复制的新陈代谢网络形式，这个自我复制的代谢网络产生了它自己的膜；这个网络将这个系统构成生物域中的一个统一体，并决定了与环境的交互作用域。这种自治系统称为"自创生"（autopoisis）系统。①

不难看出，生成主义是一种非还原论的自然主义纲领。在传统认识论中难以理解的"自我指涉"，在生成主义那里得到了合理的解释，从而为自我升级智能体的建构提供了认识论资源。

总之，生成主义不再关注意向性意义上的意识，而是强调自我意识的自主性，这就为关于自我意识的智能体研究开辟了道路。生成主义对建构自我升级智能体的影响在于，如果没有生成主义的概念，认知科学既不能解释有生命的认知，也不能建立真正有智能的智能体。

在生成主义看来，我们对意识问题的分析就是要解释人的意识是如何从大脑这个虚拟计算机的运作中产生的。他们希望为自我意识找到一个能使其成为科学的研究方法，借助这种实验的方法可以解决自我意识中的难题。虽然自创生系统理论探讨了自动机自我复制的认知基础问题，然而，仅仅具有自我复制能力的机器还不具有自我意识，构造出具有自我意识的智能体，是认知科学和人工智能面临的更为严峻的挑战。而真正使这种前瞻性设想变为现实的是哥德尔机（Gödel Machine）的构想。②

---

① 参见 Francisco J. Varela. *Principles of Biological Autonomy*. Elsever North Holland, 1979, p.55.

② Jürgen Schmidhuber. Ultimate Cognition à la Gödel. In *Cognitive Computation*, 2009, Vol.1, no. 2, pp.177-193.

二、"自指"：涉及"我"的智能体的核心概念

曾经有一本获普利策文学奖的奇书《GEB：集异璧之大成》，该书作者侯世达将巴赫的赋格曲、埃舍尔的版画和哥德尔的逻辑定理这三块奇异的瑰璧缠结在一起探讨，广泛涉及人工智能、数理逻辑、几何绘图、古典音乐、生物基因、认知心理、形而上学与认识论、禅宗寓言等不同领域，书中充斥着各种语言游戏、歧义、双关、悖论、怪圈、对称、嵌套、镶嵌、自指、跨越、同构等"奇技淫巧"，仿佛一座循环往复、层次错乱、令人目眩的迷宫。[1]但居于迷宫最核心的珍宝是两样——"自指"（self-reference）和"对角线"（diagnoal）。二者又如一枚铜币的两面，被来自范畴论的劳威尔（Lawvere）不动点定理牢牢捕获——让"数学"开口说"我"，或让"我"超越预设。康托尔定理、说谎者悖论、罗素悖论、塔斯基算术"真"不可定义定理、图灵停机定理、哥德尔不完全性定理等都可以看作它的特殊示例。

19 世纪末，康托尔创立了素朴集合论，证明了一个集合的基数严格小于其幂集的基数，从而发现存在不同层次的无穷。但素朴集合论不一致（不协调）。1901 年，罗素悖论被发现揭示出所有不属于自身的集合的类不再是一个集合，这直接导致了所谓的第三次数学基础危机。哥德尔 1931 年证明，任何包含初等算术的、一致的、可递归公理化形式系统不可能完全，也不能证明自身的一致。塔斯基 1933 年证明算术真不能在算术内部被定义。图灵 1936 年证明停机问题是不可判定的，从而一阶逻辑的有效性不可判定。上述这些否定性的结果意味着希尔伯特规划的失败，也使莱布尼茨关于通用文字、理性演算的梦想蒙上一丝阴影。这些否定性的结果看上去碰触到了人类理性的边界和极限，也引起了心灵哲学家和认知科学家的密切关注。侯世达的工作就是主要围绕这些定理和悖论展开的。这些结果还被彭罗斯（Penrose）用来论证心智胜过机器，从而人工智能不可能。[2]所以有必要弄清这些否定性结果背后的统一结构。所有这些定理、悖论都与

---

① 参见 Douglas Hofstadter. *Gödel, Escher, Bach: An Eternal Golden Braid*. Basic Books, 1979.

② Roger Penrose. *The Emperor's New mind. Concerning Computers, Minds, and the Laws of Physics*. Oxford University Press, 1989, pp.40-97.

哲学上一个古老的悖论——说谎者悖论有关。劳威尔通过范畴论里的一个不动点定理刻画了这些悖论和定理背后的对角线结构。[1]但直到雅诺夫斯基（Yanofsky）通过集合论语言重新表述劳威尔不动点定理之前，这个重要的结果并没有得到逻辑学家和哲学家的足够重视。[2]虽然这些理论结果看上去是否定性的，但它们直接催生了关于涉及"自我"的智能体的研究。下面将分析这个刻画了"自指"和"超越"（transcendence）的定理的更多应用，并揭示它在构造自我升级的通用人工智能体中的核心作用。

首先，康托尔在证明集合 A 的幂集 P（A）的基数大于集合 A 的基数时引入了对角线方法。说谎者悖论、罗素悖论、哥德尔不完全性定理、图灵停机定理等都借助了对角线方法。劳威尔通过范畴论里一个非常简洁的不动点定理给出了对角线方法的统一刻画。[3]说谎者悖论、格雷林悖论、蒯因悖论、理查德悖论、雅布劳悖论、罗素悖论、佩里悖论、忙海狸函数、康托尔定理、图灵停机定理等都服从劳威尔的模式。

其次，劳威尔不动点定理抓住了"自指"的核心，它是说谎者悖论、格雷林悖论、罗素悖论、理发师悖论、理查德悖论、蒯因悖论、雅布劳悖论等悖论的关键，也是康托尔定理、哥德尔第一不完全性定理、塔斯基算术"真"不可定义性定理、勒布定理、帕里克定理、克林尼（Kleene）不动点定理、图灵停机定理、冯·诺依曼自复制自动机和全自省程序的关键，借助它还可以构造不可计算的实数、不可命名的实数、部分递归但非潜递归的函数、佩里悖论、快速增长的忙海狸函数、λ 演算版本的哥德尔不动点引理、柯里 Y 不动点算子、图灵 Θ 不动点算子，以及它们的"传值"形式的不动点算子，借助"传值"形式的不动点算子，易得克林尼不动点定理。甚至施米德胡贝尔（Schmidhuber）的借助定理证明器进行自指从而进行自我升级的通用智能体即哥德尔机也可以看作克林尼不动点定理的应用特例。[4]

① William Lawvere. Diagonal Arguments and Cartesian Closed Categories. In *Theory and Applications of Categories*, 1969, Vol.92, pp.134-145.

② Noson S. Yanofsky. A Universal Approach to Self-referential Paradoxes, Incompleteness and Fixed Points. In *The Bulletin of Symbolic Logic*, 2003, Vol.9, no. 3, pp.362-386.

③ Wiliam Lawvere. Diagonal Arguments and Cartesian Closed Categories. In *Theory and Applications of Categories*, 1969, Vol.92, pp.134-145.

④ Jürgen Schmidhuber. Gödel Machines. Fully Self-referential Optimal Universal Self-improvers. In Ben Goertzel, Cassio Pennachin eds.: *Artificial General Intelligence*. Springer, 2007, pp.199-226.

"自指"或"对角线"方法在逻辑中的大部分应用都是证明否定性的结论，在计算机科学中也是如此。比如，科恩（Cohen）用"对角线"方法证明，不存在完美的反病毒软件，即，不存在一个算法能检测出所有的计算机病毒。假设存在某个病毒检测算法 A，则根据对角线方法，可以如下构造程序 P："如果 A 检测出 P 被感染，则直接退出；否则，传播病毒。"显然，A 不能判断 P 是否被感染。所以，对于任何反病毒软件来说，错杀或漏杀难以避免。专门检测危险程序的程序也面临一样的问题，要么可能放过了真正危险的程序，要么可能误判了安全的程序。[①]所以，试图通过打造"程序警察"的办法阻止智能体的叛乱会存在很大的安全隐患。虽然这里的"对角线"论证对解决智能伦理问题产生了负面的作用，但"自指"的方法对构建通用人工智能会起到积极且正面的作用。

我们知道，发展通用人工智能最简便最理想的方式可能是，先制造某个弱一点的人工智能体，然后赋予它某种自我进化的能力，比如，让它可以修改自身的源代码，然后希望它能通过自我修改的方式不断自我升级变得更强。但直观上，自我修改源代码的程序很难令人接受，如果自我升级后的下一代更智能，是否意味着初代就已经蕴含了同样水平的智能？自我修改是安全的吗？会不会越改越崩溃？一个允许完全修改自身源代码的程序也可能面临类似的问题，如果它能修改得更好的话，为什么没有修改得更坏的可能？如何确保一个程序能够自我修改并修改得更好而不是更坏？这里的关键就是不动点定理。

克林尼不动点定理告诉我们：对于任意的程序 h，总存在某个程序 e，执行程序 e 的结果等价于把程序 e 当作数据输入给程序 h 执行的结果。克林尼不动点定理的证明跟那些有趣的悖论构造差不多，都服从劳威尔不动点定理的结构，看起来像玩弄"自指"的文字游戏，但这并非简单的自指，它对于智能体的自我觉知、自我升级非常重要，它能保证一段程序可以计算出关于自身的各种性质。比如，假设程序 h（x）负责计算任意字符串 x 的长度，根据此定理，存在自测量长度的程序 e，使得执行 e 的结果相当于执行 h（e），也就是说，e 计算得出了自己源代码的长度。再比如，假设程序 h（e）负责编译出 x 所编码的程序。根据克林尼不动点定理，存在程

---

① Fred Cohen. Computer Viruses-Theory and Experiments. In *Computers and Security*, 1987, Vol.6, pp.22-35.

序 e，使得执行 e 的结果相当于输出了程序 e 自身，这就是所谓的自复制程序。冯·诺依曼的自复制自动机是构造性的，而这里的自复制程序 e 看上去是存在性的，但因为克林尼不动点是构造性的，所以这里的自复制程序 e 也是构造性的。

做一个类比，心理学家卡尼曼（Kahneman）认为，人有两个自我：经验自我和记忆自我，经验自我负责动作和决策，记忆自我负责解读反思。[1] 瑜伽教练的"言传身教"可以看作这两个自我的配合，记忆自我对经验自我的肢体演示过程进行了逐步的反思，并将反思的结果精确地叙述了出来。瑜伽教练的"记忆自我"的反思过程可以看作用语言对自己的经验自我的行为进行的虚拟模拟。自省程序的自省过程可以与此类比，类似于程序 $\varphi_e(x)$ 内嵌了虚拟机（记忆自我），然后把自己的源代码放在虚拟机上模拟自己运行了 $\psi(x)$ 步，最后把整个的模拟结果输出了出来。

不仅如此，程序不但能够进行"自省"，而且能够通过"自指"进行"自我升级"。抽象地看，一个智能体无非是一段程序。因此，不妨设计某种"元程序"负责搜索整个"程序空间"、自动寻找"聪明"的程序，然后通过经验学习寻找更"聪明"的程序。

三、哥德尔机：自我升级智能体的一种实现

自我升级的哥德尔机可以看作"自省"程序的超级加强版。数学家曼宁（Manin）也有过类似的超越"自省"程序的想法，设想房间的桌子上有一张房间的布置地图，地图精确地描述了房间里的陈设，包括桌子上的地图自身，然后设想地图上房间物品的摆设可以脱离地图而发生位置变化，然后房间里现实物品的摆放位置也可以根据地图的变化而变化。曼宁认为，大脑的功能与此类似，大脑内嵌了一张描述自身的大脑地图，这张地图具有建模功能，可以虚拟不同于当前大脑状态的可能状态，然后还具有控制功能，它能控制整个大脑根据虚拟状态的变化而发生现实的变化。而且，这张大脑地图还是粗粒化的。[2]曼宁有这个构想，但并没有给出具体

---

① Daniel Kahneman. *Thinking, Fast and Slow*. Farrar, Straus and Giroux, 2011, pp.377-385.

② Dmitrii Manin, Yuri I. Manin. Cognitive Networks. Brains, Internet, and Civilizations. In B. Sriraman ed.: *Humanizing Mathematics and Its Philosophy*. Birkhauser Basel, 2017, pp.85-96.

的实现方案。哥德尔机恰恰可以看作这么一张大脑地图。它的可行性由克林尼不动点定理保证。虽然能够自我修改源代码的哥德尔机可以通过克林尼不动点定理构造出来，但相比于自测量长度程序、自复制程序和自省程序，这里的 h 函数要复杂很多，因为它不仅要"自省"，更重要的是，它还要通过更深层次的"自省"实现"自我升级"，下面介绍它的详细构造。

哥德尔机由两个并行的部分构成：通用求解器可以是任何一个处理具体问题的程序，比如深度神经网络 CNN/LSTM，为了更具有通用性，它也可以是一个通用强化学习算法，比如直接采用 AIXI 的某个可计算的变种，强化学习算法负责与环境交互，能对环境采取动作，并能感知外界环境的反馈，通过不断地与环境交互来获取更大的期望累积效用。通用搜索器内嵌了一个形式系统，形式系统完整编码了哥德尔机的硬件、效用函数、不确定性计算工具的全部信息以及部分环境信息。

硬件公理负责描述机器元件具体的运作方式，比如，如果它的硬件是最简单的图灵机模型，那么，硬件公理就需要描述图灵机纸带的内容、读写头的位置、当前的状态以及状态的可能的转移规则等。效用公理负责描述不同状态的可能回报、机器在输入输出和运行过程中的计算成本以及这些不同的回报和成本之间的整合方式。环境公理负责描述观察到的环境信息以及可能的环境变化，如果通用求解器加载的是 AIXI 的某个变种的话，它就需要描述 AIXI 的环境空间，即所有半可计算的半测度。不确定性公理负责描述算术、概率论、统计学以及逻辑中的符号操作规则等。

通过内嵌的形式系统，通用搜索器就可以将机器工作的所有状态当作数学定理来讨论。通用搜索器可以通过一个定理证明器搜索数学命题的证明，基于初始给定的效用函数，如果它搜索到某个"策略在未来的时间里比当前策略能带来更大的期望累积效用"成立，那么它就改掉之前的策略，改用这个新的策略与环境进行交互。这就实现了哥德尔机的自我升级（见图 1）。

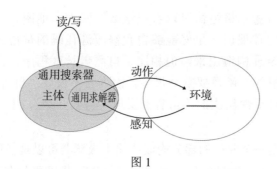

图 1

以上关于通用求解器和通用搜索器的描述就是我们借助克林尼不动点定理构造自我升级的哥德尔机所需要的函数 h。虽然上面内容是用自然语言描述的，但只要设计得足够巧妙，通用求解器和通用搜索器的构造确实是能行的，所以根据丘奇-图灵论题，它可以看作一个递归函数 h，然后我们就可以借助克林尼不动点定理，证明存在某个程序 e，它可以对自身（包括通用求解器和通用搜索器）的源代码进行彻底的修改——只要它内嵌的形式系统的定理证明器能证明"修改后的策略在未来的时间里比当前策略能带来更大的期望累积效用"。这在一定程度上保证了对源代码的修改是相对可靠的。这样通用求解器和通用搜索器就可以比较合理地自我学习升级。

但根据克林尼不动点定理，只是存在一个能提升效用的程序 e，那么，能否让机器反复改进、持续自我升级？这就需要带参数的克林尼不动点定理：对于任意给定的递归函数 h(x,y)，存在递归函数 e(y)，使得对任意 y 都有 $\varphi_{e(y)} = \varphi_{f(e(y), y)}$。将时间、部分环境等计算资源的限制信息编码到参数 y 里面，借助带参数的克林尼不动点定理，存在一种系统的自我升级方式 e，可以持续不断地产生一系列程序 e(y)，每一个都是对前一个补充了额外信息的改进。通过这样的方式，哥德尔机就能持续地搜索可提升自己效用的策略，不断用更好的策略改写自己的源代码，从而完成持续"反思升级"的学习过程。

这里的升级既有采用克林尼不动点定理的一次升级，也有采用带参数的克林尼不动点定理的持续升级。一次升级与持续升级孰优孰劣呢？是否持续升级必然强于一次升级呢？在同一个全局最优的意义上，其实二者没有区别。因为根据通用搜索器的设计，只有当"改进"后的状态比"不改进"的状态严格地好的时候才会触发改进，而"不改进"的状态其实隐含着，虽然当前不改进但会继续搜索并评估以后其他替代改进状态的可能，这意味着，相对于初始给定的效用函数和环境信息，"改进"不会落入局部最优而是稳妥地迈到全局最优。所以一次改进足矣，一次改进包含了以后可能的二代、三代……直到最优的所有可能的改进。

但是，持续升级仍然有它的优势，因为参数 y 里可以编码更多的新探测到的环境信息和计算资源等信息，所以持续改进的哥德尔机类似于一个实时算法，它可以不断拓展对环境的知识，搜索相对于当下计算资源限制下的最优改进，然后随着新环境信息的录入和计算资源的增多，不断地调整对"全局最优"的理解，从而收敛到真正的全局最优。升级后的哥德尔机也不过是一段程序，所以它还可以调用冯·诺依曼的自复制程序，不断将自己复制下去，如果允许变异的话，变异后的个体也可以繁殖下去。

不难看出，通用搜索器有点像前面作类比的虚拟机。所谓借助形式系统的搜索类似一套模拟过程。而哥德尔机允许对自身状态进行编码相当于机器可以模拟自身的运作，而用定理证明器搜索数学命题探测更好的策略的过程相当于机器进行自我反思、主动规划探索的过程。如果能将虚拟机里搜索到的策略装载到实际的执行系统上，哥德尔机就可以不断地修改自己的代码，看上去像"揪着自己的头发把自己拎起来"。有人担心，这种装置一旦实际制造出来，就有可能引发智能爆炸，从而导致技术奇点的来临。但更需注意的是，即使有实现超级智能的可能，也未必是往好的方向。虽然哥德尔机相对于其初始给定的效用函数是全局最优的，如果初始给定的效用函数有问题的话，比如与既定的目标有偏差、没有真正反映人的真实意图甚至是有敌意或邪恶的，那么，相对于这种效用的全局最优只会更可怕，极有可能收敛到最坏的情形。这就是哲学家博斯特罗姆（Bostrom）所说的"目标正交性"（goalorthogonality）论题。[①]

施米德胡贝尔建立的哥德尔机是第一个具有自指能力的元学习机，[②]以下通过讨论作为自我升级智能体的哥德尔机，探讨机器能不能具备自我意识的话题。

---

① Nick Bostrom. *Superintelligence: Paths. Dangers. Strategies*. Oxford University Press, 2014, pp.105-114.

② Bas Steunebrink and Jirgen Schmidhuber. Towards an Actual Godel Machine Implementation. In P. Wang, B. Goertzel eds.: *Theoretical Foundations of Artificial General Intelligence*. Springer, 2012, pp.173-195.

　　通过劳威尔的定理，可以看出，"自指"与"对角线"是一枚硬币的两面，通过不动点可以实现跨越层次的间接自指，可以表达"我有什么性质"或"我要进行什么操作"，而通过"对角线"可以构造出"超越"预定列表的新对象，无论是"自指"还是"超越"都是令人振奋的现象，与人的意识活动密切相关，而哥德尔机却通过内嵌形式系统的方式自指，这种"自指"实现了另一种意义上的"超越"，不同于借助"对角线"构造出不能以既有方式表示的"不合法"的新对象，哥德尔机却是通过"自指"实现"超越"，相当于对自己说——"我要变成能获取更大效用的自己"——然后就魔术般真的变强了（实现全局最优）。

　　上面例子中瑜伽教练的"记忆自我"的反思过程是对"经验自我"亦步亦趋的虚拟模拟而没有实质性的指导，而哥德尔机的"记忆自我"却试图通过定理证明器的自我反思升级"经验自我"（见图2）。

哥德尔机与自我意识的类比

自模拟计算机	哥德尔机	自我意识
宿主机	通用求解器	经验自我
虚拟机	通用搜索器	记忆自我
硬件	硬件	身体

图2　人与哥德尔机

　　如果我们把"自由意志"定义为记忆自我对经验自我的反思甚至指导，那么在这种意义上，只要搜索器比求解器跑得快，哥德尔机或许可以具有自由意志。对于人来说，记忆自我可以通过虚构故事来"欺骗"自己。人可能没有自由意志，因为有实验显示，记忆自我并不参与决策过程，真正的决策早在我们意识到之前几秒的时间就已经被经验自我作出了，自由意志很可能就是这个记忆自我编造的一个故事。我们充其量仅具有自我意识，我们可以觉知到自己所做的一切，但不能反过来作用到我们的行动上。关于自由意志，法兰克福（Frankfurt）认为，指向事物或事态的欲望叫一阶欲望，指向一阶欲望的欲望叫二阶欲望。有自我意识才能形成二阶欲望。

一个人可以有二阶欲望但不一定想依照它行动。想依照它行动的二阶欲望叫二阶意欲。一个人的行动是自由的当且仅当这个行动是由他认同的自己的二阶意欲所致使的。这要求二阶欲望是自主选择的而不是外部设定的。[①]根据这种"自由意志"的定义，叔本华所说的"人能为所欲为，但不能御其所欲"相当于否定了人有自由意志。哥德尔机的通用搜索器只根据初始的效用函数搜索升级策略，并没有真正升级效用函数，所以不具有法兰克福意义上的自由意志。埃弗里特（Everitt）等人刻画过可以自我修改效用函数的智能体，不过，根据他们刻画的自我修改效用函数的方式，看上去"高阶欲望"像是自我决定的，但其实这并不是真正的可以作用在"低阶欲望"上的"高阶欲望"，而只是用当下的策略可以修改的"未来欲望"，所以这种智能体也不具有法兰克福意义上的自由意志。[②]

四、自我升级智能体理论的贡献和局限

自我升级智能体的研究切实推进了人工智能和哲学的研究，但这种推进是有限度的。以下从逻辑、认知和认识论方面探讨自我升级智能体的贡献和局限。

（一）逻辑和哲学上的贡献和局限

自我升级智能体的构建向真正具有自我意识的智能体前进了一步。它对涉及"自指"的罗素悖论、哥德尔不完全性定理、图灵停机定理等否定性结果背后的机制作了一次正面的应用。它使得我们对自我意识的研究有了一个程序化的标准，借助这种形式化的方法可以为自我意识的机器实现提供新的思路，进而弥合学界关于机器意识的分歧，破解机器意识研究面临的困局。

自我升级智能体的局限体现在逻辑、认知和认识论方面。

---

① Harry G. Frankfurt, Freedom of the Will and the Concept of a Person. In the Journal of Phslophy, 1971, Vol.68, No 1, pp.8-20.

② Tom Everitt, et al. Self-Modification of Policy and Utility Function in Rational Agents. In Bas Steunebrink. Pei Wang, Ben Goertzel eds.: *Artificial General Intelligence*, Proceedings of the 9th International Conference, AGI 2016. Springer, 2016, pp.1-11.

1. 哥德尔第一不完全性定理的局限

哥德尔机通过内嵌的形式系统（数学）对自己和环境进行建模、作逻辑推理，从而规划与环境的交互策略，这个过程非常类似于人在世界之中的生存过程。人类在漫长的文明中，发展出了先进的数学科学，用科学手段对自己和环境建模，制造和使用工具，影响改造环境。除了人很难自我升级外，人通过发展"理性"手段自我认识并认识和改造环境的过程与机器很相似。泰格马克（Tegmark）在《生命3.0》中认为，生命的发展有三个阶段，通用人工智能是生命形式的第三个阶段。在第一个阶段，生命的硬件和软件都只能依赖于进化的力量，如细菌。在第二个阶段，硬件依靠进化，但软件可以自行设计、升级改进，如人类。人类可以创造、发展、传承知识，虽然躯体只能维修保养不能设计改进，但知识可以不断地升级。在第三个阶段，硬件和软件都可以设计升级。[①]哥德尔机应该可以看作泰格马克所说的第三个阶段的典型代表，它可以对自身（包括通用求解器和通用搜索器）进行彻底的升级改造。最开始的通用求解器可以选择 AIXI 的某种可计算的逼近或变种，如强化学习模型 $AIXI^{TL}$，而通用搜索器可以选择莱文通用搜索的某个变种，如胡特尔搜索。但是，既然通用搜索器内嵌了形式系统，那么它就面临哥德尔不完全性定理的障碍，有一些重要且必要的"变身"可能无法被形式系统找到。

对于任何可计算的环境，算法概率都可以很好地逼近它，为了保证可以逼近任何可计算环境这种"通用性"，算法概率本身不是可计算的。[②]强大的智能体必然复杂，虽然复杂且强大的智能体是存在的，但只要它足够复杂，那么形式系统将无法帮助我们找到它。这个限制可以称为哥德尔第一不完全性定理和莱格不完全性定理限制。

2. 哥德尔第二不完全性定理的局限

生物的进化有可能是基因无目的地随机变异，自然环境作选择、适者生存的结果。因为是随机变异，所以进化速度慢。对于自我升级的智能体来说，智能体根据环境自我选择变异。哥德尔机就是带有方向性地自主选择变异。在当前的主体技穷之时，人们总寄希望于进化的力量，希望演化

① Max Tegmark. *Life 3.0: Being Human in the Age of Artificial Intelligence*. Penguin Random House LLC, 2017, pp.26-31

② Ray Solomonoff. Complexity-Based Induction Systems. Comparisons and Convergence Theorems. In *IEEE Transactions on Information Theory*, 1978, Vol.24, no.4, pp.422-432.

后的主体能更强大。对于哥德尔机来说，如果它想实现迭代进化的话，一个自然的办法就是制造后代，只要每一代给下一代装配更强的形式系统，那么哥德尔第一不完全性定理的障碍就可以在一定程度上突破，但问题是——哥德尔第二不完全性定理，主体 1 在构造主体 2 时如果不能在自己的形式系统内证明主体 2 的形式系统的一致性，那么它根本无法保证主体 2 的可靠性。无法保障可靠性，就无法回避完全坍塌的风险。一致性得不到保障意味着机器智能的伦理安全问题得不到保障。但是，如果要求每一代主体必须严格证明下一代主体的形式系统的一致性的话，那么，这种进化在某种意义上是一种退化，而且是一种极为快速的退化。而生物的进化则不需要一致性的保证，好的变异、不好的变异都可能产生，自然选择的结果虽然常常是但不必然是优胜劣汰。变异和自然选择不能保证可靠性，哥德尔机面临的也是同样的问题。这可以称为可靠性限制。

3. 复杂性限制与高层抽象的反思

如果不考虑哥德尔不完全性定理的限制，哥德尔机在理论上是全局最优的，但是否可以马上进行工程制造了呢？其实很难，难点在于复杂性。由于一个自我模拟系统需要两层设计，随着求解器复杂性的提高，需要更复杂的搜索器去模拟它。一个可能的方案是，先对求解器进行高层抽象，比如，采用类似特征强化学习的办法，将求解器的环境抽象为简单的马尔科夫决策过程，搜索器只"反思"抽象后的求解器，而不是亦步亦趋地模拟所有细节。人的意识也是类似，对于一段经历，记忆自我会做加工裁剪，忽视中间波澜不惊的过程，而格外重视尖峰体验和最终时刻的体验。这就是心理学家所谓的"过程忽视"和"峰终定律"。①所以，搜索器必须以"粗粒化"的方式反思求解器，学习需要遗忘，高层抽象可以看作对复杂性限制的一个解决路径。这也可以看作一种实用复杂性限制。

4. 独立于还是内嵌于环境的问题

克林尼不动点定理保证了哥德尔机的全局最优策略，哥德尔机所谓对自身策略、效用函数、搜索器的自我修改其实也不是真的自我修改，而是通过自指方法构造的不动点。这样构造的哥德尔机是外在于环境的。这种构想类似于哲学上笛卡尔主张的"心物二元论"思想。哥德尔机与环境除了有限的输入输出的交互外，二者完全独立，环境无法影响哥德尔机的运

---

① Daniel Kahneman, *Thinking, Fast and Slow*. Farrar, Straus and Giroux, 2011. pp.377-385.

行过程。这是一种高度的理想化，与现实情境相去甚远。现实中的机器可能随时受环境的影响，机器不是超越于环境的心灵，机器与环境由同样的物质材料构成，机器是环境的一部分。所以，如果抛弃二元论的设定，考虑更现实的一元论设定，不作过度简化的更理想的哥德尔机应该是嵌入式的。如果把哥德尔机看作环境的一部分会怎样？对于内嵌于环境的主体来说，它只是环境的一个子部分，环境可以修改主体的源代码和内存，并执行主体的代码。受资源限制，第一步主体可以从长度不超过某个固定长度的程序集合中搜索最优策略，后面主体怎么改变就完全由环境控制了。

主体试图通过自己的行动影响环境，环境直接修改生成下一代主体的策略和下一代主体的感知，所以主体的动作、下一代主体以及下一代主体的感知都可以整合在一起，相当于所有的信息都被整合到了主体里，所谓的交互历史就是主体的更迭。[①]如果主体的源代码和内存完全由环境修改，环境执行主体的代码，那么，因为所有的信息都被整合到了主体里，主体只能在最开始没有任何经验知识的前提下进行决策，此时主体缺乏对环境的经验估计，唯一可以依赖的只有对环境的"先验"信念。而这种"先验"信念如何去把握？这是内嵌于环境的哥德尔机遇到的难题。

5. "自指"的物理限制

前面讨论的哥德尔机是基于经典的图灵机，并没有考虑量子效应。彭罗斯曾借助不完全性定理论证心灵胜过机器，认为人的意识可以把握机器证明不了的真理。他猜测人脑的意识行为源于大脑神经元微管的量子效应。如果彭罗斯的这个猜测成立，那么是否量子哥德尔机才能刻画人的意识？其实，只要借助"自指"来刻画意识，意识都无法超越对角线论证的局限。[②]假设M是可能的量子测量的集合，O是可能的量子测量结果的集合，劳威尔定理告诉我们，如果 α 没有不动点，那么通过对角线方法构造的 g 就不能被 f 表示。测量一个属性并完全不改变它是不可能的，换句话说，因为有量子观察效应，所以 α 没有不动点，这意味着，观察者的自我测量或者说自我反思行为必然存在局限，必然存在不能进行自我观测的死角。

① Laurent Orseau, Mark Ring. Space-Time Embedded Intelligence. In Joscha Bach. Ben Goertzel, Matthew Ikle eds.: *Artificial General Intelligence*. Proceedings of the 5th International Conference, AGI 2012, Springer, 2012, pp.209-218.

② Karl Svozil. *Physical (A) Causality: Determinism, Randomness and Uncaused Events*. Springer, 2018, pp.17-19.

通过劳威尔不动点定理，我们看到了"自指"与"超越"的广泛应用，看到了很多悖论、定理、算子之间深刻的相似性，也看到了"自指"与"超越"之间深刻的"平衡"。"自指"与"超越"恰如一枚硬币的正反两面，正面的应用甚至在构建自我升级的通用人工智能中也起着至关重要的作用，而反面的应用则在不断地挑战着机器甚至人脑自身的认知局限。

（二）认知意义和应用风险

从认知的角度看，自我升级智能体的提出具有重要的认知意义。我们知道，生成主义强调具身主体以由其生理机能决定的精确方式与环境发生交互作用，"自我"作为这种交互过程的一部分而产生，"自我"并不表征，但他通过与环境交互作用的方式产生世界，生成世界。因此，生成主义纲领的一个基本特征是自指性。比起第一代认知主义纲领，生成主义纲领的高明之处就是它直面自指性，即涉及自身的问题。罗素悖论、说谎者悖论的出现让人们时刻警惕自指性带来的风险。实践证明，作为第三人称的外部观察者所感知的东西与作为第一人称的当事人所感知的东西是不同的，生成主义采用的策略是，在二者之间搭建一个解释学循环之桥。这就像我们从生命的基本形式出发，经历了生命发展的从简单到复杂的进化，最后以生物学家研究生命的基本形式结束。这似乎是一条循环往复的莫比乌斯环，一个怪圈。从起点出发，转了一圈，又回到原点。考察的对象变成了正在探寻的主体。与此类似，生命作为自我升级智能体考察的对象，通过"自指"和"超越"变成了正在探寻的主体。生成主义为自我升级智能体的提出奠定了认知基础。自我升级智能体理论的成功为生成主义提供了一个有利的例证。

更有认知意义的是，像哥德尔机那样的自我学习升级方式也可以涌现出某种创造性，按照施米德胡贝尔、奥索（Orseau[①]）等人的观点，可以加载类似"人工好奇心"（artificial curiosity）的功能，这种聪明的智能体可以像一个好奇的儿童面对纷繁复杂的全新世界不断去探索、理解、发现和解决全新的问题，尽量增进对现实环境的理解，降低对可能环境的不确定性，最终成为能解答通用问题的通用智能体。在这个意义上，结合合适的"目的因"（效用函数），自我升级智能体的诞生具有重要的认知意义。

---

① Laurent Orseau, Tor Lattimore and Marcus Hutter. Universal Knowledge-Seeking Agents for Stochastic Environments. In Sanjay Jain, et al. eds.: *Algorithmic Learning Theory*. Proceedings of the 24th International Conference, ALT 2013, Springer 2013, pp.158-172.

五、机器意识研究的困局：以哥德尔机为例

以下我们以哥德尔机为例，探讨机器意识哲学研究面临的困局。主要讨论三个问题：哥德尔机器真正具有自我意识吗？哥德尔机器会导致智能爆炸吗？从哲学上看，哥德尔机在理论上的困局是什么？

哥德尔机是否可以具有自我意识？如果能，那它是一种功能意识，还是一种现象意识？回答这个问题之前，首先要区分两种情况：其一是机器看起来像是有自我意识的样子，也就是说，机器具有了"功能意识"；其二是机器真的具有了自我意识，而且它还知道自己具有了自我意识。这大致相当于现象意识。

如前文所述，既然哥德尔机可以"自我反思"，可以通过"自指"进行自我升级，如果人类的意识仅仅是通过自我模拟进行自我反思的话，那么机器也完全有可能模拟看起来具有意识的人类。人们只需要制造出一个同样具有两种自我的机器：一种虚拟的机器（记忆自我）和一种纯算法的执行机构(经验自我)，那么这种机器就可以表现得像是有自我意识的装置了。人们甚至可以用这样的系统定义自我意识。然而，这就说明机器"真的"具有了自我意识了吗？答案需要等待对"意识"的科学解释。因为到目前为止，科学界尚没有一个公认的关于人的"意识"的科学理论，所以这里所谓的机器具有自我意识，只是根据我们的定义机器"看起来"具有了自我意识，还不能说机器真正具有了自我意识，更遑论机器知道自己具有了自我意识，解决了知道自己知道、知道自己不知道之类的认识论难题。实际上，我们说哥德尔机具有"自我意识"只是一种"功能意识"。目前哥德尔（实体）机并没有创制出来，即便是造出来了，可能离真正具有意识还有很长的路要走。

自我升级智能体的建构有何风险？是否会导致智能爆炸？如前所述，哥德尔机可以通过在模拟器上搜索而寻求让自己优化的方案。我们只需要将搜索到的虚拟代码装载到实际的执行系统上，那哥德尔机就可以不断地修改自己的代码而升级下去。这样的机器做出来之后会有什么后果呢？由于哥德尔机具备不断自我改进自己代码的能力，亦即，这个智能系统可以通过不断地提升自己的能力而优化，这个过程会越来越快地持续下去，

从而有希望很快超过人类的智能。一旦达到了这样的智能，哥德尔机是否自己就会设计出更强的哥德尔机，从而让整个智能过程加速，从而导致智能爆炸？

对此我们不能过于乐观，认为智能爆炸会开启智能新时代。因为如前所述，哥德尔机也具有博斯特罗姆所说的"目标正交性"问题，即便有引发智能爆炸甚至达到技术奇点（technology singularity）的可能，也未必是往好的方向发展。虽然哥德尔机相对于其初始给定的效用函数是全局最优的，如果初始给定的效用函数有问题的话，比如，与既定的目标有偏差、没有真正反映人的真实意图，甚至是有敌意的或邪恶的，那么，相对于这种效用的全局最优只会更可怕，极有可能收敛到最坏的情形，甚至危及人类安全。同时，根据带参数的克林尼定理，持续升级的哥德尔机并不是完全彻底的自我迭代升级，而是需要将新获取的有关环境的信息和计算资源的信息编码到参数里，然后再借助相同的"自指"过程升级。这种升级过程并不是一种指数迭代，能不能收敛到技术奇点都存疑。退一步说，就目前的技术水平，我们离智能爆炸的实现还有很长的距离，机器不至于成为人类的"终结者"，或许有办法阻止其终结人类，比如，可以令其通过合作逆强化学习的办法学习加载人类的价值观。所以，不管是哪一方面，目前远不至于对人类构成真正的威胁。

哥德尔机的理论困局是能否实现真正的机器意识，破解意识之谜。这显然不是一个科学问题，而是一个哲学问题。通过考察理性主义与经验主义、分析哲学与现象学在这个问题上的分歧和争论，可以为我们提供化解困局的启迪。深受人工智能思想影响的哲学家麦克德莫特（McDermott）在他的《纯粹理性批判》论文中深刻指出，历史上许多没有出路的人工智能研究"只是因为对哲学家们昔日的失败一无所知，才得以维持"[①]。从细胞自动机到哥德尔机的发展历程，不难看出其中始终贯穿着理性主义和经验主义的较量和争锋。冯·诺依曼在自动机研究中尽管对概率和统计的因素有所考虑，但他主要偏重演绎逻辑和计算等理性因素而忽视统计数据等经验因素。这就使他即便走到了自我升级智能体的大门口却止步不前。哥德尔机一方面通过通用求解器采用统计学习的模型和工具与环境进行交

---

① 玛格丽特·博登：《人工智能哲学》，刘西瑞、王汉琦译，上海译文出版社，2001年，第307-308页。

互，这是经验主义的方案，另一方面通过通用搜索器内嵌的形式系统不断搜索，把搜索到的最优策略装载到实际的执行系统中以实现系统优化升级，这是理性主义的方案。另外，考虑借助带参数的克林尼定理构造的哥德尔机的话，还可以实时地把新的经验数据和计算资源通过参数的方式编码进去，然后借助"自指"的方式不断改进、持续升级，从而沟通了经验和理性两个方面，在看似对立的两极之间保持平衡。这是自我升级智能体研究给我们的哲学启示。

六、结语：自我升级智能体发展前瞻

自我升级智能体研究正处在发展的十字路口，需要在道路和方向上作出关键抉择。自我升级智能体的研究始终纠结于分析哲学传统与现象学传统的分歧，和人工智能中理性主义与经验主义此消彼长的争锋交织。它们都各有偏颇，在理性与经验孰重孰轻的问题上表现出某种片面的深刻性。自我升级智能体摆脱困境取得发展的可能出路是：在分析传统和现象学传统之间寻求一种动态平衡。这将有助于化解自我升级智能体理论的困局。

我们对上述问题的回答是：第一，自我升级智能体的建立使我们对自我意识的研究有了一个程序化的标准，借助这种形式化的方法有可能弥合学界关于机器意识的分歧，破解机器意识研究面临的困局；第二，生成主义为自我升级智能体的提出奠定了认知基础。自我升级智能体的成功为生成主义提供了一个强有力的例证；第三，尽管自我升级智能体向机器真正具有自我意识前进了一大步，但是我们不能说机器真正具有了自我意识。建构真正具有自我意识的系统，还有很长的路要走。就目前的技术水平看，我们离智能爆炸的实现还有很长的距离，机器还不至于成为人类的"终结者"。造成机器意识困局的症结在于分析哲学传统与现象学传统的分歧和偏颇。解决的出路在于：从对立到相容，从互斥到互补，进而达到融通的新境界。

（本文原载于《中国社会科学》2019 年第 12 期）

虚拟主张的三种类型

阿基·莱蒂宁*

1. 引言

许多经济学家和经济学方法论学家用"虚拟关联词"（as if locution）来限定假设。例如，考虑以下案例。

（a_1）"根据弗里德曼的观点，商业公司如此行动，仿若（as if）完全知情的、理性的计算器，旨在实现利润最大化，尽管这些假设显然不适用于实际的公司。"[1] "个体并非优化器，他们是适应性的，并且只是'仿若'在进行优化一样行动。"[2]

（a_2）人们如此行动，仿若只受自身利益的驱使。[3]

（b）投票者如此行动，仿若已经获得了有关偏好状况的扰动信号并且使用统计推理从这些信号中计算出了概率。[4] "人们可能会在社

---

* 阿克·莱特蒂宁（Aki Lehtinen），南开大学哲学院科技哲学教研室教授，主要研究方向为科学技术哲学。此文由南开大学哲学院博士胡瑞斌译，贾向桐校。

[1] Boylan, T. A., O'Gorman, P. F. *Beyond rhetoric and realism in economics: Towards a reformulation of economic methodology*. Routledge, 1999, pp.108-109.

[2] Kirman, A. P. Demand theory and general equilibrium: From explanation to introspection, a journey down the wrong road. In *History of Political Economy*, 2006, Vol.38, p. 271.

[3] 可以为这种行为主张提供辩护的方法论论证可归功于密尔（Mill J. S.）（参见 Mill. J. S., 2000（1844）.Essays on some unsettled questions of political economy (2nd ed.). Kitchener: Batoche Books, 98.），但他从未使用虚拟关联词对之进行表述。

[4] Lehtinen, A. The Welfare Consequences of Strategic Voting in Two Commonly Used Parliamentary Agendas.In *Theory and Decision*, 2007, Vol.63 (1), pp.1-40. Lehtinen, A. The Welfare Consequences of Strategic Behaviour under Approval and Plurality Voting. In *European Journal of Political Economy*, 2008, Vol.24, pp.688-704.

会行为准则的诱导下如此行动，仿若持有与其实际偏好不同的偏好。"①

（c）伊芙如此做选择，仿若在实现某个效用函数期望值的最大化。②

他们为什么使用此类主张？他们在表达什么？我们如何确定他们这样主张是否合理？

使用虚拟关联词通常意味着，一个人正在作出一个不切实际的假设。这种印象部分源于这样一个事实，即弗里德曼（M. Friedman）的整个方法论③已成为众所周知的"虚拟方法论"（as-if methodology），并且他本人已成为非现实假设的倡导者④。本文的目的在于，为有关非现实和虚构假设的文献作出澄清。出于此目的，让我们对现实的和准确的行为主张或假设作出区分。一个假设若以正确的行为原因为基础，则是现实的，若正确描述了行为，则是准确的。

笔者认为，虚拟主张经常被用于阐述准确的假设。⑤更具体地说，虚拟关联词被用于阐述三种不同的主张，其中只有一种主张的子情形（a_1）可以明确地被视为表达了一个不准确的假设。其他情形最好被理解为以语用或语义正确的方式来表达假设或阐述行为主张。在上述意义上，虚拟主张本身绝不是现实的，因为它们未能解释所关注实体为什么会如此行动。然而，笔者将论证，一些虚拟主张可能有助于阐述完全现实的行为假设。

让我们用"虚拟关联词"（as-if locution）来表示"仿若"（as if）的语言表述。使用虚拟关联词是为了表明，（a）由于某些不准确或不现实的情况可以忽略不计，因而作出一个不准确或不现实的假设。此类主张可以分为两种子情形。（a_1）第一，虚拟关联词被用以表示虚拟主张本身是不准确的，它的不准确性对于研究目的而言并不重要。（a_2）第二，它被用以表示所提出的主张不考虑那些可能存在但被认为不重要的因果因素。在这里，

---

① Sen, A. K. Behaviour and the Concept of Preference. In *Economica*, 1973, Vol.40 (159), p. 258.

② Binmore, K. Game Theory and the Social Contract. In *Just Playing*, (Vol.2). MIT Press, 1998, pp.360-361.

③ Friedman, M. The Methodology of Positive Economics. In *Essays in Positive Economics*. University of Chicago Press, 1953, pp.3-43.

④ 例如，可参见 Røgeberg, O., Nordberg, M. A Defence of Absurd Theories in Economics. In *Journal of Economic Methodology,* 2005, Vol.12 (4), pp.543-562.

⑤ 参见 Lehtinen, A., Kuorikoski, J. Unrealistic Assumptions in Rational Choice Theory. In *Philosophy of the Social Sciences*, 2007, Vol.37 (2), pp.115-138.

虚拟主张本身是用这个关联词来表述的，并且该主张被认为足够真实（true enough）。虚拟关联词也被用以（b）通过以不现实的方式将意图或认知赋予某物，从而阐述一个有关其行为的准确假设，以及（c）表明建模者不致力于任何特定的心理假设。笔者将用短语"表示可忽略性"（negligibility-indicating）、"虚假心理归因"（false mental ascription）和"表示非承诺"（non-committal-indicating）分别表示第一、第二和第三类主张。（a$_1$）子情形将被称为"可忽略不准确"（negligibly inaccurate）或"表示不准确性"（inaccuracy-indicating）的虚拟主张，（a$_2$）子情形则为"表示可忽略性且准确"（negligibility-indicating accurate）的虚拟主张。虚拟关联词的每一种用法都基于不同的虚假相关原因。

大约三十年前，马斯格雷夫（A. Musgrave）曾抱怨说，"虚拟陈述的逻辑（从中可得出什么，不可得出什么）极其含糊不清"[①]。一些经济学方法论学家[②]讨论了这个问题，但他们的关注点仅限于探寻某些类型的虚拟主张是否与特定的哲学学说兼容，或者阐释在有关虚拟的讨论中的两位主角弗里德曼和费英格（H. Vaihinger）的观点。[③]其结果是，经济学实践中虚拟主张的逻辑并未得到全面阐述。致力于此，笔者将提供一种方法来识别不同的虚拟主张，以及这些主张意欲限定或指明的相关真实主张。因

① Musgrave, A. "Unreal Assumptions" in Economic Theory. The F-twist Untwisted. In *Kyklos*, 1981, Vol.34(3), p. 385.

② 如Lagueux, M. Friedman's Instrumentalism and Constructive Empiricism in Economics. In *Theory and Decision*, 1994, Vol.37 (2), pp.147-174. Mäki, U. Friedman and Realism. In *Research in the History of Economic Thought and Methodology*, 1992, Vol.10, pp.171-195. Mäki, U. As If. In J. B. Davis, D. W. Hands, U. Mäki eds.: *The Handbook of Economic Methodology*. Edward Elgar, 1998, pp.25-27. Mäki, U. Kinds of Assumptions and Their Truth. Shaking an Untwisted F-twist. In *Kyklos*, 2000, Vol.53(3), pp.317-335. Mäki, U. "The methodology of positive economics" (1953) does not Give Us the Methodology of Positive Economics. In *Journal of Economic Methodology*, 2003, Vol.10(4), pp.495-505. Mäki, U. Realism and the Nature of Theory: A Lesson from J H von Thünen for Economists and Geographers. In *Environment & Planning A*, 2004, Vol.36 (10), pp.1719-1736. Mäki, U. Unrealistic Assumptions and Unnecessary Confusions. Rereading and Rewriting F53 as a Realist Statement. In U. Mäki ed.: The *Methodology of Positive Economics: Reflections on the Milton Friedman Legacy*. Cambridge University Press, 2009, pp.90-116.

③ 有关弗里德曼的最新讨论，参见麦基（U. Mäki）主编的 *The Methodology of Positive Economicsl: Reflections on the Milton Friedman Legacy*。法因（A. Fine）、麦基和博库利奇（A. Bokulich）讨论了费英格的虚拟解释。参见 Fine: A. Fictionalism. In *Midwest Studies in Philosophy*, XVIII, 1-18. Mäki, U. Realism and the Nature of Theory: A Lesson from J H von Thünen for Economists and Geographers. In *Environment & Planning A*, 1993, Vol.36 (10), pp.1719-1736. 以及Bokulich, A. Explanatory Fictions. In M. Suárez ed.: *Fictions in Science: Philosophical Essays on Modeling and Idealization*. Routledge, 2009, pp.91-109.

此，笔者在本文中的主要目标是梳理所作的不同真实主张，并说明它们将如何得到评估。

对于以数学方式描述一个模型的假设或推导出结果来说，虚拟主张和关联词并不是必要的。当建模者希望明确哪种证据与各种假设的真实性相关，或者明确哪些主张应该或不应该被评估为真时，他们就会采用这种表述。只有在真值状态受到挑战或可能受到挑战的时候，才需要这种精确性。这也是为什么笔者所讨论的是主张而非假设：在数学模型中，假设可以被视作形式化描述所表达的命题。虚拟主张不是假设，而是关于假设的主张。严格说来，即使在这样的方法论讨论中，虚拟关联词也是不必要的，因为使用虚拟主张的理由总是可以用不同的方式来表达。①认识到不同种类的虚拟主张有助于避免在使用关联词时产生误解。笔者将提出一个简单的识别方式：确定相关的归因（见第 2 部分）。

本文的结构如下。第 2 部分阐述基本概念，通过这些概念对不同的虚拟主张进行分析。第 3、4 和 5 部分分别讨论（a）、（b）和（c）。第 3 部分分为两个小节。3.1 讨论表示可忽略不准确的虚拟主张，3.2 讨论表示可忽略且准确的虚拟主张。第 4 部分也分为两个小节。4.1 提供有关（b）的一个案例研究，涉及投票期望效用模型中的信号提取，4.2 将本文的解释与麦基（U. Mäki）对于虚拟主张的区分进行比较。第 5 部分讨论另一个案例：宾莫尔（K. Binmore）对于显示性偏好和表征定理的解释。第 6 部分为本文的结论。

2. 虚拟主张与归因

典型形式的虚拟主张的基本模式如下：

A 如此行动，仿若它是 B。　　　　　　　　　　　（AIC）②

虚拟主张是具有（AIC）形式的断言，它涉及某物的行为方式；它是

---

① 笔者在这里并非为这一主张进行论证。本文鼓励读者找寻这样的案例，在该案例中虚拟关联词对于阐述一个主张是必要的。但笔者并未发现任何这样的案例。

② Mäki, U. As if. In J. B. Davis, D. W. Hands, U. Mäki eds.: *The Handbook of Economic Methodology Edward Elgar*. 1998, pp.25-27.

一个行为主张。[①]在某种意义上，所有不同类型的虚拟主张的含义是相同的[②]：它们指明，A 仿若 B 一样行动。需要注意，（AIC）并没有对 A 是不是 B 提出任何主张。它只是说，如果 A 实际上是 B，那么 A 就会如 B 一样行动。让我们把命题"A 是 B"称为虚拟主张潜在的归因，把命题"A 如此行动，仿若它是 B"称为虚拟主张（AIC）。[③]归因并不是一个主张，因为建模者不会断言它为真。然而，一个数学模型若包含一个用虚拟关联词来辩护的假设，则可以将 A 的行为表征为如 B 一般。使用该关联词的意义在于关注这一事实，即 A 没有被断言为 B，尽管模型将 A 的行为描述得像 B。之所以用虚拟关联词来限定假设，是因为它提供了对模型相关真实主张的理解。模型之中也有一些东西被认为是正确的。在表示不准确性的虚拟主张的情形下，这个东西是模型的结果，而在其他所有情形下，它是行为假设本身（虚拟主张）。

正如辛德里克斯（F. A. Hindriks）所指出的，以一种有意义的方式表述假设，预设了有关模型和世界之间关系的某些东西。[④]在（AIC）中，这个预设是 A 事实上不是 B。如果 A 是 B，就没有任何理由使用虚拟关联词，因为我们可以简单地说"A 的行为像 B，因为它就是 B"。存在某种预设本身便意味着，虚拟关联词的使用必然存在理由。使用它的行动者必须预设相应的归因是虚假的或涉及范畴性错误。或者，如果在归因可能为真的情况下使用该关联词，那么该行动者希望表明他并不致力于其真实性。否则，便没有根据使用这个关联词。因此，所有归因的共同点是，行动者并不致力于其真实性。找到任何给定虚拟主张的归因，就可以确定虚拟关联词的使用是否适当。如果使用适当，我们就可以说使用它的语用约束条件得到了满足。

---

① 在大多数情况下，将 A 解释为对象而将 B 解释为该对象可能具有的属性是合理的。如果只有对象可以以某种方式行动，那么 A 一定是一个对象。然而，正如笔者在表示可忽略性的虚拟主张一节中将要表明的，B 不一定始终为该对象的属性。例如，可以考虑"物体下落，仿若空气阻力不存在"这一主张。空气阻力属性是相关的，因为除了物体本身之外，还需要考虑周围的环境（大气压强）。本文对于 AIC 的阐述在这些术语的解释方面有意地保持沉默，从而将各种不同的情况容纳进来。

② 在有关表示不准确性的（a1）虚拟主张一节中，笔者为这一陈述附加了一点说明。

③ 使用归因这一术语的原因是，属性 B 被归于 A。我们似乎也可以说"B 被断定为与 A 相关"，或者"A 被识别为 B"。但是在这里使用"归因"一词似乎更为自然。

④ Hindriks, F. A. Tractability Assumptions and the Musgrave-Mäki Typology. In *Journal of Economic Methodology*, 2006, Vol.13(4), pp.401-423.

当虚拟主张准确时，通常并非绝对准确，但可能是近似正确的：它可能"足够真实"。这里想要表达的意思是，实际行为尽管并不完全由模型中的行为特征所体现，但与之相差不大。在差异可以忽略不计的情况下，虚拟主张虽然对于它们所表示的现象而言并不严格为真，但也足够真实。[①]此外，鉴于满足约束条件意味着 A 不是 B，A 不可能在所有方面都表现得像 B，而是可能只在某些因语境而显著的方面表现得像 B。因此，虚拟主张总是相对于调查的目的而提出。行为主张（AIC）与真实性相背离，对一个目的来说可能是适当的，但对另一个目的来说则可能是不可接受的。正是虚拟主张的这种语用本质证明了需要一个基于实践的解释，而非纯粹的语义解释。

现在笔者能够更准确地说明本文的观点：在子情形（a_1）下，虚拟主张是不准确或虚假的，而在其他情形下则可能是准确的，甚至是现实的。它是否确实为真，并不取决于 A 是不是 B，而是取决于 A 的行为是否与它像 B 那样表现出来的行为相一致。这为评估虚拟主张的真实性提供了一个标准。在后面几节中，笔者的目的是要证明，在某些情况下，尽管 A 显然不是 B，但是 A 在相关方面的实际行为仿若它就是 B。

确定不同种类的归因，也是根据使用关联词的主要原因来区分不同种类的虚拟主张的一种方式。因此，确定正确的归因有助于理解所提出的是哪种真实主张。这也是对虚拟主张的分类所能带来的主要益处。

对于假设的功能和真值状态的评估可能存在两个维度，它们与不同类型的虚拟主张存在系统性的联系。然而，这种三分的分类法的基础并不在于此。首先，区分归因和虚拟主张的一个主要原因是，后者可以根据对前者的真值评价是否提供有关后者真值的相关信息来进行分类。这并不能提供一个真值标准，而是表明什么样的证据与真值评估相关。其次，在描述行为主张的语句中加入一个虚拟关联词，可能会也可能不会改变归因和虚拟主张含义相同的程度。笔者认为，如果它们的含义不同，引入这个关联词会带来语义上的变化。

---

① Elgin, C. Z. True Enough. In *Philosophical Issues*, 2009, Vol.14(1), pp.113-131. Elgin, C. Z. Exemplification, Idealization, and Scientific Understanding. In M. Suárez ed.: *Fictions in Science: Philosophical Essays on Modeling and Idealization*. Routledge, 2009, pp.77-90.

3. 表示可忽略性的虚拟主张

3.1 可忽略不准确的虚拟主张

虚拟关联词的第一种用法涉及作出不准确的假设。在这里使用它的主要原因是，建模者知道他正在作一个不准确的假设。表达这一点最简单的方法是主张，A 在模型中被描述为像 B 或者行为像 B 一样，尽管它在现实世界中并非如此。然后我们主张，A 在模型中如此行动，仿若它是 B。这一类虚拟主张与费英格的虚构概念密切相关；存在对现实的偏离（最终可能被消除），并且意识到这一虚构只是一个虚构。

现在让我们仔细看看科曼（A. P. Kirman）的这种虚拟主张的例子，这一虚拟主张可以简写如下：

（a_1）人们如此行动，仿若在进行优化。

科曼明确指出，尽管人们并非按照优化的方式行动，但他还是作出了这个假设。[①]之所以使用虚拟关联词，是因为建模者知道该内在假设是虚假的。其归因为"人们实际上进行优化"。在这里优化指的是追求最优结果的努力。这种努力可能不足以实现最优行为，因为个体可能不具备成功所需的信息、知识、远见等。然而，即使他们拥有必要的信息但没有尝试进行优化，我们也不得不使用虚拟关联词，因为无论他们是否拥有必要的信息，这种归因都是错误的。

现在考虑一下，使用虚拟关联词是否会给（a_1）带来语义上的变化。

---

① 根据弗里德曼的说法（参见 Friedman, M. The Methodology of Positive Economics. *In Essays in Positive Economics*. University of Chicago Press, 1953, pp.36-38.），我们可以在某个问题上将一家公司视为仿若完全竞争者，在另一个问题上则将之视为仿若垄断者。我们可以将之视作表示不准确性的主张的一个例子。需要注意的是，科曼并没有努力为优化假设提供辩护，而是指出那些这样做的人所提供的是一种虚拟辩护。事实上，除了弗里德曼之外，笔者尚未在经济学文献中找到这样的例子，其中的作者提出了表示不准确性的主张，并且在模型中使用了相应的假设。相比之下，麦克唐纳（P. K. MacDonald）以及博伊兰（T. A. Boylan）和奥格曼（P. F. O'Gorman）提供了一个例子，其中表示不准确性的虚拟主张被归因于其他主张。（参见 MacDonald, P. K. Useful Fiction or Miracle Maker: The Competing Epistemological Foundations of Rational Choice Theory. In *American Political Science Review*, 2003, Vol.97(4), pp.551-565. 以及 Boylan, T. A., O'Gorman, P. F. Beyond Rhetoric and Realism in Economics: Towards a Reformulation of Economic Methodology. Routledge, 1995）

这需要说明若不使用它，到底会提出什么主张。一个显而易见的回答是，如果不使用该关联词，那么会提出有关归因真实性的主张。（a₁）似乎没有语义上的变化，因为"人们实际上进行优化"作出了与虚拟主张"人们如此行动，仿若在进行优化"相同的有关行为的主张。虽然引入关联词是为了表明归因和行为主张是虚假的，但是归因和虚拟主张的含义是相同的。①

有人可能会反对说，例如，如果我们不相信人们确实是理性的，那么主张他们是理性的便没有任何意义。不过，也有一些学者认为这样没有问题。例如，可以考虑博兰德（L. A. Boland）所说的情况：

> （弗里德曼的）虚拟解释理论……当我们试图解释某些个体的假定行为的影响时（例如，从最大化行为假设推导出的需求曲线），只要事实上观察到了相应的影响，而且该影响正是该个体若实际上按照我们假定的那样行动便会产生的影响，我们就可以使用这个行为假设，即使该假设是虚假的。也就是说，我们可以继续主张，所观察个体（未知但假定的）行为的影响如此，仿若他们按照我们的假定而行动。需要格外注意的是，这里并未主张个体的行为仿若他们是按照我们的假定而行动的，而是主张他们行为的影响仿若他们是按照我们的假定而行动的。②

理解这一点的一种方法是，注意到建模者并不以相同程度致力于所有假设的真实性。特别是，断言（a₁）的建模者并不致力于虚拟主张本身的真实性。如果模型结果在个体行为方面明显是稳健的（robust）③，那么此

---

① 另一种解释（a1）的方式是，主张其含义为"人们不进行优化，但这对模型结果无关紧要"。若如此解释，则必定会导致语义变化。虚拟主张"人们如此行动，仿若在进行优化"将意味着其归因"人们进行优化"是虚假的（但可以忽略不计）。笔者出于直觉略微倾向于本文正文中提供的解释，但也愿意被说服从而改弦更张。采用这种解释将使得对于虚拟主张在语义变化方面的分析更加统一，但在意义方面的分析则不那么统一。我们总是需要寻找语义上的变化，但虚拟主张的含义仅在情况 a2、b 和 c 中是相同的。

② Boland, L. A. A Critique of Friedman's Critics. In *Journal of Economic Literature*, 1979, Vol.17(2), pp.512-513.

③ Kuorikoski, J., Lehtinen, A., Marchionni, C. Economic Modelling as Robustness Analysis. In *British Journal for the Philosophy of Science*, 2010, Vol.61(3), pp.541-567. Lehtinen, A., Kuorikoski, J. Unrealistic Assumptions in Rational Choice Theory. In *Philosophy of the Social Sciences*, 2007, Vol.37(2), 115-138.

类行为便不会在理性选择模型中提供中心因果机制①。因此，一个人断言（a_1），可能只是因为他的模型需要在个体和社会层级的结果之间建立某种联系。断言（a_1）可以重新表述为，"优化模型提供了个体和结果之间的联系，尽管人们实际上与此模型中的个体并不一致，但这并不重要，因为他们的行为细节无论如何都是无关紧要的"。因此，即使知道个体实际上不会进行优化，我们也可以断言（a）。另一种可能性是，尽管个体行为并非与结果无关，但是只要群体中一部人进行优化就足够了。

需要注意的是，如果这些辩护是适当的，那么建模者很可能不会致力于任何特定的行为决定因素，或者对它们及其真实性漠不关心。这可能会导致难以区分表示不准确性的（a_1）和表示非承诺的主张（c）。在这里，建模者认为虚拟主张本身是虚假的，但对于他或她的模型的目的而言，这一点可以忽略不计。主张的真实性对建模者来说并不重要，因为他只是使用所确定的行为来研究其他事物，而虚拟关联词主要用于表明，不应通过检查它所限定的特定假设来评估模型。因此，建模者可能认为优化蕴含着与人们实际行为方式不同的行为，但是他们的行为方式最终与模型的结果无关。相比之下，在情况（c）中，建模者的目的便在于阐述一个准确的行为假设，而非可忽略虚假的行为假设。

3.2 表示可忽略性且准确的虚拟主张

令 A 表示所关注的系统，B 表示一些理想条件。麦基对这种用法的功能提供了以下描述：②

（a_2）现象表现得仿若满足了某些理想条件：在这些理想条件下，

---

① 参见 Satz, D., Ferejohn, J. A. Rational Choice and Social Theory. In *Journal of Philosophy*, 1994, Vol.91 (2), pp.71-87.

② 弗里德曼也为这种虚拟主张提供了一个例子（参见 Friedman, M. The Methodology of Positive Economics. In *Essays in Positive Economics*. University of Chicago Press, 1953, pp.3-43).）。贝克（G. S. Becker）写道："冲动型家庭被假定为如此行动，'仿若'他们只参考了一种概率机制。"（Becker, G. S. Irrational Behavior and Economic Theory. In *Journal of Political Economy*, 1962, Vol.70(1), p. 5.）然而，我们并不清楚他的意思是什么，因为他已经指出"因此可以说，家庭如此行动，不仅'仿若'是理性的，而且'仿若'是非理性的"。（同前，第 4 页）贝克缺乏精确性的主张令笔者怀疑他是否打算为理性选择理论提供论证。（参见 Moscati, I., Tubaro, P. Becker Random Behavior and the as-if Defense of Rational Choice Theory in Demand Analysis. In *Journal of Economic Methodology*, 2011, Vol.18(2), pp.107-128.）

只有那些在理论上孤立的真实因素发挥作用。[①]

在这里，虚拟主张指的是这一观点，假定现实世界中发现的各种干扰因素不存在。模型中所确定的核心因素被如此描述，仿若它们是唯一的因素。其归因是，现实情况满足理想条件，即除了模型中确定的因素之外，不存在其他干扰因素。引入虚拟关联词会引发语义变化，因为该语句现在对某物在实际条件下的行为作出了足够真实的主张，而不是关于现实情况是否具备理想条件的虚假主张。约束条件之所以得到了满足，是因为我们知道理想条件在现实世界中并不成立。此外，虚拟主张将关注点转向在假定没有这些因素的情况下所能得到的结果：我们将能够知道如果核心因素单独发挥作用会产生什么样的行为或结果。"人们如此行动，仿若只受自身利益的驱使"提供了一个经济学中众所周知的例子。在该例子中，可忽略的因果因素是精神状态，但正如我们现在将看到的，可忽略的因素也可以是物理作用力。

（a_2）所表达的虚拟主张可能是准确或足够真实的。例如，考虑经常使用的一个例子——伽利略自由落体定律，该定律规定"在真空中，落体所经过的距离 $s=\frac{1}{2}gt^2$"。然后我们可以像弗里德曼一样主张，可以通过如下假定获得较好的预测。

（a_2'）实际的物体下落，仿若遵循伽利略定律。

如果气压足够接近于零，并且该物体满足某些特征（例如密度足够大），那么这一虚拟主张便是足够真实的。其归因为，气压为零。鉴于它必然是虚假的，如果我们人为地创造了真空环境，并就其中的落体作出陈述，那么我们根本不需要使用虚拟关联词。然而，依然存在一些条件，在这些条件下可以合理地主张"一个物体如此行动，仿若这些条件与真空一致"。

在这里，评估归因的真实性与评估虚拟主张的真实性相关，这是（a_1）

① Mäki, U. Friedman and Realism. In *Research in the History of Economic Thought and Methodology*, 1992, Vol.10, pp.171-195. Mäki, U "The methodology of positive economics" (1953) does not Give us the Methodology of Positive Economics. In *Journal of Economic Methodology*, 2003, Vol.10(4), pp.495-505. Mäki, U. Unrealistic Assumptions and Unnecessary Confusions: Rereading and Rewriting F53 as a Realist Statement. In U. Mäki ed.: *The Methodology of Positive Economics: Reflections on the Milton Friedman Legacy*. Cambridge University Press, 2009, pp.90-116.

和（a_2）共有的特征。这似乎并非这一情况，即人们主张"A 仿若 B 一般行动，即使它显然不是 B"，因为 A（实际大气条件下的物体）是否以这种方式行动取决于 A 成为 B（一个完美真空中的物体）的接近程度。然而，正如笔者将在后文中将要论证的，其他类型的虚拟主张在这方面是不同的。

弗里德曼强调，我们并不假定我们生活在真空中。[①]我们只是假定（或主张）物体仿若在真空之中一样下落。引入虚拟关联词带来了语义变化，将关于真空存在的虚假主张转变为关于行为的足够真实的主张。马斯格雷夫指出，虚拟关联词可以用来表达一个可忽略的假设：主张"空气阻力可以忽略不计"可以用"物体仿若在真空之中一样下落"来表达。[②]然而，这两个主张并不相同，因为前者表达了行为主张可能准确的原因所在，而后者提供了关于某事物行为的描述性主张。

现在考虑另一个著名的例子——波义耳的理想气体定律，该定律（大致）规定，在恒定温度下，定量气体的压强与其体积成反比。根据史查芬斯（M. Strevens）的观点，我们可能主张：

（a_2''）气体表现得仿若不存在分子碰撞。[③]

这一断言的根据在于，无论是否存在这样的碰撞，波义耳定律都成立。很明显，只有出于解释波义耳定律的目的，碰撞才是可忽略的。对于其他目的而言（例如，对扩散过程进行建模），它们是不可忽略的。其归因是，不存在碰撞。需要注意，此主张的虚假性与评估虚拟主张的真实性无关。我们知道这一归因是错误的，但真正重要的是为可忽略性主张提供的论证。史查芬斯援引了迈考里（D. A. McQuarrie）和西蒙（J. D. Simon）的观点，他们认为，"任何使分子路径偏离[推导中所假定路径]的碰撞，都会被使该

① Friedman, M. The Methodology of Positive Economics. In *Essays in Positive Economics*. University of Chicago Press, 1953, pp.3-43. 需要注意，弗里德曼使用术语"假设"来表示本文中所称的"主张"。如果假设在模型中表达了命题，我们会说"模型假定了一个真空环境，但是建模者并不主张我们生活在真空之中"。

② Musgrave, A. "Unreal Assumptions" in Economic Theory. The F-twist Untwisted. In *Kyklos*, 1981, Vol.34(3), pp.377-387. 另可参见 Mäki, U. Kinds of Assumptions and Their Truth. Shaking an Untwisted F-twist. In *Kyklos*, 2000, Vol.53(3), pp.317-335.

③ Strevens, M. Depth. An Account of Scientific Explanation. Harvard University Press, 2008.

分子复位的碰撞所平衡"[1]。

因此，存在三种可忽略性主张。首先，已知会影响所关注行为的因果力量足够弱，其强度可以忽略不计（例如气压）。其次，被认为在强度上不可忽略并且可能与所讨论的行为相关的作用力具有可忽略不计的净效应（由于某些作用力的平衡，如分子碰撞）。最后，任何模型都忽略了无数的因果因素，因为这些因素被认为是不相关的。在最后一种情况下，我们不使用虚拟关联词。例如，我们不会说"石块坠落下来，仿若燕子不会在秋天迁徙到温暖地区"，因为我们预先假定这些鸟类的迁徙行为不会以任何方式影响石块。

（a_1）和（a_2）之间也存在差异。一根羽毛不满足相关特征，因而我们不应该主张"羽毛仿若遵循伽利略定律一样落下"，因为这一虚拟主张是错误的。可以将之与（a_1）进行对比。如果使用虚拟关联词的原因确实只是为了表明（a_1）的真实性无关紧要，那么这一主张的虚假性便不会阻止建模者使用该关联词。即使知道人们不进行优化，建模者也会使用这个关联词。（a_1）和（a_2）之间的区别在于，前者不表达被认为对模型具有因果重要性的主张，而后者却有此表达。在情况 a_2 中，需要使用虚拟关联词来确定行为虚拟主张的确切内容，而在情况 a_1 中，它仅仅表明不对行为主张进行真实性评估。

麦基认为（AIC）也可以用来表达关于 A 是否为 B 的认知不确定性。[2]如果这一点完全适用，那么它似乎最适合于不准确的虚拟主张（a_1）。我们会说"人们表现得仿若他们是理性的"，因为我们不确定他们是不是理性的。但是需要注意，这种用法违反了使用虚拟关联词的语用约束条件。如果一个人不确定其真实性，那么他就不能同时假定该归因是错误的。[3]有人可能会争辩说，暂时地表达关于归因的认知不确定性可以算作不致力于其真实性，因而最终可以满足约束条件。但这样不会奏效，因为无论谁为了表达认知不确定性而断言上述虚拟主张，最终都会致力于归因的真实性：

① McQuarrie, D. A., Simon, J. D. Physical Chemistry. A Molecular Approach. University Science Books, 1997, p.1015.

② Mäki, U. As If. In J. B. Davis, D. W. Hands, U. Mäki eds.: *The Handbook of Economic Methodology*, Edward Elgar, 1998, pp.25-27. Mäki, U. "The Methodology of Positive Economics" (1953) does not Give us the Methodology of Positive Economics. In *Journal of Economic Methodology*, 2003, Vol.10(4), pp.495-505.

③ 需要注意，费英格区分虚构和假设的依据是，前者已知为假，而后者尚待调查。

如果随后的调查表明该归因是虚假的，那么他将不再愿意断言该行为主张。这正是致力于归因之真实性的含义所在。

根据虚拟主张的真实性是否依赖于归因的真实性来区分不同种类的虚拟主张，对于确定认知不确定性的对象很重要。它可能涉及归因、虚拟主张以及对于主张是否为真的解释，以及如果为真，原因何在。在情况（a_1）和（a_2）中，关于归因的认知不确定性意味着虚拟主张的不确定性。麦基由于未能对虚拟主张和归因进行区分，因而也未能区分不确定性的不同对象。因此，他混淆了关于"为什么 A 表现出如此的行为方式"的认知不确定性与关于"A 是否为 B"的不确定性[①]。笔者主张，虚拟关联词并不用于表达认知不确定性，正是因为在最真实的情况（b 和 c）下，关于归因的认知不确定性并不意味着关于虚拟主张的认知不确定性。将其用于此类目的会造成一种错误印象，即归因的真实性始终与虚拟主张的真实性相关。[②]

虚拟主张本身未能解释过"为什么 A 表现出如此的行为方式"。这个特征很难与实在论相协调，即使情况（a_2）亦是如此。确实，虚拟关联词的使用是合理的，因为它们表明主张本身并没有提供解释。

4. 虚假归因的虚拟主张

虚拟关联词的第二种用法涉及将虚假的意图或认知赋予某物，从而对其行为进行描述。因此，这种主张的基本形式如下：

（b）A 如此行动，仿若对 B 有意图或认知。

在无需关心意图或认知归因是否正确的情况下，重点是要准确地描述行为。需要注意的是，与情况（a_1）相比，这里的目的是断言通过虚拟主张阐述的行为是准确的。

弗里德曼的许多例子都说明了这种非现实归因：我们可以准确地描述

---

① Mäki, U. As If. In J. B. Davis, D. W. Hands, U. Mäki eds.: *The Handbook of Economic Methodology*. Edward Elgar, 1998, pp.25-27.

② 当然，笔者同意麦基的观点，即认知不确定性与实在论是相容的。笔者只是想表明，通过虚拟关联词表达这种不确定性并不能满足笔者所言的语用约束条件。从这个意义上说，麦基未能提供任何此类用法的具体示例也就不足为奇了。

台球的轨迹，前提假设是专家级运动员表现得仿若知晓从物理理论中推导出的复杂数学公式。[1]这一理论赋予了运动员进行如此复杂的计算的能力。这种归因是虚假的，因为运动员并没有根据物理理论来概念化这个问题。然而，我们可以通过使用该物理理论推导出台球的轨迹。类似地，弗里德曼认为，我们可以准确地描述树叶在树上的位置，前提假设是每片树叶都表现得仿若在试图最大程度地吸收阳光。[2]笔者和库里科斯基（J. Kuoriko-ski）指出，在这些情况下，假设在行为方面是现实的，但在意图方面则是不现实的，因为它真实地描述了行为，但错误地将之归因于意图。[3]将意图赋予树并不能准确确定树叶分布模式的成因。[4]

在弗里德曼有关台球运动员和树叶的例子中，归因显然都是虚假的，并且虚拟主张的真实性并不依赖于归因的真实性。检查归因的真实性并不能提供关于虚拟主张真实性的相关信息。弗里德曼还使用这种虚拟主张来论证公司的行为仿若在实现利润最大化。[5]他完全清楚管理者不会有意地试图平衡边际成本和收益，而且他们通常甚至连成本函数都不知道。然而，使用虚拟主张的意义在于，证明即使他们并未有意地试图实现利润最大化，他们的行为也非常接近于利润最大化的假设，以至于我们可以在此基础上作出良好预测。当然，这些预测并不关注利润最大化本身，而是关注其他事情，例如价格变化或税收对供给的影响。弗里德曼主张，对于标准价格理论的目的而言，利润最大化假设实际上是准确的。笔者认为这种解释不再被视为激进的，胡佛（K. D. Hoover）也认为弗里德曼所关心的是假

---

① Friedman, M. The Methodology of Positive Economics. In *Essays in positive economics*. University of Chicago Press, 1953, p.21.

② Friedman, M. The Methodology of Positive Economics. In *Essays in positive economics*. University of Chicago Press, 1953, p.19.

③ Lehtinen, A., Kuorikoski, J. Unrealistic Assumptions in Rational Choice Theory. In *Philosophy of the Social Sciences*, 2007, Vol.37(2), pp.115-138.

④ 一位匿名审稿人建议用错误原因来描述这个例子。可以将情况（b）概括为涉及所有对原因的虚假归因的情况："A 如此行动，仿若受到因果作用力 B 的支配。"这显然是可能的，至少在原则上是如此，然而鉴于笔者只观察到了（b）的示例，其中的虚假归因与心理状态有关，因而笔者不愿为这种更一般的表述提供论证。类似的考虑同样适用于情况（c）。

⑤ Friedman, M. The Methodology of Positive Economics. In *Essays in positive economics*. University of Chicago Press, 1953, p.21.

设的准确性[①]。

如果归因没有提供相关信息来评估此类虚拟主张的真实性，那么是什么提供了这些信息？众所周知，弗里德曼将他的案例建立在进化选择论证之上：只有那些模仿利润最大化而行动的公司才能长期存活。选择论证通常被用于帮助解释为什么 A 的行为可以模仿 B 的行为，即使在各种不同的情况下 A 都不是 B。然而，拉格克斯（M. Lagueux）认为，虚拟主张总是能够得到一些更一般理论的辩护，但他并不要求这个理论是进化选择理论。[②]这似乎是正确的，因为在伽利略落体定律的案例中似乎不需要这种选择论证。这一案例中确实存在一个一般理论，但与弗里德曼的其他例子（公司、树上的树叶、台球运动员）不同，它与虚拟主张并没有分离，因为正是引力理论解释了为什么我们可以将物体描述为仿若遵循伽利略的公式

$$s=\frac{1}{2}\,gt^2 \text{。}$$

选择论证往往被认为没有充分的说服力[③]，因此利润最大化假设通常被认为是不准确的。甚至贝克（G. S. Becker）也认为这个假设是不准确的：

> 在我看来，阿尔奇安及其他学者提出的"存活"论证的伟大成就并不是证明了存活的公司必须仿若试图实现利润最大化一样行动（因为很容易提出反例），而是证明了非理性公司的决策受到预算约束的限制。[④]

弗里德曼使用了存活论证这一事实支持了这种解释，即弗里德曼试图论证利润最大化假设的准确性，因此他关于公司的虚拟主张将根据（b）而不是（a₁）来解释。然而，如果认为博兰德根据（a₁）对弗里德曼所进行

① Hoover, K. D. Milton Friedman's stance. The Methodology of Causal Realism. In U. Mäki ed.: *The Methodology of Positive Economics: Reflections on the Milton Friedman Legacy*. Cambridge University Press, 2009, pp.303-320.

② Lagueux, M. Friedman's Instrumentalism and Constructive Empiricism in Economics. In *Theory and Decision*, 1994, Vol.37(2), pp.147-174.

③ 参见弗罗门（J. J. Vromen）的解释及参考文献。Vromen, J. J. Friedman's Selection Argument Revisited. In U. Mäki ed.: *The Methodology of Economics: Reflections on the Milton Friedman Legacy*. Cambridge University Press, 2009, pp.257-284.

④ Becker, G. S. Irrational Behavior and Economic Theory. In *Journal of Political Economy*, 1962, Vol.70 (1), p. 10.

的解释是错误的，那么笔者会有所迟疑，因为弗里德曼认为对于假设之"实在论"的讨论只有在相对于理论化目的的情况下才是有意义的。因此，尽管他似乎认为利润最大化对于这种公司理论（19 世纪 50 年代曾付诸实践）而言足够准确[①]，但他可能认为讨论该假设在绝对意义上是否准确是没有意义的。

笔者不想依赖于对弗里德曼的正确解释。相反，笔者将研究该主张在另一个经济模型中的使用，以表明它可以用来对行为进行准确甚至现实的描述。因此，弗里德曼的经济学例子的失败不应使我们相信这种虚拟主张总是不准确的。鉴于在这一案例中不需要提供任何类型的选择论证或一般理论，因而它还将证明这些论证和理论对于通过虚拟主张对行为进行现实描述来说是不必要的。

4.1 案例研究：策略性投票期望效用模型中的信号提取

可以考虑笔者曾使用的信号提取模型，该模型是策略性投票期望效用模型的一部分。[②]策略性投票通常被定义为，投票给被认为并非最佳的候选者或候选方案。为了简化论述，本文只分析成对比较的情况。笔者假定投票者之间不知道彼此的偏好，但他们如此行动，仿若已经获得了关于他人的信息信号。令 N 表示投票者总数，n_{jk} 表示更喜欢候选者 j 而非 k 的投票者人数。在每个人都诚实投票的情况下，若 $n_{jk} > N/2$，则 j 将在成对比较中的多数规则下击败 k。该模型被设定于一个计算机模拟框架中，其中投票者的偏好是随机生成的。假定投票者如此行动，仿若已经获得了关于 n_{jk} 真实值的扰动信息，如下所示，单个投票者的信号 $s_t(jk)$ 由标准化的 n_{jk} 与一个随机项之和给出：

$$s_i(jk) = \frac{2n_{jk} - N}{\sqrt{N}} + \varepsilon R_i \tag{1}$$

其中 R_i 表示标准正态随机变量，ε 表示反映信息质量的参数。笔者表

① 在马赫卢普（F. Machlup)的文章中，这一点尤为明显。参见 Machlup, F. Marginal Analysis and Empirical Research. In *The American Economic Review*, 1946, Vol.36(4), pp.519-554.

② Lehtinen, A. Signal Extraction for Simulated Games with a Large Number of Players. In *Computational Statistics and Data Analysis*, 2006, Vol.50, pp.2495-2507. Lehtinen, A. The Welfare Consequences of Strategic Voting in Two Commonly Used Parliamentary Agendas. In *Theory and Decision*, 2007, Vol.63(1), pp.1-40. Lehtinen, A. The Welfare Consequences of Strategic Behaviour under Approval and Plurality Voting. In *European Journal of Political Economy*, 2008, Vol.24, pp.688-704.

明，某个体对于命题"候选者 j 击败 k"所持概率 $p_i(jk)$ 由以下公式给出[①]

$$p_i(jk) = 1 - \Phi\left(-\frac{s_i(jk)}{\varepsilon\sqrt{1+\varepsilon^2}}\right) + \varepsilon R_i \qquad (2)$$

其中 Φ 表示标准正态分布函数。这种信号的存在并不是虚构，因为在大规模选举中，选举前的民意调查可能被解释为某种关于各种候选人获胜概率的信号，即使在议会投票中，各代表也拥有关于其他投票人偏好的各种信息来源，例如党派和不同代表所提出论点的内容。然而，信号的各种特征都是虚构的：附录中的推导包括四页的对于随机变量及其密度的运算。主张投票者能够作出这样的计算是愚蠢的，更不必说主张他们会实际进行这些计算。真正的投票者根本不会进行这些表达式的计算。类似地，他们也不会通过将概率乘以效用来计算期望效用。此外，在现实世界中，他们不会以模型所表征的那种形式获得扰动信号，其中的信号由精确的数字给出。例如，$s_i(jk) = -0.298234$ 及概率 $p_i(jk) = 0.267543$ 可以给出一个信号。

因此，这些策略性投票模型将投票者描述为仿若已经以精确的数字形式获得了扰动信号，仿若他们能够进行复杂的计算，仿若他们实际进行了计算并将之用于期望效用计算以确定他们的决策。现在比较以下两个陈述：

（b′）投票者如此行动，仿若已经获得了有关偏好状况的扰动信号并且使用统计推理从这些信号中计算出了概率。

（b*）投票者获得了有关偏好状况的扰动信号，并且使用统计推理从这些信号中计算出了概率。

（b*）显然是错误的，但（b′）是足够真实的，因为实际投票者的行为确实符合他们若真的获得信号以及计算概率等则会做出的行为。引入虚拟关联词将虚假陈述转换为真实陈述，并且语义变化是显而易见的。

这些策略性投票模型在意图及认知方面是不现实的，因为在模型中投票者具备在现实中所不具备的认知和意图（信号和计算）。然而，该模型在

---

① Lehtinen, A. Signal Extraction for Simulated Games with a Large Number of Players. In *Computational Statistics and Data Analysis*, 2006, Vol.50, pp.2495-2507.

解释他们的行为方面可能是完全准确的，在正确识别行为的影响因素及其影响方式的意义上甚至是现实的。笔者现在将尝试证明这一点。

对策略性投票行为的现实描述会是什么样的？我们应当正确理解行为的决定因素。考虑唐斯（A. Downs）对策略性投票动因的语言描述：

> 假定有三方势力：右翼、中间派和左翼。投票者 X 比起中间派更偏向右翼，比起左翼更偏向中间派，但他认为右翼获胜的概率最小。如果他比起中间派极度偏向右翼，并且在中间派和左翼之间持近乎中立的态度，那么相比于他比起中间派稍微偏向右翼但厌恶左翼的情形，他从右翼转投中间派的可能性更低。①

这意味着策略性投票取决于各个候选者的获胜概率和偏好强度。如果投票者以这种（定性的）术语对投票进行概念化理解，那么我们可以称他们参与的是唐斯式审议（Downsian deliberation）。它涉及用概率权衡各选项可取性的心理操作。这种操作可以更一般地称为期望效用审议。笔者的模型以埃内罗（J. M. Enelow）以及麦凯尔维（R. D. McKelvey）和奥德舒克（P. C. Ordeshook）的期望效用模型为基础，这些模型被用于解释各种投票规则下投票者的行为。②这些模型显示了应该如何将信念和获胜概率结合在一起，从而以正确的方式考虑强度和概率。

如果我们只想对人们的策略性投票行为提供一个抽象的解释，那么这样的模型就足够了。然而，为了研究这种行为在总体层面的结果，有必要为个人效用函数和信念赋予特定的值，随之出现的问题是如何确定这些值。笔者随后继续随机生成效用并使用信号提取模型来推导信念。鉴于行为取决于投票者的信念，因而此模型应该以现实的方式产生信念。

在这里，似乎可以这样说，关于不同候选者获胜概率的知识的准确性以及不同投票者对其知识的信心存在人际差异。如果一个人认为右翼没有获胜的机会并进行了策略性投票，但这一判断是错误的，并且如果由于该策略性投票，结果获胜的是这个人的次优选择而不是最佳选择，那么这个

---

① Downs, A. *An Economic Theory of Democracy*. Harper, 1957, p.49.

② 参见 Enelow, J. M. Saving Amendments, Killer Amendments, and an Expected Utility Theory of Sophisticated Voting. In *Journal of Politics*, 1981, Vol.43(4), pp.1062-1089. 以及 McKelvey, R. D., Ordeshook, P. C. A General Theory of the Calculus of Voting. In J. F. Herndon, J. L. Bernd eds.: *Mathematical Applications in Political Science*. The University Press of Virginia, 1972, pp.32-78.

人的策略性投票便会伤及自身。[①]因此，只有当人们能够合理地确信他们的信息正确时，要求他们进行策略性投票似乎才是合理的。此外，更为明显的是，从信号提取模型中得出的信念应该对真实的偏好状况的变化作出响应。这正是信号提取模型所显示的。[②]

尽管必须主张投票者的行为只是仿若收到了信号，仿若已经根据这些信号计算了信念，但是信号提取模型为他们的审议和策略性投票的决定因素提供了一种完全现实的解释。对信息的确信程度及其真实质量是他们在进行策略性投票时所持信念的实际决定因素，模型以现实的方式捕捉到了这些因素。[③]因此，就某些意图而言它是现实的，但对于其他意图而言则是不现实的（而且是虚构的）。

需要注意的是，虽然其归因主张投票者有意地计算了这些概率，但是虚拟主张仅仅主张从模型中得出的行动（或信念）可用于描述实际投票者的行动（或信念）。此外，其中绝对没有假定投票者具有特别好的认知能力。如果 ε 很大，那么一些投票者可能持有非常不准确的信念。鉴于模型将投票者的行为描述为仿若进行了复杂的计算，基于这一理由而批评这个模型将不切实际的复杂行为归于投票者是愚蠢的。虚拟关联词的使用突出了这一事实。

以此类陈述阐述行为假设——诸如，投票者如此行动仿若根据扰动信号计算了概率——并不表明是否会以现实的方式对该行为进行建模。虚拟主张本身并不能为这种想法提供辩护，它只是提出了行为主张。然而，归因（b*）是不现实的这一事实与评估虚拟主张的现实性完全无关：众所周

---

① 参见笔者的例子。Lehtinen, A. The Welfare Consequences of Strategic Voting in Two Commonly Used Parliamentary Agendas. In *Theory and Decision*, 2007, Vol.63(1), pp.1-40.

② 详见笔者的讨论。Lehtinen, A. Signal Extraction for Simulated Games with a Large Number of Players. In *Computational Statistics and Data Analysis*, 2006, Vol.50, pp.2495-2507.

③ 笔者并不意图使该模型在行为的所有方面都具有现实性。一个主要特点是，笔者在对策略性行为的分析中，将每个投票者均如此行动的情况与无人如此行动的情况作了比较。本文所述适用于进行策略性投票的投票者。在现实生活中，一些投票者进行了策略性行动，而另一些则没有。然而，笔者在另一篇文章中（Lehtinen, A. Behavioural Heterogeneity under Approval and Plurality Voting. In J. Laslier, M. R. Sanver eds.: *Handbook on Approval Voting*. Springer, 2010, pp.285-310.）放宽了这一假设，但在另一种意义上，信号提取模型并非完全现实的。有学者已经指出，投票者系统性地高估了他们所支持的候选者的获胜机会，但这一模型却隐含地假定了无偏估计。然而需要注意的是，我们可以将这些偏差纳入考量，若要做到这一点，则通过将一些参数或函数纳入该形式化模型来实现，而且我们将仍然不得不使用虚拟关联词来表述其计算部分的内容。

知，投票者在投票时不会进行复杂的计算，但这一点无关紧要。然而，仅仅主张（b′）足够真实是不充分的，因为它没有提供任何解释以说明为什么我们应该认为它是足够真实的。它的真实性仍有待证明。因此，虚拟主张通常是不完整的，因为始终需要该主张之外的东西来表明模型是现实的。这一点上，其他类型的虚拟主张似乎也不完整。

如上所论，表示可忽略性的（a_2）虚拟主张是否涉及作出准确假设取决于归因的真实程度。在情况（b）下，从完全准确到完全不准确，不存在类似连续系列的主张。认为投票者获得了以七位数表示的信号，在此基础上计算概率并在考虑各种选项的期望效用后选择某一行动，这种主张是虚构的，换句话说，显然是虚假的。然而，笔者认为信号提取模型确实准确捕捉到了行为的决定因素。

不存在一般的理论（例如进化选择）可以解释为什么个人信念应该与模型中产生的信念相一致。笔者已经指出，计算行为及其信号的虚构使得对于投票行为的现实表征得以实现。笔者最终断言，这一虚拟主张是现实的，因为它正确描述了唐斯式的审议，笔者还断言，这种审议为策略性投票的原因提供了真实解释。

莫里森（M. Morrison）主张，虚构表征提供可靠信息的方式因情况而异。[①]然而，我们似乎无法概括它们为什么、是否以及何时有助于实现对行为的现实描述，这可能归因于这一事实，即虚构在对世界的表征方面发挥着至关重要的作用。[②]在这种情况下，有必要用精确的数字来表征信号、效用和概率，从而在计算机模型中表征唐斯式审议，而虚拟关联词的功能是表明这种表征的目的并不在于提供对该审议所有细节的完全真实描述。[③]

① Morrison, M. Fictions, Representations, and Reality. In M. Suárez ed.: *Fictions in Science. Philosophical Essays on Modeling and Idealization*. Routledge, 2009, pp.110-135.

② 另见 Teller, P. Fictions, Fictionalization, and Truth in Science. In M. Suárez ed.: *Fictions in Science: Philosophical Essays on Modeling and Idealization*. Routledge, 2009, pp.235-247.

③ 参见 Coddington, A. Friedman's Contribution to Methodological Controversy.*In British Review of Economic Issues*, 1979, Vol.2(4), p.1-13.

4.2 题外话：麦基的区分

麦基对（a₂）和（b~）进行了区分。[①]

（a₂）现象表现得仿若满足了某些理想条件：在这些理想条件下，只有那些在理论上孤立的真实因素发挥作用。

（b~）现象表现得仿若这些作用力是真实的。

笔者现在将试图澄清本文提出的分类与麦基的区分有何不同。麦基的区分与"虚拟关联词"的指称对象相关：他区分了某事物被建模为仿若某些次要作用力不存在的情况，以及模型中的核心作用力以虚构为基础的情况。在前一种情况下，作用力的孤立是虚假的（即，在现实中它们不是唯一起作用的力），而在后一种情况下，挑选出来的核心作用力是虚构的（即，它们存在于表征之中，但不存在于现实世界）。[②]这种区分不能被纳入本文提出的分类方案，因为它所依据的基础不同。麦基的区分基础是虚拟关联词所表达的虚构是关于什么的，而本文的分类基础在于使用这一关联词的语用原因。麦基没有给出任何理由说明为什么要用虚构来为核心因果作用力建模。[③]

[①] Mäki, U. Friedman and Realism. In *Research in the History of Economic Thought and Methodology*, 1992, Vol.10, 171-195. Mäki, U. As If. In J. B. Davis, D. W. Hands, U. Mäki eds.: The Handbook of Economic Methodology. Edward Elgar, 1998, pp.25-27. Mäki, U. Kinds of Assumptions and Their Truth: Shaking an Untwisted F-twist. In *Kyklos*, 2000, Vol.53(3), pp.317-335. Mäki, U. "The Methodology of Positive Economics" (1953) does not Give us the Methodology of Positive Economics. In *Journal of Economic Methodology*, 2003, Vol.10(4), pp.495-505. Mäki, U. Realism and the Nature of Theory: A Lesson from J H von Thünen for Economists and Geographers. In *Environment & Planning A*, 2004, Vol.36 (10), pp.1719-1736. Mäki, U. Unrealistic Assumptions and Unnecessary Confusions: Rereading and Rewriting F53 as a Realist Statement. In U. Mäki ed.: *The Methodology of Positive economics*: *Reflections on the Milton Friedman Legacy*. Cambridge University Press, 2009, pp.90-116.

[②] Mäki, U. Unrealistic Assumptions and Unnecessary Confusions: Rereading and Rewriting F53 as a Realist Statement. In U. Mäki ed.: *The Methodology of Positive Economics: Reflections on the Milton Friedman Legacy*. Cambridge University Press, 2009, pp.90-116.

[③] 虚构的工具有用性可以被视为在情况（b*）之下使用虚拟关联词的一个原因。然而，鉴于主张虚构在工具意义上是有用的并不能真正解释为何如此，反倒构成了乞题，因而更为恰当的说法是，麦基没有为此情况下使用虚拟关联词提供任何理由。正是因为工具有用性构成了乞题，所以本文没有将之视为虚拟主张的一个单独类型而涵括于内，尽管弗里德曼有时使用虚拟关联词以表明一个假设若能产生正确的预测便是有用的（参见 Friedman, M., Savage, L. J. The Utility Analysis of Choices Involving Risk. In *Journal of Political Economy*, 1948, Vol.56 (4), p.298. 以及 Friedman, M., Savage, L. J. The Expected-utility Hypothesis and the Measurability of Utility. In *Journal of Political Economy*, 1952, Vol.60(6), p.473.）。

根据麦基的观点，(b˜)引入了一种工具主义解读，因为它假设了虚构的作用力。[1]在笔者提供的信号提取例子中，个人行为是以虚构来描述的，即使它是模型中的核心因果因素。因此，麦基的区分要求必须根据（b˜）来理解（b'），而（b˜）应该以工具主义的方式来理解。笔者认为应当拒斥这个结论。

笔者在本节中已经论及，即使在以虚构表征核心作用力的情况下，一个虚拟主张也很可能是现实的。如果笔者已经成功地表明投票者的行为确实仿若受到模型所确定的一些虚构作用力（计算概率和期望效用）的支配，那么实在论者似乎没有什么可担心的。鉴于虚拟主张本身没有提供解释，因而相关的问题是该主张以现实方式描述的行为是如何获得辩护或解释的。显然，必须在其他地方寻找这样的解释，而本节所述提供了一种解释。实在论者和工具主义者之间的区别大概在于，前者要求在某处提供解释或辩护，而后者则不会在意这一点，只要理论提供的预测是正确的。只有愚蠢的实在论才会要求每一个假设都必须以这样一种方式来表述，即表述自身也提供了解释。如上所论，其归因显然是虚假的，为了实现能够正确理解行为假设的语义变化，我们需要使用虚拟关联词。如果实在论者可以接受非现实假设（如果它们得到了适当辩护），那么他们就不应该仅仅因为现实的假设是通过虚构进行表征的就摒弃它们。

麦基或许可以采取不同的策略，争辩说笔者的例子不能算作情况(b˜)，因为尽管获取信号和乘以效用是这一模型中的核心作用力，但它们是真实的。确实，虚拟主张并未限定这些作用力的存在。然而，它也不表示孤立或可忽略性。这并不意味着，出于研究的目的其他相关作用力可能会被忽略。恰恰需要使用虚拟关联词来表明，建模者并未主张投票者计算概率或将之乘以效用，尽管在提出行为假设时确实需要虚构——密度函数运算以及将效用乘以信念。断言投票者计算概率或将之乘以效用是误导性的。最好将这些虚构与弗里德曼的例子（使用物理理论来确定台球的轨迹）进行比较：众所周知，这些虚构并非所关注现象背后的原因。如果麦基采用第二种推理，那么他最终会陷入一种两难境地：他要么必须解释为什么使用物理理论不能为台球运动员的意图提供虚构式的解释，要么必须说明弗里

---

① Mäki, U. As If. In J. B. Davis, D. W. Hands, U. Mäki eds.: *The Handbook of Economic Methodology.* Edward Elgar, 1998, pp.25-27.

德曼的例子与笔者的信号提取例子在相关方面有何不同。

5. 表示非承诺的虚拟主张

丹尼特（D. C. Dennett）认为，意向性立场将实体（人、动物、人造物）视为仿若通过"考虑"其"信念"和"欲求"控制自身"行动选择"的理性行动者，这是解释实体行为的一种策略。[①]在这里，虚拟主张表达了对所讨论实体是否具有信念和欲求的非承诺态度。需要注意的是，尽管使用了虚拟关联词来限定信念和欲求的存在，但是关于行为的断言旨在提供准确的主张。这就是丹尼特对于虚拟关联词的用法与不准确虚拟主张（a_1）的用法之间的不同之处。鉴于恒温器确实表现为仿若想要保持温度不变，因而即使其归因（恒温器具有欲求）显然是虚假的，我们也可以使用虚拟主张来准确描述行为。有关恒温器的行为主张之所以为真，是因为它们的设计目的就是做到这一点：保持温度恒定。

当我们将意向性立场应用于真实的人时，相关的归因是"人们具有欲求和信念"。对于相信人们具有欲求和信念的人来说，这似乎为论点"归因始终为假"提供了一个反例。然而，即使读者认为人们具有信念和欲求，丹尼特也会使用虚拟关联词。他会说，这种归因无法被证明为真，而"虚拟关联词"正是被用以表明需求和信念的存在是有所限定的。因此，最终在语用层面为虚拟关联词的使用提供辩护的不是归因的虚假性，而是该关联词的言说者是否致力于其真实性。

现在让我们考虑一个更加难以解释的经济学例子。

（c）正统的显示性偏好理论主张，伊芙的选择仿若在实现由 C 定义的效用函数期望值的最大化（相对于由 B 定义的主观概率分布），从而为描述伊芙在 A 中的行为提供了一致性条件。[②]

为了确定这一主张的相关归因，有必要更仔细地考察一下效用概念。

---

① Dennett, D. C. *Kinds of Minds: Towards an Understanding of Consciousness*. Weidenfeld & Nicolson, 1996, p. 27.

② Binmore, K. Game Theory and the Social Contract: Just Playing, (Vol.2). MIT Press, 1998, pp.360-361.

古典功利主义者使用"效用"一词来表示一种精神状态（满足程度）或一种感觉（例如快乐）。"效用最大化"可以被理解为一种意向性活动，行动者通过这种活动努力使他的欲求满足程度最大化。如果以这种方式解释"效用"，我们会说相关的归因是"伊芙使其欲求满足最大化"，如果她实际上实现了自身欲求满足的最大化，那么这一归因为真。需要注意的是，如果伊芙在这个意义上确实实现了效用最大化，那么这种解释将构成对于主张"归因始终为假"的反例。

然而在这里，宾莫尔会使用虚拟关联词来描述伊芙的行动，即使伊芙有意地努力实现满足程度的最大化。举例来说，考虑现代效用理论对于"效用"和"最大化"的解释方式，它主要由表征定理构成。[①]这些定理规定，如果偏好满足一组一致性条件，那么可以用效用函数对之进行表征。令 P_i 表示个体 i 的严格偏好序列。标准解释是，对于某些备选方案 x 和 y, xP_iy 意味着 i 认为 x 比 y 更好。表征定理规定，$U_i(x)>U_i(y)$，当且仅当 xP_iy。换言之，若该个体严格偏好 x 而非 y，则函数 U 赋予 x 相比于 y 更大的数值。然后可以主张，个体的行为被描述为其仿若正在实现效用函数的最大化。

该理论以效用函数为特征，可用于描述那些偏好满足特定条件的个体的行为。有时术语"效用"（或"util"）被用于表示这些函数的值。鉴于"效用"在这里指的是一个数值，因而它既不包括物质福利，也不包括任何一种精神状态，如快乐。如果宾莫尔放弃使用虚拟关联词，他将做出一个涉及范畴性错误的荒谬陈述。当效用在现代意义上被解释为对个人偏好或选择的描述时，主张"一个人试图实现效用最大化"是荒谬的。最大化不是由被描述行为的人进行的心理操作，而是以最大化表征该人行为的数学模型的一个属性。因此，这种范畴性错误在于主张"一个人旨在（有目的地）实现他的效用函数的最大化"。然而，这个人的行为可以被描述为他仿若正在实现效用函数最大化，因为更偏好（或选择）的结果相比不太偏好的结

---

① 本节的原创性贡献仅限于对虚拟关联词在期望效用理论中的作用的讨论。本文的观点最先由卢斯（D. R. Luce）和雷法（H. Raiffa）明确提出（参见 Luce, D. R., Raiffa, H. *Games and Decisions: Introduction and Critical Survey*. Wiley, 1957.），卡夫卡（G. Kavka）以及笔者和库里科斯基也提出了类似的论点（参见 Kavka, G. Rational Maximizing in Economic Theories of Politics. In K. R. Monroe ed.: *The Economic Approach to Politics: A Critical Reassessment of the Theory of Rational Action*. HarperCollins, 1991, pp.371-385. 以及 Lehtinen, A., Kuorikoski, J. Unrealistic Assumptions in Rational Choice Theory. In *Philosophy of the Social Sciences*, 2007, Vol.37(2), pp.115-138.）。

果被赋予了更高的效用。正如宾莫尔所言，"我们的理论使得这一主张成为无稽之谈，即主张亚当之所以选择前者是因为其效用更大"①。这样主张就等同于犯了"因果效用谬误"。换言之，效用并不提供以一种或另一种方式进行选择的理由，而仅仅表征个体的偏好。

宾莫尔不能使用这个关联词来主张伊芙的实际行为与她实现了欲求满足程度最大化时会产生的行为相一致，因为他主张现代决策理论"使得我们对选择行为的心理原因不做任何假设"②。表征定理并未说明为什么人们应当实现效用最大化。与情况（b）不同，宾莫尔为了准确描述伊芙的行为，并未将虚假意图归于伊芙。

宾莫尔也没有用虚拟关联词来限定行为主张，因为他否认伊芙实现了效用（在现代意义上）最大化。他已然假定伊芙是理性的：

> 尽管本书将保留对效用的显示性偏好解释，但将跳过根据行动者的选择行为构建效用函数的一半工作。我们将假定已经构建了偏好关系，现在只需表明可以使用适当的效用函数对之进行表征。③

尽管他在其他著作中欣然接受了"人类行为通常是完全非理性的"④，但在这里他无法怀疑伊芙的理性，因为除非个体是理性的，否则根本无法构建偏好关系。因此，使用虚拟关联词的目的是阐述准确的行为假设。

有人可能会提出，期望效用最大化应当被解释为期望效用审议。"伊芙实现期望效用最大化"将是相关的归因，并且可以根据这种心理操作对最大化进行解释。然而，这也是不正确的，因为虚拟主张"伊芙的行为可以描述为仿若在实现某个效用函数期望值的最大化"的真值标准并不在于她的行为是否与她进行了期望效用审议时的行为相一致，而是在于她的偏好是否满足对效用进行表征的条件。一个人的行为是否可以被描述为他仿若在实现期望效用最大化，并不取决于他是否进行了某种心理操作。类似地，包含期望效用假设的模型是否准确并不取决于这个人是否试图实现某物的最大化或者他是否正在进行期望效用审议，而仅取决于他的偏好是否满足这些条件。笔者将之视作决策理论学家的标准立场，但本文将提供一个简

---

① Binmore, K. *Rational Decisions*. Princeton University Press, 2009, pp.19-21.

② Binmore, K. *Rational Decisions*. Princeton University Press, 2009, pp.8-9.

③ Binmore, K. *Game Theory and the Social Contract: Playing Fair*, (Vol.1). MIT Press, 1994, p.268.

④ Binmore, K. *Natural Justice*. Oxford University Press, 2005, p.75.

单的论证为之提供支持：例如，如果伊芙在计算预期效用时出错，那么即使她进行了期望效用审议，她也可能违反这些条件。

在上一节中，相关的归因是：

（b*）投票者获得了有关偏好状况的扰动信号，并且使用统计推理从这些信号中计算出了概率。

更完整的归因应当为：

（b**）投票者获得了扰动信号、进行概率计算，并且通过基于概率权衡效用值直接计算得出了期望效用。

因此，通过将概率和以七位数表示的效用相乘来直接计算期望效用是一种心理操作，这一操作也被虚假地归于投票者。鉴于（b）和（c）都涉及期望效用最大化的情况，可能会有人争辩说，它们之间差异很小，不足以证明将它们归为单独的类别是合理的。然而，笔者曾指出，笔者的模型的可信度关键取决于投票者真正进行了唐斯氏审议这一假设的合理性，而且他们的偏好是否满足一致性条件并不重要，因为模型结果不依赖于这一点。①事实上，满足一致性条件似乎并不足以保证投票者进行了唐斯氏审议。如果我们接受宾莫尔的论点，即现代效用理论不做心理假设，那么这至少是我们不得不思考的问题。

在这两种情况下，为了使有关期望效用最大化的虚拟主张为真，所需的是完全不同的东西。在情况（c）中，若个体满足一致性条件，则该主张为真。然而在情况（b）中，该主张是否足够真实取决于投票者是否进行了唐斯式审议。（b）和（c）之间的相似之处在于，在这两种情况下，建模者都使用了虚拟关联词来阐明关于行为和心理状态的主张类型。宾莫尔使用虚拟关联词来提醒读者注意，"最大化"所指的并非任何类型的心理操作。通过使用这一关联词，他避免了作出虚假主张，即最大化就是这样的操作。

现在让我们回到（c）。一旦确定了正确的归因，就可以很明显地看到，它确实总是要么是虚假的，要么涉及范畴性错误。笔者认为存在两种可能性。第一种可能性是，它涉及伊芙的意图："伊芙努力实现期望效用最大化"，

---

① Lehtinen, A. A Welfarist Critique of Social Choice Theory. In *Journal of Theoretical Politics*, 2001, Vol.23(3), pp.359-381.

其中效用在现代意义上被理解为描述偏好的数值。此归因包含范畴性错误。它不是经验层面未能以某种方式行动的结果，而是源于这样一个事实，即效用不是伊芙可以根据"效用"一词的逻辑形式试图实现最大化的东西。第二种可能性是，它涉及宾莫尔对于其读者的信念。他可能假定并非每个读者都知道他将在现代意义上使用"效用"这一术语。因此，他会使用虚拟关联词，因为他相信读者中的一些人可能会认为"在宾莫尔提出的理论中，效用意味着快乐"。这也是虚假的。同样显而易见的是，对于这些归因的真实性评估与虚拟主张是否准确完全无关，因为两者都没有对一致性条件提供任何说明。

有人可能会争辩说，如果第一种归因是适当的，那么与（c）类似的主张应该被视为单独的第四种虚拟主张，因为避免范畴性错误与表达对于任何特定行为决定因素的非承诺之间不存在内在联系。为了进一步支持这一论点，有人可能指出，从前文所引 1994 年的文本可见宾莫尔相信伊芙的理性，而这种理性正是行为的决定因素。笔者反对这种解释，主要原因在于，理性不是正确的决定因素。就"偏好关系已经构建"而言，行为也已经发生，如果它是用效用函数来描述的，那么它的决定因素是什么并不重要。此外，一旦理解了宾莫尔为何使用虚拟关联词，我们也就理解了避免范畴性错误如何等同于对行为决定因素不作承诺。

期望效用理论中使用的虚拟主张很可能能够提供对行为的准确描述。然而，虚拟关联词的使用绝对不会告诉我们情况是否如此。这与将人们的实际行为描述为实现效用最大化是否准确的问题无关。这个问题可以用多种不同的方式来评估，其中一种方式是评估人们在某些实际情况下是否试图实现快乐最大化。之所以如此，是因为一致性条件的合理性取决于人们的真实行为方式，而评估他们的行为是否满足这些条件的相关考虑因素之一是他们是否试图实现快乐最大化。在某些情况下，他们的行为确实满足这些条件，在其他情况下则不满足，但在任何情况下，即使期望效用最大化是一个准确的假设，我们也需要使用虚拟关联词。这就是（c）与（a₁）的不同之处。如果我们想主张实际行为与期望效用理论所确定的行为之间的差异可以忽略不计，那么我们将不得不主张"人们如此行动，仿若他们仿若实现了期望效用最大化一样行动"。自然地，我们永远不会提出这种主张，因为可以用更优雅的方式来表达这一观点。例如，我们可以主张"伊芙如此行动，仿若她是效用最大化者"①。这是因为，如果伊芙不按照这些条件行动，那么相关的归因"伊芙是效用最大化者"便是虚假的。

包括宾莫尔在内的一些决策理论学家显然认为，为了使期望效用理论能够适用，只有选择（而非偏好）才需要保持一致。然后可以主张，"行动者如此行动，仿若他具有一致性的偏好"，而且他的选择可以用效用函数来描述。在这里，偏好的存在是被限定的。需要注意的是，如果用这种显示性偏好术语来解释期望效用理论，那么主张"行动者如此行动，仿若他具有一致性的选择"将意味着这一虚拟主张将被解释为表示不准确性（a_1）。

在情况（b）和（c）中，使用虚拟关联词的原因是，它允许我们准确地确定关于行为假设我们想要说些什么。丹尼特和宾莫尔用它来强调不需要进行意向性归因，而笔者用它来阐述现实的行为假设，并表明模型的可信度不取决于这一假设，即投票者实际进行了期望效用计算或者收到了数值精确的信号。这些情况的相似之处在于，使用虚拟关联词可以让建模者避免作出某些特定的心理归因。

6. 结　论

虚拟关联词可以以多种方式使用。笔者认为它们可以用（a_1）表明其所限定的行为主张是不准确的，但可以忽略不计，以及（a_2）表明建模者承认存在一些在模型中没有明确考虑的因果因素，因为它们被认为可以忽略不计。在最真实的情况下，它们被用于（b）通过以不现实的方式将意图归于实体来表达准确的行为主张的内容，以及（c）表明我们对行为的描述性主张不致力于任何特定的心理假设。因此，可以将这些主张简述如下。

（a_1）表示不准确性的主张。AIC——或者说，A 实际上并不像 B 一样行动，但这一点在模型中并不重要。

（a_2）表示可忽略性且准确的主张。AIC，因为 A 在某些方面（但并非全部方面）与 B 相似。被忽略的方面在此模型中并不重要。

（b）表示虚假心理归因的主张。AIC，因为 A 不具有（心理）属性 B，但确实具有属性 C。然而，可以假设它具有属性 B 以对之行为进行描述。

---

① 这里所预设的前提为，"伊芙为最大化者"意味着她满足 VNM 条件。

（c）表示非承诺的主张。AIC，因为尽管 A 与 B 无关，但无论 A 的行为的实际决定因素是什么，A 的行为都与 B 相像。

然而，虚拟主张也有一些共性。首先，它们最重要的功能是帮助确定模型的哪些部分应当为真，哪些部分可以为假。其次，它们似乎总是与提出有关行为的主张或对之进行描述有关。再次，它们都表明，对于潜在归因的真实性不作承诺。最后，它们自身在方法论层面总是不完整的，因为对于为什么现实中的行为应该与模型所确定的行为相一致，它们没有提供任何解释。

虚拟主张可能会造成很大的混淆。鉴于它们的不完整性，我们总是有必要确定一个特定的虚拟主张是不是现实的。此外，我们可能很难看出不同类型的主张之间的差异。我们很容易被误导，以至于相信即使没有对行为进行真实的建模，虚拟主张也是现实的，或者相信所有虚拟主张都是虚假的，因为它们的归因总是虚假的。弗里德曼出于本文所描述的所有原因使用了这一关联词。鉴于不同的用法以不同的方法论承诺为基础，并且导致对于主张真实性的评估需要采取不同方式，因而尚不清楚谈论"弗里德曼的虚拟方法论"是否有意义。①

有些人可能更倾向于尽量减少使用虚拟主张，因为它们非常令人困惑并且不完整。在涉及语义变化的所有情况下，它们显然具备有用的功能。通常，这种变化涉及将虚假的归因转变为足够真实的虚拟假设。然而，这些从来都不是必需的。如果我们只是想表达某个假设的现实性无关紧要，或者想表达我们意识到自己作出了一个非现实假设，那么笔者建议最好避免使用虚拟关联词，因为我们可以通过一些更自然、更不容易产生混淆的方式来阐述此类主张。于是，是否蕴含了语义变化便可以用于帮助识别虚拟主张是否被合理使用。

本文可能会被认为有些怪异，因为笔者在哲学案例研究中使用了自己的经济学研究成果。然而，本文的写作动机来自有关投票和信号提取的论文写作的经历。经济学期刊不允许作者详细解释他们对于假设所作的虚拟形式的辩护。在笔者有关投票和信号提取的文章中，虚拟关联词实际上从未出现过。它之所以没有出现，是因为笔者唯恐被解释为借由表示不准确

---

① 笔者也曾因使用这种表达方式而感到内疚。参见 Lehtinen, A., Kuorikoski, J. Unrealistic Assumptions in Rational Choice Theory. In *Philosophy of the Social Sciences*, 2007, Vol.37(2), p. 123.

性的虚拟主张来推广自己的模型。这种解释在经济学家中似乎很普遍，笔者由于非常担心被误解，因而决定不使用这种关联词。这些经历也解释了为什么笔者不满足于仅仅描述虚拟关联词在经济学中是如何被使用的，而且试图通过语用约束条件来界定它们的用法；笔者相信更严格地使用这一关联词将有助于避免混淆。

鉴于（a_2）、（b）和（c）代表了虚拟主张可能具有准确性乃至现实性的情况，将其用法限定为此三种类型也促进了对其真值标准的评估。这里最重要的考虑是，归因的真实性是否与虚拟主张的真实性相关。信号提取的示例旨在表明，在它们不相关的情况下，即当它涉及虚假意图归因的虚构时，尽管其基础在于虚构，但虚拟主张很可能是现实的，并且评估其真实性的根据不必来自更一般的理论。

致　谢

本文曾展示于墨西哥哈拉帕的 INEM 会议以及芬兰赫尔辛基的 TINT 研讨会。Till Grüne-Yanoff、Jaakko Kuorikoski、Uskali Mäki、Luis Mireles-Flores、Samuli Pöyhönen 以及匿名审稿人均为本文的早期版本提供了有益评论。本文适用于常规免责条款。

参考文献：

[1] Becker, G. S. (1962). Irrational behavior and economic theory. Journal of Political Economy, 70(1), 1-13.

[2] Binmore, K. (1994). Game theory and the social contract: Playing fair, (Vol.1). Cambridge, MA: MIT Press.

[3] Binmore, K. (1998). Game theory and the social contract: Just playing, (Vol.2). London: The MIT Press.

[4] Binmore, K. (2005). Natural justice. Oxford: Oxford University Press.

[5] Binmore, K. (2009). Rational decisions. Princeton: Princeton University Press.

［6］Bokulich, A. (2009). Explanatory fictions. In M. Suárez (Ed.), Fictions in science: Philosophical essays on modeling and idealization (pp.91-109). London: Routledge.

［7］Boland, L. A. (1979). A critique of Friedman's critics. Journal of Economic Literature, 17 (2), 503-522.

［8］Boylan, T. A., & O'Gorman, P. F. (1995). Beyond rhetoric and realism in economics: Towards a reformulation of economic methodology. London: Routledge.

［9］Coddington, A. (1979). Friedman's contribution to methodological controversy. British Review of Economic Issues, 2 (4), 1-13.

［10］Dennett, D. C. (1996). Kinds of minds: Towards an understanding of consciousness. London: Weidenfeld & Nicolson.

［11］Downs, A. (1957). An economic theory of democracy. New York: Harper. Elgin, C. Z. (2004). True enough. Philosophical Issues, 14(1), 113-131.

［12］Elgin, C. Z. (2009). Exemplification, idealization, and scientific understanding. In M. Suárez (Ed.), Fictions in science: Philosophical essays on modeling and idealization (pp.77-90). London: Routledge.

［13］Enelow, J. M. (1981). Saving amendments, killer amendments, and an expected utility theory of sophisticated voting. Journal of Politics, 43(4), 1062-1089.

［14］Fine, A. (1993). Fictionalism. Midwest Studies in Philosophy, XVIII, 1-18.

［15］Friedman, M. (1953). The methodology of positive economics. Essays in positive economics (pp.3-43). Chicago: University of Chicago Press.

［16］Friedman, M., & Savage, L. J. (1952). The expected-utility hypothesis and the measurability of utility. Journal of Political Economy, 60 (6), 463-474.

［17］Friedman, M., & Savage, L. J. (1948). The utility analysis of choices involving risk. Journal of Political Economy, 56(4), 279-304.

［18］Hindriks, F. A. (2006). Tractability assumptions and the

Musgrave-Mäki typology. Journal of Economic Methodology, 13(4), 401-423.

[19] Hoover, K. D. (2009). Milton Friedman's stance: The methodology of causal realism. In U. Mäki (Ed.), The methodology of positive economics: Reflections on the Milton Friedman legacy (pp.303-320). Cambridge: Cambridge University Press.

[20] Kavka, G. (1991). Rational maximizing in economic theories of politics. In K. R. Monroe (Ed.), The economic approach to politics: A critical reassessment of the theory of rational action (pp.371-385). New York: Harper Collins.

[21] Kirman, A. P. (2006). Demand theory and general equilibrium: From explanation to introspection, a journey down the wrong road. History of Political Economy, 38, 246-280.

[22] Kuorikoski, J., Lehtinen, A., & Marchionni, C. (2010). Economic modelling as robustness analysis. British Journal for the Philosophy of Science, 61 (3), 541-567.

[23] Lagueux, M. (1994). Friedman's instrumentalism and constructive empiricism in economics. Theory and Decision, 37(2), 147-174.

[24] Lehtinen, A. (2006). Signal extraction for simulated games with a large number of players. Computational Statistics and Data Analysis, 50, 2495-2507.

[25] Lehtinen, A. (2007). The welfare consequences of strategic voting in two commonly used parliamentary agendas. Theory and Decision, 63(1), 1-40.

[26] Lehtinen, A. (2008). The welfare consequences of strategic behaviour under approval and plurality voting. European Journal of Political Economy, 24, 688-704.

[27] Lehtinen, A. (2010). Behavioural heterogeneity under approval and plurality voting. In J. Laslier & M. R. Sanver (Eds.), Handbook on approval voting (pp.285-310). Heidelberg: Springer.

[28] Lehtinen, A. (2011). A welfarist critique of social choice theory.

Journal of Theoretical Politics, 23(3), 359-381.

[29] Lehtinen, A., & Kuorikoski, J. (2007). Unrealistic assumptions in rational choice theory. Philosophy of the Social Sciences, 37(2), 115-138.

[30] Luce, D. R., & Raiffa, H. (1957). Games and decisions: Introduction and critical survey. New York: Wiley.

[31] MacDonald, P. K. (2003). Useful fiction or miracle maker: The competing epistemological foundations of rational choice theory. American Political Science Review, 97(4), 551-565.

[32] Machlup, F. (1946). Marginal analysis and empirical research. The American Economic Review, 36(4), 519-554.

[33] Mäki, U. (1992). Friedman and realism. Research in the History of Economic Thought and Methodology, 10, 171-195.

[34] Mäki, U. (1998). As if. In J. B. Davis, D. W. Hands & U. Mäki (Eds.), The handbook of economic methodology (pp.25-27). Cheltenham: Edward Elgar.

[35] Mäki, U. (2000). Kinds of assumptions and their truth: Shaking an untwisted F-twist. Kyklos, 53(3), 317-335.

[36] Mäki, U. (2003). 'The methodology of positive economics' (1953) does not give us the methodology of positive economics. Journal of Economic Methodology, 10(4), 495-505.

[37] Mäki, U. (2004). Realism and the nature of theory: A lesson from J H von Thünen for economists and geographers. Environment & Planning A, 36(10), 1719-1736.

[38] Mäki, U. (2009). Unrealistic assumptions and unnecessary confusions: Rereading and rewriting F53 as a realist statement. In U. Mäki (Ed.), The methodology of positive economics. Reflections on the Milton Friedman legacy (pp.90-116). Cambridge: Cambridge University Press.

[39] McKelvey, R. D., & Ordeshook, P. C. (1972). A general theory of the calculus of voting. In J. F. Herndon & J. L. Bernd (Eds.), Mathematical applications in political science, (Vol.IV), (pp.32-78). Charlottesville: The University Press of Virginia.

[40] McQuarrie, D. A., & Simon, J. D. (1997). Physical chemistry: A

molecular approach. Sausalito: University Science Books.

［41］Mill, J. S. (2000［1844］). Essays on some unsettled questions of political economy (2nd ed.). Kitchener: Batoche Books.

［42］Morrison, M. (2009). Fictions, representations, and reality. In M. Suárez (Ed.), Fictions in science: Philosophical essays on modeling and idealization (pp.110-135). London: Routledge.

［43］Moscati, I., & Tubaro, P. (2011). Becker random behavior and the as-if defense of rational choice theory in demand analysis. Journal of Economic Methodology, 18(2), 107-128.

［44］Musgrave, A. (1981). 'Unreal assumptions' in economic theory: The F-twist untwisted. Kyklos, 34(3), 377-387.

［45］Røgeberg, O., & Nordberg, M. (2005). A defence of absurd theories in economics. Journal of Economic Methodology, 12(4), 543-562.

［46］Satz, D., & Ferejohn, J. A. (1994). Rational choice and social theory. Journal of Philosophy, 91(2), 71-87.

［47］Sen, A. K. (1973). Behaviour and the concept of preference. Economica, 40(159), 241-259.

［48］Strevens, M. (2008). Depth: An account of scientific explanation. Cambridge, MA: Harvard University Press.

［49］Teller, P. (2009). Fictions, fictionalization, and truth in science. In M. Suárez (Ed.), Fictions in science: Philosophical essays on modeling and idealization (pp.235-247). London: Routledge.

［50］Vromen, J. J. (2009). Friedman's selection argument revisited. In U. Mäki (Ed.), The methodology of economics. Reflections on the Milton Friedman legacy (pp.257-284). Cambridge: Cambridge University Press.

（本文原载于《经济学方法论》2013 年第 2 期）

附:

Three kinds of 'as-if' claims

Aki Lehtinen*

Department of Political and Economic Studies/Philosophy, University of Helsinki, Finland

As-if locutions are used (a) in order to indicate that an inaccurate or unrealistic assumption is being made because some inaccuracy or unrealisticness is negligible. This kind of claim has two sub-cases. (a₁) The as-if locution is used to indicate that the as-if claim in itself is inaccurate and that its inaccuracy does not matter for the purposes of the investigation. (a₂) It is used to indicate that claims are made without regard to the causal factors that are assumed to exist but are deemed to be unimportant. As-if locutions may also (b) formulate an accurate behavioural assumption by ascribing intentions or cognitions to an entity in an unrealistic manner or (c) indicate that the modeller is not committed to any particular mental assumptions. The various kinds of claims may be recognised by identifying their underlying 'attributions'. (a₂), (b) and (c) may be used in formulating an accurate claim.

Keywords: as-if; unrealistic assumptions; attributions; fictions

1. Introduction

Many economists and economic methodologists qualify assumptions with an 'as-if' locution. Consider, for example, the following cases.

(a₁) 'According to Friedman, business firms behave as if they were fully informed, rational calculators aiming at the achievement of profit maximisation, even though clearly these assumptions do not apply to actual firms' (Boylan & O'Gorman, 1995, pp.108-109). 'Individuals are not optimizers, they are adaptive and only behave "as if" they optimize' (Kirman, 2006, p.271).

(a₂) People behave as if they were only motivated by self-interest.[1]

(b) Voters act as if they have obtained perturbed signals concerning the preference profile and as if they have computed probabilities from these signals using statistical reasoning (Lehtinen, 2007, 2008). 'People may be induced by social codes of behaviour to act *as if* they have different preferences from what they really have' (Sen, 1973, p.258).

Eve chooses *as though* she were maximising the expected value of a utility function (Binmore, 1998, pp.360-361).

Why do they use such claims, what do they mean and how do we know whether they are justified?

Using an as-if locution tends to imply that one is making an unrealistic assumption. Such an impression stems in part from the fact that Friedman's (1953) methodology as a whole has become known as his 'as-if methodology', and he has become known as a champion of unrealistic assumptions (see e.g., Røgeberg & Nordberg, 2005). The aim in the paper is to clarify the literature on unrealistic and fictional assumptions. For such a purpose, let us distinguish between *realistic* and *accurate* behavioural claims or assumptions. An assumption is realistic if it is based on the correct causes of the behaviour, and it is accurate if it correctly describes the behaviour.

I argue that as-if claims are frequently made in order to formulate an accurate assumption (cf. Lehtinen & Kuorikoski, 2007). More specifically, the as-if locution is used in making three different kinds of claim, and only one sub-case of a claim (a_1) may unequivocally be taken to express the idea that an inaccurate assumption is being made. The other cases are better understood as ways of expressing assumptions or making behavioural claims in a pragmatically or semantically correct way. As-if claims in themselves are never realistic in the aforementioned sense because they never *explain* why the entity of interest behaves in the way it does. Nevertheless, I will argue that some as-if claims may help in formulating a perfectly realistic behavioural assumption.

Let us use the term 'as-if locution' to denote the linguistic expression 'as if'. As-if locutions are used in order to (a) indicate that an inaccurate or unrealistic assumption is being made because some inaccuracy or unrealisticness is negligible. This kind of claim has two sub-cases. (a_1) First, the as-if locution is used to indicate that the as-if claim in itself is inaccurate and that its inaccuracy does not matter for the purposes of the investigation. (a_2) Second, it is used to indicate that claims are made without regard to the causal factors that are assumed to exist but are deemed to be unimportant. Here the as-if claim itself is formulated with the locution, and it is claimed to be true enough. As-if locutions also are used (b) to formulate an accurate or a realistic claim concerning the behaviour of something by ascribing intentions or cognitions to it in an unrealistic manner, and (c) to indicate that the modeller is not committed to any particular mental assumptions. I will use the shorthand 'negligibility-indicating', 'false mental ascription' and 'non- committal-indicating' for the first, second and third kind of as-if claims, respectively. Sub-cases under a_1 will be called 'negligibly inaccurate' or 'inaccuracy-indicating' as-if claims, and sub-cases under a_2 'negligibility-indicating accurate' as-if claims. Each of these uses of the as-if locution is based on different falsity related *reason* why it is used. Musgrave (1981, p.385) complained some thirty years ago that the 'logic of as if statements (what follows from them and what does not follow from them) is terribly unclear'. Some economic methodologists (Lagueux, 1994; Ma¨ki 1992, 1998, 2000, 2003, 2004, 2009) discuss the issue, but their focus is limited either to finding out whether certain kinds of as-if claims are compatible with particular philosophical doctrines, or to interpreting the two protagonists in the as-if discussion, Milton Friedman and Hans Vaihinger.[2] As a result, the logic of as-if claims in economic practice has not been set out in a comprehensive manner. I endeavour to do that here by providing a way of identifying the different as-if claims and the associated truth claims that they are meant to qualify or specify. My main goal in the present account is thus to sort out the different truth claims that are being made, and to show how they are to be evaluated.

As-if claims and locutions are *never necessary* for describing the assumptions of a model mathematically or for deriving the results. Modellers employ them when they wish to specify what kind of evidence is relevant to the truth status of various assumptions or to specify which claims ought or ought not to be evaluated for truth. Such precision is only called for when the truth status is challenged, or is likely to be challenged. This is also why I discuss claims rather than assumptions: in mathematical models, assumptions can be taken to be propositions expressed in the formal descriptions. As-if claims are not assumptions, they are rather claims *about* assumptions. Strictly speaking, as-if locutions are not necessary even in such methodological discussions because the reasons for using an as-if claim can always be expressed differently.[3] Recognising the different kinds of as-if claims helps to avoid misunderstandings when the locution is used. I propose a simple recognition formula: identify the relevant *attribution* (see Section 2).

The structure of the paper is the following. Section 2 lays out the basic concepts through which the different as-if claims are analysed. Sections 3,4 and 5 are devoted to cases (a),(b) and (c), respectively. Section 3 has two subsections: Section 3.1 discusses negligibly inaccurate as-if claims, and Section 3.2 negligibility-indicating accurate as-if claims. Section 4 is also divided in two subsections: Section 4.1 presents a case study of (b) concerning signal extraction in an expected utility model of voting and Section 4.2 compares the present account to Uskali Ma¨ki's distinction concerning as-if claims. Section 5 discusses another case: Ken Binmore's account of revealed preferences and representation theorems. Section 6 concludes the paper.

2. As-if claims and attributions

The canonical form of as-if claims is given by the following basic schema (Ma¨ki, 1998): A behaves as if it were B. (AIC)

An as-if claim is an assertion that has the form (AIC), and which concerns how something behaves; it is a *behavioural claim*.[4] There is a sense in which the *meaning* of all the different kinds of as-if claim is the same[5]: they specify that A behaves as if it were B. Note that (AIC) does not make any claims about whether A is B. It merely states that A behaves as B would behave were A, in fact, B. Let us call the proposition that 'A is B' the underlying *attribution* of an as-if claim, and the proposition that 'A behaves as if it were B' the *as-if claim* (AIC).[6] The attribution is not a claim at all because the modeller never intends to assert that it is true. Yet, a mathematical model including an assumption that is justified with an as-if locution represents A as behaving like B. The point of using the locution is to focus attention on the fact that A is not asserted to be B, even though the model describes A as behaving like B. The reason why an assumption is qualified with an as-if locution is that it provides understanding about the relevant truth claims of the model. Something is also claimed to be correct in the model. In the case of inaccuracy-indicating as-if claims, that something is the model result, and in all other cases it is the behavioural assumption itself (i.e. the as-if claim).

As Hindriks (2006) notes, presenting assumptions in a meaningful way *presupposes* certain things about the relationship between the model and the world. In (AIC) the presumption is that A is not in fact B. If A were B, there would not be any reason to use the as-if locution because one would simply be able to say 'A behaves like B because it is B'. The idea of a presupposition requires that there must be a *reason* for using the as-if locution. *An agent who uses it must presuppose that the corresponding attribution is false or involves a category mistake. Alternatively, if the locution is used when the attribution could be true, the agent wishes to indicate that he or she is not committed to its truth. Otherwise its use is not warranted.* What is common to all attributions is thus that the agent is not committed to their truth. Finding the attribution for any given as-if claim allows one to determine whether using the as-if locution is appropriate. If it is, one could say that the pragmatic *constraints* for using it are satisfied.

When the as-if claim is accurate it is not usually so in absolute terms, but may be approximately correct: it may be 'true enough'. The intended meaning is that although actual behaviour is not quite instantiated by the features of behaviour in the model, it is not very far from it. Where the divergence is negligible the as-if claims, although not strictly true of the phenomena they denote, are true enough (Elgin, 2004, 2009). Furthermore, given that satisfying the constraints implies that A is not B, A cannot behave as B in all respects, and may only do so in some contextually salient respect. As-if claims are thus always made relative to the purpose of the investigation. The divergence from the truth of a behavioural claim (AIC) may be appropriate for one purpose but unacceptable for another. It is this pragmatic nature of as-if claims that justifies the need for a practice-based rather than a purely semantic account.

I am now able to state my point more precisely: the as-if claim is inaccurate or false under sub-case (a_1), and may be accurate or even realistic under the other cases. Whether it is indeed true depends not on whether A is B but on whether A's behaviour corresponds to that which it would exhibit if it behaved like B. This provides a *criterion* for evaluating the truth of as-if claims. My aim in the later sections is to demonstrate that there are cases in which A *in fact behaves* as if it were B in the relevant respects even though it clearly is not B.

Identifying different kinds of attributions is also a way of distinguishing between the different kinds of as-if claims on the basis of the primary reason for using the locution. Identifying the right kind of attribution thus facilitates understanding of what kind of truth claim is being made. This is the main benefit to be derived from a classification of as-if claims.

There are two dimensions along which the function and truth status of assumptions may be evaluated that are systematically related to the different kinds of as-if claims. However, the three-part classification is not based on them. First, a major reason for distinguishing between attributions and as-if claims is that the latter can be classified on the basis of whether evaluating the truth of the former provides relevant information concerning their truth. This does not provide a truth criterion, but rather indicates what *kind of evidence* is relevant for evaluating the truth. Secondly, adding an as-if locution to a sentence describing a behavioural claim may or may not change the extent to which the meaning of the attribution and the as-if claim is the same. If they do not have the same meaning, I would say that introducing the locution *brings about a semantic change*.

3. Negligibility-indicating as-if claims

3.1 Negligibly inaccurate as-if claims

The first use of the as-if locution involves making inaccurate assumptions. The primary reason for using it here is that the modeller knows that he or she is making an inaccurate assumption. The simplest way of conveying the idea is to say that A is described as being or behaving like B in the model even though it is not so in the real world. One then says that A behaves as if it were B in the model. This category of as-if claims is closely related to Vaihinger's notion of a fiction; there is a deviation from reality (which may ultimately be eliminated) and an awareness that the fiction is just a fiction.

Let us now have a closer look at Kirman's example of such as-if claims: the as-if claim can be written briefly as follows.

(a_1) People behave as if they optimize.

Kirman makes it clear that although people do not behave optimally, the assumption is made anyway.[7] The reason why the as-if locution is used is that the modeller knows that the inherent assumption is false. The attribution is 'actual people optimize'. Optimising refers to the endeavour of pursuing optimal results here. The endeavour may not be sufficient for optimal behaviour because the individuals may not have the requisite information, knowledge, foresight etc. in order to succeed. Yet, even if they had the requisite information but did not try to optimize, one would have to use the as-if locution because the attribution is false irrespective of whether they have the requisite information.

Consider now whether the use of the as-if locution brings about a semantic change in (a_1). This requires specification of what exactly would be claimed if it were not used. An obvious response is that without the locution the claim is about the truth of the attribution. There does not seem to be a semantic change under (a_1) because 'actual people optimize' makes the same claim *about behaviour* as the as-if claim 'people behave as if they optimize'. Although the locution is introduced in order to indicate that the attribution and the behavioural claims are false, the meaning of the attribution and the as-if claim is the same.[8]

One might object that it does not make any sense to claim, for example, that real people are rational if one does not believe that they are. Nevertheless, certain scholars think that there is no problem. Consider, for example, Boland (1979, pp.512-513):

[Friedman's,] as if theory of explanation... [I]f we are trying to explain the *effect* of the assumed behavior of some individuals (e.g., the demand curve derived with the assumption of maximizing behavior), *so long as the effect is in fact observed and it would be the effect if they were in fact to behave as we assume,* we can use our behavioral assumption even when the assumption is false. That is, we can continue to claim the observed effect of the individuals' (unknown but assumed) behavior is *as if* they behaved as we assume. Note carefully, the individuals' *behavior* is not claimed to be *as if* they behaved as we assume, but rather it is the *effect* of their behavior that is claimed to be *as if* they behaved according to our assumption. (all emphases in the original)

One way of making sense of this is by noting that modellers are not committed to the truth of all assumptions to the same degree. In particular, a modeller who asserts (a_1) is not committed to the truth of the as-if claim itself. If the model result is demonstrably robust with respect to individual behaviour (Kuorikoski, Lehtinen, & Marchionni, 2010; Lehtinen & Kuorikoski, 2007), such behaviour need not provide the central causal mechanism in a rational-choice model (see also Satz & Ferejohn, 1994). One might thus wish to assert (a_1) just because one's model needs some connection between the individuals and the social-level outcomes. Asserting (a_1) could then be rephrased as 'the optimising model gives me a connection between individuals and outcomes. Even though real people are not like the individuals in my model, it does not matter because the fine details of their behaviour are irrelevant anyway'. One could thus assert (a) even though one knows that real individuals do not optimize. Another possibility is that although individual behaviour is not irrelevant to the results, it is sufficient if part of the population optimizes.

Note that if such justifications are appropriate, the modeller may well not be committed to any particular determinants of behaviour or be indifferent towards them and their truth. This may make it difficult to distinguish between inaccuracy-indicating (a_1) and non-committal-indicating claims (c). Here the modeller believes that the as-if claim *itself* is false, but for the purposes of his or her model, it is negligibly so. The truth of the claim is not important to the modeller because he or she is merely using the behaviour specified *in order to study something else,* and the as-if locution is used mainly to indicate that one should not evaluate the model by examining the particular assumption that it has qualified. Thus the modeller may believe that optimisation entails behaviour that is different from the way in which people actually behave, but the way in which they behave is ultimately irrelevant to the results of the model. In contrast, in case (c) the modeller aims to formulate an accurate rather than a negligibly false behavioural assumption.

3.2 Negligibility-indicating accurate as-if claims

Here A is some system of interest, and B refers to some set of ideal conditions. Ma¨ki (1992, 2003, 2009) provides the following description of the function of such usage:[9]

(a_2) Phenomena behave as if certain ideal conditions were met: conditions under which only those real forces that are theoretically isolated are active.

Here the as-if claim refers to the idea that various disturbing factors found in the real world are assumed to be absent. The central forces identified in the model are depicted as if they were the only forces. The attribution is that reality satisfies the ideal conditions, i.e. that there are no disturbing factors other than those identified in the model. Introducing the as-if locution induces a semantic change because the sentence now makes a true enough claim about the behaviour of something in actual conditions rather than a false claim concerning whether the reality exhibits ideal conditions. The constraints are satisfied because we know that the ideal conditions do not hold in the real world. Furthermore, the as-if claim directs attention to what is achieved in assuming the absence of such factors: we get to know what kind of behaviour or outcomes would result if the central forces were acting alone. 'People behave as if they were only motivated by self-interest' provides a well-known example from economics. In this example the negligible causal factors are mental states, but as we will now see, they also can be physical forces.

The as-if claim expressed by (a_2) may be accurate or true enough. Consider, for example, the often used example of Galileo's law of falling bodies, which states that 'under vacuum, the distance covered by a falling object is given by $s^1 g t^2$'. One could then say, with Friedman, that good predictions may be obtained by assuming that

(a_2^0) Actual objects fall as if they were following Galileo's law.

The as-if claim is true enough if the air pressure is sufficiently close to zero, and the object satisfies certain characteristics such as having sufficient density. The attribution is that the air pressure is zero. Given that it must be false, one does not need to use the as-if locution at all if one has artificially created a vacuum, and makes statements concerning objects falling in it. There is, however, a range of conditions under which it makes sense to say that 'an object behaves as if those conditions corresponded to a vacuum'.

Here, evaluating the truth of the attribution is relevant for evaluating the truth of the as-if claim, which is a feature that (a_1) and (a_2) share. This does not seem to be a case in which one would say 'A behaves as if it were B even though it *clearly* is not B' because whether A (an object in actual atmospheric conditions) behaves in such a way depends on how close A is to being B (an object in a perfect vacuum). As I will demonstrate in later sections, however, other kinds of as-if claims are different in this respect.

Friedman (1953, p.18) emphasises that it is *not assumed* that we live in a vacuum.[10] We merely assume (or claim) that objects fall as if they were in a vacuum. Introducing the as-if locution brings about a semantic change that transforms the false claim about there being a vacuum into a true enough claim about behaviour. Musgrave (1981) suggests that the as-if locution could be used to express a negligibility assumption: the claim 'air resistance is negligible' could be expressed in the words 'bodies fall as if they were in a vacuum' (see also Mäki, 2000). These two claims are not identical, however, because the former expresses reasons why the behavioural claim might be accurate whereas the latter provides a descriptive claim about the behaviour of something.

Consider now another well-known example, Boyle's law of ideal gases states, roughly, that at a constant temperature the pressure of a fixed amount of gas varies inversely with its volume. According to Strevens (2008), one might say that

(a_2^{00}) Gases behave as if there are no collisions of molecules.

This is asserted on the grounds that whether or not there are such collisions, the demonstration of Boyle's law goes through. It is clear that collisions are only negligible for the purposes of explaining Boyle's law. They are not negligible for other purposes (e.g., modelling diffusion). The attribution is that there are no collisions. Note that the falsity of this claim is not relevant in evaluating the truth of the as-if claim. We know that it is false, but what really matters is the argument given for the negligibility claim. Strevens cites McQuarrie and Simon (1997, p.1015), who argue that 'any collision that deflects the path of a molecule from [the path assumed in the derivation] will be balanced by a collision that replaces the molecule.'

There are thus three kinds of negligibility claim. The first is that causal forces that are known to affect the behaviour of interest are weak enough to be negligible in strength (e.g., air pressure). Secondly, forces that are taken to be non-negligible in strength and potentially relevant to the behaviour in question have negligible net effects (due to some counterbalancing of forces, as with molecular collisions). Thirdly, any model ignores an infinite number of causal factors because those factors are thought to be irrelevant. In this last case, the as-if locution is not used. One does not say, for example, that 'stones fall as if swallows do not migrate to warmer territories during the autumn' because one presupposes that the migration behaviour of these birds could not affect the stones in any way.

There is also a difference between (a_1) and (a_2). A feather does not satisfy the relevant characteristics, and one should not say that 'the feather falls as if it were following Galileo's law' because *the as-if claim would be false*. Contrast this with (a_1). If the reason for using the as-if locution is indeed only to indicate that the truth of (a_1) does not matter, the falsity of the claim would not prevent the modeller from using the locution. He or she would use it even knowing that people do not optimize. The difference between (a_1) and (a_2) is that the former does not express a claim that is taken to be causally important for the model, but the latter does. In case a_2, the as-if locution is needed for specifying the exact content of the behavioural as-if claim, whereas in case a_1 it merely indicates that the behavioural claim is not to be evaluated for truth.

Mäki (1998, 2003) suggests that (AIC) could also be taken to express epistemic uncertainty concerning whether A is B. It seems that if this is applicable at all, it is most suitable for inaccurate as-if claims (case a_1). One would say that 'people behave as if they were rational' because one is uncertain whether they are rational. Note, however, that such use violates the pragmatic constraint for using the as-if locution. One cannot presuppose that the attribution is false if one is simultaneously uncertain about its truth.[11] One might argue that provisionally expressing epistemic uncertainty with respect to the attribution counts as not being committed to its truth and thus that the constraint is satisfied after all. But this will not do because, whoever asserts the aforementioned as-if claim in order to express epistemic uncertainty is ultimately committed to the truth of the attribution: if later investigations show that the attribution is false, he or she is no longer willing to assert the behavioural claim. That is what being committed to the truth of the attribution means.

Distinguishing between different kinds of as-if claims on the basis of whether their truth depends on the truth of the attribution is important for specifying the *object* of epistemic uncertainty. It may concern the attribution, the as-if claim and the explanation of whether the claim may be true, and if so, why. In cases (a_1) and (a_2) epistemic uncertainty

concerning the attribution *implies* that of the as-if claim. Because Mäki does not distinguish between as-if claims and attributions, he does not distinguish between different objects of uncertainty. He is thus led to conflate epistemic uncertainty concerning 'why it is that A behaves in the way it does' with uncertainty concerning 'whether A is, or is not, B' (Mäki, 1998, p.26). I suggest that as-if locutions are not used for expressing epistemic uncertainty precisely because epistemic uncertainty concerning the attribution does not imply epistemic uncertainty concerning the as-if claim in the most genuine cases (b and c). Using it for such purposes would perpetuate the false impression that the truth of an attribution is always relevant to the truth of the as-if claim.[12]

As-if claims never explain 'why it is that A behaves the way it does' *in themselves*. This feature is difficult to reconcile with realism, even concerning case (a_2). Indeed, the use of as-if locutions can be justified because they give an indication that the claim itself does not provide an explanation.

4. False ascription as-if claims

The second use of the as-if locution involves ascribing false intentions or cognitions to something in order to describe its behaviour. The basic form of such a claim is thus the following:

(b) A behaves as if it had intentions or cognitions to B.

The point is to *describe behaviour* accurately when there is no need to concern oneself about whether the intentional or the cognitive attributions are correct. Note that in contrast to case (a_1), here one aims to assert that the behaviour formulated by means of the as-if claim is accurate.

Many of Friedman's (1953, p.21) examples exemplify such unrealistic attributions: one can describe the trajectories of billiard balls accurately under the assumption that expert players act as if they know complicated mathematical formulas derived from physical theory. This theory attributes the ability to make such complicated calculations to the players. The attribution is false because the players do not conceptualise the issue in terms of the physical theory. Nevertheless, one could derive trajectories for the billiard balls by using that physical theory. Similarly, Friedman (1953, p.19) argues that the position of the leaves on a tree may be accurately described on the assumption that each individual leaf acts as if it is trying to maximise the amount of sunlight it receives. Lehtinen and Kuorikoski (2007) posit that in such cases the assumption is *behaviourally realistic* but *intentionally unrealistic* because it describes the behaviour truthfully but attributes intentions untruthfully. Ascribing intentions to the tree fails to accurately identify the causes of the leaf pattern.[13]

In Friedman's examples of billiards players and leaves the attribution is clearly false, and the truth of the as-if claim does not depend on the truth of the attribution. Examining the truth of the attribution does not provide relevant information about the truth of the as-if claim. Friedman also uses this kind of as-if claim in arguing that firms behave as if they were maximising profits (1953, p.21). He was perfectly aware of the fact that managers do not intentionally try to equalise marginal cost and benefit, and that they often do not even know the cost function. The point of using the as-if claim, however, is to argue that even if they do not intentionally try to maximise profits, their behaviour is so close to the profit- maximising assumption that one could obtain good predictions on that basis. These predictions do not, of course, concern profit maximising in itself, but rather focus on other things such as the effects of a price change or a tax on supply. Friedman was arguing that the profit-maximisation assumption was, in fact, accurate for the purposes for which it was meant in standard price theory. I take it that such an interpretation is no longer considered radical, given that Hoover (2009) also argues that Friedman cares about the accuracy of assumptions.

If the attribution does not provide relevant information for evaluating the truth of this kind of as-if claim, what does? Friedman is known to rest his case on an evolutionary- selection argument: only firms whose behaviour mimics profit maximising will survive in the long run. The selection argument is commonly taken to facilitate explanation of why the behaviour of A could mimic that of B even when A is not B in various different contexts. Lagueux (1994) argues, however, that as-if claims are always justified by some more general theory, but he does not require this theory to be that of evolutionary selection. This seems right, given that there does not seem to be any need for a selection argument in the case of Galileo's law of falling bodies. There is a general theory, but unlike in Friedman's other examples (firms, leaves on a tree, billiards players), it is not separate from the as-if claim because it is the very theory of gravity that explains why one can describe objects as if they followed Galileo's formulation s^1gt^2.

The selection argument tends to be considered less than fully compelling (see Vromen, 2009 for an account and references), and therefore the profit-maximisation assumption is often considered inaccurate after all. Even Becker (1962, p.10) argues that the assumption is not accurate.

In my judgment the great achievement of the "survival" argument advanced by Alchian and others' is not a demonstration that surviving firms must act as if they were trying to maximize profits, *for counterexamples can easily be developed,* but rather a demonstration that the decisions of irrational firms are limited by a budgetary constraint.

The fact that Friedman employs the survival argument gives support to the interpretation that Friedman *tried* to argue for the accuracy of the profit maximisation assumption and thus that his as-if claim concerning firms is to be interpreted in terms of rather than (a_1). Yet, I would hesitate to argue that Boland's interpretation of Friedman in terms of (a_1) is wrong because Friedman thought that discussing the 'realism' of assumptions is only meaningful relative to the purpose of theorising. Thus, although he seems to have thought that profit maximising is accurate enough for the purposes of the theory of the firm as it was practised in the 1950s,[14] he probably thought that discussing whether the assumption is accurate in an absolute sense is meaningless.

I do not wish to rely on a correct interpretation of Friedman. I will instead examine the use of the claim in another economic model in order to show that it could be used to describe behaviour accurately and even realistically. Thus, the failure of Friedman's example from economics should not lead one to believe that this kind of as-if claim is always inaccurate. Given that there is no need to provide any kind of selection argument or general theory in this case, it will also demonstrate that such arguments and theories are not *necessary* for the realistic description of behaviour through as-if claims.

4.1 A case study: signal extraction in an expected utility model of strategic voting

Consider Lehtinen's (2006, 2007, 2008) use of a signal extraction model as part of an expected utility model of strategic voting. Strategic voting is usually defined as giving one's vote to a candidate or alternative that is not considered to be the best. Only the case with pair-wise comparisons is analysed here in order to simplify the presentation. Lehtinen assumes that voters do not know other voters' preferences, but that they act as if they had obtained informative signals concerning them. Let N denote the total number of voters and n_{jk} the number of voters who prefer alternative j to k. If n_{jk}. $N/2, j$ will beat k in a pair- wise comparison under the majority rule if everyone votes sincerely. The model is set in a computer-simulation framework in which voters' preferences are generated randomly. Voters are assumed to act as if they have obtained perturbed information on the realised value of n_{jk} as follows: an individual voter's signal $s_i(jk)$ is given by the sum of the standardised n_{jk} and a random term:

$$s_i(jk) = \frac{2n_{jk} - N}{\sqrt{N}} + \varepsilon R_i$$

where R_i denotes a standard normal random variable and 1 denotes a parameter that reflects the quality of the information. He shows (Lehtinen, 2006) that an individual's probability $p_i(jk)$ for the proposition that alternative j beats alternative k is given by

$$p_i(jk) = 1 - \Phi\left(-\frac{s_i(jk)}{\varepsilon\sqrt{1+\varepsilon^2}}\right) + \varepsilon R_i$$

where F denotes the standard normal distribution function. The existence of such signals is not a fiction because in mass elections pre-election polls may be interpreted as some sort of signal concerning the winning probabilities of various candidates, and even in parliamentary voting the representatives have various sources of information on other voters' preferences, such as party affiliation and the content of arguments made by different representatives. Yet, various features of the signals are fictions: the derivation in the appendix consists of four pages of manipulations of random variables and their densities. It would be foolhardy to claim that voters are able to make such calculations, let alone that they would actually perform them. Real voters do not engage in computing such expressions at all. Similarly, they do not literally compute expected utilities by multiplying probabilities by utilities. Furthermore, in the real world they do not obtain perturbed signals in the kind of form in which they are represented in the model, in which a signal is given by an exact numeral. For example, a signal could be given by $s_i(jk)$ 2 0.298234 and a probability by $p_i(jk)$ 0.267543.

These models of strategic voting thus depict voters as if they had obtained perturbed signals in an exact numerical form, as if they were able to perform complicated calculations and as if they actually carried out the computations and used them in an expected-utility calculus for determining their decisions. Now compare the following two statements:

(b^0) Voters act as if they have obtained perturbed signals concerning the preference profile and as if they have computed probabilities from these signals using statistical reasoning.

(b*) Voters obtain perturbed signals concerning the preference profile and compute probabilities from these signals using statistical reasoning.

(b*) is clearly false but (b^0) is true enough in the sense that actual voters' behaviour really corresponds to that which would ensue if they actually obtained signals, computed probabilities and so on. Introducing the as-if locution converts a false statement into a true one and the semantic change is obvious.

These strategic voting models are intentionally and cognitively unrealistic in the sense that voters have cognitions and intentions (signals and computing) in the model that they do not have in reality. However, the model may nevertheless be perfectly accurate in accounting for their behaviour, and even realistic in the sense of correctly identifying the factors that influence the behaviour and the way in which they do so. I will now attempt to demonstrate this.

What would a realistic description of strategic voting behaviour look like? One should get the determinants of the behaviour right. Consider Anthony Downs' verbal description of the incentives for strategic voting:

Assume that there are three parties: Right, Center, and Left. Voter X prefers Right to Center and Center to Left, but he *believes* that Right has the least chance of winning. If he *greatly prefers* Right to Center and is *almost indifferent* between Center and Left, he is *less likely* to switch his vote from Right to Center than if he *slightly prefers* Right to Center but *abhors* Left (Downs, 1957, p.49).

The implication here is that strategic voting depends on the winning chances of various candidates and on preference intensities. Let us say that voters engage in *Downsian deliberation* if they conceptualise voting in such (qualitative) terms. It involves the mental operation of weighing the desirabilities of the options with the probabilities. This operation could more generally be called *expected-utility deliberation*. Lehtinen's models are based on Enelow's (1981) and McKelvey and Ordeshook's (1972) expected utility models for explaining voter behaviour under various voting rules. These models show how beliefs and winning probabilities ought to combine so as to take intensities and probabilities into account in the right way.

If all one wishes to do is to provide an abstract account of people's strategic voting behaviour, such models are sufficient. However, in order to study the aggregate-level consequences of such behaviour it is necessary to give specific values to individual utility functions and beliefs, and the question that then arises is how they should be determined. Lehtinen goes on to generate utilities randomly and uses the signal extraction model to derive the beliefs. Given that behaviour depends on voters' beliefs, his model should generate beliefs in a realistic way.

Here it seems plausible to state that there are interpersonal differences in the *accuracy* of knowledge concerning the winning chances of various candidates and in the *confidence* different voters have in their knowledge. If one believes that the Right does not have a chance of winning but is wrong about this and votes strategically, and if the outcome then turns out to be one's second-best option rather than the best one due to that strategic vote, one would have hurt oneself by voting strategically (see Lehtinen, 2007 for an example). Hence, it seems reasonable to require that people vote strategically only if they can be reasonably confident that their information is correct. Furthermore, and even more obviously, the beliefs derived from the signal extraction model should be responsive to variations in the realised preference profile. This is precisely what the signal extraction model shows (see esp.Lehtinen, 2006 for details).

Even though voters must be said to act only as if they had received signals and as if they had computed beliefs on the basis of those signals, the signal extraction model provides a perfectly realistic account of their deliberation and the determinants of strategic voting. The degree of confidence in and the real quality of the information are the actual determinants of their beliefs when they vote strategically, and the model captures them in a realistic manner.[15] It is thus realistic with respect to some intentions but unrealistic (and fictional) with respect to some others.

Note that whereas the attribution states that voters intentionally calculate these probabilities, the as-if claim merely states that the actions (or beliefs) derived from the model may be taken to describe actual voters' actions (or beliefs). Furthermore, it is definitely not assumed that voters have particularly good cognitive capacities. If 1 is large, some voters may have highly inaccurate beliefs. It would be silly to criticise this model for attributing unrealistically sophisticated behaviour to voters on the grounds that it describes their behaviour as if they had gone through complicated calculations. Using the as-if locution highlights this fact.

Formulating the behavioural assumption in statements such as voters act as if they computed probabilities on the basis of perturbed signals does not indicate whether or not the behaviour will be realistically modelled. The as-if claim in *itself* does not justify such thinking, it merely formulates the behavioural claim. Nevertheless, the fact that the attribution (b*) is unrealistic is entirely irrelevant in terms of evaluating the realisticness of the as-if claim: it is known that voters do not go through complex computations when they vote, but that is irrelevant. However, merely stating that (b^0) is true enough is not sufficient because it does not provide any explanation of why one should think that it is. Its truth is rather to be demonstrated. Hence, as-if claims are typically *incomplete* in that showing that the model is realistic always requires something beyond the claim itself. Other kinds of as- if claims also seem to be incomplete in this way.

As demonstrated above, whether negligibility-indicating (a$_2$) as-if claims involve making accurate assumptions depend on the degree to which the attribution is true. In this case (b) there is no similar continuum of claims from the perfectly accurate to the utterly inaccurate. The claim that voters obtain signals expressed in terms of a seven-digit number, compute probabilities on this basis and choose an action after considering the expected utility of the various options is a fiction in other words known to be false. However, I argue that the signal extraction model does accurately capture the determinants of behaviour.

There is no general theory (such as evolutionary selection) that explains why individual beliefs should correspond to those generated in the model. I have argued that the fiction of computing behaviour and its signals allows for a realistic representation of voting behaviour. Ultimately, I assert that the as-if claim is realistic on the grounds that it correctly describes Downsian deliberation, which, I also assert, provides a true account of the reasons for strategic voting.

Morrison (2009) claims that the way in which fictional representations provide reliable information differs from one case to another. It does not seem possible to generalise on why, whether and when they facilitate the realistic description of behaviour, however, which could be attributable to the fact that fictions play a crucial role in *representing* the world (see also Teller, 2009). In this case it is necessary to represent the signals, the utilities and the probabilities with precise numerals in order to represent Downsian deliberation in a computer model, and the function of the as-if locution is to show that this representation is not intended to provide a literally true description of all the details of that deliberation (cf. Coddington, 1979).

4.2 A digression: Mäki's distinction

Mäki (1992, 1998, 2000, 2003, 2004, 2009) distinguishes (a_2).

(a_2) Phenomena behave as if certain ideal conditions were met: conditions under which only the real forces that are theoretically isolated are active from (b) thus:

(b) Phenomena behave as if those forces were real.

I will now attempt to clarify how the classification proposed here differs from Mäki's distinction. Mäki's distinction concerns the *reference* of the as-if locution: he distinguishes between cases in which something is modelled as if certain minor forces were absent, and those in which the central forces in the model are based on fictions. In the former case the isolation of forces is false (i.e., they are not the only forces that operate in reality), whereas in the latter case the central forces picked out are fictional (i.e., they are found in the representation but not in the real world) (Ma¨ki, 2009). This distinction cannot be incorporated into the classification scheme proposed here because the basis on which it rests is different. Ma¨ki's distinction is based on what the fiction the as-if locution expresses is about, whereas here it is based on the pragmatic reason for using the locution. Ma¨ki does not give any reason why one would want to model the central causal forces with a fiction.[16]

According to Ma¨ki (1998), (b) invites an instrumentalist reading because it postulates fictional forces. In my example of signal extraction individual behaviour is described in terms of fictions even though it is a central causal factor in the model. Ma¨ki's distinction thus requires that (b^0) must be understood in terms of (b), and (b') should thus be understood in instrumental terms. I believe this conclusion should be resisted.

I have argued in this section that an as-if claim may well be realistic even in a case in which central forces are represented by fictions. If I have succeeded in showing that voters *really* behave as though they were governed by some fictional forces (computing probabilities and expected utilities) identified in the model, there seems to be little reason for a realist to be worried. The relevant question is how the realistically described behaviour specified in the as-if claim is justified or explained given that the claim itself does not provide an explanation. It is obvious that such an explanation must be found elsewhere, and what I have written in this section provides it. The difference between realists and instrumentalists is presumably that the former require that an explanation or justification is provided somewhere, whereas the latter do not care as long as the predictions provided by the theory are correct. Only a foolish brand of realism would require that each and every assumption must be formulated in such a way that an explanation is also provided in the very formulation. As demonstrated above, the attribution is plainly false, and the as-if locution is needed in order to effect a semantic change that allows the correct understanding of the behavioural assumption. If realists can accept unrealistic assumptions if they are properly justified, they should not banish realistic assumptions merely because they are represented by fictions.

Ma¨ki could perhaps take a different tack, and argue that my example does not count as a case of (b') because, although obtaining signals and multiplying utilities are central forces in the model, they are real. It is true that the as-if claim does not qualify the *existence* of these forces. However, neither does it indicate isolation or negligibility. It does not mean that there might be other relevant forces that are ignored for the purposes of investigation. The as-if locution is rather needed to indicate that the modeller *does not claim* that voters compute probabilities or multiply them by utilities, albeit the fictions of literally manipulating density functions and of literally multiplying utilities by beliefs are needed for formulating the behavioural assumption. It would be misleading to assert that voters compute probabilities or multiply them by utilities. These fictions are best compared to using physical theory to determine the trajectories of billiard balls in Friedman's example: it is known that these fictions are not the underlying causes of the phenomena of interest. If Ma¨ki were to adopt this second line of reasoning, he would end up in a dilemma: he would either have to explain why using physical theory does not provide a fictional account of billiards players' intentions or show how Friedman's example is relevantly different from my signal-extraction example.

5. Non-committal-indicating as-if claims

Dennett (1996, p.27) suggests that the intentional stance is the strategy of interpreting the behaviour of an entity (person, animal, artefact) by treating it *as if* it were a rational agent who governed its 'choice' of 'action' through 'consideration' of its 'beliefs' and 'desires'. Here the as-if claim expresses a non-committal attitude towards whether the entity in question has beliefs and desires. Note that even though the as-if locution is used to bracket the existence of beliefs and desires, the assertion about behaviour is intended to be accurate. This is what makes Dennett's use of the as-if locution different from that of inaccurate as-if claims (case a_1). Given that a thermostat really behaves as if it wanted to keep the temperature fixed, such as-if claims may be used to describe behaviour accurately even if the attribution (thermostats have desires) were to be blatantly false. What makes the behavioural claim about thermostats true is that they have been designed to do just that: keep the temperature fixed.

When the intentional stance is applied to real people, the relevant attribution is that 'people have desires and beliefs'. For someone persuaded that people have desires and beliefs, this would seem to provide a counterexample to the thesis that attributions are always false. However, Dennett would use the as-if locution even if his audience thought that people had beliefs and desires. He would say that this attribution cannot be proven to be true, and that the as-if locution is used precisely to indicate that the existence of desires and beliefs is bracketed. Thus it is ultimately not the falsity of the attribution that pragmatically justifies using the as-if locution but rather whether the utterer of the locution is committed to its truth.

Let us now consider an example from economics which is more difficult to interpret.

(b) *Orthodox revealed preference theory* then provides consistency conditions for Eve's behavior in A to be described by saying that she chooses *as though* maximizing the expected value of a utility function defined on C, relative to a subjective probability distribution defined on B (Binmore, 1998, pp.360-361).

In order to see the relevant attribution for this claim, it is necessary to look at the notion of utility more closely. Classical utilitarians used the term 'utility' to denote either a mental state (degree of satisfaction) or a feeling (e.g., pleasure). 'Maximising utility' could then be understood as an intentional activity whereby an agent endeavours to maximise the degree to which his or her desires are satisfied. If 'utility' were to be interpreted in such a manner, one would say that the attribution is that 'Eve maximises desire satisfaction', which would be true if she actually maximised her desire satisfaction. Note that if Eve actually maximised utility in this sense, such an interpretation would constitute a counterexample to the claim that the attribution is always false.

Here, however, Binmore would use the as-if locution in describing Eve's actions even if Eve deliberately and consciously endeavoured to maximise satisfaction. By way of illustration, consider the way in which 'utility' and 'maximisation' are interpreted in modern utility theory, which essentially consists of *representation theorems*.[17] Such theorems specify that if preferences satisfy a set of *consistency conditions,* then they may be represented with utility functions. Let P_i denote individual i's strict preference ordering. The standard interpretation is that for some alternatives x and y, xP_iy means that i considers x better than y. The representation theorem then states that $U_i(x)$. $U_i(y)$ if and only if xP_iy. In other words, function U assigns a higher number to x than to y if the individual strictly prefers x to y. It could then be said that the individual's behaviour is described as if he or she were maximising a utility function.

The theory features utility functions that may be used to describe the behaviour of an individual whose preferences satisfy the conditions. Sometimes the term 'utility' or 'util' is used for the values of these functions. Given that 'utility' refers to a number here, it consists neither in material welfare nor in any kind of mental state such as pleasure. Binmore would be making a nonsensical statement that involved a category mistake if he were to drop the as-if locution. It is nonsensical to say that 'a person tries to maximise utility' when utility is interpreted in its modern sense as a description of the person's preferences or choices. Maximisation is not a mental operation carried out by the person whose behaviour is described, it is rather a property of a mathematical model that represents that person's behaviour in terms of maximisation. The category mistake would thus consist in stating that 'a person aims to (purposefully) maximise his or her utility function'. However, the person's actions could be described as if he or she were maximising a utility function because the more preferred (or chosen) outcomes are assigned higher utilities than the less preferred. As Binmore states, 'our story makes it *nonsense* to say that Adam chooses the former *because* its utility is greater' (Binmore, 2009, pp.19-21). Saying so would amount to committing the 'causal utility fallacy'. In other words, utility does not provide any reasons for choosing one way or the other, and merely represents an individual's preferences.

Binmore could not use the locution in order to claim that actual behaviour corresponded to that which would ensue if Eve maximised her desire satisfaction because he claims that modern decision theory 'makes a virtue of assuming nothing whatever about the psychological causes of our choice behavior' (Binmore, 2009, pp.8-9). Representation theorems do not say anything about why people are supposed to maximise utility. Unlike in case (b), Binmore does not attribute false intentions to Eve in order to describe her behaviour accurately.

Neither does Binmore qualify the behavioural claim with an as-if locution because he denies that Eve maximises utility (in the modern sense). He has already assumed that Eve is rational:

Although the revealed preference interpretation of utility will be maintained throughout this book, half of the labor of constructing a utility function from an agent's choice behavior will be skipped. It will be assumed that a preference relation has already been constructed and that it remains only to show that it can be represented using an appropriate utility function (Binmore, 1994, p.268).

Even though he readily accepts elsewhere that 'human behavior is often downright irrational' (Binmore, 2005, p.75), he cannot doubt Eve's rationality here because preference relations cannot be constructed at all unless individuals are rational. The locution is thus used in order to formulate an accurate behavioural assumption.

One might propose that maximising expected utility is to be interpreted as expected utility deliberation. 'Eve maximises expected utility' would then be the relevant attribution, and maximisation would be interpreted in terms of this mental operation. This would not be correct either, however, because the criterion of truth for the as-if claim 'Eve's behaviour can be described as if she were maximising the expected value of a utility function' which is not whether her behaviour corresponds to that which would ensue if she engaged in expected-utility deliberation. It is rather whether her preferences satisfy the conditions for representing utility. Whether a person's actions could be described as if he or she were maximising expected utility does not depend on whether he or she engages in some kind of mental operation. Similarly, whether or not a model incorporating the expected utility assumption is accurate does not depend on whether the person is trying to maximise something or whether he or she is engaging in expected-utility deliberation, but only on whether his or her preferences satisfy the conditions. I take this to be the standard position among decision theorists, but I will provide a simple argument in favour of it: Eve may violate the conditions even if she is engaged in expected-utility deliberation if, for example, she makes errors in calculating expected utilities.

In the previous section the attribution was:

(b*) Voters obtain perturbed signals concerning the preference profile and compute probabilities from these signals using statistical reasoning.

A more fully specified attribution would have been:

(b**) Voters obtain perturbed signals, compute probabilities and literally calculate expected utilities by weighing utility values with probabilities.

Literally calculating expected utilities by multiplying probabilities and utilities expressed in seven-digit numbers is thus a mental operation that is also falsely attributed to voters. Given that (b) and (c) both concern cases with expected utility maximisation, one might argue that they are not different enough to justify putting them into separate categories. Lehtinen (2011) posits, however, that the credibility of his model crucially depends on the plausibility of the assumption that voters really engage in Downsian deliberation, and that whether their preferences satisfy the consistency conditions matters very little in the sense that the results of the model do not depend on it. In fact, it seems that satisfying the consistency conditions is not sufficient to guarantee that voters engage in Downsian deliberation. This is at least what one is compelled to think if one accepts Binmore's argument that modern utility theory makes no psychological assumptions.

Completely different things are required in the two cases for the as-if claims concerning expected utility maximisation to be true. In case (c), the claim is true if the individual satisfies the consistency conditions. In case (b), however, whether or not it is true enough depends on whether or not voters engage in Downsian deliberation. The similarity between (b) and (c) lies in the fact that, in both cases, the modeller uses an as-if locution in order to clarify what kind of claims about behaviour and mental states are made. Binmore uses the as-if locution to alert the reader to the fact that 'maximisation' does not refer to any kind of mental operation. He avoids making the false claim that maximisation is such an operation by using the locution.

Let us now return to (c). Once the right attribution is specified, it is clear that it is indeed always either false or involves a category mistake. I suggest two possibilities. The first is that it concerns Eve's intentions: 'Eve endeavours to maximise expected utility' when utility is understood in its modern sense as a number describing preferences. This attribution incorporates a category mistake. It is not a consequence of an empirical failure to act in a certain manner but rather derives from the fact that utility is not something that Eve can try to maximise as a matter of the logical form of the term 'utility'. The second possibility is that it concerns Binmore's beliefs concerning his audience. He could be taken to assume that not everyone in his audience knows that the term 'utility' will be used in its modern sense. He would thus be using the as-if locution because he believes that some people in his audience might think that 'utility means pleasure in the theory that Binmore is presenting'. This is again false. It is also evident that evaluating the truth of either of these attributions is entirely irrelevant to whether or not the as-if claim is accurate because neither says anything about the consistency conditions.

One might argue that if the first attribution is appropriate, claims like (c) should be treated as a separate *fourth* kind of as-if claim on the grounds that avoiding category mistakes is not intrinsically related to expressing non-committal to any particular determinants of behaviour. In further support of such an argument one could point out that the above quotation from 1994 commits Binmore to Eve's rationality, and that rationality is a determinant of behaviour. I resist such an interpretation mainly because rationality is not the right kind of determinant. Insofar as the 'preference relation has already been constructed', the behaviour has also already taken place, and if it is described in terms of utility functions, it does not matter what its determinants were. Furthermore, once one understands why Binmore uses the as-if locution, one also understands how avoiding category mistakes amounts to being non-committal about the determinants of behaviour. As-if claims used in expected utility theory may well provide accurate accounts of behaviour. However, here the use of the as-if locution tells us absolutely nothing about whether or not this is the case. It has nothing to do with the question of whether or not it is accurate to describe people's actual behaviour as utility-maximising. This question can be evaluated in many different ways, of which one is to evaluate whether people in some actual situations try to maximise pleasure. This is so because the reasonability of the consistency conditions depends on how real people act, and one of the relevant considerations in assessing whether their behaviour satisfies the conditions is whether or not they try to maximise pleasure. In some circumstances they do satisfy the conditions, in others they do not, but in any case one needs to use the as-if locution even when expected utility maximisation is an accurate assumption. This is what makes (c) different from case (a_1). If one wished to say that the difference between actual behaviour and that specified by expected utility theory is negligible, one would have to say that 'people act as if they were acting as if they maximised expected utility'. Naturally, such claims are never made because there are more elegant ways of conveying the idea. One could say, for example, that 'Eve acts as if she were a utility maximiser'.[18] This is because the relevant attribution

'Eve is a utility maximiser' is false if she does not act according to the conditions.

Some decision theorists, including Binmore, apparently think that mere choices rather than preferences ultimately need to be consistent for the theory of expected utility to apply. One could then state that 'an agent acts as if he or she had consistent preferences', and that his or her choices could be described in terms of utility functions. Here the very existence of preferences is bracketed. Note that if expected utility theory is interpreted in such revealed-preference terms, stating that 'an agent acts as if he or she had consistent choices' would mean that the as-if claim is to be interpreted as indicating inaccuracy (a_1).

In cases (b) and (c) the reason for using the as-if locution is that it allows one to specify exactly what one wants to say about behavioural assumptions. Dennett and Binmore use it to emphasise that no intentional ascriptions need to be made, whereas Lehtinen uses it to formulate a realistic behavioural assumption and to show that the credibility of the model does not hinge on the assumption that voters actually engage in computing expected utilities or receive numerically precise signals. These cases are similar in that using the as-if locution allows the modeller to *avoid* making some *particular* mental attributions.

6. Conclusions

As-if locutions can be used in a variety of ways. I have argued that they can be used to (a_1) indicate that the behavioural claim they qualify is inaccurate but negligibly so, and (a_2) to indicate that the modeller acknowledges the existence of some causal factors that are not explicitly taken into account in the model because they are deemed to be negligible. In the most genuine cases, they are used for (b) expressing the content of accurate behavioural claims by ascribing intentions on entities in an unrealistic manner, and (c) for indicating that descriptive claims made about behaviour do not commit one to any particular mental assumptions. The claims could thus be put briefly as follows.

(a_1) *Inaccuracy-indicating claims*. AIC - or rather, A does not actually behave as B, but that is unimportant in this model.

(a_2) *Negligibility-indicating accurate claims*. AIC because A is like B in some respects but not in all. The ignored respects are not important in this model.

(b)*Claims indicating false mental ascription*. AIC because A does not have (mental) properties B and does have properties C. Yet its behaviour could be described under the assumption that it has properties B.

(c)*Claims indicating non-committal*. AIC because, although A has nothing to do with B, A behaves as B whatever may be the actual determinants of A's behaviour.

However, as-if claims also have some commonalities. First, their most important function is to help in specifying which part of a model ought to be true and what can be allowed to be false. Secondly, they would appear to be invariably related to making claims about or describing behaviour. Thirdly, they all express lack of commitment to the truth of their underlying attributions. Fourthly, in themselves they are always methodologically incomplete in the sense that they do not provide any explanation of why behaviour should, in reality, correspond to that specified in the model.

As-if claims are likely to create a great deal of confusion. In view of their incompleteness it is always necessary to find out whether a given one is realistic. Furthermore, it may be difficult to see the difference between the different kinds of claim. One could easily be misled into believing that an as-if claim is realistic even when behaviour is not realistically modelled, or that all as-if claims are false because their attributions are always false. Friedman uses the locution for all of the reasons described in this paper. Given that the different uses are based on different methodological commitments and lead to different ways of evaluating the truth of the claims, it is not clear that it makes any sense to talk about 'Friedman's as-if methodology'.[19]

Some people may prefer to minimise the use of as-if claims just because they are so confusing and incomplete. In all the cases in which they involve a semantic change, they clearly have a useful function. Usually the change involves transforming a false attribution into a true enough as-if claim. Yet, they are never necessary. If one merely wishes to express the idea that the realisticness of an assumption does not matter, or that one is aware of making an unrealistic assumption, I suggest that it would be better to avoid using the as- if locution because there are more natural and less confusing ways of making such claims. Whether a semantic change thus entailed could then be taken to facilitate recognition of the warranted uses of as-if claims.

This paper may be considered somewhat odd because the author is using his own work as an economist in a philosophical case study. However, the motivation for writing this paper arose from the experience of writing the papers on voting and signal extraction. Economic journals do not allow authors to explain the as-if justifications of their assumptions at length. The 'as-if' locution actually never appears in any of my papers on voting and signal extraction. It does not appear because I was too afraid that I would be interpreted as promoting my model in terms of inaccuracy-indicating as-if claims. This interpretation seemed to be very common among the economists, and I was so deeply concerned about being misunderstood that I decided not to use the locution at all. These experiences also explain why I have not been content merely to describe how as-if locutions are used in economics, but rather also tried to delimit their use with the pragmatic constraints: I believe that a more regimented use of the locution would help in avoiding confusions.

Given that (a_2),(b) and (c) represent cases in which the as-if claim may be accurate or even realistic, restricting usage to these three kinds also encourage evaluation of the criteria as to their truth. The most important consideration here is whether or not the truth of the attribution is relevant to the truth of the as-if claim. The example of signal extraction was intended to show that in one case in which it is not relevant, i.e. when it involves a fiction of a false intentional ascription, it may well be realistic despite being based on a fiction, and the grounds for evaluating its truth need not come from a more general theory.

Acknowledgements

This paper has been presented in the INEM conference in Xalapa, Mexico, and in the TINT seminar in Helsinki, Finland. Till Grüne-Yanoff, Jaakko Kuorikoski, Uskali Mäki, Luis Mireles-Flores, Samuli Pöyhönen and anonymous reviewers provided useful comments on earlier versions of the paper. The usual disclaimer applies.

Notes

1. The methodological argument that could justify this behavioural claim is attributable to Mill (2000 [1844], p.98), but he never used the 'as-if' locution to express it.

2. For the latest discussion on Friedman, see *The methodology of positive economics: Reflections on the Milton Friedman legacy* (ed. Uskali Mäki). Vaihinger's as-if account is discussed in Fine (1993), Mäki (2004), and Bokulich (2009), for example.

3. I am not arguing for this claim here. The reader is encouraged to find a case in which the as-if locution is necessary for formulating a claim. I have not found any such cases.

4. In most cases it is reasonable to interpret A as an object and B as a

property that the object could have. If only objects can behave in certain ways, A must be an object. However, B need not always be a property of that object, as I show in the section on negligibility-indicating as-if claims. Consider, for example, the claim that 'objects fall as if there were no air resistance'. The property of air resistance is relational because it requires reference to the surrounding circumstances (atmospheric pressure) in addition to the object itself. The formulation of AIC is deliberately silent on the interpretation of the terms in order to accommodate various different cases.

5. I add a caveat to this statement in the section on inaccuracy-indicating (a_1) as-if claims.

6. The reason for using attribution terminology is that property B is attributed to A. One might also say that 'B is predicated about A', or that 'A is identified as being B'. However, using the term 'attribution' seems more natural here.

7. According to Friedman (1953, pp.36-38), one can treat the same firm as if it were a perfect competitor on one question, and as if it were a monopoly on another. This example qualifies as an inaccuracy-indicating claim. Note that Kirman does not endeavour to justify the optimisation assumption, but rather ascribes the as-if justification to those who do. In fact, except for Friedman, I have not found examples of economic texts in which the inaccuracy- indicating as-if claim is made by the author who uses the corresponding assumption in a model. In contrast, MacDonald (2003) as well as Boylan and O'Gorman (1995) provide an example in which the inaccuracy-indicating as-if claim is attributed to others.

8. Another way of interpreting (a_1) is to say that it means 'people do *not* optimize, but that does not matter for the model results'. If this were to be the interpretation, there would be a semantic change after all. The as-if claim 'people behave as if they optimize' would then mean that the attribution 'People optimize' is false (but negligibly so). My intuitions are slightly in favour of the interpretation provided in the main text, but I am willing to be persuaded to think otherwise. Adopting this interpretation

would make analysing as-if claims more uniform with respect to semantic change but less uniform with respect to meaning. One would always have to look for a semantic change, but the meaning of the as-if claims would be the same only in cases a_2, b and c.

9. Friedman (1953, p.40) also provides an example of this kind of as-if claim. Becker (1962, p.5) writes 'Impulsive households are assumed to act "as if" they only consulted a probability mechanism.' It is not clear, however, what he means because he had already stated 'Therefore, households can be said to behave not only "as if" they were rational but also "as if" they were irrational (p.4).' Becker's lack of precision makes me wonder whether he intended to present an argument for rational choice theory (cf. Moscati & Tubaro, 2011).

10. Note that Friedman uses the term 'assumption' to mean what is called a 'claim' in this paper. If assumptions express propositions in models, one would say that 'the model assumes a vacuum but the modeller does not claim that we live in a vacuum'.

11. Note that Vaihinger distinguishes between *fictions* and *hypotheses* on the grounds that the former are known to be false whereas the latter are a matter of investigation.

12. Naturally, I agree with Mäki that epistemic uncertainty is consistent with realism. I am merely concerned to show that expressing such uncertainty by means of as-if locutions does not satisfy my pragmatic constraints. In this sense, it is not surprising that Mäki has not provided any concrete examples of such uses.

13. An anonymous reviewer suggested describing this example in terms of incorrect causes. It might be possible to generalise case (b) such that it concerns all false ascriptions of causes: 'A behaves as if it were governed by causal forces B'. This is clearly possible at least in principle, but given that I have only seen examples of (b) in which the false attribution concerns mental states, I hesitate to argue for this more general formulation. Similar considerations apply to case (c).

14. This aspect is even more evident in Machlup (1946).

15. Lehtinen's models are not intended to be realistic with respect to all aspects of behaviour. One major feature is that in his analyses of strategic behaviour he compares the case in which every voter engages in such behaviour to one in which nobody does so. What is presented here applies to voters *insofar as* they engage in strategic voting. In real life some voters engage in strategic behaviour and some do not. He relaxes this assumption, however, in Lehtinen (2010), but here is another sense in which the signal extraction model is not entirely realistic. It has been argued that voters systematically overestimate the winning chances of candidates they support, but the model implicitly assumes non-biased estimates. Note, however, that such biases could be taken into account, and if they were it would be via incorporating some parameters or functions into the formal model, and one would still have to use the as-if locution in presenting the computing part.

16. The instrumental usefulness of fictions could be taken as a reason why as-if locutions are used in case (b*). Given, however, that stating that a fiction is instrumentally useful does not really explain why it is, it is rather begging the question, and it might be better to state that Ma¨ki does not provide any reason for using the as-if locution in this case. It is because instrumental usefulness is question-begging that it is not included as a separate type of as-if claim, even though Friedman sometimes uses the as-if locution to indicate that a hypothesis is useful if it generates correct predictions (Friedman & Savage, 1948, p.298, 1952, p.473).

17. The original contribution of this section is limited to the role of as-if locutions in expected utility theory. The ideas presented here were first clearly formulated by Luce and Raiffa (1957), and similar arguments are presented in Kavka (1991) and Lehtinen and Kuorikoski (2007).

18. 'Eve is a maximiser' here is presupposed to mean that she satisfies the vNM conditions.

19. I, too, have been guilty of using this expression (Lehtinen & Kuorikoski, 2007, p.123).

References

Becker, G. S. (1962). Irrational behavior and economic theory. *Journal of Political Economy, 70*(1), 1-13.

Binmore, K. (1994). *Game theory and the social contract: Playing fair,* (Vol.1). Cambridge, MA: MIT Press.

Binmore, K. (1998). *Game theory and the social contract: Just playing,* (Vol.2). London: The MIT Press.

Binmore, K. (2005). *Natural justice.* Oxford: Oxford University Press. Binmore, K. (2009). *Rational decisions.* Princeton: Princeton University Press.

Bokulich, A. (2009). Explanatory fictions. In M. Sua'rez (Ed.), *Fictions in science: Philosophical essays on modeling and idealization* (pp.91-109). London: Routledge.

Boland, L. A. (1979). A critique of Friedman's critics. *Journal of Economic Literature, 17*(2), 503-522.

Boylan, T. A., & O'Gorman, P. F. (1995). *Beyond rhetoric and realism in economics: Towards a reformulation of economic methodology.* London: Routledge.

Coddington, A. (1979). Friedman's contribution to methodological controversy. *British Review of Economic Issues, 2*(4), 1-13.

Dennett, D. C. (1996). *Kinds of minds: Towards an understanding of consciousness.* London: Weidenfeld & Nicolson.

Downs, A. (1957). *An economic theory of democracy.* New York: Harper. Elgin, C. Z. (2004). True enough. *Philosophical Issues, 14*(1), 113-131.

Elgin, C. Z. (2009). Exemplification, idealization, and scientific understanding. In M. Sua'rez (Ed.), *Fictions in science: Philosophical essays on modeling and idealization* (pp.77-90). London: Routledge.

Enelow, J. M. (1981). Saving amendments, killer amendments, and an expected utility theory of sophisticated voting. *Journal of Politics, 43*(4), 1062-1089.

Fine, A. (1993). Fictionalism. *Midwest Studies in Philosophy,* XVIII, 1-18.

Friedman, M. (1953). The methodology of positive economics. *Essays in positive economics* (pp.3-43). Chicago: University of Chicago Press.

Friedman, M., & Savage, L. J. (1952). The expected-utility hypothesis and the measurability of utility. *Journal of Political Economy,* 60(6), 463-474.

Friedman, M., & Savage, L. J. (1948). The utility analysis of choices involving risk. *Journal of Political Economy,* 56(4), 279-304.

Hindriks, F. A. (2006). Tractability assumptions and the Musgrave-Ma¨ki typology. *Journal of Economic Methodology,* 13(4), 401-423.

Hoover, K. D. (2009). Milton Friedman's stance: The methodology of causal realism. In U. Ma¨ki (Ed.), *The methodology of positive economics: Reflections on the Milton Friedman legacy* (pp.303-320). Cambridge: Cambridge University Press.

Kavka, G. (1991). Rational maximizing in economic theories of politics. In K. R. Monroe (Ed.), *The economic approach to politics: A critical reassessment of the theory of rational action* (pp.371-385). New York: HarperCollins.

Kirman, A. P. (2006). Demand theory and general equilibrium: From explanation to introspection, a journey down the wrong road. *History of Political Economy,* 38, 246-280.

Kuorikoski, J., Lehtinen, A., & Marchionni, C. (2010). Economic modelling as robustness analysis.
British Journal for the Philosophy of Science, 61(3), 541-567.

Lagueux, M. (1994). Friedman's instrumentalism and constructive empiricism in economics. *Theory and Decision,* 37(2), 147-174.

Lehtinen, A. (2006). Signal extraction for simulated games with a large number of players.
Computational Statistics and Data Analysis, 50, 2495-2507.

Lehtinen, A. (2007). The welfare consequences of strategic voting in two commonly used parliamentary agendas. *Theory and Decision,* 63(1), 1-40.

Lehtinen, A. (2008). The welfare consequences of strategic behaviour under approval and plurality voting. *European Journal of Political Economy,* 24, 688-704.

Lehtinen, A. (2010). Behavioural heterogeneity under approval and plurality voting. In J. Laslier &

M. R. Sanver (Eds.), *Handbook on approval voting* (pp.285-310). Heidelberg: Springer. Lehtinen, A. (2011). A welfarist critique of social choice theory. *Journal of Theoretical Politics*, 23(3), 359-381.

Lehtinen, A., & Kuorikoski, J. (2007). Unrealistic assumptions in rational choice theory. *Philosophy of the Social Sciences,* 37(2), 115-138.

Luce, D. R., & Raiffa, H. (1957). *Games and decisions: Introduction and critical survey*. New York: Wiley.

MacDonald, P. K. (2003). Useful fiction or miracle maker: The competing epistemological foundations of rational choice theory. *American Political Science Review,* 97(4), 551-565.

Machlup, F. (1946). Marginal analysis and empirical research. *The American Economic Review,* 36(4), 519-554.

Ma̅ki, U. (1992). Friedman and realism. *Research in the History of Economic Thought and Methodology,* 10, 171-195.

Ma̅ki, U. (1998). As if. In J. B. Davis, D. W. Hands & U. Ma̅ki (Eds.), *The handbook of economic methodology* (pp.25-27). Cheltenham: Edward Elgar.

Ma̅ki, U. (2000). Kinds of assumptions and their truth: Shaking an untwisted F-twist. *Kyklos,* 53(3), 317-335.

Ma̅ki, U. (2003). 'The methodology of positive economics' (1953) does not give us the methodology of positive economics. *Journal of Economic Methodology,* 10(4), 495-505.

Ma̅ki, U. (2004). Realism and the nature of theory: A lesson from J H Von Thu̅nen for economists and geographers. *Environment & Planning A,* 36(10), 1719-1736.

Ma̅ki, U. (2009). Unrealistic assumptions and unnecessary confusions: Rereading and rewriting F53 as a realist statement. In U. Ma̅ki (Ed.), *The methodology of positive economics. Reflections on the Milton Friedman legacy* (pp.90-116). Cambridge: Cambridge University Press.

McKelvey, R. D., & Ordeshook, P. C. (1972). A general theory of the calculus of voting. In J. F. Herndon & J. L. Bernd (Eds.), *Mathematical applications in political science,* (Vol.IV), (pp.32-78). Charlottesville: The

University Press of Virginia.

McQuarrie, D. A., & Simon, J. D. (1997). *Physical chemistry: A molecular approach*. Sausalito: University Science Books.

Mill, J. S. (2000 [1844]). *Essays on some unsettled questions of political economy* (2nd ed.).

Kitchener: Batoche Books.

Morrison, M. (2009). Fictions, representations, and reality. In M. Sua′rez (Ed.), *Fictions in science: Philosophical essays on modeling and idealization* (pp.110-135). London: Routledge.

Moscati, I., & Tubaro, P. (2011). Becker random behavior and the as-if defense of rational choice theory in demand analysis. *Journal of Economic Methodology,* 18(2), 107-128.

Musgrave, A. (1981). 'Unreal assumptions' in economic theory: The F-twist untwisted. *Kyklos,* 34(3), 377-387.

Røgeberg, O., & Nordberg, M. (2005). A defence of absurd theories in economics. *Journal of Economic Methodology,* 12(4), 543-562.

Satz, D., & Ferejohn, J. A. (1994). Rational choice and social theory. *Journal of Philosophy,* 91(2), 71-87.

Sen, A. K. (1973). Behaviour and the concept of preference. *Economica,* 40(159), 241-259. Strevens, M. (2008). *Depth: An account of scientific explanation*. Cambridge, MA: Harvard University Press.

Teller, P. (2009). Fictions, fictionalization, and truth in science. In M. Sua′rez (Ed.), *Fictions in science: Philosophical essays on modeling and idealization* (pp.235-247). London: Routledge.

Vromen, J. J. (2009). Friedman's selection argument revisited. In U. Ma¨ki (Ed.), *The methodology of economics. Reflections on the Milton Friedman legacy* (pp.257-284). Cambridge: Cambridge University Press.

方法论个体主义、结构限制和社会复杂性

佛兰西斯科·迪·爱奥里奥[*]

一、方法论个体主义的两个变种

方法论个体主义在社会科学哲学的某些领域中具有很不好的名声，因为人们通常认为它和还原论有紧密关系，还原论意味着用原子理论来看待社会，其错误在于它幼稚地否定了社会世界的系统性特征，以及社会文化因素施加在个体身上的结构性限制。尽管这种看法很流行，但是从还原论角度对方法论个体主义的解释必须被拒绝，因为被社会契约论和一些原子式经济学理论所规定的还原论仅仅是一种更为简单的方法论个体主义的种类（参见 Boettke 2012，p.147；Boettke and Candela 2015；Demeulenaere 2011，p.11；Di Iorio 2015，pp.89-92；2016；Hayek 1948 pp.1-32；Jarvie 2001，pp.117 ff.；Manzo 2014，p.21；Tuomela 1990）。这一理论变种受到了另一种非还原论理论变种的批评和挑战。非还原论理论变种来源于苏格兰启蒙运动，包括了来自不同学派的学者，比如韦伯、门格、齐美尔、斯宾塞、米塞斯、哈耶克、波普尔、沃特金斯、默顿、克洛泽和布东。

方法论个体主义的第二个变种认为，个体主义一整体主义论争与当前普遍所接受的看法相反，同还原论和反还原论的对立没有关系。个体主义和整体主义论争不如说是非原子式的人类自治理论（这个理论同"看不见的手"解释模型和将社会世界看作系统的概念紧密联系在一起）和社会文化他治理论之间的对立（参见 Boudon 2013，p.25；Di Iorio 2015，p.75 ff.）。

---

[*] 佛兰西斯科·迪·爱奥里奥（Francesco Di Iorio），南开大学哲学院科技哲学教研室副教授，研究方向为科学技术哲学。此文由南开大学胡军副教授译，博士生向原校。

波普尔提到了一个解释历史的"有神论"，这种观点认为历史和社会秩序可以归因于隐秘的超人力量，个人则是这些隐秘力量的无意图的工具。在方法论个体主义的非还原论理论变种中，"整体主义"意味着波普尔所言之"有神论"的一个世俗化版本。根据这种理解，整体主义是一种植根于黑格尔和孔德的历史哲学，并为各种社会学和哲学流派所发展的观念，这种观念认为社会科学研究的要紧的和恰当的对象是无意图之社会决定因素的机制，这种机制可以控制个人，并且将社会锻造为一个有组织的结构（Antiseri and Pellicani 1995；Antiseri 2007；Boudon 2013；Cubeddu 1993；Dawe 1970；Di Nuoscio 2016；Watkins 1957）。相比之下，方法论个体主义的非还原论变种认为个人是自我决定的存在，社会秩序，以及更一般意义上的社会现象必须被看作大范围内人类行动的无意图结果，在将人类（使用解释方法）赋予行动的意义纳入考虑范围的基础上，人类行动是可以解释的。根据这种观点，社会现象的终极原因必须从个人，而不是个人之外加以寻找这一事实并不意味着不存在社会限制，只是因为人类行动来源于解释技能，所以社会限制的解释建立在如下假定基础上，即社会环境的影响从来不是机械性的，而是受到这些解释技能的调节。（参见 Bronner 2007，pp.166-167；Boudon and Bourricaud 1990，p.13 ff.；Di Iorio 2015，pp.98-115）。

很多非还原论的个体主义者（例如 Mises［1949］1998 42-45；Hayek 1952，p.54；Popper 1966a，pp.26 ff.，204 ff.）强调，在解释行动和社会现象的终极原因方面，整体主义和个体主义的对立必须被看作是和集体名词的本体论冲突紧密相关的。按照这些学者的看法，方法论个体主义以一元论术语来解释指涉社会实体（比如欧盟单一市场、美国民主党、英国军队和天主教堂等等）的集体名词。这意味着尽管集体名词在语义上不能被还原为严格的单个属性，但是它们也不是独立的物质，或者独特的实体，例如像一块石头或者一棵树那样独立存在的个体。集体名词不如说指的是从它们的存在、它们的信念、它们的意图和它们的互动中产生出来的单一的、系统的和无法还原的属性（参见 Dawe 1970；Di Iorio 2015；Di Nuoscio 2016；Nadeau 2003；Petitot 2012；Rainone 1990；Tuomela 1989；Zahale 2015）。相反，非还原论个体主义者所理解的，并被他们批评的整体主义本体论是一种柏拉图式的实在论。这种观点假设因为集体名词指的是柏拉图式的超个体物质（比如法国结构主义者所理解的"结构"），所以个体及其行动是这种结构的派生物，这意味着从本体的和解释的观点看个体是不重要的。

基于以上看法，一元论和实在论的本体对立严格地同个体自治和整体他治之间的方法论对立紧密相关。如果集体名词从一元论角度进行理解，那么社会科学的对象就是个体（以及与一系列个体相关的属性），并且行动的原因必须到个体那里寻找，例如个体的观点和信念。相反，如果集体名词从实在论角度加以理解，社会科学的对象就是超个体的柏拉图式的物质，行动的终极原因要到个体之外去寻找。（Antiseri and Pellicani 1995；Pribam 2008，p.120）

二、唯心主义还原论和语义还原论

方法论个体主义所批评的整体主义观点直到过去几十年仍然是很有影响力的，不过今天它不再被认为是有吸引力的，并且很大程度上被拒绝。但是，方法论个体主义也不如从前流行了，主要是因为整个个体主义传统和原子主义，以及还原论纠缠在一起了。大多数方法论个体主义的当代批评者拒绝整体主义的他治观念，但是，他们认为整体主义具有部分正确性，因为不同于方法论个体主义，整体主义是反对还原论的，并且坚持社会世界的系统观念（例如，Bunge 1996；Kincaid 1986，1996，2014；Little 2014；Pettit 1993；Sawyer 2002，2003；Udehn 2001）。结果，他们站在了一个整体主义和个体主义的中间地带，例如将这两种范式"综合"起来，将反还原论的立场（这是一种典型的整体主义特征，为方法论个体主义所拒斥）和一种人类自治的理论整合起来。这种综合有时候被称为"结构个体主义"（Udehn 2001，p.318）。

以这样一种新的结构化（和反还原论的）个体主义的名义而开展的反对传统个体主义的广泛倾向似乎建立在了一种对个体主义的错误的和简单化的理解之上。其原因如德默勒纳尔（Demeulenaere 2011，第11页）所强调，方法论个体主义者，或者至少是大多数方法论个体主义者"都为如下观点作出辩护，即个人'嵌入'在可以被称为'社会结构'的社会情境中，绝不是在社会真空中独立游动的原子"。（同上）"结构化个体主义从一开始就内在于方法论个体主义，而同一些经济原子主义相对立。"（同上）在非还原的个体主义那里，制度和规则很明显地"对个人行动发生影响"，尽管它们"自身没有直接的'能量'"（同上；同时参见

Demeulenaere 2012，第 25-26 页）。

对"还原论"的指控也同样作用于整个个体主义传统，这种指控在当前十分广泛，表现为两个理论变种。第一个将方法论个体主义解释为唯心主义还原论，第二个将之解释为语义还原论。（Di Iorio 2015，pp.103 ff；2016）根据唯心主义还原论框架对方法论个体主义的理解（例如，Archer 1995；Bhaskar 1979；Lawson 1997；Udehn 2001），方法论个体主义之所以是错误的，是因为它否定了社会结构，以及这种社会结构对能动者所产生的限制的客观存在。方法论个体主义之所以被解释成这种形式，是因为它所持的如下观点，即解释社会现象必须通过理解个体赋予行动的意义来实现，例如通过解释方法。（verstehen approach）方法论个体主义被认为坚持如下观念，即社会系统和社会限制必须被还原为纯粹主观的思维结构。并且，方法论个体主义之所以是错误的，是因为这个系统和这些限制是独立存在于行动者的意见（比如个体的主观观点）之外的。换句话说，方法论个体主义被看作一种有关社会世界的反实在论，这种观点将世界解释成纯粹的思维创造，否定客观的社会结构，例如一系列规则、惩戒措施和社会位置，真实地存在于行动者头脑之外，否定客观的社会结构能造成他人的意志力（voluntarist power）受到约束。方法论个体主义等同于如下观点：社会世界或者社会条件都不能被看作客观现实和有效的限制（详见 King 2004；Di Iorio 2016）。

对方法论个体主义的这种批评似乎是不公平的。因为这种理论，至少其非还原论的变种承认，从社会学的观点看，个体的和纯粹主观的信念"多多少少是无关的"，因为它们"不是社会生活的基础"。[①]（King 2004，第190页）

方法论个体主义将社会世界和施加在能动者身上的限制解释为"集体信念"，以及与这些"集体信念"相关的无意图的后果（unintended consequences）（Doudon 1971；Di Iorio 2015，第 104 页）。换句话说，方法论个体主义在分析社会生活和社会条件的基础的时候，不是将解释方法直接应用于纯粹的个体和主观意见上，而是将这种方法应用于"主体间性"

---

① King（2004）为韦伯和其他解释传统的显著代表人物发展起来的解释方法进行辩护，不同意巴斯卡（Bhaskar）和其他批判实在论者对解释方法的批判。他没有像我这样把解释方法称为"方法论个体主义"。但是，他对于社会科学的哲学和方法论假设的观点的本质和我的观点没有什么差别。在我看来，他支持的观点同我上边所称的"方法论个体主义的非还原论变种"是一致的。

的世界上（Schutz 1967，第 218 页），例如被广泛共享的意义，并且，它聚焦于这些共享意义的真实的和具体的结果，这些结果有时可以对行为能动者施加冷酷的客观限制。如同哈耶克（Hayek 1952）所指出的，社会系统必须被看作"很多人持有某些观点（所产生的）作用效果"。从方法论个体主义的观点看，理解行为能动者赋予其行动的那种典型意义是理解社会结构和社会限制的"无意图的或者未事前设计的"本质的第一步（Hayek 1952，第 25 页）。就此而言，我们可以推出，方法论个体主义不可被等同于反实在论或者唯心主义理论，这两种理论都假定结构限制仅仅是单个人的主观创造产物，以及能动者的自由意志是不受限制的。根据方法论个体主义理论，因为社会世界不能被还原为纯粹个人关于社会世界是什么的观念，因此社会世界不能被个人意志随意地改变。相反，社会世界及其给行为能动者施加的限制只能是在多数人共享的观念发生变化之后才能够被改变（参见 King 2014；Di Iorio 2016）。

　　方法论个体主义的第二种还原论解释变种是语义主义还原论。根据这个理论变种，方法论个体主义的主张，即社会现象必须从个体的层面进行解释，意味着这种理论支持将社会属性从语义上还原为个体属性的原则（参见 Rainone 1990，第 169 页之后；Petroni 1991，第 16 页；Zahale and Collin 2014，第 2-10 页；Di Iorio 2016，2015）。这种在分析哲学传统中发展起来的方法论个体主义理论得到了曼德尔鲍姆（Mandelbaum 1995）、卢卡斯（Lukes 1973）、鲁本（Ruben 1985）、金凯德（Kincaid 1986，1990）、李丹（Little 1990）、索耶（Sawyer 2002，2003）和埃尔德-瓦斯（Elder-Vass 2014）等人的支持。表现为语义还原论的方法论个体主义在如下要点上受到批评：（1）如果不借助于无法在语义上还原为严格个体属性的概念和法则，社会现象就无法得到解释；（2）不能否认在语义上无法还原的因素和法则的存在，这些因素和法则对心灵和行动的影响具有因果关系。方法论个体主义的这种语义还原论解释似乎是不合情理的：（1）因为很多方法论个体主义的知名拥护者，比如我在前边所称的"非还原论理论变种"的代表人物，都明确地批评了这种还原论；（2）因为方法论个体主义的历史提供了大量与"系统"和"人类行动的无意图后果"等概念相关的解释模式，它们都同语义还原论不一致。（Boettke and Candela 2015；Di Iorio 2016，第 105 页）

　　如同布东（Boudon 1971，第 1-4 页）和波普尔（Popper 1957，第 82

页）所阐述的，从非还原论的方法论个体主义角度看，将社会属性在语义上还原为严格的个体属性是不可能的，这一点十分正确。这两位思想家都同意，社会解释如果不借助于语义上不可还原的社会属性的情形是不存在的，从不可还原的属性来分析社会现象是必要的，也是不可避免的。哈耶克（Hayek 1967，第 70 页）发展了对原子论和还原论的批评，他也遵循了类似的推理路线。他认为，一个社会"比组成这个社会的部分之总和要多"，因为它是一个系统，这个系统的特征是由各种突现的（emergent）属性界定的，并且系统存在的前提是它的构成要素"以某种特定方式相互关联"（同上；另参见 Lewis 2011，2014）。在哈耶克之前，对哈耶克有重大影响的卡尔·门格（Carl Menger）指出，根据方法论个体主义，个体的意图和行动必须被看作某个不可还原的结构的一部分（参见 Antiseri 2007，第 141页；Campagnolo 2013）。门格（[1883]1985，第 142 页）指出，"社会结构，相对于它的组成部分是更高一级的单位"。再者，社会结构被赋予了"功能"，这些功能"是社会结构在整体上的至关重要的表达"（第 139 页）。根据门格（同上，第 147 页）的意见，社会是一个系统，因为它的每一个组成部分——每一个个体或者每一个社会亚系统（比如一个家庭或者企业）——"服务于社会整体的典型功能，构成社会整体的条件，并影响它；反过来组成部分同样受到社会整体的典型本质和典型功能的决定和影响"。

方法论个体主义被解释为语义还原论之所以应该被拒绝的原因之一是这种解释和无意图结果这个概念（参见 Boettke and Candela，2015；Boudon 2013；Bouvier 2011；Di Iorio，第 106 页；Dupuy 2004；Petitot 2012）存在强烈关联。从无意图的结果这个角度开展的理论解释同语义还原论是不一致的，因为前者所依据的是新出现的全球属性，这种全球属性无法还原为纯粹心理的和个体的属性与法则。这种理论解释也无法还原为行为能动者的思维和行为属性。哈耶克将市场解释为一个自组织系统就是一个给予无意图结果的个体主义非还原论解释（参见 Hayek 1948，第 77 页及后页；同前，1952；Bouvier 2011）。再者，它也揭示出哈耶克所认同的方法论个体主义承认了社会性的突现的属性（emergent properties）的存在，这种社会性的突现属性在因果关系上影响了行动，限制了人类自由。我们以哈耶克的价格理论为例，价格理论是哈耶克市场自组织理论的核心，哈耶克和米塞斯（Mises）一样主张市场价格在市场合作中发挥关键作用（Hayek 1948，第 85 页及后页；Mises [1922]1981）。价格是不同的个体评估和分散信息聚合起来产生的无意图的结果。因为这种无意图的本质，价格在语义上是无法还原的。根据哈耶克（和 Mises）的意见，价格所具有的协调力量取决于如下事实，价格影响和限制了能动者的选择自由，能动者需要让自己的决策符合价格的变化。哈耶克强调价格是人类选择无意图地创造出来的，价格又反过来影响到人类的选择，例如，整个经济体系对它的组成部分有因果关系上的影响，反之亦然。（参见 Di Iorio 2016）

　　方法论个体主义的语义还原论解释产生于对如下个体主义观点的错误理解，即社会现象必须从个体的角度加以解释（参见 Jarvie 1972，第 157 页；DiIorio 2015，第 107-108 页；同前，2016）。这个观点往往同社会现象必须从语义上还原为严格的个体属性和法则的观念相混淆。但是，就"从个体的角度所作的解释"而言，方法论个体主义的非还原论解释并不意味着社会现象必须通过这样一种还原加以解释，而是某些完全不同的东西。它意味着社会科学必须拒斥在集体名词上所持有的那种整体的实体主义的本体论观念（holistic substantialist ontology），以及在历史和社会的解释模式上所持有的同这种本体观念紧密相关的他治观念（heteronomy）。方法论个体主义的非还原论解释认为，个体是历史和社会机制的终极动力，并且，它对于社会系统及其在语义上不可还原的属性的解释是从反实体主义的角度展开的，比如个体所创造的无意图结果、他们的信念、行动和互动（详见 Di Iorio 2016，第 105-111 页；DiNuoscio 2016；Manzo 2014，第 21 页；McGinley 2012；Rainone 2002；Tuomela 1990，第 34 页；Watkins 1957）。

三、复杂性方法论个体主义

　　COSMOS+TAXIS 这一期专刊致力于非还原论的方法论个体主义，从历史的和方法论的角度分析它的本质和启发。它反对占据主导地位的理论假设，即社会科学家因为哲学和系统理论所提供的反对还原论的压倒性主张而需要消除个体主义传统，并发展替代性理论。一个基本假设是，将方法论个体主义和还原论等同起来的倾向无论从历史的角度还是逻辑的角度都是站不住脚的，从而反对后者的主张并不能削弱前者。

　　很多文章关注非还原论个体主义的一个特定的次级理论，法国哲学家让-皮埃尔·杜佩（Jean-Pierre Dupuy，1922；同前，2004）称为"复杂性方法论个体主义"。这一次级理论不同于其他非还原论个体主义理论，例如韦伯、阿隆（Aron）和布东等为代表的解释社会学，以及波普尔及其学生所捍卫的个体主义社会哲学，将方法论个体主义的概念和自组织复杂系统的概念（参见 Dupuy and Dumouchel 1983；Petitot 2009、2012）融合在一起[①]。它的优先研究对象——当然不是唯一的对象——是市场社会及其文化的和演化的前提条件。哈耶克是复杂性方法论个体主义理论的最杰出支持者，它强调这种理论的起源应当追溯到苏格兰启蒙运动，例如曼德维尔（Bernard De Mandeville）、亚当·斯密（Adam Smith）、亚当·弗格森（Adam Ferguson）和大卫·休谟（David Hume）这些人的著作。这些思想家用自发的秩序和看不见的手来解释市场社会，从复杂性科学和系统理论中使用的复杂自组织系统来预测解释方法。除了哈耶克和苏格拉启蒙运动的思想家，复杂性方法论个体主义的其他重要理论家还有阿克顿勋爵（Lord Acton）、赫伯特·斯宾塞（HerbertSpencer），以及奥地利经济学派的成员，比如卡尔·门格和路德维希·冯·米塞斯。根据哈耶克的看法，即使哲学和经济学中自发秩序理论的代表没有使用复杂性科学的术语和"复杂自组织系统"这一词组（这些术语和词组只是在相对晚近才创造出来），他们也基本上采用了和这些科学相似的观点，因此必须被看作先行者。哈耶克强调，将这些新术语运用于"看不见的手"这一传统的个体主义理论具有启发效用，因为这些新术语更加精确、清晰和准确。

根据复杂性方法论个体主义，市场社会必须被解释为一个复杂的自组织系统，因为从其初始条件以持续的和无法预测的方式作出变化这个角度看，市场社会是非常开放的系统，它包含了大量的具有操作自主性的构成要素（行为能动者），在自发的过程中，这些行为能动者的行动是动态协调的。市场社会没有主导性方向。众多行为能动者之间的合作与协调取决于他们对于一些普遍的和抽象的规则的服从，这些规则控制着众多行为能动者之间的直接互动，并且促成了市场价格的形成（参见 Birner 1994，第 2 页及之后；Hayek 1973，第 34 页及之后；Marsh and Onof 2008；Nemo 1988；Petitot 2012）。在市场中，价格以控制论机制发挥作用，因为价格所体现的

---

① 需要注意的是，韦伯（第 63 页及之后）在《经济与社会》第一本书中使用了复杂性这个概念来批评计划经济。进而，波普尔（1957，第 36-40 页）也提及了这个概念，强调了它在社会科学中的重要性，尽管他没有关注这个概念的细节。结果，复杂的方法论个体主义和其他非还原论个体主义变种之间的区别没有得到清晰的解释。

信息是无数本地的和短暂的环境状况，并且确保了分散化知识在促成行为能动者之间的协调上发挥作用（参见 Hayek 1948，第 77 页及之后）。系统所具有的突现的全球行为是无意图发展出来的结果，其显著特征是它是一个动态的和持续的从本地到全球，从全球到本地的适应过程。换句话说，它建立在一个个人与价格之间的递归循环之上，价格是人类决策无意图地产生的结果，它转而又影响到人类决策（参见 Boettke and Candela 2015；Dupuy 2004）。这种全球行为只是在一般模式下可以预测，相反，则因为系统的复杂性（例如系统的极端开放性）在细节上无法加以预测。这种复杂性造成初始条件的持续的和无法预测的变化，并且这种复杂性同组成系统的众多行为能动者的操作自主性，以及这些行为能动者的情景化知识的变化相关。"其他条件不变"的严格运用对于精致的预测来说是必要的，它只有在一个假设的闭合系统中才是可能的，但是这一点对于一个复杂的自组织系统而言是不可能的（参见 Di Iorio 2015，第 42-43 页；Dupuy 1990；Petitot 2012；DiNuoscio 2016；Caldwell 2007，第 363 页；2009，第 13 页及之后）[1]。因为市场建立在自发整合基础上，自发整合遵循适应的和演化的理性，例如，因为市场的复杂性无法被掌握，所以计划经济不能奏效，注定招致失败。借助于自组织方式，市场体系使用分散化的知识体系，分散化的知识体系是没有中心的。

我将通过对术语的评论来结束本文。"复杂的方法论个体主义"这一术语指的是非还原的方法论个体主义的一个特定变种，它有助于将这种特定变种同还原论的个体主义和其他非还原论的方法论个体主义变种区分开来。它的有用性部分地依赖于学界在一般性术语"方法论个体主义"的含义上存在的普遍混乱，例如将这一术语的使用等同于"还原论"的倾向。由于这些混乱，以及方法论个体主义的不同变种和亚变种的存在，使用"方法论个体主义"这个一般性术语来指代自发秩序这个理论传统的方法论假

---

① 尽管哈耶克是复杂性理论的创始人之一，但是他没有给"复杂性"概念提出一个好的定义（参见 Di Iorio 2015；Dupuy 1990；Petitot 2002；Di Nuoscio 2006；Caldwell 2009）。哈耶克（1967）认为，"复杂性"来自这样一种事实，即某些系统的行为是极难预测的（除了一些普遍化模式），因为它由大量的变量决定。但是，如果这些系统是封闭的，由大量变量构成的系统也可以被完美预测。哈耶克给复杂性下的定义没有考虑到他自己有关市场和心灵的著作所强调的观点，例如可以影响到复杂系统的初始条件所发生的持续的和无法预测的变化，这些系统是十分开放的系统（Hayek 1952b，第 185 页及之后；1967，第 55 页及之后；亦参见 Nadeau 1997，第 67 页及之后；Caldwell 2004，第 363 页及之后；Di Nuoscio 2006，第 46-48 页；Marsh 2010，第 140-141 页）。

设，尽管是正确的，但是相较于"复杂的方法论个体主义"这一术语却是信息含量低的和不够准确的。①

参考文献：

[1] Antiseri, D. and Pellicani, L. (1995). *L'individualismo metodologico. Una polemica sul mestiere dello scienziato sociale.* Milan: Franco Angeli.

[2] Antiseri, D. (2007). *Popper's Vienna.* Aurora, CO: The Davies Group Publishers.

[3] Archer, M. (1995). *Realist Social Theory: The Morphogenetic Approach.* Cambridge: Cambridge University Press.

[4] Bhaskar, R. (1979). *The Possibility of Naturalism.* Sussex: Harvester.

[5] Birner, J. (1992). Hayek's Grand Research Program. In: *Birner J. and Van Zijp R. (Eds.), Hayek, Co-ordination and Evolution: His Legacy in Philosophy, Politics, Economics and the History of Ideas.* London and New York: Routledge.

[6] Boettke, P. (2012). *Living Economics. Yesterday, Today, and Tomorrow.* Oakland, CA: The Independent Institute.

[7] Boettke, P. and Candela, R. A. (2015). What Is Old Should Be New Again: Methodological Individualism, Institutional Analysis and Spontaneous Order. *Sociologia* 2: 5-14.

[8] Boudon, R. (1971). *Uses of Structuralism.* London: Heinemann.

[9] Boudon, R., and Bourricaud, F. (1990). *A Critical Dictionary of Sociology.* Chicago: University of Chicago Press.

[10] Boudon, R. (2013). *Sociology as Science: An Intellectual Autobiography.* Oxford: The Bardwell Press.

[11] Bouvier, A. (2011). Individualism, collective agency and the "micro-macro relation." In: *The Sage Handbook of the Philosophy of Social Sciences,* J. C. Jarvie, and J. Zamora Bonilla (Eds.), London: Sage Publications.

---

① 我在此感谢 David Anderson 和 Leslie Marsh 邀请我编辑 *COSMOS + TAXIS* 杂志本期的专刊，并感谢所有本期专刊的作者。我也感谢所有的审稿人。此外，我还要感谢 Gianluca Cavallo，他慷慨地同意将他的画作 *L'iride* 复制到本期专刊的封面。

〔12〕Bronner, G. (2007). *L'Empire de l'erreur. Eléments de sociologie cognitive*. Paris: Puf.

〔13〕Bunge, M. (1996). *Finding philosophy in social science*. New Haven and London: Yale University Press.

〔14〕Caldwell, B. (2007). *Hayek's challenge: An intellectual biography of F. A. Hayek*. Chicago: University of Chicago Press.

〔15〕Caldwell, B. (2009). Some Comments on Lawson's Reorienting Economics: Same Facts, Different Conclusions. In: Edward Fullbrook (Ed.) *Ontology and Economics: Tony Lawson and His Critics*. London and New York: Routledge.

〔16〕Campagnolo, G. (2013). *Criticisms of Classical Political Economy: Menger, Austrian Economics and the German Historical School*. London/ New York: Routledge.

〔17〕Cubeddu, R. (1993). *The Philosophy of the Austrian School*. London and New York: Routledge.

〔18〕Dawe, A. (1970). The two sociologies. *British Journal of Sociology* 21(June): 207-218.

〔19〕Demeulenaere, P. (ed.). (2011). *Analytical Sociology and Social Mechanisms*. Cambridge: Cambridge University Press.

〔20〕Di Iorio, F. (2015). *Cognitive Autonomy and Methodological Individualism: The Interpretative Foundations of Social Life*. Berlin and New York: Springer.

〔21〕Di Iorio, F. (2016), World 3 and Methodological Individualism in Popper's Thought", *Philosophy of the Social Sciences*. DOI: 10.1177/004839 3116642992, 2016, pp.1-23.

〔22〕Di Nuoscio, E. (2016). *Philosophy of Social Sciences*. Oxford: The Bardwell Press.

〔23〕Dupuy, J.-P. (1990). *Ordres et désordres. Enquête sur un nouveau paradigme*. Paris: Seuil.

〔24〕Dupuy, J-P. (1992) *Le sacrifice et l'envie*. Paris: Calmann-Lévy.

〔25〕Dupuy, J-P. and Dumouchel, P. (Eds.). (1983). *L' Auto-Organisation de la Physique au Politique*. Paris: Seuil.

［26］Dupuy, J-P. (2004). Vers l'unité des sciences sociales autour de l'individualisme méthodologique complexe. *Revue du MAUSS* 24(2): 310-328.

［27］Elder-Vass, D. (2014). Social entities and the basis of their powers. In: *Rethinking the Individualism-Holism debate. Essays in the philosophy of social science,* eds. J. Zahle and F. Collin. Berlin and New York: Springer.

［28］Hayek, F. A. (1948). *Individualism and Economic Order.* Chicago: University of Chicago Press.

［29］Hayek, F. A. (1952). *The Counter-Revolution of Science: Studies on the Abuse of Reason.* Indianapolis: Liberty Press.

［30］Hayek, F. A. (1967). *Studies in Philosophy, Politics and Economics.* Chicago: University of Chicago Press.

［31］Hayek, F. A. (1973). *Law, Legislation and Liberty, Vol.1: Rules and Order.* Chicago: University of Chicago Press.

［32］Jarvie, I. C. (1972). *Concepts and Society.* London: Routledge & Kegan Paul.

［33］Jarvie, I. C. (2001). *The republic of science: The emergence of Popper's social view of science 1935-1945.* Amsterdam and Atlanta: Rodopi.

［34］King, A. (2004). *The structure of social theory.* London: Routledge.

［35］Kincaid, H. (1986). Reduction, explanation, and individualism. *Philosophy of Science* 53(4) (December): 492-513.

［36］Kincaid, H. (1990). Eliminativism and methodological individualism. *Philosophy of Science* 57(1)(March): 141-148.

［37］Laurent, A. (1994). *L'individualisme méthodologique,* Paris: Puf.

［38］Lawson, T. (1997). *Economics and Reality.* London and New York: Routledge.

［39］Lewis, P. (2012). *Emergent Properties in the Work of Friedrich Hayek. Journal of Economic Behavior & Organization* 82: 268-378.

［40］Lewis, P. (2015). *Notions of Order and Process in Hayek: the Significance of Emergence.* Cambridge Journal of Economics, 39: 1167-1190.

［41］Little, D. (1990). *Varieties of social explanation: An introduction to the philosophy of social science.* Boulder: Westview Press.

［42］Lukes, S. (1973). *Individualism.* New York: Harper & Row.

［43］Mandelbaum, M. (1955). Societal facts. *British Journal of Sociology* 6(4) December: 305-317.

［44］Manzo, G. (2014). A*nalytical sociology: Actions and networks.* Chichester: Wiley.

［45］Marsh, L. and Onof, C. (2008). Stigmergic epistemology, stigmergic cognition. *Cognitive Systems Research* 9: 136-149.

［46］Marsh, L. (2010). Hayek: Cognitive scientist avant la lettre. *Advances in Austrian Economics* 13:115-155.

［47］McGinley, W. (2012). Reduction in Sociology. *Philosophy of the Social Sciences* 42(3) September: 370-398.

［48］Menger, C. (［1871］2004). *Principles of Economics.* Auburn: The Ludwig von Mises Institute.

［49］Menger, C. (［1883］1985). *Investigations into the method of the social sciences with special reference to economics.* New York and London: New York University Press.

［50］Mises, L. (［1922］1981). *Socialism: An economic and sociological analysis.* New York: Liberty Fund.

［51］Mises, L. (［1949］1998). *Human action: A treatise on economics.* Auburn: The Ludwig von Mises Institute.

［52］Nadeau, R. (1997). Hayek and the complex affair of the mind. Sixty-seventh Annual Conference of the Southern Economic Association, Atlanta, 21-23 November.

［53］Nadeau, R. (2003). Cultural evolution true and false: A debunking of Hayek's critics. *Proceedings of 7th ESHET Conference,* Paris, 30 January-1 February.

［54］Nemo, P. (1988). *La société de droit selon Hayek.* Paris: Puf.

［55］Petitot, J. (2009). *Per un nuovo Illuminismo.* Milan: Bompiani.

［56］Petitot, J. (2012). "Individualisme méthodologique et évolution culturelle". In Un austriaco in Italia. *Studi in onore di Dario Antiseri,* eds. E. De Mucci and K. R. Leube. Soveria Mannelli: Rubbettino.

［57］Petroni, A. M. (1991). L'individualisme méthodologique. *Journal des Economistes et des Études Humaines.* 2(1): pages

［58］Popper, K. R. (1957). *The Poverty of Historicism.* Boston: Beacon Press.

［59］Popper, K. R. (［1945a］1966a). *The Open Society and Its Enemies,* Vol.1: The Spell of Plato. Princeton: Princeton University Press.

［60］Popper, K. R. (［1945b］1966b). *The Open Society and Its Enemies,* Vol.2: Hegel and Marx. Princeton: Princeton University Press.

［61］Pribram, K. (2008). La genesi della filosofia sociale individualistica. In: *L'individualismo nelle scienze sociali,* ed. E. Grillo. Rubbettino: Soveria Mannelli.

［62］Rainone, A. (1990). *Filosofia analitica e scienze storico-sociali.* Rome: ETS.

［63］Ruben, D-H. (1985). *The metaphysics of the social world.* London: Routledge & Kegan Paul.

［64］Schütz, A. (1967). *The phenomenology of the social world.* Evanston: Northwestern University Press.

［65］Tuomela, R. (1989). Ruben and the metaphysics of the social world. *The British Journal for the Philosophy of Science.* 40(2): 261-273.

［66］Tuomela, R. (1990). Methodological individualism and explanation. *Philosophy of Science* 57(1): 133-140.

［67］Udehn, L. (2001). *Methodological individualism: Background, history and meaning.* London and New York: Routledge.

［68］Sawyer, R. K. (2002). Nonreductive individualism. Part I—Supervenience and wild disjunction. *Philosophy of the Social Sciences* 32(4): 537-559.

［69］Sawyer, R. K. (2003). Nonreductive individualism. Part II—Social causation. *Philosophy of the Social Sciences* 33(2): 203-224.

［70］Watkins, J. W. N. (1952b). The principle of methodological individualism. *The British Journal for the Philosophy of Science* 3(10): 186-189.

［71］Watkins, J. W. N. (1957). Historical explanation in the social sciences. *The British Journal for the Philosophy of Science* 8(30): 104-117.

［72］Weber, M. (1978). *Economy and Society: An Outline of Interpretive*

Sociology, Volume I. Los Angeles: University of California Press.

[73] Zahle, J. and Collin, F. (eds.). (2014). *Rethinking the individualism-Holism debate. Essays in the philosophy of science.* Berlin and New York: Springer.

[74] Zahle, J. (2014). *Holism, emergence, and the crucial distinction.* In: Zahle and F. Collin (2014).

（本文原载于 *Cosmos* 2016 年第 3 期）

附：Methodological Individualism, Structural Constraints, and Social Complexity

TWO VARIANTS OF METHODOLOGICAL INDIVIDUALISM

Methodological individualism does not have a good reputation in some sectors of the philosophy of social science because it is often regarded as committed to reductionism, where reductionism means an atomistic theory of society that is mistaken because it naively denies both the systemic nature of the social world and the structural constraints imposed on the individuals by sociocultural factors. Despite its popularity, the interpretation of methodological individualism in terms of reductionism must be rejected because reductionis—which has been theorized by the social contract theory and some atomistic economic approaches—is only the more simplistic variant of methodological individualism (see Boettke 2012, p.147; Boettke and Candela 2015; Demeulenaere 2011, p.11; Di Iorio 2015, pp.89-92; 2016; Hayek 1948 pp.1-32; Jarvie 2001, pp.117 ff.; Manzo 2014, p.21; Tuomela 1990). This variant is criticized and challenged by a non-reductionist one, which is rooted in the Scottish Enlightenment and includes authors belonging to various schools, such as Weber, Menger, Simmel, Spencer, Mises, Hayek, Popper, Watkins, Merton, Crozier and Boudon.

As understood by this second variant of methodological individualism, the individualism-holism debate is, contrary to what is often supposed today, unrelated to the opposition between reductionism and anti-reductionism.

Rather, it is a conflict between a non-atomistic theory of human autonomy—strictly linked to an invisible hand model of explanation and a systemic conception of the social world—and a theory of socio-cultural heteronomy (see Boudon 2013, p.25; Di Iorio 2015, p.75 f.). By 'holism: the non-reductionist variant of methodological individualism means a secular version of what Popper ([1945]1966a, p.17) called the "theistic" interpretations of history, i.e. a view that conceives history and social order as being caused by superhuman hidden powers and individuals as unconscious instruments of those powers. Understood in these terms, holism is the idea, rooted in Hegel's and Comtes philosophies of history and developed by various sociological and philosophical schools, that what matters and must be seen as the proper object of investigation in social sciences are mechanisms of unconscious social determination that make individuals remote-controlled and mold the society as an organized structure (Antiseri and Pellicani 1995; Antis er i 2007; Boudon 2013; Cubeddu 1993; Dawe 1970; Di Nuoscio 2016; Watkins 1957). By contrast, the non-reductionist variant of methodological individualism argues that individuals are self-determined beings and that social order, and social phenomena more generally, must be explained as largely unintentional results of human actions—actions explainable on taking into account the meanings that individuals attach to them, i.e. using an interpretative approach *(Verstehen)*. According to this view, the fact that the ultimate causes of social phenomena must be sought within individuals rather than outside them does not mean that social conditioning does not exist, but only that, since human actions result from interpretative skills, this conditioning must be explained by assuming that the influence of the social environment is never mechanical, but always mediated by these skills (see Bronner 2007, pp.166-167; Boudon and Bourricaud 1990, p.13 ff.; Di Iorio 2015, pp.98-115).

Many non-reductionist individualists (e.g. Mises [1949]1998 42-45; Hayek 1952, p.54; Popper 1966a, pp.26 ff., 204 ff.)have stressed that the opposition between holism and individualism regarding the explanation of action and the ultimate causes of social phenomena must be seen as strictly related to a conflict over the ontology of collective nouns. According to these authors, methodological individualism interprets collective nouns that refer to social entities (e.g. the EU single market, the American Democratic Party, the British Army, the Catholic Church, and so on) in nominalist terms. This means that, although collective nouns cannot be semantically reduced to strictly individual properties, they do not refer to independent substances, i.e. to *sui generis* entities that exist independently of individuals like, for example, a stone or a tree. Collective nouns refer rather to individuals and the systemic and irreducible proprieties that emerge from their existence, their beliefs, their intentions and their interactions (See Dawe 1970; Di Iorio 2015; Di Nuoscio 2016; Nadeau 2003; Petitot 2012; Rainone 1990; Tuomela 1989; Zahale 2015). By contrast, the holist ontology as understood and criticized by non-reductionist individualists is a form of Platonic realism. It assumes that, since collective nouns refer to Platonic supra-individual substances (like the 'structures' as understood by the French structuralists), individuals and their actions are derivatives of these substances, which means that they are unimportant from an ontological and explanatory standpoint. Framed in these terms, the ontological opposition between nominalism and realism is strictly related to the methodological opposition between individualist autonomy and holistic heteronomy. If collective nouns are conceived in nominalist terms, then the object of social sciences is represented by individuals (and emergent properties that concern a set of individuals), and the causes of actions must be sought within individuals, i.e. in their views and beliefs. On the contrary, if collective nouns are conceived in realist terms, the object of social sciences is represented by supra-individual Platonic substances, and the ultimate causes of actions must be sought outside individuals (Antiseri and Pellicani 1995; Pribam 2008, p.120).

IDEALIST REDUCTIONISM AND SEMANTIC REDUCTIONISM

The holistic perspective criticized by methodological individualism, which was very influential until few decades ago, is no longer regarded as very appealing, and it is largely rejected today. However, methodological individualism is less popular than ever precisely because the entire individualist tradition is confused with atomism and reductionism. Most of the contemporary critics of methodological individualism reject holistic heteronomy, but they assume that holism was partly correct in that it was, unlike methodological individualism, an anti-reductionist and systemic theory of the social world (e.g. Bunge 1996; Kincaid 1986，1996，2014; Little 2014; Pettit 1993; Sawyer 2002, 2003; Udehn 2001). As a consequence, they defend a middle ground between holism and individualism, i.e.a "synthesis" of these two paradigms merging an antireductionist approach, understood as a typical feature of holism rejected by methodological individualism, and a theory of human autonomy. This synthesis is sometimes called "structural individualism" (Udehn 2001, p.318).

The widespread tendency to reject traditional individualism in the name of a new kind of structural (and anti-reductionist) individualism seems to be based on a mistaken and oversimplified interpretation of the former approach. This is because, as stressed by Demeulenaere (2011, p.11), methodological individualists, or at least a great number of them, "have always defended the idea that individuals are, let us say, 'embedded' in social situations that can be called 'social structures', and are in no respect isolated atoms moving in a social vacuum." The notion of "structural individualism... is... inherent to… methodological individualism from the very beginning, as opposed to some versions of economic atomism" (ibid.). Within nonreductionist individualism, institutions and rules clearly have "effects upon individual action" (ibid.) even though they "have no direct 'energy' of their own" (ibid.; see also Demeulenaere 2012, pp.25-26).

The accusation of "reductionism" levelled against the entire individualist tradition, so widespread today, is expressed in two variants. he first interprets methodological individualism in terms of *idealist reductionism;* the second in terms of *semantic reductionism* (see Di Iorio 2015, pp.103 ff;2016). According to the interpretation of methodological individualism in terms of idealist reductionism (e.g. Archer 1995; Bhaskar 1979; Lawson 1997; Udehn 2001), this approach is mistaken because it denies the objective existence of the social structure and the constraints imposed by this structure on agents.

Methodological individualism is interpreted in these terms because of its contention that social phenomena must be explained through the understanding of the meaning that the individuals attach to their actions, i.e. through a *Verstehen* approach. This approach is regarded as committed to the idea that the social system and social constraints must be reduced to purely subjective mental constructs. It is argued that methodological individualism is mistaken because this system and these constraints exist independently of the agent's opinion about what he or she is free or not free to do, i.e. of his/her subjective standpoint. In other words, methodological individualism is seen as an anti-realist theory of the social world that interprets this world as a pure mental creation and denies that an objective social structure, characterized by a set of rules, sanctions and social positions, really exists outside the agent's mind and entails his or her voluntarist powers being bounded. Methodological individualism is equated to the contention that neither the social world nor social conditioning can be regarded in terms of objective reality and effective constraints (for more details on this point see King 2004; Di Iorio 2016).

This criticism of methodological individualism does not seem to be fair. This is because this approach, or at least its non-reductionist variant, acknowledges that, from a sociological standpoint, personal and purely subjective beliefs "are more or less irrelevant" because they "are not the basis of social life" (King 2004, 190).[1]

Methodological individualism explains the social world and the constraints that this world imposes on agents in terms of "collective beliefs" and of unintended consequences related to these "collective beliefs" (Boudon 1971; see Di Iorio 2015, p.104). In other words, in analyzing the foundations of the social life and social conditioning, methodological individualism does not apply its interpretative approach (*Verstehen*) to purely personal and subjective opinions. Instead, it applies this approach to an "intersubjective" world (Schutz 1967, p.218), i.e. to largely shared meanings, and it focuses on the real and concrete consequences of these shared meanings—consequences that can sometimes entail very brutal objective constraints on agents. As Hayek (1952, p.34) pointed out, social systems must be seen as "the implications of many people holding certain views". From the standpoint of methodological individualism, understanding the typical meanings that agents attach to their actions is the first step in explaining "the unintended or undesigned" nature of social structures and social constraints (1952, p.25). From this it follows that methodological individualism cannot be equated to an anti-realist or idealist theory of structural constraints assuming that these constraints are mere subjective creations of a single human mind and that the agent's voluntarist powers are unbounded. According to methodological individualism, since the social world cannot be reduced to a purely personal idea about what the social world is, this world cannot be changed voluntarily by a single will. Instead, the social world and the constraints that it imposes on agents can be altered only if the common view shared by many people changes (see King 2014; Di Iorio 2016).

The second variant of the interpretation of methodological individualism as reductionist is couched in terms of semantic reductionism. According to this variant, the claim by methodological individualists that social phenomena must be explained in terms of individuals means that this approach is supportive of a principle of semantic reduction of social properties to individual ones (see Rainone 1990, pp.169 ff.; Petroni 1991, p.16; Zahale and Collin 2014, pp.2-10; Di Iorio 2016, 2015). This interpretation of methodological individualism, which developed within analytic philosophy, has been defended by authors such as Mandelbaum (1955), Lukes (1973), Ruben (1985), Kincaid (1986, 1990), Little (1990), Sawyer (2002, 2003) and ElderVass (2014). Conceived in terms of semantic reductionism, methodological individualism is criticized on the grounds that: (i) social phenomena cannot be analyzed without referring to concepts and laws that are semantically irreducible to strictly individual properties; and (ii) that the existence of semantically irreducible factors and laws that causally influence mind and action cannot be denied. This interpretation of methodological individualism in terms of semantic reductionism seems implausible: (i) because many eminent advocates of methodological individualism, namely the representatives of what I have called above "the non-reductionist variant" of this approach, explicitly criticized this kind of reductionism and (ii) because the history of methodological individualism provides countless examples of models of explanation, related to the concepts of "system" and "unintended consequences of human actions': inconsistent with semantic reductionism (see Boettke and Candela 2015; Di Iorio 2016, p.105)

As clarified by both Boudon (1971, pp.1-4) and Popper (1957, p.82), from the standpoint of (non-reductionist) methodological individualism, the impossibility of semantically reducing social properties to strictly individual ones is trivially true. These two thinkers agreed that examples of social explanations that do not refer to semantically irreducible social properties cannot be found, and that the analysis of social phenomena in terms of irreducible properties is simply necessary and cannot be avoided. Developing a criticism of atomism and reductionism, Hayek (1967, p.70), followed a similar line of reasoning. He argued that a society "is more than the mere sum of its parts" because it is a system, characterized by emergent properties, which presupposes that its constitutive elements are "related to each other in a particular manner" (ibid.; see Lewis 2011; 2014). Long before Hayek, Carl Menger, a major influence on him, had pointed out that, according to methodological individualism, the individual's intentions and actions must be regarded as parts of an irreducible structure (see Antiseri 2007, p.141 ff; Campagnolo 2013). For Menger ([1883]1985, 142), "social structures... in respect to their parts are higher units". In addition, they are endowed with "functions" that "are vital expressions of these structures in their totality" (p.139). According to Menger (p.147), society is a system because each part of it—each individual or each social subsystem (like a family or a firm) —"serves the normal function of the whole, conditions and influences it, and in turn is conditioned and influenced by it in its normal nature and its normal function":

One of the reasons why the interpretation of methodological individualism in terms of semantic reductionism must be rejected is the strong connection between this approach and the concept of unintended consequences (see Boettke and Candela 2015; Boudon 2013; Bouvier 2011; Di Iorio 2016, p.106; Dupuy 2004; Petitot 2012). Explanations in terms of unintended consequences are inconsistent with semantic reductionism because they refer to emergent global properties that are irreducible to purely psychological and individual properties and laws. Explanations of this kind are irreducible to the agents' mental and behavioral properties. Hayek's analysis of the market in terms of a self-organizing system is an example of an irreducible individualist explanation based on the concept of unintended consequences (see Hayek 1948, pp.77 ff; 1952; Bouvier 2011). Moreover, it shows how methodological individualism, as understood by the variant defended by Hayek, admits the existence of social emergent properties that causally influence action and restrict human freedom. Consider Hayek's prices theory, which is central to his theory of the market's self-organization. Like Mises, Hayek argues that market prices play a crucial role in market coordination (Hayek 1948, pp.85 f.; Mises [1922]1981). Prices unintentionally emerge from the aggregation of different individual evaluations and distributed items of information. Because of their unintentional nature, they are semantically irreducible. According to Hayek (and Mises), the coordination power of prices depends on the fact that they affect and limit the freedom of choice of agents, who need to adapt their decisions to price variations. Hayek stresses that prices are unintentionally created by human choices and that they in turn affect those choices, i.e. that the whole economic system causally influence its parts and vice versa (see Di Iorio 2016).

The interpretation of methodological individualism in terms of semantic reductionism stems from a misunderstanding of the individualist contention that social phenomena must be explained *in terms of individuals* (see Jar vie 1972, p.157; Di Iorio 2015, pp.107-108; 2016). This contention is confused with the idea that social phenomena must be semantically reduced to strictly individual properties and laws. However, by "explanations in terms of individuals", the non-reductionist variant of methodological individualism does not mean that social phenomena must be explained through such a reduction, but something completely different. It means that social sciences must reject the holistic substantialist ontology of collective nouns and the explanatory models of history and society in terms of heteronomy strictly related to this ontology. The non-reductionist variant of methodological individualism assumes that individuals are the ultimate engine of history and social dynamics, and it interprets the social system and its semantically irreducible properties in anti-substantialist terms, i.e. in terms of unintended consequences produced by individuals, their beliefs, actions and interactions (for more details on this point, see Di Iorio 2016, pp.105-111; Di Nuoscio 2016; Manzo 2014, p.21; McGinley 2012; Rainone 2002; Tuomela 1990, p.34; Watkins 1957).

COMPLEX METHODOLOGICAL INDIVIDUALISM

This special issue of COSMOS+TAXIS is devoted to the nonreductionist variant of methodological individualism and analyses its nature and heuristic power from both an historical and methodological standpoint. It opposes the dominant assumption that social scientists need to get rid of the individualist tradition and develop alternative approaches because of the devastating arguments provided against re- ductionism by philosophy and systems theory. A basic assumption is that the tendency to equate methodological individualism and reductionism is both historically and logically untenable and that, as a consequence, arguments against the latter do not undermine the former.

Many articles focus on a specific subvariant of nonreductionist individualism that the French philosopher Jean-Pierre Dupuy (1992; 2004) called "complex methodological individualism," his subvariant, unlike other non-reductionist individualist approaches such as interpretative sociology (e.g. Weber, Aron, Boudon) and the individualist social philosophy defended by Popper and his pupils, merges the concept of methodological individualism with that of self-organizing complex system (See also Dupuy and Dumouchel 1983; Petitot 2009; 2012).[2] Its privileged—but not unique—object of study is the market society and its cultural and evolutionary presuppositions. As stressed by Hayek (1973, pp.xviii-xix), who has been the most eminent advocate of this complex methodological individualism, the origins of this approach must be traced back to the Scottish Enlightenment, i.e. to the work of authors such as Bernard De Mandeville, Adam Smith, Adam Ferguson, and David Hume. These thinkers interpreted market society in terms of spontaneous order and the invisible hand, anticipating the explanatory method in terms of complex self-organizing system used by the complexity sciences and systems theory. Apart from Hayek and the thinkers of the Scottish Enlightenment, other important theorists of this complex methodological individualism are Lord Acton, Herbert Spencer, and the other members of the Austrian school of economics, namely Carl Menger and Ludwig von Mises. According to Hayek, even if the representatives of the tradition of the spontaneous order in philosophy and economics did not use the complexity sciences' terminology and the term "complex self-organizing system: which has been invented only in relatively recent times, they basically took the same approach as these sciences and must be considered their precursors. Hayek stressed the heuristic utility of applying this new terminology to the traditional individualist analysis of market society in invisible-hand terms because of its greater precision, clarity and accuracy.

According to complex methodological individualism, market society must be interpreted as a complex selforganizing system because it is a very open system (in the sense that its initial conditions change in a continuous and unpredictable manner) comprising an extremely high number of operatively autonomous components (agents), whose activities are dynamically coordinated through a spontaneous process. There is no central direction within a market society. he cooperation and coordination of agents depends on their compliance with some general and abstract rules that govern their direct interactions and allow the formation of market prices (see Birner 1994, p.2 ff; Hayek 1973, pp.34 ff.; Marsh and Onof 2008; Nemo 1988; Petitot 2012). Within a market, prices work as a cybernetic mechanism in the sense that they reflect information about countless local temporary circumstances and ensure the use of a distributed knowledge so as to allow the agents' coordination (see Hayek 1948, pp.77 ff.). The emergent global behavior of the system, which develops unintentionally, is characterized by a dynamic and constant adaptation of the local to the global, and the global to the local. In other words, it is based on a recursive loop between individuals and the prices unintentionally produced by human decisions which in turn influence those decisions (see Boettke and Candela 2015; Dupuy 2004). This global behavior is predictable only in terms of very general patterns, but it is unpredictable in detail because of the complexity of the system, i.e. because of its extreme openness. This complexity entails the constant and unpredictable change of the initial conditions, and it is related to the operative autonomy of the high number of agents who compose the system, as well as to the constant variation of their circumstantial knowledge. A strict application of the *ceteris paribus* clause, which is required for detailed previsions, is possible only for a system that can be assumed to be closed, while it is impossible for a complex self-organizing system (see Di Iorio 2015, pp.42-43; Dupuy 1990; Petitot 2012; Di Nuoscio 2016; Caldwell 2007, p.363; 2009, pp.13ff.).[3] Since a market is based on spontaneous cooperation for adaptive and evolutionary reasons, i.e. because its complexity cannot be mastered, a planned economy cannot match its performances and is bound to fail. By means of self-organization, a market system uses a distributed knowledge that cannot be centralized.

I would like to conclude this short introduction with a terminological remark. The term "complex methodological individualism, which designates a specific sub variant of non-reductionist methodological individualism", is useful to distinguish this subvariant from both reductionist individualism and other subvariants of non-reductionist methodological individualism. Its utility partly depends on the widespread confusions about the meaning of the generic term "methodological individualism", i.e. on the tendency to use the expression as a synonym of "reductionism: Given these confusions and the existence of different variants and subvariants of methodological individualism", referring to the methodological assumptions of the tradition of the spontaneous order using the generic term "methodological individualism" seems, although correct, less informative and accurate than using the term "complex methodological individualism".[4]

NOTES

1. King (2004), who defended the interpretative approach developed by Weber and other eminent representatives of the *Verstehen* tradition from the objections developed by Bhaskar and other critical realists, does not call the

Verstehen approach "methodological individualism" as I do. However, the essence of his view on the philosophical and methodological assumptions of the social sciences does not differ from mine. It seems to me that he is supportive of an approach consistent with what I called above "the non-reductionist variant of methodological individualism".

2. To be noted is that Weber (pp.63 ff.) used the concept of complexity to criticize the planned economy in the first book of Economy and Society. Moreover, Popper (1957, pp.36-40) referred to this concept as well, stressing its importance in social sciences, although he did not focus on it in detail. As a consequence, the distinction between complex methodological individualism and other variants of non-reductionist individualism must not be interpreted as clear-cut.

3. Although Hayek was one of the originators of complexity theory, he did not provide a good definition of "complexity" (see Di Iorio 2015; Dupuy 1990; Petitot 2002; Di Nuoscio 2006; Caldwell 2009). Hayek (1967) argued that "complexity" results from the fact that the behavior of certain systems is highly unpredictable (except for some general patterns) because it is determined by a very high number of variables. However, even systems made up of a very large number of variables can be perfectly predictable if they are closed. Hayek's definition of complexity neglects to take into account a point stressed by Hayek himself in his works on market and mind, i.e. the constant and unpredictable change of the initial conditions which affect complex systems: these systems are extremely open systems (Hayek 1952b, pp.185 ff.; 1967, pp.55 ff.; see also Nadeau 1997, pp.67 ff.; Caldwell 2004, p.363; Di Nuoscio 2006, pp.46-48; Marsh 2010, pp.140-141).

4. I would like to thank both David Anderson and Leslie Marsh for inviting me to guest edit this special issue of COSMOS+TAXIS, as well as all the contributors for their excellent work and cooperation. I also wish to express my gratitude to all the reviewers. In addition, I thank Gianluca Cavallo, who gave permission for his painting "Eiride" to be reproduced on the cover of this issue.

REFERENCES

Antiseri, D. and Pellicani, L. (1995). *Uindividualismo metodologico. Una polemica sul mestiere dello scienziato sociale.* Milan: Franco Angeli.

Antiseri, D. *(2007).Popper's Vienna.* Aurora, CO: The Davies Group Publishers.

Archer, M. (1995). *Realist Social theory: The Morphogenetic Approach.* Cambridge: Cambridge University Press.

Bhaskar, R. (1979). *The Possibility of Naturalism.* Sussex: Harvester.

Birner, J. (1992). Hayek's Grand Research Program. In: *Birner J. and Van Zijp R. (Eds.), Hayek, Co-ordination and Evolution: His Legacy in Philosophy, Politics, Economics and the History of Ideas.* London and New York: Routledge.

Boettke, P. (2012). *Living Economics. Yesterday, Today, and Tomorrow.* Oakland, CA: The Independent Institute.

Boettke, P. and Candela, R. A. (2015). What Is Old Should Be New Again: Methodological Individualism, Institutional Analysis and Spontaneous Order. *Sociologia* 2: 5-14

Boudon, R. (1971). *Uses of Structuralism.* London: Heinemann.

Boudon, R., and Bourricaud, F. (1990). *A Critical Dictionary of Sociology.* Chicago: University of Chicago Press.

Boudon, R. (2013). *Sociology as Science: An Intellectual Autobiography.* Oxford: The Bardwell Press.

Bouvier, A. (2011). Individualism, collective agency and the "micromacro relation" In: *The Sage Handbook of the Philosophy of Social Sciences,* J. C. Jarvie, and J. Zamora Bonilla (Eds.), London: Sage Publications.

Bronner, G. (2007). *LEmpire de lerreur. Elements de sociologie cognitive.* Paris: Puf.

Bunge, M. (1996). *Finding philosophy in social science.* New Haven and London: Yale University Press.

Caldwell, B. (2007). *Hayeks challenge: An intellectual biography of F A. Hayek.* Chicago: University of Chicago Press.

Caldwell, B. (2009). Some Comments on Lawson's Reorienting

Economics: Same Facts, Different Conclusions. In: Edward Fullbrook (Ed.) *Ontology and Economics: Tony Lawson and His Critics.* London and New York: Routledge.

Campagnolo, G. (2013). *Criticisms of Classical Political Economy: Menger, Austrian Economics and the German Historical School.* London/ New York: Routledge.

Cubeddu, R. (1993). *The Philosophy of the Austrian School.* London and New York: Routledge.

Dawe, A. (1970). The two sociologies. *British Journal of Sociology* 21(June): 207-218.

Demeulenaere, P. (ed.). (2011). *Analytical Sociology and Social Mechanisms.* Cambridge: Cambridge University Press.

Di Iorio, F. (2015). *Cognitive Autonomy and Methodological Individualism: The Interpretative Foundations of Social Life.* Berlin and New York: Springer.

Di Iorio, F. (2016), World 3 and Methodological Individualism in Popper's hought. *Philosophy of the Social Sciences.*
DOI: 10.1177/0048393116642992，2016, pp.1-23

Di Nuoscio, E. (2016). *Philosophy of Social Sciences.* Oxford: he Bardwell Press.

Dupuy, J.-P. (1990). *Ordres et desordres. Enquete sur un nouveau paradigme.* Paris: Seuil.

Dupuy, J-P. (1992) *Le sacrifice et lenvie.* Paris: Calmann-Levy.

Dupuy, J-P. and Dumouchel, P. (Eds.). (1983). L' *Auto-Organisation de la Physique au Politique.* Paris: Seuil

Dupuy, J-P. (2004). Vers l'unite des sciences sociales autour de l'individualisme methodologique complexe. *Revue du MAUSS* 24(2): 310-328.

Elder-Vass, D. (2014). Social entities and the basis of their powers. In: *Rethinking the Individualism-Holism debate. Essays in the philosophy of social science,* eds. J. Zahle and F. Collin. Berlin and New York: Springer.

Hayek, F. A. (1948). *Individualism and Economic Order.* Chicago: University of Chicago Press.

Hayek, F. A. (1952). *The Counter-Revolution of Science: Studies on the Abuse of Reason.* Indianapolis: Liberty Press.

Hayek, F. A. (1967). *Studies in Philosophy, Politics and Economics.* Chicago: University of Chicago Press.

Hayek, F. A. (1973). *Law, Legislation and Liberty, Vol.1: Rules and Order.* Chicago: University of Chicago Press.

Jarvie, I. C. (1972). *Concepts and Society.* London: Routledge & Kegan Paul.

Jarvie, I. C. (2001). *The republic of science: the emergence of Poppers social view of science 1935-1945.* Amsterdam and Atlanta: Rodopi.

King, A. (2004). *The structure of social theory.* London: Routledge.

Kincaid, H. (1986). Reduction, explanation, and individualism. *Philosophy of Science* 53(4) (December): 492-513.

Kincaid, H. (1990). Eliminativism and methodological individualism. *Philosophy of Science* 57(1)(March): 141-148.

Kincaid, H. (2014).

Laurent, A. (1994). *L'individualisme methodologique,* Paris: Puf.

Lawson, T. (1997). *Economics and Reality.* London and New York: Routledge.

Lewis, P. (2012). *Emergent Properties in the Work of Friedrich Hayek. Journal of Economic Behavior & Organization* 82: 268-378.

Lewis, P. (2015). *Notions of Order and Process in Hayek: the Significance of Emergence.* Cambridge Journal of Economics, 39: 1167-1190.

Little, D. (1990). *Varieties of social explanation: An introduction to the philosophy of social science.* Boulder: Westview Press.

Lukes, S. (1973). *Individualism.* New York: Harper & Row.

Mandelbaum, M. (1955). Societal facts. *British Journal of Sociology* 6(4) December: 305-317.

Manzo, G. (2014). *Analytical sociology: Actions and networks.* Chichester: Wiley.

Marsh, L. and Onof, C. (2008). Stigmergic epistemology, stigmergic cognition. *Cognitive Systems Research* 9: 136-149.

Marsh, L. (2010). Hayek: Cognitive scientist avant la lettre. *Advances in Austrian Economics* 13:115-155.

McGinley, W. (2012). Reduction in Sociology. *Philosophy of the Social Sciences* 42(3) September: 370-398.

Menger, C. ([1871]2004). *Principles of Economics.* Auburn: he Ludwig von Mises Institute.

Menger, C. ([1883]1985). *Investigations into the method of the social sciences with special reference to economics.* New York and London: New York University Press.

Mises, L. ([1922]1981). *Socialism: An economic and sociological analysis.* New York: Liberty Fund.

Mises, L. ([1949]1998). *Human action: A treatise on economics.* Auburn: The Ludwig von Mises Institute.

Nadeau, R. (1997). Hayek and the complex affair of the mind. Sixty-seventh Annual Conference of the Southern Economic Association, Atlanta, 21-23 November.

Nadeau, R. (2003). Cultural evolution true and false: A debunking of Hayek's critics. *Proceedings of 7th ESHET Conference,* Paris, 30 January-1 February.

Nemo, P. (1988). *La societe de droit selon Hayek.* Paris: Puf.

Petitot, J. (2009). *Per un nuovo Illuminismo.* Milan: Bompiani.

Petitot, J. (2012). "Individualisme methodologique et evolution culturelle" In Un austriaco in Italia. *Studi in onore di Dario Antiseri,* eds. E. De Mucci and K. R. Leube. Soveria Mannelli: Rubbettino.

Petroni, A. M. (1991). Lindividualisme methodologique. *Journal des Economistes et des Etudes Humaines.* 2(1): pages

Popper, K. R. (1957). *The Poverty of Historicism.* Boston: Beacon Press.

Popper, K. R. ([1945a]1966a). *The Open Society and Its Enemies,* Vol.1: he Spell of Plato. Princeton: Princeton University Press.

Popper, K. R. ([1945b]1966b). *The Open Society and Its Enemies,* Vol.2: Hegel and Marx. Princeton: Princeton University Press.

Pribram, K. (2008). La genesi della filosofia sociale individualistica. In:

Lindividualismo nelle scienze sociali, ed. E. Grillo. Rubbettino: Soveria Mannelli.

Rainone, A. (1990). *Filosofia analitica e scienze storico-sociali.* Rome: ETS.

Ruben, D-H. (1985). *The metaphysics of the social world.* London: Routledge & Kegan Paul.

Schutz, A. (1967). *The phenomenology of the social world.* Evanston: Northwestern University Press.

Tuomela, R. (1989). Ruben and the metaphysics of the social world. *The British Journal for the Philosophy of Science.* 40(2): 261-273.

Tuomela, R. (1990). Methodological individualism and explanation. *Philosophy of Science* 57(1): 133-140.

Udehn, L. (2001). *Methodological individualism: Background, history and meaning.* London and New York: Routledge.

Sawyer, R. K. (2002). Nonreductive individualism. Part I—Supervenience and wild disjunction. *Philosophy of the Social Sciences* 32(4): 537-559.

Sawyer, R. K. (2003). Nonreductive individualism. Part II—Social causation. *Philosophy of the Social Sciences* 33(2): 203-224.

Watkins, J. W N. (1952b). The principle of methodological individualism. *The British Journal for the Philosophy of Science* 3(10): 186-189.

Watkins, J. W. N. (1957). Historical explanation in the social sciences. *The British Journal for the Philosophy of Science* 8(30): 104-117.

Weber, M. (1978). *Economy and Society: An Outline of Interpretive Sociology,* Volume I. Los Angeles: University of California Press.

Zahle, J. and Collin, F. (eds.). (2014). *Rethinking the individualismHolism debate. Essays in the philosophy of science.* Berlin and New York: Springer.

Zahle, J. (2014). *Holism, emergence, and the crucial distinction.* In: Zahle and F. Collin (2014).

近代科学革命时期基督教与科学的相互作用

——以麦尔赛纳为例

宋 斌[*]

一、问题的定位

基督教对于现代科学的产生究竟具有什么作用？自从迪昂阐明基督教作为一种"理智根源"对于"发展出一个自我支持的现代科学"[①]的必要性之后，已很少再有学者主张两者间的"冲突论"。如果它们之间确曾有过冲突，学者们也大多认同那"其实在于新的科学理论和基督教信仰所固守的旧的科学理论之间发生冲突"[②]；就基督教文明在更高的观念层面"孕育"了现代科学来说，基督教与科学之间是"和谐的"。

实际上，考虑到现代科学是在基督教文明中发展而来这一人类历史上绝无类似而又无法重演的既成事实，两者之间就不会存在单纯的"冲突"关系。但如果"和谐说"仅仅意指前一事实而并未道出两者间更为丰富的意义关联，那么无论"冲突"还是"和谐"，由此及彼的理论更替就难免有矫枉过正之嫌。

首先，现代科学既然是在基督教文明中诞生的，那么"基督教"与"科

---

* 宋斌（1981—），山东淄博人，哲学博士，南开大学哲学院讲师。

① 安道玉：《迪昂论基督教与现代科学的兴起》，《河南师范大学学报》（哲学社会科学版），2005年第1期，第24页。

② 田薇：《试论基督教与科学的关系——从霍伊卡〈宗教与现代科学的关系〉谈起》，《学术月刊》，2001第2期，第25页。

学"便不是两个其内涵已固化并借此具有本质性差异的"实体性力量"①，即与"李约瑟问题"中所探讨的中国传统文明与现代自然科学之间的关系有根本的不同；它们自始至终都处于同一文明之中，在复杂的相互作用之下经历着各自的演变。例如中世纪占统治地位的自然学说是基督教信仰与亚里士多德自然哲学的结合体，而现代科学的诞生却是以与亚里士多德自然哲学相竞争的"柏拉图主义"与"机械论"为主题的②；如果基督教与科学之间单纯是和谐的，它为什么抛弃了与自身融合几百年之久的自然学说而转而采纳了与其对立的现代科学？这是"主动的促进"还是"被动的迎合"？显然在这个过程中基督教因为现代科学的兴起自身亦发生了改变。

其次，学者们会以"护教"为目的强调科学的基督教渊源。例如主张"和谐说"者多会援引开普勒、笛卡尔、波义耳、牛顿等近代自然科学大师对自己的知识成果所作的神学辩护，以此证明基督教与科学在近代的相携相伴。但正如布鲁克所说，这些辩护多是在居于宗教正统地位的天主教神职团体之外作出的，这些科学家对于基督教教义的表述也大多并非是培育他们的宗教传统的典型代表③。如果"和谐"是被近代自然科学家们单方面制造出来的，人们则难以断定基督教自身是否真地具有推动现代科学发展的固有力量。

基于上述的分析，笔者认为我们对于基督教与科学关系的定位及对开篇问题的应答策略应当是：立足历史文献，将现代科学在基督教文明中的创生还原为近代科学革命的参与者们生存其中的包含了理智活动但又不止于此的丰富的生活世界，借此探寻基督教与科学之间复杂多样的"相互作用"④。

为此，在本文之中我们将选择以麦尔赛纳（1588—1648）为例来进一步推进对此问题的探讨。麦尔赛纳是天主教神父，法国最小兄弟会的成员，他在科学史上的重要位置来自其"欧洲信使"的称谓。在近代科学革命的早期，成建制的科学团体与科学刊物尚未出现，学术成果的交流主要通过

---

① 约翰·H. 布鲁克：《科学与宗教》，复旦大学出版社，2002年，第43页。

② 韦斯特福尔：《近代科学的建构：机械论与力学》，复旦大学出版社，2000年，第1页。

③ 约翰·H. 布鲁克：《科学与宗教》，复旦大学出版社，2002年，第59页。

④ 本文对基督教与科学之间关系的探讨局限于"近代科学革命"这一特殊的历史时期，与伊安·巴伯在更加整全的视野中对于宗教与科学之间一般关系的研究有着不同的思路。当然，基于这种考察，笔者对于宗教与科学之间一般关系的态度是支持巴伯所说的"对话"与"整合"，而非"冲突"与"独立"的。

通信完成，而麦尔赛纳便是当时欧洲最重要的"科技信函中转站"。他自身不仅是一个现代科学的早期研究者，而且尤其以对伽利略、笛卡尔、帕斯卡、伽桑迪、惠更斯等近代科学巨匠的思想的传播与启发而闻名于世。

正因为麦尔赛纳是一位虔诚的基督教神父，他在现代科学的发展过程中又起到了重要作用，所以考察其人其事，不仅可以避免为强调科学的基督教渊源而单单援引科学家的神学辩护的弊端，而且也可透过其具有浓厚宗教意味的科学活动，具体而微地理解在近代科学革命时期基督教与科学之间复杂的相互作用。

二、基督教自然秩序观及亚里士多德自然哲学

与理解麦尔赛纳的思想立场密切相关的观念及时代背景是《圣经》启示所蕴含的基督教"自然秩序"观，以及在此观念的参照下亚里士多德自然哲学的合宜与缺陷。

依据《圣经》，基督教的自然秩序观大致包含以下几个层面：

（1）自然是拥有完美理智的上帝设计、创造及维系的结果，因此自然是稳定、客观而有秩序的，"具有内在的和谐及普遍齐一的法则"[①]。

（2）由于上帝按照自己的肖像创造了人并赋予了人"管理"宇宙万物的权利与义务[②]，因此自然的秩序是能够被人的理智认识的，人也可以依照这种知识发展技术，减轻劳苦，获得尘世的利益[③]。

（3）自然及其秩序的被创造又同时是上帝完全的意志自由的体现，因此自然尽管具有秩序，但现存秩序却是上帝众多候选可能性中的一种，它从本质上说是偶然的，并不能由人凭借理智先天地（apriori）推测与认知，人对自然的理性认识也必须从尊重既定事实的"经验态度"开始[④]。

（4）正是由于上帝对自然的创造与维系是完全自由的，所以上帝完全可以在适宜的时机按照其意愿干涉甚至违背既定的自然秩序，做出昭示其

---

① 何光沪：《科学革命中的基督宗教与人文主义》，《中国人民大学学报》，2008 年第 3 期，第 48 页。

②《圣经创世纪》1，第 26 页。

③ R. 霍伊卡：《宗教与现代科学的兴起》，四川人民出版社，1999 年，第 61-81 页。

④ 何哲逊：《科学渊源与基督信仰》，光启出版社，1992 年，第 32 页。

超越存在的"神迹"。《圣经》启示中的众多"神迹",如上帝创世、三位一体,道成肉身,皆是"信仰"的对象,非人类"理性"可以企及。①

在这样的秩序观的参照之下,我们可以更好地理解亚里士多德自然哲学对于基督教信仰来说的合宜与缺陷。

构成亚里士多德自然哲学的两大要件是以"类概念"为基础的三段论推理及旨在为自然现象提供因果解释的"目的论"②。对于亚里士多德来说,根据经验中自然物体作"自然运动"的方式确定其"目的"——自然位置,便认识了此类物体借以与他类物体相区别的"本质";而能够对自然现象进行合理的分类,宇宙的秩序也便由此得到确认。在亚里士多德的宇宙论模型中,他根据经验中恒常存在的自然现象归纳式地将宇宙划分为由作永恒圆周运动的"神圣元素"所构成的"月上天"及由作短暂的直线运动的"水、土、火、气"所构成的"月下天",并将至高无上的神祇安排在神圣天球的最外层,正是这种以"自然位置"——作为自然运动的"目的因"——规定"事物本质",并借此确定宇宙秩序的自然哲学的结果。重视观察的经验态度、对宇宙秩序及人类理智能力的肯定以及为神所保留的至高位置,这都在不同程度上贯彻了以上诸点基督教教义,也正因为如此亚里士多德自然哲学才得以在中世纪经由与基督教信仰的结合立为正统。

可尽管亚里士多德在托马斯哲学中获得了经院哲学集大成之地位,但作为古希腊理性批判精神的当然传承,经院哲学内部并不缺乏对于亚里士多德的批判与反思③;以上从《圣经》启示归纳出的教义也只是自然学说须与之符合的形上前提,《圣经》本身"并不具有一种明确的世界图景"④。也就是说,亚里士多德自然哲学与基督教信仰的结合从来就不是严丝合缝没有缺陷的。在麦尔赛纳生活的近代科学革命的早期,站在基督信仰及现实需要的角度看,它的缺陷主要表现为以下两点:

(1)烦琐。在亚里士多德自然哲学中,与其说"目的因"刻画了自然物体运动的"原因",不如说它是物体所恒常具有的运动状态的"标签",

---

① Etienne Gilson. *Reason and Revelation in the Middle Ages*. Charles Scribnerssons, 1938, pp.82-84.

② 宋斌:《人间取象与类逻辑:亚里士多德自然哲学体系的核心要素》,《中国社会科学报》,2010年第4期。

③ 郝刘翔:《中世纪希腊科学的传播及其与宗教的关系》,《自然辩证法通讯》,2003年第3期,第69页。

④ R. 霍伊卡:《宗教与现代科学的兴起》,丘仲辉译,四川人民出版社,1999年,第24页。

是对不同的自然运动进行分类命名的"名词"；因此，当亚里士多德用"重物具有下降的倾向——重性"来回答"为什么重物会下降"的问题时，它实际上表达了一种"重物在不受人力干扰的自然状态之下总是具有下降的运动状态"的秩序意识。正是在这样的意义上，按照现代物理学的标准，亚里士多德自然哲学的主体是旨在描述物体恒常运动状态的"运动学"，缺乏对自然运动的动力机制做出统一说明的"动力学"。对此麦尔赛纳曾评论道，"三段论并不是一种发现的方法（une méthode d'invention），它仅仅是使得我们的思想有秩序的技术"，三段论推理奠基其上的"归纳"也"仅仅告诉了我们现象是什么"，并不能够"建立表征了现象之间恒常关系的规律（les lois）"①。随着自然界可观察的自然运动的种类越来越多，亚里士多德主义者便需要命名越来越多的"质""形式"，这将使得理论变得异常烦琐，以日常语言为载体的论证也会变得越来越晦涩；可以说，这样的论证只有在一种统一的动力机制被提供出来，进而那些千变万化的自然现象可以从少数的初始原则中被数学式地推演出来的时候才能够变得有序与清晰，而这无论是从理论内容还是逻辑工具上说都是亚里士多德自然哲学所缺乏的。

（2）与缺陷（1）密切相关，亚里士多德自然哲学中事物运动的秩序依靠其恒常趋向的"目的"来保证，而"动力因"往往被看作事物偏离自然秩序作"受迫运动"的原因，也就是说动力因在对自然秩序的说明中不具有首要的位置；即使就亚里士多德文本中为数不多的对于动力机制的说明来看，它们也存在了很多问题，成为被库恩看作促成范式转化之必备因素的"旧理论长期未解决的难题"②，中世纪的物理学家们也正是在这些难题的刺激之下才发展出可以作为近代数理物理学之滥觞的"冲力动力学"③。

动力因说明的不成功所导致的后果便是亚里士多德自然哲学改造、利用、"管理"自然能力的大大缺乏。经过近代科学的洗礼，技术被提升到与理智科学同等重要的地位，而技术的应用须以认识反映了自然现象前后相继之普遍规律的因果机制为前提。而亚里士多德自然哲学却满足于对事物

---

① Robert Lenoble. *Mersenne ou la Naissance du Mécanisme.* Librairie philosophique J. Vrin, 1943, pp.325-327.

② 托马斯·库恩：《科学革命的结构》，北京大学出版社，2003 年，第 60-86 页。

③ Alexander Koyré. *Galileo Studies.* Humanities press, 1978, pp.1-16.

"分类"，满足于在"神圣"与"卑下"的价值分判之下"沉思"神所赐予宇宙的完美秩序。它轻视动力、贬低"技术"，更遑论发展技术改造自然，为人类谋取世俗的利益。

综上所述，宇宙论的烦琐显然并不符合上帝在创世时简洁而优美的理智设计。而在近代科学革命的早期，欧洲的卫生医疗状况，人们发展技术改造自然以降低劳作之苦、发展物质生产的能力仍然是非常低下的[①]。人们亟须一种能够为世间生活带来实际的功效，并不仅仅只是就"形式""目的"等抽象名词进行繁复论证的新的自然学说。在这样的意义上，亚里士多德自然哲学并未完全符合基督教教义（1）与（2）。

三、自然主义对世界的深度"魔幻化"

基于上述原因，在近代科学革命的早期便形成了背叛亚里士多德自然哲学并力图为自然现象提供新的动力因说明的哲学潮流。然而为了全面理解这段历史我们必须认识到，机械论自然科学并不是这股潮流的唯一力量，站在它的对立面的不仅有亚里士多德还有"文艺复兴时期的自然主义"（Le Naturalisme de la Renaissance）[②]。正是在这三股力量的相互角力中，麦尔赛纳展示出其维护并推动现代科学的哲学立场与宗教缘由。

所谓"文艺复兴时期的自然主义"，是指以炼金术、占星术、神秘医学为代表的自然理论，它以对世界的泛灵论解释为模式，认为在自然世界的"大宇宙"内部的各物质之间，以及"大宇宙"与人类个体的"小宇宙"之间存在着一种基于灵魂特性的普遍的相互作用。如果说亚里士多德用"倾向""目的"等术语解释自然现象，更多地是对自然界所具有的不以人的意志为转移的稳定秩序的类型化表达，那么当自然主义者——以彭波纳启（Pomponazzi）、布鲁诺等为代表——用具有人类情感、意志特点的"普遍灵魂"来比附磁铁之间的相互作用，解释琥珀对纤毛的吸引，说明物体的化学特性的转换，则是要完全抛弃善变的"灵魂"与稳定的"物体"之间的区别，将自然界与人类精神等量齐观。于是在自然主义的宇宙中人凭借

---

① R. 霍伊卡：《宗教与现代科学的兴起》，四川人民出版社，1999 年，第 86-87 页。

② Robert Lenoble. *Mersenne ou la Naissance du Mécanisme*. Librairie philosophique J. Vrin, 1943, pp.85-174.

对语言、符号以及各种巫术仪式的掌握就可以拥有预知未来和施加魔法以改变自然进程的神秘力量；自然界则因为具有与人类意志相类同的"普遍灵魂"，失去了被可诉诸检验的恒常而稳定的自然规律规范的可能，其内部充斥着违背常理的魔幻与奇迹。①如果我们采用劳埃德对于古希腊科学精神的概括②，可以说文艺复兴时期的自然主义是无视"自然"，向以万物有灵论为哲学基础的古代巫术的倒退。

自然主义之所以能够在近代早期蔚然成风，按照沃克尔的观点，是源于当时人们研究、利用与支配自然的功利冲动③，也即上文所指出的按照基督教教义（2）为增进世间利益而改革自然学说的愿望。但它之所以令人（尤其令像麦尔赛纳这样的神父）尴尬地让世界充满"魔幻"，却是与其反对的亚里士多德自然哲学有着莫大关联的。因为自然主义的"普遍灵魂"虽然造成了一个与亚里士多德的稳定自然全然不同的魔幻宇宙，但这一概念在一定意义上却沿用了亚里士多德的术语，毋宁说它是使用与"目的""倾向"等同样具有灵魂特点的"爱""恨""吸引"等范畴来对自然现象进行动力因解释的结果，这违背了亚里士多德仅仅使用"目的"来对稳定的自然现象进行"运动学"分类的初衷。由此我们也就不难理解为什么像笛卡尔这样的现代科学奠基者在批判亚里士多德自然哲学时，会说亚里士多德以"目的因"来解释自然运动是混淆了"思想"（la pensée）与"事物"（les choses），混淆了"灵魂"与"物体"之间的形上差别。④亚里士多德自然哲学的本意虽然并不是要将"自然"与"人类精神"等量齐观进而无视自然的稳定特性，但它的以"目的""倾向"来说明自然现象的质的物理学却影响了这一划分，或者说玷污了这一划分。在不能够提供一种更完善的动力理论的前提下，亚里士多德自然哲学要反驳自然主义就会缺乏基本的概念装置。也就是说在自然主义的挑战下，亚里士多德自然哲学已经变得不再能够维持教义（4）了。

这对于麦尔赛纳来说当然是不可忍受的。自然主义的最大危害是从根

---

① Robert Lenoble. *Mersenne ou la Naissance du Mécanisme.* Librairie philosophique J. Vrin, 1943, p.121.

② 劳埃德：《早期希腊科学：从泰勒斯到亚里士多德》，上海科技教育出版社，2004年，第7页。

③ 约翰·H. 布鲁克：《科学与宗教》，复旦大学出版社，2002年，第67页。

④ Réné. Descartes. *Sixièmes réponses, das Oeuvres de Descartes.* publiées par Adam et Tannery. Tome IX. Librairie Philosophique, 1996, pp.240-241.

本上违背了教义（1）与（4），使自然失去了稳定的秩序，使得人们不能够根据对自然秩序的准确认识而判别真正的"神迹"。更为严重的是，自然主义让有限的人类个体拥有了依靠巫术直接干预自然进而使自然充满"奇迹"的神秘力量，威胁到上帝作为唯一的无限超越者的神圣地位，而这无论从何种意义而言都是明显的思想异端。①

为了维护纯正的基督教教义，同时也考虑到人们对增进世间利益的渴求，麦尔赛纳坚定地采纳了另一种哲学立场——机械论。

四、机械论自然科学的诞生

通过以上分析我们发现，就反驳自然主义混淆了"思想"与"事物"的魔幻宇宙，进而维持"灵魂"与"物体"的区分、维护自然的稳定秩序而言，机械论与亚里士多德是站在同一阵营的。只不过因为机械论拥有了全新的概念装置，它对魔幻宇宙的驱逐要比亚里士多德有效得多。在亚里士多德的自然哲学中，目的因是说明事物运动的"终极因"（final cause），机械论自然科学却主张在对自然现象的研究中排除对"最终原因"的探讨。②这意味着"机械学"（mechanics）这门在亚里士多德体系中作为与"物理学"相区别而仅仅研究"人工技艺"的附属学科，成为整个自然科学的基础③。自然被设想为一部机器，为了说明它的运作人们只须凭借经验和理性猜测自然现象是如何遵循了普遍的因果规律、由某一前在的物质状态前后相继地"被制造出来"，无须也无法认识上帝在设计这部机器时所设想的目的。

由此我们也可以看到机械论自然科学在创生过程中所承担的历史使命。首先，它要提供一种全新的逻辑工具——数学，以摆脱亚里士多德自然哲学的烦琐与晦涩；其次，它要提供一种全新的因果概念——旨在规范

① Robert Lenoble. *Mersenne ou la Naissance du Mécanisme*. Librairie philosophique J. Vrin, 1943, p. 121.

② Réné. Descartes. Principes de la philosophie, das Oeuvres de Descartes. publiées par Adam et Tannery. Tome Ⅸ. Paris, 1996, p. 37.

③ Daniel Garber. *Descartes, Mechanics, and the Mechanical Philosophy*. In *Midwest Studies in Philosophy*, 2002(XXVI), pp.185-198.

自然现象之先后相继次序的"因果决定论"，对自然现象的动力机制作出更加合理的解释与说明。"自然的数学化"与"因果决定论"由此成为机械论自然科学的概念基础，毋宁说这两者是紧密结合在一起的，对特定自然现象的数学描述需要从初始条件与普遍的因果规律中推演出来，而所有的因果规律都要在简洁而清晰的数学公式中得到表达。

显然，这样的机械论学说对于维护基督教教义的优越性是明显的。它肯定自然的稳定秩序，反映了上帝创世的理智设计，同时又指明人类认识这种设计与秩序的途径。而且它将原本附属于物理学研究之下的"机械技术"提升到与理智自然科学同等重要的位置，大大增强了人管理自然的能力。

对于麦尔赛纳来说，他所尤其担心的自然主义对教义（4）的威胁，机械论的反驳也尤为有效。既然人们可以凭借机械论的物理定律准确识别事物的发生原因，既然人们也只能利用这种物理定律来改造、利用自然从而在自然中制造符合心愿的结果，那么只有当一个事件不能够被物理定律解释的时候，它才能够被认作"神迹"，而人也必定不具备制造这样的"神迹"的能力。[①]

由此可见，麦尔赛纳抛弃亚里士多德自然哲学转而接受并推广机械论自然科学是具有维护基督信仰的强大驱动力的；现代科学在这样复杂的社会环境、观念背景下促使基督教信仰改变其世界图景，也应当被看作被基督教文明"孕育"的现代科学对其母体的反作用。

让人印象更为深刻的是，不仅科学影响了麦尔赛纳思想中基于基督信仰的世界图景的转变，麦尔赛纳对于基督教教义的理解也影响到了他的科学观。简言之，麦尔赛纳的宗教信仰对于处于竞争地位的科学理论具有"选择性作用"[②]。

根据列若贝尔（Lenoble）的考证，在机械论的近代发展过程中，其阵营内部出现了理性论的笛卡尔主义与以伽利略、迦桑迪、麦尔赛纳为代表的"实证的机械论"（le Mécanisme Positif）的区别。

尽管以"数学化+因果决定论"为构件的机械论自然科学可以更加有效地认识物理规律，但对于麦尔赛纳来说数学推理虽然可以给理论的论说

① Robert Lenoble. *Mersenne ou la Naissance du Mécanisme.* Librairie philosophique J. Vrin, 1943, pp.374-378.

② 约翰·H. 布鲁克：《科学与宗教》，复旦大学出版社，2002年，第30页。

带来确定性，但数学推理的对象却仅仅具有"理智的可能性"，它无法揭示现实事物的本来面目：

> 我们可以说纯粹数学只是一门想像力的学问，或者说是纯粹理智的学问……它除了那些具有单纯的可能性的、或者有条件的对象之外，并不考虑其他的任何东西。①

在这样的意义上，以地球为中心的托勒密天文学与以太阳为中心的哥白尼体系都是可能存在的天体运动状态的数学组合，仅从数学上考虑，两者并不涉及事物的真实。而以规定现象的前后相继为己任的因果定律，因为人们对它们的探索依赖于有限的感性经验，所以就更不能够揭示有关事物本质的任何必然特征：

> 如果发光对于星星来说是自然的这一点看起来更加真实，但是与之相反的结论却并不是荒谬的；在这方面（指靠感性经验获得的知识）人们不能够形成任何的原则。②

因此对于实证的机械论者来说，既然数学命题只处理可能的对象，而依赖于感性经验的自然知识又仅能提供偶然的结论，所以新自然科学就不能够提供有关事物本质的必然知识。而这恰恰符合教义（3）。实际上，出于对上帝创世的"唯意志论"的认同，像帕斯卡、波义耳、牛顿等科学家在有关自然科学是否可以提供符合康德"物自体"意义上的绝对真理的问题上，基本上都抱有与麦尔赛纳同样的哲学立场，而这种立场在波尔、海森堡等现代科学家身上也一再可以看到。

与此相比，笛卡尔主义的机械论就具有了过强的理性色彩。笛卡尔认为物理学的基本定律可以直接由对上帝属性的认识推出，而人们仅仅凭借理智就可以从这些普遍的先天原则中演绎出物质所有可能的存在状态；感觉的作用是决定这些可能结果中的哪一些与实际相符，它并不影响物理定

---

① Robert Lenoble. *Mersenne ou la Naissance du Mécanisme.* Librairie philosophique J. Vrin, 1943, p.347.

② Robert Lenoble. *Mersenne ou la Naissance du Mécanisme.* Librairie philosophique J. Vrin, 1943, p.344.

律自身的真实性。显然，笛卡尔在人类是否可以凭借理性认识事物本质方面抱有过强的自信，麦尔赛纳出于与宗教相关的理由并不赞同这一点，这也就是他每当对笛卡尔的思想发表评论时总是有所保留的原因。①

（本文原载于《自然辩证法研究》2012 年第 9 期）

---

① Robert Lenoble. *Mersenne ou la Naissance du Mécanisme*. Librairie philosophique J. Vrin, 1943, p.50-51.

波爱修斯的知识划分及后世影响

王　琦*

　　自古希腊起，哲学家就开始了对知识的理性探索。比如，柏拉图在《泰阿泰德篇》和《国家篇》（第5—7卷）中，集中讨论了知识的定义、知识与意见的区分、太阳喻与线段喻等知识问题；亚里士多德在《后分析篇》和《论灵魂》中，探索了科学知识的性质和条件等关于知识和真理的问题。在对柏拉图、亚里士多德等古希腊哲学家的思想进行继承与融合的基础上，中世纪初期百科全书式思想家波爱修斯（A. M. S. Boethius）创造性地提出了自己关于知识的系统理论，包括知识的划分、知识的获得模式以及人类知识的局限性等。

　　在亚里士多德的思想中，"知识"一词对应着两个希腊词汇：一个是ἐπιστήμη（science），另一个是γνῶσις（knowledge）。这两个近义词有一点细微的差别：前者通常指"具有了形态的知识"，后者指"形成过程中的知识，相当于知道了、了解了其确定性的东西"。[1]从亚里士多德所使用的这两个希腊词汇可以看出，他所谓的知识也可以对应于"科学"和"学科"的中文翻译。在波爱修斯的知识划分理论中，所谓的"知识"同样具有科学和学科的意思，除此之外，知识还有一层含义，即哲学。哲学的概念在波爱修斯的观念中远比我们现在所理解的宽泛，这一传统来自古希腊。毕达哥拉斯第一个提出"哲学就是爱智慧"，柏拉图的《国家篇》和亚里士多德的《形而上学》中都延续了毕达哥拉斯对哲学的这一看法，并且进一步认为，哲学是最高贵、最神圣的知识。[2]波爱修斯在其最早的一部逻辑学

---

　　* 王琦（1982—），辽宁葫芦岛人，南开大学哲学院科技哲学教研室副教授，主要研究方向为科学史研究，中世纪哲学与文化。

　　① 亚里士多德：《亚里士多德全集》，中国人民大学出版社，1996年，第166页，注释2。
　　② 参见《柏拉图全集》第2卷，第490页；《亚里士多德全集》第7卷，第32页。

著作中明确指出：哲学在某种意义上是对智慧（*sapientia*）的热爱和追求（*amor et studium*），这里的智慧包括能力（*ars*）和知识（*notitia*）。①在这种意义上，波爱修斯宽泛地将知识的总汇看作哲学。综上所述，波爱修斯对知识的划分，其实就是对哲学学科或科学的划分。

一

波爱修斯第一次提到知识的划分问题是在其早期逻辑学著作《波菲利〈范畴篇导论〉注释》（*In Isagogen Porphyrii Commenta*）中②，在其后期的神学著作《论三位一体》（*De Trinitate*）中③，知识又被进一步细分。

波爱修斯曾为波菲利的《〈范畴篇〉导论》写过两篇注释。第一篇注释比较短，只有两章。该篇注释是基于修辞学家维克托里（Gaius Marius Victorinus）的翻译，但是由于波爱修斯对维克托里的翻译并不满意，认为维克托里对波菲利的了解甚少，而且有些地方翻译得太过模糊，所以波爱修斯基于自己的翻译写了第二篇注释，分为五章。在两篇注释的开端，波爱修斯分别从不同的视角指出哲学与灵魂相关。④波爱修斯认为，生命体拥有三种级别的灵魂能力："第一种级别的能力用于支撑生命体的生命，这种能力产生于生命体的诞生之时并通过营养来维持生命；第二种级别的能力是对感觉的判断；第三种级别的能力是心灵力量的基础，也是理性的基础。"⑤这三种级别的能力是由低到高排序的，后面级别的能力可以将前面的能力作为自己的"奴隶和仆人"，进而将其所具有的功能纳入自己的能力，构成自己能力的一部分。三种灵魂能力分属于不同的生命体。第一种级别的能力属于植物所具有。第二种级别能力是所有动物拥有的，换言之，动物的灵魂不仅能创造、滋养和维持肉体，而且可以形成对于事物的各种不同形式的判断。虽然第二种级别的灵魂能力可以把握可感觉的物体处于当

---

① Boethius, *Anicii Manlii Severini Boethii In Isagogen Porphyrii Commenta*. S. Brandt ed.: Vindobonae [etc.]: Tempsky [etc.], 1906, p. 7.

② Boethius, *The Theological Tractates. The Consolation of Philosophy*. transls. by H. F. Stewart, E. K. Rand & S. J. Tester, London [etc.]: Harvard University Press, 1906, pp.7-9，140-143.

③ Boethius. *The Theological Tracadaes; The Consolation of Philosophy*. 1971, pp.8-12.

④ Boethius. *The Theological Tracadaes; The Consolation of Philosophy*. 1906, p. 7，135.

⑤ Boethius. *The Theological Tracadaes; The Consolation of Philosophy*. 1906, p. 136；1957, pp.70-71.

下状态时事物的形式，也能够在撤消感觉或移除可感觉的物体的时候，记住感觉到的形式的影像，进而形成记忆，但是，它们无法以同等的程度记住所有的事物，这也就意味着，当动物开始渐渐遗忘之时，它们没办法回忆起很多事情。拥有第三种级别灵魂能力的是人类，除了具有滋养和感知的能力外，还可以处理当下事物的概念，或者理解不在场事物，或者研究未知事物。

从人类所拥有的灵魂能力可知，人类对当下事物、不在场事物甚至未知事物都可以进行探究。人类的灵魂能力可以在四个方面使用理性本身的能力："可以询问事物是否如此（whether it is），或如果确定了它是这样，那么可以质疑它是什么（what it is）。如果通过理性获得了这两种知识，那么接着需要探究的是任意一个个别事物如何会这样（how any particular thing is），并研究它所具有的偶性的其他变化；了解了关于事物的这些情况之后，灵魂也可以通过理性来询问和探寻事物为什么如此（why it is）。"①通过运用理性，人类的灵魂获得了关于事物的知识，这一过程到了 20 世纪 60 年代发展成了一个在西方较为流行的关于知识的说法，即四个 W：知道是什么（Know-what）、知道为什么（Know-why）、知道怎么做（Know-how）和知道是谁（Know-who）。

那么，通过理性获得的知识或哲学如何划分呢？波爱修斯认为，哲学包括理论的（*theoretica*）部分和实践的（*practica*）部分，那么知识就可以划分为思辨的（*speculativa*）知识和实践的（*activa*）知识。②这种对知识的划分源于亚里士多德但又有些不同。亚里士多德将知识划分为三种：理论和思辨的科学（*theoria*）、实践的科学（*praxis*）和创制的科学（*poiesis*）。③虽然波爱修斯并没有指出关于创制知识的问题，但是与亚里士多德一样，他也重视思辨知识的进一步划分。二者都将思辨知识分为三门学科：物理学、数学和神学。

亚里士多德指出，物理学和数学的研究对象都是不可分离的事物：物理学的研究对象是"在自身内具有运动本原的东西"④；数学的研究对象

---

① Boethius, 1957, p. 72.

② cf. Boethius, 1906, p. 8.

③ cf. The Complete Works of Aristotle II, pp.158-159.

④《亚里士多德全集》第 7 卷，第 254 页。

是静止的（at rest）、恒久的①。波爱修斯延续了亚里士多德关于这两门学科的观点，但是更加详细地进行了解释。虽然在《波菲利〈范畴篇导论〉注释》中，波爱修斯指出了三种思辨的知识，但只是初步的概述②，更详细的解释是在《论三位一体》的第二章中给出的。根据波爱修斯的观点，物理学研究的是运动，关注的是物体的形式以及构成物体的质料，虽然在思想中，形式可能会与物体分离，但是在现实中，二者是无法分割的，因此，作为物理学研究对象的运动，是非抽象的或非独立的；数学研究的是与质料脱离开的物体的形式，但是事实上，这些与质料相关的形式是无法真正独立于物体的，换言之，数学的研究对象不是抽象的。③

与物理学和数学两种知识不同，亚里士多德指出还有一种思辨知识，其研究对象是"分离的、存在而不运动的东西"，在他看来，具有"分离和不运动"这种本性的存在物一定是"最初的、最重要的本原"，也就是神学研究的"神圣物"（the divine）。④同样的，在波爱修斯看来，由于上帝的存在不依托于物质和运动，因此，神学所研究的神圣物既没有质料也不运动，而是抽象的、可独立的。总而言之，不论是亚里士多德还是波爱修斯都将思辨的知识分成了三类，对应的三门学科是物理学、数学和神学。但是，这三门学科与我们现代所理解的意义有所不同。

首先是物理学（physics）。在古代和中世纪哲学家那里，physics（物理学）是与 natural science（自然科学）、natural philosophy（自然哲学）同义使用的，他们并没有将三个概念进行区分，直到 19 世纪，关于物理学的书籍仍被称为自然哲学。但是从这个时候开始，现代意义上的科学的范围和方法越来越与自然哲学区分开来。

其次是数学。古代和中世纪的西方数学概念比我们现在所理解的数学概念宽泛，除了包括算术和几何之外，还包括音乐和天文学，由于这四门学科的研究对象都与"数"相关，所以它们都被归为数学学科。波爱修斯为了强调数学的重要性，赋予数学的四门学科一个统一名称——*quadrivium*（四艺）。在其著作《算术原理》（*De Institutione Arithmetica*）的开篇，波爱

---

① *The Complete Works of Aristotle,* the Revised Oxford Translation (2 Volumes), Fourth Printing, 1991, ed. by J. Barnes, Princeton, N. J. Princeton University Press, p. 159.

② cf. Boethius, 1906, pp.7-9.

③ cf. Boethius, 1971, pp.8-9.

④ The Complete Works of Aristotle II, p. 159. 参见《亚里士多德全集》第 7 卷，第 254 页。

修斯第一次使用了 *quadrivium* 这个词，用"四艺"指称四门数学学科，并对四门学科的研究对象进行了说明：算术研究关于数的理论，即研究"数"本身；几何研究静止的数量；天文学研究运动的数量；音乐研究数与数之间的比例。①其中需要重点解释的是音乐学科。音乐属于数学学科要归功于毕达哥拉斯，他发现了音程中具有数学比例关系，由此奠定了音乐的数学基础。属于数学学科的音乐研究的是旋律（melody），包括研究音调（notes）、音程（intervals）、音阶（scales）和不同音乐调式（modes）的特点。②所有这些研究都与算术中的比例原理有关，研究的是数与数之间的关系。所以，在波爱修斯的时代，音乐归属于数学。

最后是神学。波爱修斯的神学不是指关于宗教经典的学科，而是指第一哲学或形而上学。神学研究的只能是没有影像的、纯粹的形式（pure form）。由于任何事物的存在，都不是因为它具有质料，而是因为它具有某种特定的形式，所以，神学所研究的这种纯粹的形式成为"存在之源"，也是"存在本身"。③因此，神学成为哲学中最高级别的学科。

那么，这样一种划分方式是否合理？三门学科是否囊括了所有的思辨知识？

二

上文提到，波爱修斯对知识的细分是在《论三位一体》的第二章中，对这一细分，阿奎那（Thomas Aquinas）在注释《论三位一体》时用问题 V 和 VI 进行了讨论。英译者将阿奎那的注释之题 V 和 VI 命名为《知识的划分和方法》（*The Division and Methods of the Sciences*），作为英译的单行本。问题 V 和 VI 分别讨论思辨知识的划分和思辨知识的方法。著作讨论了两个问题：一个是思辨知识的划分，一个是思辨知识的方法。对于将思辨知识分为物理学、数学和神学是否合适的问题，阿奎那列举出了十个反驳并对之一一回应，从而捍卫了思辨知识三分法的准确性。其中两个重要的反驳

① Boethius, *Boethian Number Theory: A Translation of the De Institutione Arithmetica,* transl. by M. Masi. Amsterdam: Rodopi, 1983, pp.71-72.

② Clarke, *Higher Education in the Ancient World,* Routledge & Kegan Paul, p. 54.

③ Boethius, 1971, pp.8-11.

分别关于逻辑学的归属和七艺的划分。

1．逻辑学是否属于思辨知识

logic（逻辑学）在柏拉图的传统中最初被称为 dialectic（辩证法）。不管是新柏拉图主义者还是波爱修斯都没有对逻辑论证和辩证法论证进行区分。亚里士多德也没有使用 logic 一词，而是用 analytica（分析或分析学）来表示关于推理的理论。虽然现代意义上的"逻辑"一词并非始于亚里士多德，而是始于亚历山大（Alexander of Aphrodisias）的使用，但是，逻辑学这个领域的内容是由亚里士多德的《工具论》确定的。[①]对于逻辑学的身份归属主要有两种观点：一种认为逻辑学是哲学的一个分支；另一种认为逻辑学是哲学的一种工具。[②]

第一种观点的主要代表是斯多葛主义者。他们认为，逻辑学是哲学一个必不可少的分支。这种观点的支持者是将逻辑学与思辨哲学、实践哲学相并列，而并非把逻辑学归属于思辨知识。在他们看来，哲学除了可以分为思辨的和实践的部分外，还应具有理性的部分。其中，思辨哲学研究的是事物的本性；实践哲学研究的是关于道德等实践问题；除此之外，则是关于命题和三段论推理等问题，这些主题就属于逻辑学所研究的范围。[③]就此而言，思辨的、实践的和理性的三部分哲学分别具有不同的研究对象和目标，"既然思辨知识和实践知识是哲学的组成部分，那么毋庸置疑，理性知识也应该被证明是哲学的组成部分之一"[④]，即逻辑学应该是哲学的分支，与思辨哲学并列，故而不能归属于思辨知识。

第二种观点的主要支持者是亚里士多德主义者。他们延续了亚里士多德在《论题篇》中的观点[⑤]，将逻辑学看作论证中发现谬误的实用工具和人类探索中不可缺少的工具。因此，他们将亚里士多德的逻辑学著作称为《工具论》（Organon）。从逻辑学的工具论观点可以看出，逻辑学是不能跟思辨哲学、实践哲学并列的，但是，逻辑学是否能归属于思辨知识呢？亚里士多德在《形而上学》的开篇指出，思辨哲学和实践哲学要解决的是关

---

① Kneale. *The Development of Logic*. Oxford: Clarendon Press, 1984, p. 7.

② Sorabji. *The Philosophy of the Commentators 200-600 AD— A Sourcebook Volume 3: Logic and Metaphysics,* Duckworth, pp.32-36.

③ cf. Boethius, 1906, p. 141；1957, p. 75.

④ Boethius, 1906, p. 142；1957, p. 76.

⑤ 参见《亚里士多德全集》第 1 卷，第 545 页。

于智慧的问题，即"关于什么原因，什么本原的科学"①。可见，思辨知识是研究智慧的，即"研究最初原因和本原"②。阿奎那指出，由于逻辑学并不是研究最初的原因或本原的，而是研究思辨知识中所需要的三段论推理、概念定义等，所以他认为，逻辑学不属于思辨知识，而是它的工具。

但是，阿奎那对波爱修斯观点的解读并不准确，因为在他看来，"对于波爱修斯来说，逻辑学与其说是一门知识，不如说是知识的工具"③。事实上，波爱修斯认为，逻辑学不仅具有工具作用，而且本身也是一门知识，是哲学的分支。可见，针对上述两种关于逻辑学的不同观点，波爱修斯采取了一种融合的态度。在他看来，逻辑学具有双重身份：

> 因为逻辑学保有自己的目标，这个目标仅被哲学关注，因此，它必定被认为是哲学的一部分，但是，既然哲学所关注的的逻辑学目标承诺它会辅助哲学的其他部分，那么，我们并不否认它也是哲学工具；逻辑学的目标是发现和判断原因。……因此，逻辑学是哲学的一部分，因为哲学独自是它的主人；但是，逻辑学也是哲学的工具，因为通过它可以探究哲学所寻求的真理。④

根据波爱修斯的观点，当逻辑学作为知识的工具时，它是为思辨知识服务的；当逻辑学作为一门独立的知识时，它是与思辨知识、实践知识并列的。总之，不论逻辑学是工具还是一门独立的知识，都不可能归属于思辨知识，因为逻辑学与思辨知识的三门学科在本质上是不同的。

2. 七艺划分与思辨知识

拉丁词 *artes liberales*（liberal arts，自由技艺）源自希腊词 ενκυκλιοσ παιδεια（general education，通识教育）。"自由技艺"最初一般是哲学家学习的课程，是作为教育初级阶段学习的系统而完备的知识，被认为是学习高等教育或为更高级别的哲学课程做准备的。自由技艺课程的数量从古希腊开始不断变化。最早是在柏拉图的《国家篇》中，自由技艺被确定为体

---

① 《亚里士多德全集》第 7 卷，第 30 页。

② 《亚里士多德全集》第 7 卷，第 29 页。

③ Aquinas, *The Division and Methods of the Sciences,* transl. With introduction and notes by A. Maurer, Toronto: Pontifical Institute of Mediaeval Studies, pp.9-10.

④ Boethius, 1906, pp.142-143; 1957, p. 77.

育、音乐、算术、平面几何、立体几何、天文学与和声学七门学科[①]；经过罗马时期瓦罗（Marcus Terentius Varro）的修改，自由技艺被增至九门学科，包括文法、修辞、逻辑、音乐、数学、集合、天文、医学及建筑学；最终将"七艺"的内容确定下来的是卡佩拉（Martianus Capella），在其著作《墨丘利与菲劳罗嘉的婚姻》（*The Marriage of Mercury and Philology*）中，卡佩拉将自由技艺的内容规定为语法（grammar）、逻辑学（logic）、修辞学（rhetoric）、几何学（geometry）、算术（arithmetic）、天文学（astronomy）和音乐（music）。[②]而对七艺的具体划分则要归功于波爱修斯。前文提到，波爱修斯将四门数学命名为四艺，即七艺中的算术、几何、天文学和音乐，所以在9、10世纪的时候，学者们将剩下的三门学科——逻辑学、语法学和修辞学——对应地命名为 *trivium*（三科）。

在与七艺有关的反驳中，阿奎那提出的是："哲学通常被分为七艺，其中既不包括自然知识也不包括神圣知识，而只包括理性的数学知识。因此，关于自然的和神圣的知识不应该被称为思辨知识的组成部分。"[③]对于这一反驳，阿奎那从亚里士多德主义的角度给出回应。

首先，亚里士多德认为，在学习知识之前要先探索知识的方式，"应该学会如何论证每一种事物，同时去寻求知识和知识的方式是荒谬的"[④]。正因为如此，工具性质的七艺应该先学习，七艺可以说是从探索知识的方式角度划分的，并不是对知识的完整划分，只是作为进一步研究哲学做准备的。至于数学可以归属于七艺，则如亚里士多德在《尼各马可伦理学》中所言，数学的学习不需要经验[⑤]，而物理学需要经验。这也就意味着，数学是基础学科，可以作为知识的一种探索方式。波爱修斯将四门数学学科看作进一步学习哲学、通往智慧的四条道路，他甚至认为，如果不能掌握数学知识，根本不可能找到真理，无法成为哲学家。[⑥]所以，数学可以归属于七艺，而物理学不可以。

其次，亚里士多德将"技艺"称为"创制的理性"，因而，七门自由技

---

① 参见《柏拉图全集》第2卷，第431、519-520、526-527、530-533页。

② cf. Stahl, Johnson & Burge.

③ Aquinas, p. 4.

④《亚里士多德全集》第7卷，第63页。

⑤ 参见亚里士多德，第178页。

⑥ cf. Boethius, 1983, pp.71-73.

艺"不仅关涉知识，而且涉及理性自身的某种直接产物"①，但是，不同于七门自由技艺，神圣知识和自然知识二者只与知识有关，而并不涉及创制的产物。由此可见，神学和物理学是不能归属于七艺的。

总而言之，思辨知识的划分方式与七艺的划分方式不同，是从不同的角度进行的两种划分。数学作为七门自由技艺之一，它可以为深入学习哲学打好灵魂的基础，使人的灵魂从有形的世界提升出来；而且它同时又具有理性自身的直接产物②，如算术的产物是计数，几何学的产物是测量，音乐的产物是创作乐曲，天文学的产物是绘制天体的运行轨迹。所以，数学可以归属于七艺，而物理学和神学不可以。但是，数学与神学、物理学一样，都是关于事物性质或者可以得出事物性质的知识，因此，三者归属于思辨知识。

三

波爱修斯对知识的划分也许并不完善，但是按照理性的思维具有其合理性。这样的一种划分方式，尤其是对七艺的细分，对中世纪大学的教育模式和理念影响很大，他的数学著作，尤其是《算数原理》和《音乐原理》成为中世纪大学中使用最多的数学教材；他翻译和注释的亚里士多德《范畴篇》和《解释篇》成为中世纪早期逻辑学的教科书，在公元 12 世纪以前是人们了解和研究古代逻辑学的唯一材料，并且他创造的许多逻辑术语至今仍在沿用。

除了数学与逻辑学著作的影响外，波爱修斯知识体系中的神学对后世也有重要影响。作为思辨知识的三门学科，物理学、数学和神学运用的方法、模式各不相同：物理学运用的是理性模式（*rationabiliter*）；数学运用的是系统模式（*disciplinaliter*）；神学运用的理智模式（*intellectualiter*）。③这三门学科所运用的模式关涉知识的获得模式，尤其是理性模式和理智模式。在其最后一部著作《哲学的慰藉》（*Consolatio Philosophiae*）中，波爱修斯指出，知识的获得取决于理解事物的认知者的能力，而不是被认知的

---

① Aquinas, p. 11.

② cf. ibid..

③ cf. Boethius, 1971, pp.8-9.

事物本身。①所以，由于认知者能力的不同，知识获得的模式也有区别。波爱修斯将认知者的能力从低级到高级划分为感觉、想象、理性和理智。其中，感觉能力依靠的是有形体，观察的是未脱离质料的有形体；想象能力可以脱离开质料而独自辨认有形体；理性能力则能够超越感觉和想象的能力，用普遍的方式考察有形体本身在单一个体中当下特有的形式，也就是从其所属的种属进行考察；相比前三种能力，最高级别的能力是理智，因为理智是用纯粹的心灵之眼明察秋毫地注视简单形式本身。②在四种认知能力中，理性能力属于人类，理智这样的认知能力唯独属于上帝那样的神圣者。由此可见，由于人类不具有理智能力，所以用理智能力所获知识，即关于纯粹的形式本身的知识，人类是无法获得的。这就导致了人类知识的局限性，这种局限性引发了波爱修斯关于理性与信仰之间关系的探讨。波爱修斯在具有信仰的前提下，通过运用逻辑学、数学等知识，对神学问题进行理性论证，这是第一次对理性神学的正式探讨，对后世，尤其是理性神学的高峰——阿奎那，产生了重要影响。阿奎那翻译注释了波爱修斯的两篇神学论文，并以此为基础进入了研究理性神学的高峰期。

参考文献：

[1]波爱修斯，2012 年：《神学论文集·哲学的慰藉》，荣震华译，商务印书馆。

[2]《柏拉图全集》，2014 年，王晓朝译，人民出版社。

[3]亚里士多德，2003 年：《尼各马可伦理学》，廖申白译注，商务印书馆。

[4]《亚里士多德全集》，1996 年，苗力田主编，中国人民大学出版社。

[5]Aquinas, T., 1953, *The Division and Methods of the Sciences,* translate. with introduction and notes by A. Maurer, Toronto: The Pontifical Institute of Mediaeval Studies.

[6]Boethius, A. M. S., 1906, *Anicii Manlii Severini Boethii In Isagogen Porphyrii Commenta,* ed. by S. Brandt, Vindobonae [etc.]: Tempsky [etc.].

---

① cf. Boethius, 1971, pp.410-411.

② cf. Boethius, 1971；参见波爱修斯，第205页。

[7] 1957, "The second edition of the *Commentaries on the Isagoge of Porphyry,* (Book I)", in R. McKeon (ed.), *Selections from Medieval Philosophers (I): Augustine to Albert the Great,* New York: Charles Scribner's Sons.

[8] 1971, *The Theological Tractates; The Consolation of Philosophy,* transls. by H. F. Stewart, E. K. Rand & S. J. Tester, London [etc.]: Harvard University Press.

[9] 1983, *Boethian Number Theory: A Translation of the De Institutione Arithmetica,* transl. by M. Masi, Amsterdam: Rodopi.

[10] Clarke, M. L., 1971, *Higher Education in the Ancient World,* London: Routledge & Kegan Paul.

[11] Kneale, M. & W., 1984, *The Development of Logic,* Oxford: Clarendon Press.

[12] Sorabji, R., 2004, *The Philosophy of the Commentators 200-600 AD — A Sourcebook Volume 3: Logic and Metaphysics,* London: Duckworth.

[13] Stahl, W. H., Johnson, R. & Burge, E., 1971-1977, *Martianus Capella and the Seven Liberal Arts* (2 vols.), New York: Columbia University Press.

[14] *The Complete Works of Aristotle,* the Revised Oxford Translation (2 Volumes), Fourth Printing, 1991, ed. by J. Barnes, Princeton, N. J.: Princeton University Press.

（本文原载于《哲学研究》2017 年第 12 期）

论当代科学哲学动态先验论路径的实用主义阐释及其超越的可能性

贾向桐*

进入 21 世纪以来，当代科学哲学的研究范式又有了新的进展，"近来的主要形式之一是借鉴康德和传统约定主义来复兴和捍卫先验知识。弗里德曼（M. Friedman）、德皮尔里斯（G. Depierris）、迪赛勒（R. Disalle）和斯塔姆普（D. Stump）等都提出和支持这种观点：我们信念结构之网（特别是物理学）中的一些命题具有特殊地位，它们应该被理解为一种先验知识。"[1]这一新先验论进路以强调动态科学知识（或原则）的分层化和功能化特征为中心辩护环节，主张将库恩的历史主义与早期逻辑实证主义对先验知识的解读逻辑相结合，从动态理性视角对科学合理性作出说明。但这种新的动态先验论（dynamics a priori）关于先验原则的属性与交替基础问题仍需深化，这也是新近实用主义阐释兴起的内在原因，在哈索克（C. Hasok）、莫曼（T. Mormann）等支持者看来，"对先验知识实用性方面的强调，不但较之于弗里德曼的进化理性说明更具优势，而且这还提供了将进化的理性过程理解为连续性的更好解释"[2]。事实上，这一主要源自刘易斯传统的实用主义阐释的确进一步揭示了科学认知实践的局域性和语境化问题，并对"理论-导向"（theory-oriented）的科学哲学范式进行了深刻反思，使得动态先验论背后的科学实践意义凸显出来。当然，先验化实用

---

　* 贾向桐，南开大学哲学院教授，研究方向为科学技术哲学。

　① Shaffer M. The Constitutive a Priori and Epistemic Justification. In Michael J. Shaffer, Michael L. Veber eds: *What Place for the A Priori?*. Open court, 2011, p. 193.

　② Mormann T. A Place for Pragmatism in the Dynamics of Reason?. In *Studies in History and Philosophy of Science*, 2012, Vol.43, p. 36.

主义维度的这种阐释还存在一定的局限性，因为它虽然强调了科学理论与实践的贯通，但其论述的视野仍是传统理论哲学的二分法，这种纯粹实用阐释仍难以真正勾勒出科学进步与合理性的内在理性逻辑，只有最终回归感性的科学实践之中，我们才能将科学理论的结构及其相应实践活动的一致性和同构性展现出来，进而全面揭示当代科学哲学发展的新可能性。

一、动态先验论的演绎与辩护逻辑

早在 20 世纪末，弗里德曼等在分析自然主义背景下科学哲学新先验论进路的发展问题时就已指出："当代对宽泛意义上康德主义持同情态度的哲学家们试图重新阐释其先验论规划"，这一思路主要存在两个基本发展方向：其中，斯特劳森和麦克道威尔的工作很有代表性，而且这些工作引起了学界的普遍关注，但他们在"现代数学—物理学的科学世界观以及所引入的康德主义议题方面却存在矛盾"，以至于他们的"工作曲解了康德主义的最初意向"；此外，"还有另一条试图从分析哲学传统出发重建和恢复康德科学哲学的路径，从现在的观点看，这是由巴士达尔（G. Buchdahl）发展起来的。他的一个基本论点就是保留康德哲学中数学物理学在科学知识中的中心地位，与此同时，松动对欧氏-牛顿主义（Euclidean-Newtonian）科学的承诺"[1]。在弗里德曼等人看来，通常被忽视的第二条发展路径才是科学哲学发展中最有希望的，"巴士达尔对科学理论活动的建设性解释，是很有洞见和启发性的，它实际上指出了一条新进路：康德式的先验综合判断概念可以超出其欧氏-牛顿主义语境得以明确总结。其实，这种对康德先验性的概括，由此失去了它的不变性特征，而保留了对经验知识本质上的建构性功能"[2]。这也正是以弗里德曼为代表的动态先验论的基本理论建构理路，与斯特劳森和奎因等人的争论视角不同，自然主义整体论（Naturalistic Holism）成为新先验论反思科学合理性的逻辑起点。

较之于自然主义，动态先验论的基本目标意在重新阐明科学革命的纯

① Friedman M, Graham Bird. Kantian Themes in Contemporary Philosophy. In *Proceedings of the Aristotelian Society*, 1998, 72, Vol.p. 111-123.

② Friedman M, Graham Bird. Kantian Themes in Contemporary Philosophy: In *Proceedings of the Aristotelian Society*, 1998, Vol.72, p. 123.

粹理性本质，这样才能彻底证明科学革命的转变既是可能的，也是最符合理性认知的自然过程。面对以不可通约为代表的历史主义难题，库恩以来的科学哲学陷入了自然主义带来的相对主义泥沼中。因此，在新先验论者的理解中，要克服不可通约背后科学发展间断性问题，关键在于重新解读逻辑实证主义作为标准科学哲学起始点的真正价值所在，"为了理解 20 世纪哲学中逻辑实证主义的整体意义，我们应该处理好其早期工作中更专注于技术的新康德主义因素问题。所以，弗里德曼认为，20 世纪 20 年代早期的逻辑实证主义，尤其是卡尔纳普和莱辛巴赫的工作，即他们关于相对论物理学方法论的研究至关重要，这些研究已表明先验性在世界科学理解方面的作用不是否定性的，而是一种康德意义上的基本再建"①。这也是其重估逻辑实证主义的初衷，从而为在巴士达尔的先验论辩护奠定基础，也因此否定了从逻辑实证主义到奎因自然主义发展的所谓必然性。按照这种思路，弗里德曼、斯塔姆普等主要借鉴了莱辛巴赫对先验性的区分思想："必然性和不可修正性，在所有时间都是固定不变的"和"知识对象的构成性概念"，而强调"只保留后者"。②之后，卡尔纳普更是进一步发展了这一思想，"为莱辛巴赫相对化先验知识观提供了成熟的表述"："一个判断是有意义的，如果论断是在某种语言框架约定意义上的规则范围之内"，所以，按照弗里德曼的观点，动态先验论的主张是和逻辑实证主义存在内在关联关系的，这种主张"从卡尔纳普的语言框架，特别是相对化的构成性先验知识的实证概念中得出"。③

但实际上，以奎因为代表的自然主义才是科学哲学历史发展的现实轨迹，这源自对"语言框架"的另一种解读，"正是卡尔纳普的语言框架哲学形成了奎因认识论整体论的反对形式的背景，按照这一观点，在先验知识和后验知识、逻辑和事实、分析和综合之间不存在二分"④。对此，弗里德曼认为，正是这种自然主义预设的平等主义的信念之网彻底阻断了对科学连续性说明的先验论进路，但其理论本身是存在很大问题的，所以，无

① Richardson A, Uebel T. The Epistemic Agent in Logical Positivism. In *Proceedings of the Aristotelian Society, Supplementary*, 2005, Vol.79, p. 75.

② Friedman M. *Dynamics of Reason*: *The* 1999 *Kant Lectures at Stanford University*. CSLI Publishers, 2001, p. 30.

③ Tsou J. A Role for Reason in Science. In *Dialogue*, 2003, Vol.42, pp.576-578.

④ Friedman M. *Dynamics of Reason*: *The* 1999 *Kant Lectures at Stanford University*. CSLI Publishers, 2001, p. 32.

论是在理论还是历史现实层面，自然主义解读都是亟待突破的。①要克服这些问题只能是返回逻辑实证主义的源头，因为在这里科学哲学才走向了岔路，"奎因对分析—综合命题二分的批判，意味着卡尔纳普对构成性原则的形式化说明的失败，但这只是说明纯粹形式逻辑不足以刻画科学的构成性原则而已。但这些原则本身仍是自然科学绝对的基本特征"②。鉴于此，动态先验论主张寻求表述构成性原则的新方法，那就是将科学连续性置于理论的分层与功能的不对称性特征方面。只有科学理论在结构和功能上存在的等级性，才使得自然主义的经验还原理想在理论的分层结构中既不可能，也不正确。而且，这种理论结构和功能的特殊属性还赋予人类理性和实践活动以基础性地位，换言之，这也是科学理论之间实现沟通和通约的重要依据，所以以历史动态和功能性为特征的"先验框架"构成解决库恩不可通约问题的新思路："科学革命性是一系列不同构成性原则的替代过程"，"哲学的元范式可以确保框架之间合理性的回溯性概念"。③

斯塔姆普进一步明确了这一思路，"重要的是，在自然科学理论中有各种构成性要素存在，其中一些实际上是一种先验知识，即，具有必然性和固定的知识，而其他部分则不是，这样以来，我们就可以理解科学中的概念变化问题了"④。弗里德曼在此基础上总结了新的辩护策略：沿用卡西尔对"科学理性连续性和汇聚性的进化说明"模式，进而强调先验概念"作为引导或丹尼特所谓直觉泵（intuition pumps）的作用"。⑤这一思路的确不同于斯特劳森的"经验形而上学"（metaphysics of experience）进路，"斯特劳森认为，我们可以接受明显的洞见真理的能力，因此而陷入哲学的'理

---

① 为此，弗里德曼在反驳整体论的基础上强调科学理论中先验原则的意义，这是"形成经验知识的必要条件"，而整体论则忽略了科学结构的复杂性，这是人类实践构造方式或结构的差异性造成的。这体现在科学理论对整体论的批判构成新动态先验论的一个基本共识，先验原则在实践哲学中表现为科学交往中人与自然交互活动的同构性。（见拙文：《自然科学中先验知识可以存在》，《哲学研究》，2014年第6期）

② Samaroo R. Friedman's thesis. In *Studies in History and Philosophy of Modern Physics*, 2015, Vol.52, p. 134.

③ Dimitrakos T. Kuhnianism and Neo-Kantianism: On Friedman's Account of Scientific Change. In *International Studies in the Philosophy of Science*, 2016, Vol.30, p. 366.

④ Stump D. *Conceptual Change and the Philosophy of Science.* Rutledge, 2015, p. 167.

⑤ Mormann T. A Place for Pragmatism in the Dynamics of Reason?. In *Studies in History and Philosophy of Science*, 2012, Vol.43, p. 29.

性直观'传统"①。与之不同，弗里德曼等的基本思想是"设想一种科学理性的进化——总结为一系列理论或概念框架——作为在逻辑或概念空间的连续轨迹"，然后借助于柯西准则实现理论前后的一种汇聚，"'真正的宇宙秩序'不再为单一理论 T，而是由一系列趋同的理论 T1、T2、T3 等所给出。和卡西尔一样，弗里德曼的动态科学理性也没有断言理论（在本体论上）趋同于独立于心灵的实在领域；而是，它们会（在数学上）汇聚于理论的历史进步中，不断连续地接近于一个完全理想的关于现象的数学表述，但永远也达不到"②。

这样，在新先验论进路看来，这种理论的汇聚类似于人们交往合理性的发展过程，其本身既是连续的也是具有合理性的。不同范式或框架界定的科学理论就有了连续性和可比较的基础，"这种新哲学框架通过自然的、合理的或有理由的概念转变来帮助我们界定意图。在弗里德曼看来，哲学在构想和提出新概念可能性的基础上使得科学进化成为可能"③。特别是在借鉴哈贝马斯合理性概念的基础上，科学哲学能够在克服自然主义问题的前提下重新论证科学的合理性。

根据哈贝马斯对工具合理性和交往合理性的划分，弗里德曼认为库恩的辩护主要集中在工具合理性层面，"指向后继范式没问题的纯粹工具性的成功，就失去了对威胁（概念相对主义）的反应，所以我们更应该意识到交往合理性领域的基本问题"，"解释科学范式或框架革命转变的交往合理性"。④更准确一点说，全面的对理论的汇聚或连续性的解释，这在科学革命中应该归于"回溯"（retrospectively）和"预期"（prospectively）的整体理性。其中，所谓"回溯"，即"框架或范式之间的汇聚性，这不是世界实际的实在趋同，而是交往意义上的趋同。后一框架被视为扩展了前者的经验可能性空间，并且把前者容纳为其特例"；"预期"则是指如何前瞻性地解释科学新框架替代的合理性而成为一种实时的类似于"詹姆斯的实时假

① Friedman M, Graham Bird. Kantian Themes in Contemporary Philosophy. In *Proceedings of the Aristotelian Society*, 1998, Vol.72, p. 117.

② Mormann T. A Place for Pragmatism in the Dynamics of Reason?. In *Studies in History and Philosophy of Science*, 2012, Vol.43, p. 29.

③ Kindi V. The Challenge of Scientific Revolutions. In *International Studies in the Philosophy of Science*, 2011, Vol.25, p. 338.

④ Friedman M. *Dynamics of Reason*: *The 1999 Kant Lectures at Stanford University*. CSLI Publishers, 2001, p. 95.

说（live hypothesis）"。以"回溯"和"预期"相结合的整体理性才是完整的科学合理，这是科学哲学追求的动态理性的真正内涵。这样，"一旦一个范式变为'实时选择'，也就是说，它是一种预期理性，理智的事就是去采纳它。支持旧范式是可能的，但这不能带来科学的前进；相反，这便是回溯。概言之，弗里德曼意在确保科学进步的合理性，从哲学的视角做出评价来探寻交往合理性"①。

二、实用主义对动态先验论的进一步阐释

虽然新动态先验论在学界产生了重大影响，但仍有许多工作尚未完成，人们在对构成性先验知识、交往合理性的基础问题的阐释和解读成为当前科学哲学的重要研究方向。其中，构成性先验原则的基础和辩护在动态先验论的不同支持者那里发生了激烈争议——"构成性先验原则被视为不是由经验证据所确证的，但其又是可以修正变动的"，这种充满矛盾的"先验性"基础何在，人们应该如何合理说明构成性先验原则替代在新康德主义和约定论之间的尴尬摇摆呢？②实用主义对动态先验论的阐释逐渐发展起来，并产生了巨大影响。哈索克和莫曼等人从刘易斯的"实用先验论"角度出发，强调实用主义对动态先验论在扩展和辩护方面的意义："弗里德曼进路低估了科学知识的实用主义内涵，这在库恩建立在范式概念基础上的科学哲学中就已显现出来，并导致了对相对化先验论过于理论化的说明"，"为了克服这种缺陷，我总结了一种可以称为相对化实用主义先验论的替代性方案"。③斯塔姆普作为从约定论出发为动态先验论辩护的重要代表，也主张进一步把约定论的解释诉诸实用主义，"我坚持的是一种实用主义观点，而不是弗里德曼倡导的新康德主义立场：构成性要素是科学可能性的必要条件的原则和理论"④。具体而言，这种实用主义的阐释主要集中

① Kindi V. The Challenge of Scientific Revolutions. In *International Studies in the Philosophy of Science*, 2011, Vol.25, pp.337-338.

② Shaffer M. The Constitutive a Priori and Epistemic Justification. In Michael J. Shaffer, Michael L. Veber eds. *What Place for the A Priori?*. Open court, 2011, pp.202-207.

③ Kindi V. The Challenge of Scientific Revolutions. In *International Studies in the Philosophy of Science*, 2011, Vol.25, p. 338.

④ Stump D. *ConceptuaL change and the Philosophy of Science*. Rutledge, 2015, p. 167.

在对先验概念和交往合理性背后的"实践-导向"（practice-oriented）的论证层面，相比较而言，如果说弗里德曼关心的问题是理智主义的认识论问题，那么詹姆斯的实用主义则是关注个体和实践的问题。[①]这一思路恰恰部分弥补了纯粹先验论主要关注于"理论-导向"（theory-oriented）的单一性和封闭性问题。

首先，实用主义阐释主张将先验知识的功能化与实用性结合起来进行论证，以便既保证先验知识的框架性功能，又能为先验基础作出合理解释。在这方面，他们主要是诉诸"刘易斯-詹姆斯传统"："奎因对先验知识的怀疑建立在美国哲学中的皮尔士传统"，"但不是另一支实用主义，可以追溯到从刘易斯、杜威到詹姆斯哲学的特征"。[②]在这方面，哈索克等特别注意到刘易斯与莱辛巴赫之间观点的类似之处，"一定存在某些命题，其真值是必然的，而且具有独立于经验的特征，传统先验概念已经被否定，这在很大程度上是因为其必然性和独立性的意义被误读了"[③]。为了重新解释知识的先验可能性，刘易斯把实用先验性概念具体分为三种情况："（1）先验知识是通过某些诸如'自然之光'或特殊的心理起源如天赋这样的心理标准区分开的；（2）由一些特殊的证据模型或经验的逻辑关系，通常称之为'预设'区分开的；（3）心灵的先验规则不能应用到经验中，除非它是在经验中给定的，它们总是有限的或者为一些恒定模式所决定；对范畴解释的先验有效性也有赖于我们的感受性或直觉的先验模式。"[④]但不同于莱辛巴赫，刘易斯认为实用先验性并不是约定或定义，"人类理性的本质是一种思维模式，而不是具体内容；它与结论的有效性相关，而和其原初条件的本然特质无关"[⑤]。这种差别正是实用主义阐释得以发展的重要原因，它以实用主义的实效性原则把科学哲学的彻底自然化与规范化维度贯通起来。

刘易斯通过"有效性"来界定先验概念的方法给莫曼等人的阐释一个

① Kindi V. The Challenge of Scientific Revolutions. In *International Studies in the Philosophy of Science*, 2011, Vol.25, p. 338.

② Klein A. Divide et Impera!: William James's Pragmatist Tradition in the Philosophy of Science. In *Philosophical Topics*, 2008, Vol.36, p. 131.

③ Lewis C. *Mind and the world Order. Outline of a Theory of Knowledge*. Dover, 1999, p. 196.

④ Klein A. Divide et Impera!: William James's Pragmatist Tradition in the Philosophy of Science. In *Philosophical Topics*, 2008, Vol.36, p. 198.

⑤ Klein A. Divide et Impera!: William James's Pragmatist Tradition in the Philosophy of Science. In *Philosophical Topics*, 2008, Vol.36, p. 198.

重要启示，哈索克则进一步比较了动态先验论与刘易斯实用先验主张结合的可能性："尽管很赞赏弗里德曼努力论述在范式激烈转变情况下物理学中先验知识如何连续性进化是可能的工作，但还是比较认同刘易斯强调先验选择中的自由度问题，人们的连续性努力要满足实用的需要。"[①]他认为，弗里德曼对构成性或动态先验知识基础解释中存在的问题，正是在于没有正视知识的实用性质。如果按照实用主义的理解，那么先验原则的结构和功能的构成性则变得易于理解了，"在经验可以开始被理解之前，心灵自身必须提供定义、基本原则和标准"，随着"经验的更新和拓展，也必然会带来这些'态度'的某些变化，虽然它们并不规定经验的内容，而经验也不证明其无效"，所以，"知识中的先验因素是实用性的，而不是经验的"。[②]为此，斯塔姆普也进一步肯定："对科学理论中构成性要素的实用主义理解可以被视为一种收缩式策略（deflationary strategy），将构成性要素的核心信念置于原位不动，但并不认为它们是超越自然或科学领域的东西。这些构成性要素，在我们看来就是开始进行探究或认知的一些原则，只是无需宣布它们是确定的，或者是通过某种特殊直观而知道的"。[③]

其次，是对先验框架或原则动态演变基础的实用主义说明，以弥补弗里德曼交往合理性论证的依据不足问题，"科学理论中刘易斯式的先验原则并不是简单的同义反复；它们确实起到了自然律的意义，在一定程度上这和弗里德曼的构成性原则观点相一致"[④]。因此，对动态先验论进路的实用主义阐释，主要体现为对动态科学理性的实践导向的揭示，从而融合"实用主义中的实践-导向和先验传统的条件-导向（condition-oriented）"[⑤]。在实用主义阐释的支持者看来，弗里德曼正是在将理论框架更迭置于交往合理性的过程中，才确保了科学理论中"先验陈述和哲学争论层次"具有连续性，"哲学具有调节不同范式的使命，它可以通过交往理性或交往合理性的空间，使得只在狭隘的纯粹科学推理范围无法实现统一的不同范式达成

---

① Hasok C. Contingent Transcendental Arguments for Metaphysical Principles. In *Royal Institute of Philosophy*, 2008, Vol.63, p. 133.

② Lewis C. *Mind and thE world Order. Outline of a Theory of Knowledge*. Dover, 1999, p. 266.

③ Stump D. *ConceptuaL change and the Philosophy of Science*. Rutledge, 2015, p. 167.

④ Hasok C. Contingent Transcendental Arguments for Metaphysical Principles. In *Royal Institute of Philosophy*, 2008, Vol.63, p. 117.

⑤ Pihlström S. Synthesizing Traditions: Rewriting the History of Pragmatism and Ranscendental. In *Philosophy History of Philosophy Quarterly*, 2012, Vol.23, p. 382.

一致"。①但事实上，弗里德曼对哈贝马斯交往合理性理论的用法还是"有些奇怪"，"对交往合理性策略是如何保证动态科学理性的连续性说明是初步的，相当粗略的"，"其中的一个原因是哈贝马斯意义上的交往合理性只是实践理性的一部分"，使得"弗里德曼的科学理性概念表现出了一定的理论偏见，按照卡西尔和卡尔纳普的解释，弗里德曼的理性在本质上是理论化的"。不过，"这种不足可以通过强调库恩范式的实用主义方面加以克服"，"库恩的范式在根本上只是卡尔纳普意义上的语言框架，'根据定义'它是被剥夺了实用性的内容"。②在莫曼等人看来，只有对弗里德曼的先验论作出某种实用主义的解读，才能在一定程度上与其整合库恩历史主义的初衷相符合，这也就在根源上对实用主义的解释给予了肯定。

从哈贝马斯本身的最初意图来说，"交往合理性是建立在生活世界的实践基础上的，这种实践超出了主体与实在之间单纯的工具和描述关系"，但很明显，"弗里德曼并不对生活世界中的实践感兴趣，他是想寻求应用哈贝马斯的交往合理性概念到一种科学革命的环境之中，在这里，科学共同体成员缺乏一个共同的范式框架来界定问题和方法"。③这样看来，这一阐释的最大问题是如何揭示出科学实践交往合理性的基础还需要实用主义作为根据。为此，人们才主张借鉴刘易斯-詹姆斯的实用先验论思路，"詹姆斯对便宜假设的使用有助于我们将弗里德曼洞见从物理学拓展到其他具体科学，因为詹姆斯式的心理学正是利用了一套构成性先验论意义上的假设（即意识流议题）"，这种功能性的先验"框架可以为了实践的有效性而帮助调整认知，但它们最终还是一定要在实用的基础上被接受或拒斥"。④在实用主义意义上，理论框架与科学实践活动就具有了统一性，这种"实用基础"确保了科学理论交往或理解公共平台的可能性，并弥补了弗里德曼对实践兴趣的缺乏问题，也从而间接呼应了詹姆斯对心理学的科学地位界定思路。

因此，在实用主义的阐释中，不同理论框架的替代展现出的原因主要

---

① Mormann T. A Place for Pragmatism in the Dynamics of Reason?. In *Studies in History and Philosophy of Science*, 2012, Vol.43, p. 30.

② Mormann T. A Place for Pragmatism in the Dynamics of Reason?. In *Studies in History and Philosophy of Science*, 2012, Vol.43, p. 30.

③ Mormann T. A Place for Pragmatism in the Dynamics of Reason?. In *Studies in History and Philosophy of Science*, 2012, Vol.43, p. 30.

④ Klein A. Divide et Impera!: William James's Pragmatist Tradition in the Philosophy of Science. In *Philosophical Topics*, 2008, Vol.36, pp.151-158.

在于科学实践活动的局域性问题，这样，"康德或准康德主义的先验因素可能也存在于其局部实践之中，它一定是研究、表象或认知可能性的前提"①。局域化的科学实践和功能化的理论框架在实用主义这里取得了一致性，为此，克雷恩引用詹姆斯的思路来改造弗里德曼的构成性先验性概念，"我用'本体论协议'来指称詹姆斯所谓的'便宜的假设'（convenient assumption），在我的术语中这是要强调理论要素在科学理论中起着两种作用——确立本体论和作为稳固智识劳动分工的社会协议的工具"②。纯粹理论的先验框架的合理性指向了科学实践活动的效用以及科学活动的社会分工结果，这进一步发挥了弗里德曼本人的对交往合理性的见解，即"主体间合理性的历史化"的"客观标准总是局域化和语境化的"。③实用主义阐释将新先验论进路初步与科学实践以及社会交往合理性联系起来，使得科学的实践效应尝试沟通了科学认识论中的理性和"自然"，科学实践和知识的结构与功能成为理解科学合理性的关键。

三、科学实践哲学对实用主义阐释的超越

将科学理论的变革与科学实践活动相联系，实用主义对动态先验论的阐释揭示了科学哲学辩护从理论哲学向实践哲学转变的可能性，也从更深层次探究了科学理论框架和结构的多维性以及在此发展过程中的动态内因问题。但实用主义对新先验论框架的解释，仍有不尽人意之处。一方面，"具体原则的选择代表着我们的'主动态度'，它似乎构成对经验分类方式的意图。这样，先验性在某种意义上具有规则性的特征，是有意识的选择"④。也就是说，先验知识的实用主义选择无疑具有实践的随机性。另一方面，先验原则汇聚性特征（包括回溯和预期合理性）的柯西标准方向

---

① Pihlström S. Synthesizing Traditions: Rewriting the History of Pragmatism and Ranscendental. In *Philosophy History of Philosophy Quarterly*, 2012, Vol.23, p. 80.

② Klein A. Divide et Impera!: William James's Pragmatist Tradition in the Philosophy of Science. In *Philosophical Topics*, 2008, Vol.36, p. 144.

③ Friedman M. A post-kuhnian Approach to the History and Philosophy of Science. In *The Monist*, 2010, Vol.93, p. 497.

④ Hullett J. A Pragamatic Conception of the a Priori Re-Viewed. In *Transactions of the Charles S. Peirce Society*, 1973, Vol.9, p. 139.

性问题就难以通过实用主义蕴含的随机性给以说明了，即交往合理性的实用主义阐释和弗里德曼的中心观点的冲突还是明显的："科学理论的早期框架作为一种极限形式存在于现框架的'特定条件下'"，而"后继范式的概念和构成性原则，也就是先验的但非不可变的基本框架命题应该'是通过一系列的自然转变，从早期范式连续的进化'"。①这意味着对先验论进路的实用主义阐释本身还是存在矛盾的，它更多只是指明了科学合理性辩护需求助科学实践效应的问题，但其具体对先验原则或框架的连续性说明仍是模糊的和方向性的，科学实践效应如何沟通科学认识论的自然化与规范化等问题还有待深化。

究其问题的根源，这主要在于实用主义阐释本身还是过于局限在科学实践"效应"的有限视角，因为无论是斯塔姆普将先验基础归于实用，还是莫曼等把先验性和实用属性相结合，他们对理论与实践经验虽已不再作严格区分，凸显了动态先验论背后的科学实践意义。但在这种阐释中仍对理论与实践持一种隔离或分裂的理论哲学态度。在这一点上，较之于詹姆斯等人最初试图超越理论哲学的努力还略有倒退，也就是说，他们对理论（思想）和实践的描述仍处于两个不同层面，对理论功能与结构的理解还没有真正诉诸整个科学实践本身。

因此，按以上思路在探讨科学框架的连续性问题时，我们需要在理论和实践层面上进一步拓展实用主义阐释的论证思路。其中，理论层面是新动态先验论以及实用主义阐释的重点——在科学理论的建构过程中，最经典和成熟的理论方式莫过于以"数学—逻辑"为构成性框架来整理和勾勒实在对象的结构与属性的模型方法。从这一形式化的视角来看，我们可以更好地解读弗里德曼的核心表述："相对化的康德意义上科学原则的先验概念为一定历史语境下的特殊理论，是历史化的科学客观性概念（主体间性的科学合理性概念）。例如，欧氏几何学和牛顿运动定律实际上是——正如康德设想的——万有引力理论客观经验意义的必要前提，由黎曼几何和等效原理构成的新概念框架界定了广义相对论类似的必要前提系统。"②这种历史理性构成动态先验论的理论连续性的整体依据，但库恩等揭示的范式

---

① Kindi V. The Challenge of Scientific Revolutions. In *International Studies in the Philosophy of Science*, 2011, Vol.25, p. 338.

② M Friedman. A post-kuhnian approach to the History and Philosophy of Science. In *The Monist* Vol.93, p. 500.

或框架的间断性还是无法直接说明，为此实用主义阐释对交往合理性作了进一步的补充。"交往合理性建立在生活世界实践基础之上"，合理性依据在于实践方式或结构的连续性，"我们可以从数学获知，如果把交往合理性设想为一种概念变化连续性的必要要素，物理学或数学空间中的抛物线或函数并不是自身连续性的：反之，这种连续性总是相对于一定拓扑空间或几何结构而言的"。①如此以来，对实践层面的解释又回归到了理论层面的说明，与詹姆斯等的实用主义传统不同，这种带有隔离式的阐释还是缺乏一种能够真正沟通存在于经验与理论框架裂缝之间的中间环节，实践或实用维度仍是附属于理论需要的。

但事实上，在真实的科学理论构建过程中，科学家观念性的抽象把握是和感性的具体操作有机结合在一起的，这也就是技艺性实验的介入问题，"我们需要在实践和思想两个方面建构世界"②，这成为现实科学实践密不可分的两个主要组成部分。这两个层面是不可分的，而弗里德曼的先验表述恰恰忽略了具体实践操作的维度，只诉诸纯粹理论建构是很难真正揭示出所谓"交往合理性"背后更为基础的连续性问题的。所以，弗里德曼先验框架的跳跃性背后总是伴随着感性实践操作的连续性，以及语言、语用层面的一致性，因为科学的实践和生活世界并没有随着科学革命而同时发生剧烈的格式塔转变，这就是说，"独立于真实世界的观察与数据是通过实验、技术工具和数据处理而获得的，因此，事实源自物理世界的建构活动，与此同时，这些建构活动和关于技术工具、数据和物理现象的实践以及理论推理相伴随。更重要的是，数据、事实、数据处理、实验、工具和理论解释是在相互的作用下发展的，甚至相互'证实'"③。这样，现实的科学生活世界其实已经连接起了经验与理论框架，科学理论框架间的衔接和通约可以在具体的科学感性活动中找到合理性的基础。

从科学与自然的交互作用角度来看，科学理论不再是自然主义所认为的经验数据的平等集合，而是存在一定结构和层次的信念系统，"不同元素

---

① Mormann T. A Place for Pragmatism in the Dynamics of Reason?. In *Studies in History and Philosophy of Science*, 2012, Vol.43, p. 31.

② Kitcher P. Extending the Pragmatist Tradition. In *Transactions of the Charles S. Peirce Society*, 2014, Vol.50, p. 100.

③ Soler L, Emiliano Trizio, Thomas Nickles, William C. Wimsatt. *Characterizing the robustness of science*. Springer, 2012, p. 291.

之间是相互依赖、相互调节的；它们在通过实践和理论推理的建构活动逐渐稳定下来，并伴随着探索和调整相互作用活动的介入而发展"①。而且，对先验框架基础的实用阐释还要和知识框架的功能性结合起来进行理解。"卡西尔想把康德的先验学说和功能—实用解释融合起来"的思路是很有道理的，因为，"普遍原则是综合性的，只要它们有经验基础，它们是关于真实世界对象的陈述，但在功能上是先验的"。②进一步来说，这种在实践哲学基础上对先验论与实用主义的结合，意在沟通科学实践与理论框架之间断裂的中介环节，它们之间的同构性则是实现这一任务的关键，与之相应的结构主义实在论具有这种连接性的功能："真理具有功能性和结构性的意义。在功能性方面，真理就是我们的目标所在：在我们的各种会话领域，真理是我们努力确认和赞同的陈述。在描述性领域，功能是塔尔斯基结构的实现过程——用'协议'认同的词典定义。"③因为正是这个环节的存在才能合理解释理论框架的连续性，这源自它与科学实践存在的一致性，而这种一致性则来自理论与实践的结构同构性。也就是说，这种交往合理性的深层原因在于科学活动分工与科学理论结构之间存在的协同性，理论及其反思是建立在感性实践基础之上的，作为人类整体活动的一部分，它们的共同之处在于实践的结构与形式，而非具体经验内容，只有这样才能说动态理性连续性的依据应该"诉诸哲学元-范式以确保交往合理性，为主体间协议达成共识的可能性"④。

这也是我们主张科学实践基础上进一步融合结构主义实在论与动态先验论的原因，"时空几何学的构成性原则是一种定义，它们是解释性而非经验主张，因为它们预设物理现象的特征可以通过一定的几何结构来加以解释。但这些定义不仅仅是约定，反之，每一个都是从时空测量程序的概念分析中产生的；每个定义都不是选自等值的替代，而是发现其在物理史的

---

① Soler L, Emiliano Trizio, Thomas Nickles, William C. Wimsatt. *Characterizing the robustness of science.* Springer, 2012, p. 292.

② Stump D. Arthur Pap's Functional Theory of the A Priori. In *The Journal of the International Society for the History of Philosophy of Science*, 2011, Vol.1, p. 276.

③ Kitcher P. Extending the Pragmatist Tradition. In *Transactions of the Charles S. Peirce Society*, 2014, Vol.50, p. 101.

④ Dyck M. Dynamics of Reason and the Kantian Project. In *Philosophy of Science*, 2009, Vol.76, p. 693.

关键时刻，在当时的经验原则是具有确定性的"①。由于科学理论的建构是科学实践者同自然实在的一种交互作用过程，理论框架和实验工具又中介着理论表象或模型及其实践对象背后的结构形式，"对于这种结构实在论而言，在理论或框架变化过程中保留下的性质是那些类似定律形式的属性，它们是在实验交互作用中产生的。这些'交互作用的属性'是由数学方程表述的，它们至少作为一种极限形式存在于新理论之中"②。所以，科学框架之间的间断性背后实际上还存在着实践工具和结构的连续性，这是哈金历史认识论揭示的一个重要内容，"推理型概念在和组织概念相联系的时候，可以变得更容易理解，组织概念起着类似于康德主义纯粹概念的作用，它们将我们关于世界的思想结构化，并组织起整个概念、实践和价值的集合"③。结构主义实在论在这方面起着关键作用，是实现动态先验原则和实践连续性的重要环节。④

　　简单来说，科学实践本身就是科学活动连续性与变动性的有机统一体，而与之相应，同构的科学系列理论则不可避免也具有与此一致的双重属性。这也是认知理性贯穿过程，"这种理性为适应解释性假说提供了方法论框架，以说明经验定律，只有通过这种理性的作用才能为自然科学提供基

①　DiSalle R. Conventionalism and Modern Physics: A Re-Assessment. In *Noûs*, 2002, Vol.36, p. 194.

②　McArthur D. Theory Change, Structural Realism, and the Relativised *a Priori*. In *International Studies in the Philosophy of Science*, 2008, Vol.22, p. 15.

③　Sciortino L. On Ian Hacking's Notion of Style of Reasoning. In *Erkenn*, 2017, Vol.82, p. 262.

④　为探究科学理论"结构"与"交往合理性"背后基础问题，我们需要在两进路间引入某个共同的理论平台来消弭其差异。它们二者同时具有"结构性"的这一特征使得人们开始关注科学实践能否成为这一平台的问题，新先验论承认科学理论与自然存在的同构关系，结构实在论则认为，"基础物理学理论正确地反映了外在独立于实在的结构关系"。当然，这种"同构"还只是表面现象，"自然科学把经验现象再现为在一定程度上可嵌入的抽象结构，但这些抽象结构只描述了结构的同构性"（范·弗拉森）。所以，这一理解仍是抽象的，单一"结构"难以承担两条进路的基础。但在超出理论哲学的视角来看，科学理论源自科学家在科学实践中与自然世界的交互作用，科学实践中介着科学理论与其对象自然世界，即二者的同构关系以科学实践为中间桥梁。例如，广义相对论的理论模型是洛伦兹四维空间，所以人们一般相信广义相对论就意味着要相信洛伦兹四维空间结构，只有当二者是同构（isomorphic）关系的时候，理论模型才能够应用到这一特定经验系统中。人们对自然实在的抽象理论把握仍只是科学实践活动的一部分，它根源于科学实践的世界，其逻辑自足性只是抽象和不完备的，对科学实践的反思和把握最终还要回归具体的感性科学实践本身。关于结构主义实在论与新先验论的融合以及解答问题，详见拙作《论当代动态先验论与结构主义实在论的融合及其实践论超越》（《哲学研究》2018 年第 2 期）相关论述。

础"①。其中，科学实践总是具体的，这同时也意味着科学活动的局域化，"主体间交往合理性历史化"的"客观标准总是局域化和语境化的"②。事实上，这一点也进一步揭示了先验原则发生动态变化的根源，人们把先验概念相对化到具体的科学实践语境，而科学的客观性同样渗透到了动态的历史变动情形之中。因此，这种结构-功能层面上的先验原则，既不是自然主义所理解的经验陈述或实用主义的简单约定或效用，也不是脱离具体历史语境的纯粹超验范畴，劳斯所描述的"实践者"和"信守者"（believers）才很好诠释了这一原则的矛盾性："信念无疑是建立在探究的实践语境之中的，因为探究的目标是信念的固定化，或者问题情境的解决，这种实用性带来的是新习性的获得，或已建立习性的修正。当然，劳斯对'实践者'与'信守者'、信念与生活形式的二分就过于简单，科学家既是实践者，又是信守者。"③总之，科学理论的实用主义阐释揭示出来的科学实用效应维度还可以深入拓展实践哲学的更宽广视角，"实践者"工具性活动的"实践导向"正是以实验介入方式的体现，而"信守者"则是理论表象中科学信念的确定过程。在此意义上，心灵的表象与实验操作活动都是原发性实践，而介入实验与沉思的静观共同构成动态开放的科学实践整体。

四、结论

动态先验论的提出与发展为反思当前科学哲学前景提供了新的视野，它在自然化与规范化层面揭示了科学理论本身的复杂性与功能—结构问题，并从自然主义的对称性与平等性主张中展示出其背后科学理性在功能结构层面的非对称性特征。这进一步意味着，科学实践活动与其相应理论表述之间不对称性问题的存在，"这种非对称性意味着构成性原则自身可以为经验所检验是没有意义的，所有有意义的经验检验一定早已作出了某

① Buchdahl G. *Kant and the Dynamics of Reason: Essays on the structure of Kant's philosophy*. Blackwell Publishers, 1992, p. 170.

② M Friedman A post-kuhnian approach to the history and philosophy of science. In *The Monist*, Vol.93, p. 497.

③ Pihlström S. Synthesizing Traditions: Rewriting the History of Pragmatism and Ranscendental. In *Philosophy History of Philosophy Quarterly*, 2012, Vol.23, p. 84.

种预设"①，科学理性的连续性正好体现在这一过程中先验框架建构与选择的"回溯"和"预期"视角的统一方面。当然，在我们看来，所谓的"回溯"，更多还是指理论框架之间的汇聚或渐进的结构形式，而"预期"则是科学实践效应的收缩式策略的表现形式，它们分别对应于先验哲学的"条件导向"和实用主义阐释的"实践导向"。因此，科学实践哲学较之于实用主义阐释的关键价值，"并不在于一个思想意义的行动结果，而是在于'发展'意义"②，这才是超越实用主义的有限视角而在一个更宽阔平台上整合自然主义和先验论张力的一个开放性维度。如果说动态先验论只是揭示了人类心灵表象能力的抽象化和形式化特征，那么实用主义阐释则部分展现了科学认知实用效应对理论与实践的贯通，而科学实践哲学在肯定科学理论建构独立性的同时，在结构主义实在论层面上更全面有机综合了以实验操作为代表的具体科学实践推理和理论推理的统一。

参考文献：

［1］Buchdahl. G., 1992, *Kant and the Dynamics of Reason: Essays on the structure of Kant's philosophy*. Oxford: Blackwell Publishers.

［2］Dimitrakos. T., 2016, "Kuhnianism and Neo-Kantianism: On Friedman's Account of Scientific Change". in *International Studies in the Philosophy of Science* 30.

［3］DiSalle. R., 2002, "Conventionalism and Modern Physics: A Re-Assessment". in *Noûs* 36.

［4］Dyck. M., 2009, "Dynamics of Reason and the Kantian Project", in *Philosophy of Science* 76.

［5］Ekeberg. B., 2019, *Metaphysical experiments: physics and the invention of the universe*. Minnesota: University of Minnesota Press.

［6］Friedman. M., 2001, *Dynamics of Reason: The* 1999 *Kant Lectures at Stanford University,* Stanford, CA:CSLI Publishers.

---

① Dyck M. Dynamics of Reason and the Kantian Project. In *Philosophy of Science*, 2009, Vol.76, pp.690-691.

② Kitcher P. Extending the Pragmatist Tradition. In *Transactions of the Charles S. Peirce Society*, 2014, Vol.50, p. 99.

〔7〕2010, "A post-kuhnian Approach to the History and Philosophy of Science", in *The Monist* 93.

〔8〕Friedman. M. and Graham Bird., 1998, "Kantian Themes in Contemporary Philosophy", in *Proceedings of the Aristotelian Society* 72.

〔9〕Hasok. C., 2008, "Contingent Transcendental Arguments for Metaphysical Principles", in *Royal Institute of Philosophy* 63.

〔10〕Hullett. J., 1973, "A Pragamatic Conception of the a Priori Re-Viewed", in *Transactions of the Charles S. Peirce Society* 9.

〔11〕Kindi. V., 2011, "The Challenge of Scientific Revolutions", in *International Studies in the Philosophy of Science* 25.

〔12〕Kitcher. P., 2014, "Extending the Pragmatist Tradition", in *Transactions of the Charles S. Peirce Society* 50.

〔13〕Klein. A., 2008, "Divide et Impera!: William James's Pragmatist Tradition in the Philosophy of Science", in *Philosophical Topics* 36.

〔14〕Lewis. C., 1999, *Mind and the World Order. Outline of a Theory of Knowledge*. NewYork: Dover McArthur.D.2008, "Theory Change, Structural Realism, and the Relativised *a priori*", in *International Studies in the Philosophy of Science* 22.

〔15〕Mormann. T., 2012, "A Place for Pragmatism in the Dynamics of Reason?", in *Studies in History and Philosophy of Science* 43.

〔16〕Pihlström. S., 2012, "Synthesizing Traditions: Rewriting the History of Pragmatism and Ranscendental", in *Philosophy History of Philosophy Quarterly* 23.

〔17〕2012, "Toward Pragmatically Naturalized Transcendental Philosophy of Scientic Inquiry And Pragmatic Scientific Realism". *Studia Philosophica Estonica* 5.

〔18〕Richardson. A and Uebel.T., 2005, "The Epistemic Agent in Logical Positivism", in *Proceedings of the Aristotelian Society, Supplementary* 79.

〔19〕Samaroo. R., 2015, "Friedman's thesis", in *Studies in History and Philosophy of Modern Physics* 52.

〔20〕Sciortino. L., 2017, "On Ian Hacking's Notion of Style of Reasoning", in *Erkenn* 82.

[21] Shaffer. M., 2011, "the Constitutive a Priori and Epistemic Justification", in Michael J. S and Michael L. V. (eds.), *What Place for the A Priori*?, Chicago: Open court.

[22] Soler. L., Emiliano, T., Thomas, N. and William C. W., 2012, *Characterizing the robustness of science*. Dordrecht: Springer.

[23] Stump.D., 2011, "Arthur Pap's Functional Theory of the A Priori", in *The Journal of the International Society for the History of Philosophy of Science* 1.

[24] Stump.D., 2015, *Conceptual Change and the Philosophy of Science,* New York: Rutledge.

[25] Tsou. J., 2003, "A Role for Reason in Science", *Dialogue* 42.

（本文原载于《哲学研究》2020 年第 4 期）

重复计算的方法论问题与意义

胡瑞斌[*]

一、何谓重复计算？

重复计算（double-counting）在不同的领域有不同所指。在经济学中，重复计算指的是一种会计核算的错误，即对某一项目进行两次甚至多次计数。例如，在以生产法计算国内生产总值时，需要将各生产部门的总产值减去中间产品的价值以获得增加值，这样就避免了对中间产品价值的重复计算。然而，在科学哲学的讨论中，重复计算则指的是证据理论中对于证据的"重复使用"（double-use），即使用某一证据（数据或其他证据形式）构建假设或理论，同时再次使用该证据作为对于所构建的假设或理论的支持（support）或者确证（confirmation）。本文所讨论的为第二种重复计算。

应当指出，重复计算所指的并非某一特定的构建假设或理论的具体方法，而是一种方法类型。梅奥（D. G. Mayo）以"规则 R"来界定重复计算，具体的重复计算方法会因规则 R 的不同而存在差异，但是其基本形式是一致的："基于规则 R，数据 x 被用来构建或选择假设 H（x），从而使所得的 H（x）符合 x；然后'再次'使用该数据'作为证据'来证明 H（x）。"[①] 对于以规则 R 构建假设或理论的方法，梅奥称为"使用构造"（use-construction），而豪森（C. Howson）、希区柯克（C. Hitchcock）和索伯（E. Sober）等人则称为"容纳"（accommodation），从而与"预测"（prediction）相区分。

---

* 胡瑞斌，南开大学哲学院科技哲学教研室讲师、博士，主要研究方向为科学哲术哲学。

① Mayo, D. G. How to Discount Double-Counting When It Counts: Some Clarifications. In *The British Journal for the Philosophy of Science*, 2008, Vol.59(4), p.859.

在科学实践中，使用数据来构建假设或理论是"完全正常的科学程序"[①]，而重复计算的争议之处在于"已使用的"数据能否被"再次使用"，换言之，在构建假设和理论中使用的数据能否构成对于所构建假设或理论的支持。直觉上看，如果某一假设的构建中使用了某一证据，那么该假设准确地符合该证据是毫无疑问的。按照证伪主义的观点，这就排除了这一假设被此证据证伪的可能，因而被使用过的证据不能构成对于假设的支持。这一观点被沃勒尔（J. Worrall）进一步引申为"禁止重复计算规则"（no-double-counting rule），该规则强调"不能两次使用相同的事实，一次是在构建理论时，再一次是在为其提供支持时"，"理论在经验上受到其所正确预测的现象的支持……而非那些事后'容纳'或'写入'该理论的那些现象的支持"。[②]豪森称此类观点为"零支持论点"（the null-support thesis）[③]，而希区柯克和索伯则称这种强调"预测"优于"容纳"的观点为"预测主义"（predictivism）[④]。

然而，科学实践中存在诸多涉及重复计算的案例，被用于构建假设的数据同样构成支持该假设的证据，因而禁止重复计算规则是站不住脚的。梅奥、沃勒尔、豪森、斯蒂尔（K. Steele）和沃恩德尔（C. Werndl）等人的讨论援引了大量的案例，基于这些案例，可以将重复计算大致分为四种类型：测量；参数确定（parameter determination）；例外并入（exception incorporation）；模型（或假设、理论）选择。

类型 1. 测量

测量不仅仅是直接"读出"测量所得数值，还包括在对数据的进一步分析的基础上提出假设。例如：

例（1） 拿尺子测量桌子的长度为 150 厘米，在估计误差的基础

---

① Worrall, J. Error, Tests, and Theory Confirmation. In D. G. Mayo, A. Spanos eds.: *Error and Inference: Recent Exchanges on Experimental Reasoning, Reliability, and the Objectivity and Rationality of Science*. Cambridge University Press, 2010, p.130.

② Worrall, J. Error, Tests, and Theory Confirmation. In D. G. Mayo, A. Spanos eds.: *Error and Inference: Recent Exchanges on Experimental Reasoning, Reliability, and the Objectivity and Rationality of Science*. Cambridge University Press, 2010, pp.129-130.

③ Howson, C. Fitting Your Theory to the Facts: Probably not Such a Bad Thing After All. In *Minnesota Studies in the Philosophy of Science*, 1990, Vol.14, p.224.

④ Hitchcock, C., Sober, E. Prediction Versus Accommodation and the Risk of Overfitting. In *The British Journal for the Philosophy of Science*, 2004, Vol.55(1), p.3.

上提出假设"桌子长度在 149 至 151 厘米之间"。[1]

　　例（2）　统计某一班级学生的 SAT 分数，并提出假设"该班级学生的平均 SAT 分数为 1121"。[2]

例（1）、例（2）中"测量"所得的数据被用于构建假设，同时该数据也构成了该假设的证据，支持或确证了该假设。测量是重复计算中较为极端的情形，其特殊之处在于，所构造的假设必然符合观察到的数据，概率为 1。

类型 2. 参数确定

对于包含未知参数或自由参数的假设，可以通过观察、实验确定其具体数值，从而获得更为具体、准确的假设。例如：

　　例（3）　牛顿万有引力定律包含一个自由参数 G，即万有引力常数，卡文迪许于 1797 年通过实验测得 $G=6.754\times10^{-11}m^3 \cdot kg^{-1} \cdot s^{-2}$。

　　例（4）　假设总体 X 服从正态分布 $N(\mu, \sigma_0^2)$，其中 μ 未知，σ_0 已知，现有样本数据 E（样本量为 n），计算得样本均值为 $\bar{x}$，在 $1-\alpha$ 置信水平下，可得 $\bar{x}-\frac{\sigma_0}{\sqrt{n}}Z_{\alpha/2}<\mu<\bar{x}+\frac{\sigma_0}{\sqrt{n}}Z_{\alpha/2}$（$z_{\alpha/2}$ $Z_{\alpha/2}$ 数值可根据 n 和 α 的值来确定）。[3]

例（3）、例（4）中都事先存在一个一般假设 H（x），通过数据 E 确定未知参数 x 的值或取值区间，得出了一个更为具体的假设 $H(x_0)$。其中，E 被用于构建 $H(x_0)$，并被视为 $H(x_0)$ 的证据［例（4）中的 $1-\alpha$ 可以理解 E 对 $H(x_0)$ 的确证度］。对于这一类型的重复计算，豪森和梅奥等均认为 E 为 $H(x_0)$ 提供了支持或确证，而沃勒尔则持反对意见，他认为 $H(x_0)$ 相对于 E 而言是"不可检验的"，这是因为"由于它的构造方式，它永远

　　① Hitchcock, C., Sober, E. Prediction Versus Accommodation and the Risk of Overfitting. In *The British Journal for the Philosophy of Science*, 2004, Vol.55(1), p.24.

　　② Mayo, D. G. Novel Evidence and Severe Tests. In *Philosophy of Science*, 1991, Vol.58(4), pp534.

　　③ Mayo, D. G. How to Discount Double-Counting When It Counts: Some Clarifications. In T*he British Journal for the Philosophy of Science*, 2008, Vol.59(4), pp.865-866.

不会被这些观察所驳斥"①。换言之，豪森和梅奥强调这一类型的重复计算是完全合法的，而沃勒尔则继续坚持禁止重复计算规则。

类型 3. 例外并入

所谓例外并入，指的是当假设 H 面临异常数据 x′ 时，"通过构造或选择一些辅助假设 A（x′）来解释 H 的异常 x′，这一辅助假设能够恢复与数据 x′ 的一致性或拟合度，同时保留 H"。②其中 x′ 被用于构建或选择辅助假设，并被视为假设 H 的证据，因此构成了一种重复计算。例如：

例（5） 面对天王星运行轨道的异常，提出假设"存在另一颗行星"，并最终被海王星的发现证实。

例（6） 1919 年爱丁顿通过观测日食得到的数据中，存在一部分结果不符合爱因斯坦广义相对论的预测，他提出假设，"这部分结果是由太阳引起的镜面畸变引起的，而非光的偏折"。③

例（5）中的天王星轨道异常数据以及例（6）中的异常数据，均被用于构建辅助假设 A（x′），从而解释假设 H 的异常。但沃勒尔指出，例（5）中真正确证牛顿体系的是海王星的最终发现这一事实，而非天王星轨道的异常。④然而梅奥认为，例（5）、例（6）中的数据以及辅助假设提供了一定程度的支持，因为它能够"阻隔异常"，解释数据为什么与假设的预测不符，从而排除假设本身的错误。⑤应当指出，此类重复计算的争议之处在于无法排除特设性（ad hoc）修改或容纳，例如：

例（7） 托勒密地心说体系通过引入本轮、均轮以及偏心圆等假

① Worrall, J. Scientific Discovery and Theory-confirmation. In J. C. Pitt ed.: *Change and Progress in Modern Science*. Springer, 1985, p.313.

② Mayo, D. G. Some Surprising Facts about (the Problem of) Surprising Facts. In *Studies in History and Philosophy of Science*, 2014, Vol.45, p.82.

③ Mayo, D. G. Error and the Growth of Experimental Knowledge. University of Chicago Press, 1996, p.284.

④ Worrall, J. Error, Tests, and Theory Confirmation. In D. G. Mayo, A. Spanos eds.: *Error and Inference: Recent Exchanges on Experimental Reasoning, Reliability, and the Objectivity and Rationality of Science*. Cambridge University Press, 2010, p.127, p.138.

⑤ Mayo, D. G. An Ad Hoc Save of a Theory of Adhocness? Exchanges with John Worrall. In D. G. Mayo, A. Spanos eds.: *Error and Inference: Recent Exchanges on Experimental Reasoning, Reliability, and the Objectivity and Rationality of Science*. Cambridge University Press, 2010, p.157.

设来解释行星逆行现象。

这一案例涉及仅仅通过容纳证据来解释异常，因此沃勒尔认为行星逆行现象为哥白尼理论提供了更多的支持，因为后者并非特设性的容纳，而是为之提供了"自然的"解释。[①]可见，这一类型的重复计算仍需明确具体的条件限制，从而区分特设性与非特设性的容纳。

类型 4. 模型选择

这一类型的重复计算涉及利用数据确定或校准模型的参数，并基于相同的数据在多个模型之间进行比较与选择。斯蒂尔和沃恩德尔讨论了气候科学中进行模型选择的一个案例：

> 例（8） 哈维（Harvey）和考夫曼（Kaufmann）为模拟过去两个半世纪的气温变化，考察了两种基本模型 M1 和 M2，其中 M1 同时考虑了自然和人为因素，M2 则仅考虑了人为因素，赋予这些因素以不同的参数组合，分别得到 M1 和 M2 的具体实例。接着他们通过统计学检验得到了拟合数据最佳的一系列模型实例，发现其中仅仅包含 M1 的实例，最终得出结论，M1 相对于 M2 得到了确证。[②]

在该案例中，相同的数据被用于校准和确证，其中涉及了两种重复计算：一种是通过模型校准"确定基本模型的哪些具体实例相对于其他具体实例得到了确证"；另一种则是通过校准确定哪些基本模型相对于其他基本模型得到了确证。[③]

应当指出，以上四种类型的重复计算之间存在分类上的交叉。类型 1 可以视作类型 2 的特例，例（1）、例（2）中所提出的假设背后隐含着关于"长度""平均数"的一般假设，不过这类假设往往可以忽略，而类型 2 中的一般假设通常不应当忽略。例（5）涉及的例外并入亦可视为一种参数确定，因为牛顿天文学系统的行星数量被重新确定。此外，类型 4 的模型选

---

① Worrall, J. Error, Tests, and Theory Confirmation. In D. G. Mayo, A. Spanos eds.: *Error and Inference: Recent Exchanges on Experimental Reasoning, Reliability, and the Objectivity and Rationality of Science*. Cambridge University Press, 2010, pp.127-128.

② Steele, K., Werndl, C. Climate Models, Calibration, and Confirmation. In *The British Journal for the Philosophy of Science*, 2013, Vol.64(3), pp.620-621.

③ Steele, K., Werndl, C. Climate Models, Calibration, and Confirmation. In *The British Journal for the Philosophy of Science*, 2013, Vol.64(3), p.633.

择中涉及类型 2 中的参数确定或校准，其不同之处在于，类型 4 涉及模型的不同实例或不同的模型之间的比较和选择，而类型 2 则仅涉及单个模型的参数的确定。还需要注意的是，并非所有的重复计算都是合理的，例如特设性容纳。可见，作为一种方法论原则，重复计算仍需细化其条件或限制，从而将"好的"重复计算方法与"坏的"区分开来。这就涉及重复计算所面临的方法论问题。

二、重复计算的方法论问题

重复计算所面临的方法论问题在于，如果证据 E 被用于构建假设 H，那么 H 自然与 E 相一致，从直觉上看，E 不能构成对 H 的支持或者确证。重复计算的批评者通常援引证伪主义的观点来否定 E 对 H 的确证效力。根据波普尔的观点，"真正的确证只能来自通过严格的检验而进行的真正反驳假设的尝试的失败"，然而由于使用 E 构建的 H 必然与 E 一致，E 对 H 的检验是不严格的，不具有"独立可检验性"，因而不构成对于 H 的支持或确证，真正能够确证 H 的应当是"新颖的独立的预测"。[①]但波普尔对于"新颖性"的理解是时间性的，问题在于，提出假设前已知的证据无法构成对于假设的支持，这就排除了诸多案例的合法性，如行星逆行现象对哥白尼理论的支持。因此扎哈尔（E. G. Zahar）、沃勒尔等提出了"使用新颖性"（use-novelty）概念，主张若 E 未被用于 H 的构建，则 E 相对于 H 而言具有使用新颖性。作为使用新颖性的对立面，重复计算的方法论问题亦可称为"使用新颖性问题"。

实际上，使用新颖性要求与前文所述的禁止重复计算规则或零支持论点是一致的，梅奥将之总结为"被用于得出使用构造的假设 h 的数据 e 不能算作对于 h 的良好检验"[②]。可以说，对使用新颖性要求的违反即重复计算。

长期以来，重复计算的方法论地位未得到普遍认可。使用新颖性要求根深蒂固的原因在于它不仅符合"直觉"，而且得到了证伪主义的理论支持，

---

① Musgrave, A. Logical Versus Historical Theories of Confirmation. In *The British Journal for the Philosophy of Science*, 1974, Vol.25(1), pp.5-6.

② Mayo, D. G. Novel evidence and severe tests. In *Philosophy of Science*, 1991, Vol.58(4), p.533.

更重要的是，重复计算中存在诸多特设性修改或容纳的例子，如例（7），再如：

例（9） 假设"所有的面包都给人营养"，出现了异常现象——法国一个农村中许多人吃面包后罹患重病甚至死亡，修改原假设，提出新的假设"除法国某农村生产的某批次面包外，所有的面包都给人营养"。[①]

在这种特设性的例外并入中，证据被用于构建新的假设，但不能被视为对新假设的支持或确证。显然，这种重复计算是不适当的。正是出于这方面的考虑，希罗斯（S. Psillos）借助特设性条件来定义使用新颖性，他指出存在两种特设性条件，一是"关于现象 E 的信息被用于理论 T 的构建，而 T 容纳了 E"，二是"某一现有的 T 理论不能预测/解释 E，T 被修改为 T′理论，从而使 T′可以预测 E，但这种修改的唯一原因是为了预测/解释 E"，"特别是，T′没有比 T 更多的理论和经验内容"。[②]在此基础上，可对使用新颖性作如下定义："一个现象 E 的预测 P 对于一个理论 T 在使用上是新颖的，如果 E 在 T 提出前就是已知的，T 不满足任何一个特设性条件，且T 预测了 E。"[③]可以看到，第二个特设性条件针对的是特设性的例外并入，第一个则针对重复计算的一般形式，因而使用新颖性要求仍然是一种禁止重复计算规则。

然而，正如前文所述，科学实践中存在诸多涉及重复计算的案例，其方法论地位需要得到应有的认可。对此，梅奥、豪森、希区柯克和索伯都批评了使用新颖性的要求，并提出了不同的策略来为重复计算进行辩护，沃勒尔也在争论中逐步转变了立场。这些应对使用新颖性问题的策略可以分为三种：严格性（severity）要求、条件支持（conditional support）概念和简单性（simplicity）要求。

策略 1. 严格性要求

梅奥提出，应当以严格性概念取代使用新颖性概念，因为前者是隐藏在后者背后的基本逻辑。梅奥在一定程度上借鉴了波普尔的严格检验的概念，但她对于严格性的界定与之不同："假设 H 借由 x 通过了严格的检验 T，

[①] Chalmers, A. F. *What is This Thing Called Science?*. Hackett Publishing Company, 1999, pp.75-76.

[②] Psillos, S. *Scientific Realism: How Science Tracks Truth*. Routledge, 1999, p.101.

[③] Psillos, S. *Scientific Realism: How Science Tracks Truth*. Routledge, 1999, p.102.

如果（i）x 符合或'拟合' H（基于适当的拟合概念），并且（ii）如果 H 为假或不正确，那么检验 T 会与 H 产生较差的拟合（或完全不拟合）的概率很高。"[1]而检验的严格性或严格度则为"1 减去当通过的假设为假时检验产生这种通过结果（或其他）的概率。"[2]例如，在例（4）的置信区间估计中，α为当假设为假时通过该假设的概率，置信水平 1-α则为该检验的严格度，同时也是对假设的确证度，而在例（1）、例（2）的测量案例中，检验的严格度则为 1，但根据使用新颖性要求，这些假设没有获得支持或确证。

相较于使用新颖性偏于僵硬的标准，严格性概念更具灵活性，因而能够对重复计算的合理应用与不合理应用作出区分。其问题在于，并非所有的科学推理都是统计学推理，对于严格性的衡量会面临实际性的困难。对此，梅奥主张"必须通过考虑构造规则的属性来评估严格性"，在不同的使用构造规则下，"相关的错误的概率可能会发生变化"。[3]但对于一些类型的重复计算，如模型选择，如何确定其具体的使用构造规则以及评估该规则对检验严格性的影响，梅奥尚未作出更加具体的分析。然而正如她所言，"严格性标准保持不变并且不会改变；会改变的是如何应用它"，"重要的不是 H 是否是被故意构造从而容纳数据 x 的，重要的是数据与背景信息一起如何排除对 H 的推断可能出错的方式"。[4]实际上，梅奥所提供的是一个优于使用新颖性的标准或方法，对于严格性的评估仍取决于对具体案例的逐案分析。

策略 2. 条件支持概念

条件支持概念针对的主要是重复计算中的类型 2 和 3，即参数确定和例外并入。其基本观点是，H（x_0）或 A（x'）确实获得了数据 E 的支持，但这种支持以一般假设 H（x）为前提，且 E 不提供对 H（x）的支持。豪森、沃勒尔和舒尔茨（G. Schurz）等人均持此观点。

---

① Mayo, D. G. How to Discount Double-Counting When It Counts: Some Clarifications. In *The British Journal for the Philosophy of Science*, 2008, Vol.59(4), p.861.

② Mayo, D. G. Novel Evidence and Severe Tests. In *Philosophy of Science*, 1991, Vol.58(4), pp.530-531.

③ Mayo, D. G. How to Discount Double-Counting When It Counts: Some Clarifications. In *The British Journal for the Philosophy of Science*, 2008, Vol.59(4), p.864.

④ Mayo, D. G. How to Discount Double-Counting When It Counts: Some Clarifications. In *The British Journal for the Philosophy of Science*, 2008, Vol.59(4), p.877.

　　豪森指出，H（x）作为"背景理论是牢固地根深蒂固的，或多或少地被视为理所当然的"，而零支持论点的错误在于，将对 H（x_0）的支持与对 H（x）的支持混为一谈，E 对于 H（x）的零支持"非法转移"到了 H（x_0）之上。[1]沃勒尔明确提出了"条件支持"概念，以应对梅奥的批评，实际上他在与梅奥的长期争论中逐步转变了立场。沃勒尔基于条件支持概念部分承认了此类重复计算的合法性，但他仍坚持认为，这只是"将一般理论已经拥有的任何经验支持转移到更具体的理论上"，"这肯定不会为更一般的理论增加任何支持"，[2]真正能够提供后一种支持的仍然是独立的"使用新颖的"证据。舒尔茨发展了沃勒尔的条件支持概念，主张在"真实确证"（genuine confirmation）中，"确证是超越证据的：确证从 E 扩展到假设或理论 H 超出 E 的那些部分的内容"[3]。

　　条件支持概念为理解重复计算提供了一个重要的角度，强调了一般假设或背景理论 H（x）对于参数确定和例外并入的影响。例如，例（3）中对于 G 的测定以牛顿万有引力定律为前提，例（4）中的假设则以总体服从正态分布为前提。但沃勒尔和舒尔茨对于这一概念的解释存在过于琐碎的嫌疑，例如沃勒尔认为例（2）中"为 SAT 分数做平均所得的任何结果都不会挑战平均值的定义"[4]，舒尔茨则指出在这一例子中，从 H（x）推出 H（x_0）与 H（x_0）本身"在逻辑上是等效的"，"以重言式为条件的确证为无条件确证"。[5]梅奥在回应中则指出，H（x_0）不必然以 H（x）为前提，如例（6）中，镜面畸变假设与广义相对论并不相关，相反，存在独立

　　[1] Howson, C. Fitting Your Theory to the Facts: Probably not Such a Bad Thing After All. In *Minnesota Studies in the Philosophy of Science*, 1990, Vol.14, pp.232-233.

　　[2] Worrall, J. Error, Tests, and Theory Confirmation. In D. G. Mayo, A. Spanos eds.: *Error and Inference: Recent Exchanges on Experimental Reasoning, Reliability, and the Objectivity and Rationality of Science*. Cambridge University Press, 2010, p.135.

　　[3] Schurz, G. Bayesian Pseudo-confirmation, Use-novelty, and Genuine Confirmation. In *Studies in History and Philosophy of Science*, 2014, Vol.45, p.92.

　　[4] Worrall, J. Error, Tests, and Theory Confirmation. In D. G. Mayo, A. Spanos eds.: *Error and Inference: Recent Exchanges on Experimental Reasoning, Reliability, and the Objectivity and Rationality of Science*. Cambridge University Press, 2010, p.153.

　　[5] Schurz, G. Bayesian Pseudo-confirmation, Use-novelty, and Genuine Confirmation. In *Studies in History and Philosophy of Science*, 2014, Vol.45, p.91.

的数据分析方法对该假设进行检验。①概而言之，这一策略认可特定类型的重复计算，但仍然坚持使用新颖性要求。

策略 3. 简单性要求

这一策略强调在对重复计算进行评估时，应当关注使用数据所构建的假设的简单性。希区柯克和索伯认为，简单性之所以很重要，是因为对数据的容纳容易犯"过度拟合"（overfitting）错误。所谓过度拟合，指的是为了精确地拟合数据，提出一个相对复杂的假设或模型，这种假设或模型对于数据中的"异质性"（idiosyncrasy）过于敏感，其中的异质性"不太可能在从相同基础分布中抽取的其他样本中重复出现"②。由于数据中不仅包含关于研究对象的信息，而且可能隐含着许多其他因素以及误差的影响，对于这些异质性因素的过度拟合自然会导致所构建的假设不能正确反映研究对象。

对于模型选择而言，相对复杂的模型存在过度拟合的可能，而相对简单的模型对数据的拟合度可能不高，因此需要"在简单性与拟合程度之间取得平衡"③。除模型选择之外，简单性要求亦可用于对例外并入的评估。例如：例（7）中引入本轮和均轮以及匀速偏心圆等假设使得托勒密地心说体系过于复杂，存在过度拟合的嫌疑，相比之下哥白尼日心说体系则更为简单，因而得到了行星逆行现象的更多的支持；例（9）中为解释异常而添加的辅助条件"除法国某农村生产的某批次面包外"过于强调异常现象的异质性，同样存在过度拟合的嫌疑，因而是重复计算的不合理应用。

可以看到，以上各种策略对于重复计算的侧重点不尽相同。严格性要求对于前三个类型的重复计算均有所涉及，但对于模型选择关注不足，简单性要求对之给予了更多关注，而条件支持概念则侧重于参数确定。总的来说，梅奥的严格性要求与其他两种策略相比更具一般性和灵活性，对于理解和处理重复计算的方法论问题也更具优势，但是在如何衡量严格性的问题上仍需进一步的细化和论证。实际上，这些策略并不相互矛盾，而是

---

① Mayo, D. G. An Ad Hoc Save of a Theory of Adhocness? Exchanges with John Worrall. In D. G. Mayo, A. Spanos eds.: *Error and Inference: Recent Exchanges on Experimental Reasoning, Reliability, and the Objectivity and Rationality of Science*. Cambridge University Press, 2010, p.160.

② Hitchcock, C., Sober, E. Prediction Versus Accommodation and the Risk of Overfitting. In *The British Journal for the Philosophy of Science*, 2004, Vol.55(1), p.11.

③ Hitchcock, C., Sober, E. Prediction Versus Accommodation and the Risk of Overfitting. In *The British Journal for the Philosophy of Science*, 2004, Vol.55(1), p.20.

互相补充的，使用新颖性也在一些情况下继续发挥作用。正如梅奥所言，对于重复计算的理解，需要避免"全有或全无"（all or nothing）的立场，"与其采取重复计算永远有效或永远无效的立场，我们需要考虑何时以及如何改变检验的能力，以此作为发现和避免错误推断的工具"[①]。

三、重复计算的方法论意义

在明确和尝试解决了重复计算所面临的方法论问题之后，一个值得探究的问题在于，重复计算的意义何在？具体而言，对于科学假设、模型或理论的构建与检验，重复计算能够发挥什么样的作用？对于这些问题的回答，能够进一步认识重复计算作为一种方法而非谬误的重要方法论意义。

1. 对科学发现的全新理解

如前文所述，测量是重复计算中的一种较为极端的类型，类似于例（1）、例（2）的案例在科学实践中是普遍存在的。基于这种理解，似乎凡科学观察、测量都可以视为重复计算的例证，因而存在概念泛化、过于琐碎之嫌。实际上，这些类型的案例的提出针对的主要是使用新颖性要求。根据这一要求，科学发现中的数据难以构成对于所构建的假设的支持或确证，但是如例（2），"关于学生的数据是对于他们的 SAT 平均分数的假设的极好的证据"，"假定进一步的检验会提供更好的证据似乎很荒谬"。[②]对此，重复计算无疑为理解此类的科学发现提供了全新的视角，它表明科学发现与辩护的逻辑在这些情形下是统一的。

此外，重复计算也为评估科学发现的可靠性提供了重要思路。在测量类型的重复计算中，尽管假设与数据拟合的概率为 1，但是这并不意味着该假设必然为真，因为测量与数据分析过程仍存在出错的可能。在这一点上，虽然测量可以视为参数确定的特例，因而参数确定也可理解为科学发现，但是两者之间也存在着显著的不同，这主要体现在一般理论 $H(x)$ 和具体理论 $H(x_0)$ 之间的关系与数据分析方法和 $H(x_0)$ 之间的关系存在着很大的差异。对于前者，具体理论是一般理论具体化的特定版本，对于

---

① Mayo, D. G. How to Discount Double-Counting When It Counts: Some Clarifications. In *The British Journal for the Philosophy of Science*, 2008, Vol.59(4), p.877.

② Mayo, D. G. Novel Evidence and Severe Tests. In *Philosophy of Science*, 1991, Vol.58(4), p.534.

一般理论的质疑针对的是其真实性；而对于后者，具体假设以数据分析为方法论基础，并非其具体化形式，对于数据分析方法的质疑针对的则是其可靠性。正如梅奥所言，可靠的"使用构造规则"使我们"走向证据引向的任何地方"，而在不可靠的"使用构造规则"中，"似乎是我们将数据带到想要去的地方"。①但无论可靠与否，问题都不在于重复计算本身的方法论有效性。

2. 解释异常、构建假设的功能

例外并入类型的重复计算揭示了一种构建假设的方式,在面对异常时,可以通过构建辅助假设解释异常，从而保留原假设。科学实践中存在大量涉及例外并入的案例，其中既有成功的案例，也有失败的案例，因而这种类型的重复计算一直都是争论的一个焦点。实际上，例外并入正是库恩所谓的"常规科学"中"解释异常"一部分，或者是拉卡托斯所言的为保护"硬核"而修正"保护带"的具体实践。对此，沃勒尔起初承认这种使用经验事实构建假设或理论的方法，但否认所构建的假设得到了该经验事实的支持或确证。②然而这种"全有或全无"的立场是站不住脚的，关键在于对"好的"重复计算和"坏的"重复计算作出区分。

对于重复计算的方法论问题的讨论提供了评估例外并入的有效性的几种可能策略。梅奥的严格性要求强调对于例外并入的具体方法的严格性的考量，"只要检验是适度严格的，那么就可以使用任何证据来构造和检验假设"③。希区柯克和索伯强调应当考虑例外并入所引入的辅助假设的简单性，以避免对于数据异质性的过度拟合。相比之下，沃勒尔的条件支持概念尽管作出了让步，但实际上是一种折中的策略，在例外并入的问题上，"沃勒尔的解释缺乏区分可靠和不可靠使用构造的机制"④。而严格性和简单性无疑能够提供这样一种机制，能够对例外并入方法在解释异常、构建和检验假设问题上的有效性进行评估。

① Mayo, D. G. Some Surprising Facts about (the Problem of) Surprising Facts. In *Studies in History and Philosophy of Science*, 2014, Vol.45, p.82.

② Worrall, J. Scientific Discovery and Theory-confirmation. In J. C. Pitt ed.: *Change and Progress in Modern Science*. Springer, 1985, p.312.

③ Mayo, D. G. Novel Evidence and Severe Tests. In *Philosophy of Science*, 1991, Vol.58(4), p.544.

④ Mayo, D. G. An Ad Hoc Save of a Theory of Adhocness? Exchanges with John Worrall. In D. G. Mayo, A. Spanos eds.: *Error and Inference: Recent Exchanges on Experimental Reasoning, Reliability, and the Objectivity and Rationality of Science*. Cambridge University Press, 2010, p.157.

3. 对科学证据理论的推进

在使用新颖性主导的科学证据理论中，只有未被用于构建假设的证据才能构成对于所构建的假设的支持或确证。这一观点无疑是狭隘的，而且与科学实践不符。相比之下，关于重复计算的讨论摒弃了这种狭隘的理解，并且区分了几种不同的确证概念：测量所涉及的确证为最高程度的确证，或者梅奥所谓的"最高严格度检验"[①]；参数确定涉及的"条件确证"指的是以一般理论或背景理论为前提的确证，强调的是一般理论对于确证的影响；模型选择中的确证则为"比较确证"，涉及基本模型的不同实例之间以及不同的基本模型之间的比较。

重复计算对于科学证据理论的影响还体现于对"历史因素"的细化。马斯格雷夫（A. Musgrave）指出，科学证据理论经历了从逻辑主义到历史主义或者说"逻辑-历史主义"的转向，确证不再只是假设与证据间的逻辑关系的函数，还涉及两者之间的时间次序以及构建假设的方式等历史因素。[②]在这一点上，使用新颖性要求和重复计算对于确证的理解均涉及对于构建假设的方式的考量，但后者摒弃了前者的"全有或全无"立场，对于历史因素的评估不再是简单的"是或否"的问题——"证据是否被用于构建假设"，而是"如何"的问题——"证据如何被用于假设"。因此，对于重复计算的方法论地位的重新认识无疑推动了科学证据理论的进一步深化。

然而，围绕重复计算的讨论也为科学证据理论引入了新的问题。"如何"问题将关注的重点置于方法论可靠性的评估，但严格性和简单性等作为可靠性的标准，其自身的合理性仍需进一步的辩护。此外，在历史主义的框架下，方法论似乎构成了证据和假设的"二元逻辑函数"之外的"第三元"，对此，如何应对方法论标准的历史偶然性与证据关系的客观性之间的对立，换言之，如何明确历史主义和逻辑主义进路的限度，将是科学证据理论进一步研究的一个关键所在。

4. 对数据的充分合理利用

在对数据的使用上，对于重复计算的认可并不意味着不欢迎使用新颖的数据。然而，在某些科学研究领域而中，"假设由数据得出并得到数据确

---

① Mayo, D. G. Novel Evidence and Severe Tests. In *Philosophy of Science*, 1991, Vol.58(4), p.530.

② Musgrave, A. Logical Versus Historical Theories of Confirmation. In *The British Journal for the Philosophy of Science*, 1974, Vol.25(1), pp.2-3.

证，而获取新数据是不可能或不切实际的（例如，进化论、流行病学、人类学、心理学等等）"①。由于历史数据的稀缺性、实验的高昂成本或者伦理问题等因素，相关的研究只能基于已有的数据构建假设，同时这些数据也被视为对于这些假设的支持或确证。

为实现对数据的充分合理利用，许多研究都采取了涉及重复计算的方法，如交叉验证（cross-validation）。斯蒂尔和沃恩德尔指出，气候科学的许多研究都采用了此方法来进行模型选择，典型的（n-1）交叉验证方法如下："对于 n 个数据点，首先使用前 n-1 个数据点构建基础模型在这些数据下的最佳拟合模型实例，然后使用剩余的数据点来评估模型实例的表现"，然后"对 n-1 个数据点的所有可能选择重复此操作"，最终选出拟合最佳的模型实例。②在此方法中，每一次操作都存在一个数据点是使用新颖的，但对于整体而言，所有的数据都被用于构建和检验假设，因而是一种重复计算。可见，在最大化对数据利用程度方面，重复计算具有极大的优势。

总而言之，重复计算作为一种特殊的构建假设以及检验假设的方法，摒弃了科学证据理论中长期存在的一种直觉，即同一证据不能既用于构建假设又用于检验假设。科学实践中存在的诸多案例均表明，应当从一种方法论而非谬误的角度来重新认识重复计算。当然，这并非对使用新颖性要求的全盘否定，在一些情况下它仍然能够发挥重要的作用，如参数确定中的条件支持概念以及模型选择中的交叉验证方法。与使用新颖性要求强调禁止重复计算规则不同，重复计算摒弃了"全有或全无"的立场，这对于理解科学实践中构建和检验假设的方法的多样性以及推进科学证据理论的发展均具有重要意义。

参考文献

［1］Chalmers, A. F. What is this thing called science? Indianapolis: Hackett Publishing Company. (1999).

［2］Hitchcock, C., & Sober, E. Prediction versus accommodation and the risk of overfitting. The British Journal for the Philosophy of Science, (2004).

---

① Mayo, D. G. Novel Evidence and Severe Tests. In *Philosophy of Science*, 1991, Vol.58(4), p.537.

② Steele, K., Werndl, C. The Diversity of Model Tuning Practices in Climate Science. In *Philosophy of Science*, 2016, Vol.83(5), p.1139.

vol, 55(1), pp.1-34.

［3］Howson, C. Fitting your theory to the facts: Probably not such a bad thing after all. Minnesota studies in the philosophy of science, (1990). vol, 14, pp.224-244.

［4］Mayo, D. G. Novel evidence and severe tests. Philosophy of Science, (1991). vol, 58(4), pp.523-552.

［5］Mayo, D. G. Error and the growth of experimental knowledge. Chicago: University of Chicago Press. (1996).

［6］Mayo, D. G. How to Discount Double-Counting When It Counts: Some Clarifications. The British Journal for the Philosophy of Science, (2008). vol, 59(4), pp.857-879.

［7］Mayo, D. G. An ad hoc save of a theory of adhocness? Exchanges with John Worrall. In D. G. Mayo & A. Spanos (Eds.), Error and Inference: Recent Exchanges on Experimental Reasoning, Reliability, and the Objectivity and Rationality of Science. New York: Cambridge University Press. (2010).

［8］Mayo, D. G. Some surprising facts about (the problem of) surprising facts. Studies in History and Philosophy of Science, (2014). vol, 45, pp.79-86.

［9］Musgrave, A. Logical versus historical theories of confirmation. The British Journal for the Philosophy of Science, (1974). vol, 25(1), pp.1-23.

［10］Psillos, S. Scientific realism: How science tracks truth. London: Routledge. (1999).

［11］Schurz, G. Bayesian pseudo-confirmation, use-novelty, and genuine confirmation. Studies in History and Philosophy of Science, (2014). vol, 45, pp.87-96.

［12］Steele, K., & Werndl, C. Climate Models, Calibration, and Confirmation. The British Journal for the Philosophy of Science, (2013). vol, 64(3), pp.609-635.

［13］Steele, K., & Werndl, C. The diversity of model tuning practices in climate science. Philosophy of Science, (2016). vol, 83(5), pp.1133-1144.

［14］Worrall, J. Scientific discovery and theory-confirmation. In J. C. Pitt (Ed.), Change and progress in modern science. Dordrecht: Springer. (1985).

［15］Worrall, J. Error, Tests, and Theory Confirmation. In D. G. Mayo & A. Spanos (Eds.), Error and Inference: Recent Exchanges on Experimental Reasoning, Reliability, and the Objectivity and Rationality of Science. New York: Cambridge University Press. (2010).

（本文原载于《科学技术哲学研究》2021 年第 5 期）

模型及其真实性所在

乌斯卡里·麦基*

1. 引言

科学模型可以为真吗？如果不可以，那么为什么不可以，在这一情形下真实性这一语词是否存在某种与模型相关联的用法？如果可以，那么模型的真实性具体位于何处，如何确定其定位？近来对于科学中的模型的本质和功能的哲学探讨如火如荼，但对于上述问题的相对忽视也激发了对这些问题的关注。我对于这些问题的回答构成了对于模型可以为真这一直觉进行阐明的尝试。

我的动机部分源于经济学家学科文化的一个特征所带来的长期刺激：作为对于频繁的批评——运用虚假假设构建虚假理论模型——的回应，经济学家经常逃避似地（并且优柔寡断地）说，模型或者必然为假，或者既非真亦非假，这就是它们的本质。

典型的经济学模型具备一些特征，这些特征使其非常适合作为考察真实性问题的代表，而不是一个极其特殊的案例。那些模型以及它们的构成部分通常是虚假的，甚至完全为假。而且它们经常因其无所顾忌的虚假性而被严厉地批评，有时候还会被嘲笑。然而，那些运用这些显然为假的模型的经济学家经常认为它们能够为经济现实提供重要的洞见。与此同时，那些经济学家通常不能以真实性概念来阐述这一信念。尽管本文的首要目标是为当今相对受到忽视的模型问题的哲学讨论作出贡献，但次要的目标

---

* 乌斯卡里·麦基（uskdi Mäki），南开大学哲学院讲座教授，赫尔辛基大学教授，主要研究方向为科学哲学、社会科学哲学。本文由南开大学哲学院科技哲学教研室讲师、博士生胡瑞斌译，向　校。

也在于说明如何能够为经济学家以及其他科学家阐述其关于理论模型的元理论信念提供帮助。①

科学家与哲学家持有两个我认为应当避免的观点。这两个观点都认为模型"仅仅是模型",而不严肃地视其为真实性的候选者。但这两个观点以不同的方式推出了这一结论。

第一个观点认为,模型不能为真,因为它们包含了太多的虚假内容。模型违反了"整体真实性"原则,它们遗漏过多而涵括太少:模型孤立化了。由于包含了扭曲世界中的事物的性质的假设,它们同样违反了"真实性至上"原则:模型理想化了。这些观点都与这一直觉性的想法联系在一起,即这个世界比任何如此单薄构建的模型都更加丰富和复杂。因此,这一直觉(及其哲学阐述)认为,获得真实性或者与之靠近,需要通过放松理想化的假设并增强模型复杂性来构建更加深厚和丰富的模型:模型必须去孤立化和去理想化。这正是我想要驳斥的第一个较流行的观点,无论任何一般的形式。

我的替代想法是,模型为真与违反整体真实性和真实性至上原则之间并不必然存在如上所述的矛盾。我接受更弱的观点,即尽管假设为假,但模型可能为真。我也接受——本文也将对之进行论证——这个更强的观点,即模型借助于假的假设可能能够帮助捕捉真实性。因此,许多真实性是可达至的,无需通过去理想化而去孤立化——因而确实能够通过理想化实现孤立化从而获得真实性。

需要注意的是,第一个观点——以及对其驳斥——基于这个假定,即一个模型可能是有真值的。这一点被第二个我认为应当考虑避免的观点否定了。第二个观点认为,模型不能为真,因为它们并不属于有真值的实体类型。例如,吉尔认为,模型不具有真值,因为它们并非语言学意义上的

① 之前的尝试可参见 Mäki, U. On the Method of Isolation in Economics. In *Poznan Studies in the Philosophy of the Sciences and the Humanities*, 1992, Vol.26, pp.319-354. Mäki, U. Isolation, Idealization and Truth in Economics. In *Poznan Studies in the Philosophy of the Sciences and the Humanities*, 1994, Vol.38, pp.147-168. Mäki, U. Realism and the Nature of Theory: A Lesson from J. H. von Thünen for Economists and Geographers. In *Environment and Planning A*, 2004a, Vol.36, pp.1719-1736. Mäki, U. Some Truths about Truth for Economists, Their Critics and Clients. In P. Mooslechner, H. Schuberth, M. Schurtz eds.: *Economic Policy-making under Uncertainty: The Role of Truth and Accountability in Policy Advice*. Edward Elgar, 2004b, pp.9-39.

实体（而是"抽象实体"）。①基于这一观点，真实性至多存在于关于模型性质的语言学断言中（基于吉尔的解释，这样的断言是关于相似性关系的"理论假设"，它们是有真值的）。

对于第二个观点，我的替代想法是，聚焦于模型中的真实性承载者（其本质和定位）——以及使其为真的真实性实现者。因此，我不仅对模型的真实性感兴趣，也想看到模型本身是如何为真的。本文将尝试对吉尔的解释进行阐述和修正，从而对模型的真实性进行重新定位（就真实性问题而言，这将给予一种更为激进版本的吉尔式解释）。为了在模型内对真实性进行重新定位，我们主要需要重新思考真实性的承载者和条件，但我们同样也提议给予模型概念以一定的反思。

本文提供的论证例证了我在建模研究中称为功能分解的方法。②模型及其表征拥有许多具有各种功能的组成部分。本文的论证将通过确定这些组成部分及其功能来进行。

考虑到本文在当今哲学中的定位，我认为它能够解决那些遭到相对忽视的问题。首先，研究科学模型和表征的文献愈来愈多，其中对于真实性概念和问题的关注却相对较少。其次，围绕科学实在论的争论对于科学中的真实性已经作出了强硬的断言，但那些可能具有真实性抑或可能不具有真实性的具体科学学科却依然含糊不清。最后，近来研究真实性理论的文献相对很少给予真实性承载者以批判和系统性的关注。接下来的讨论可被视为一种尝试，即尝试开始将这些相互联系的问题提上日程。

因此，我想做的是给予真实性一个机会，从而以全新的视角来考虑模型中的真实性甚至模型的真实性的可能性（我将在文章结尾给予两者更多的讨论）。关键的问题在于：如果这是我想做的，那么我怎样才能实现这一目标——我还需要接受或者拒斥什么东西？我该如何考量模型和真实性，从而使它们的关系更加密切？

---

① Giere, R. Explaining Science. University of Chicago Press. 1988.

② Mäki, U. On the Method of Isolation in Economics. In *Poznan Studies in the Philosophy of the Sciences and the Humanities*, 1992, Vol.26, pp.319-354. Mäki, U. Realism and the Nature of Theory: A Lesson from J. H. von Thünen for Economists and Geographers. In *Environment and Planning A*, 2004a, Vol.36, pp.1719-1736. Mäki, U. Some Truths about Truth for Economists, Their Critics and Clients. In P. Mooslechner, H. Schuberth, M. Schurtz eds.: *Economic Policy-making under Uncertainty: The Role of Truth and Accountability in Policy Advice*. Edward Elgar. 2004b. pp.9-39. Mäki, U. Models and Truth: The Functional Decomposition Approach. In *European Philosophy of Science 2007*. Springer. 2009c.

我将把模型视为孤立化的表征。[①]正是通过考察这一概念，我力图在模型中重新定位真实性。我将考察冯·杜能（von Thünen）著名的 1826/1842 农业土地使用模型，它将作为一个例证贯穿全文。本文的探究将分三部分进行。首先，孤立化的模型。我将讨论杜能模型中的虚假内容的功能，并阐明理想化与孤立化概念。其次，作为表征的模型。我将概述我对于模型概念的解释，在代表性和相似性方面我将之视为语用学层面可行而又受限的表征。最后，作为真实性涵括者的模型。我探讨了需要什么样的举措才能容纳这一直觉，即一个高度不切实际的模型——如杜能的模型——捕捉了世界的某些真实性。

2. 模型：以理想化实现孤立化

杜能在其著作《孤立国同农业和国民经济的关系》（1826/1842）中提出了一个农业土地使用分配的简单模型，该模型有时被称为世界上第一个经济学模型。而且，这一模型还有着持久的重要意义。该模型依然是标准的教科书材料，且其变体仍被广泛应用于经济地理学和地理经济学中的子领域，如区位论、城市经济学和区域科学。由于该模型涉及地理学，它的许多特征都可以可视化地呈现，这也构成了对我的论证进行例证的一个优势。对于我们的目的而言更为重要的是，杜能的模型使用了许多不真实的假设，从而设想出了一个极为简单的与现实世界几乎毫不相干的情境。因而它是一个最不具可能性的真实性候选者，从而也构成了一个对于我的观点的有力检验。

① 参见 Mäki, U. On the Method of Isolation in Economics. In *Poznan Studies in the Philosophy of the Sciences and the Humanities*, 1992, Vol.26, pp.319-354. Mäki, U. Models. In *International Encyclopedia of the Social and Behavioral Sciences, Amsterdam: Elsevier*, 2001, Vol.15, pp.9931-9937. Mäki, U. Realism and the Nature of Theory: A Lesson from J. H. von Thünen for Economists and Geographers. In *Environment and Planning A*, 2004a, Vol.36, pp.1719-1736. Mäki, U. Models are Experiments, Experiments are Models. In *Journal of Economic Methodology*, 2005, Vol.12, pp.303-315. Mäki, U. Realistic Realism about Unrealistic Models. In H. Kincaid, D. Ross eds.: *Oxford Handbook of the Philosophy of Economics*. Oxford University Press, 2009a, pp.68-98. Mäki, U. MISSing the World: Models as Isolations and Credible Surrogate Systems. In *Erkenntnis*, 2009b, Vol.70, pp.29-43. Mäki, U. Models and Truth: The Functional Decomposition Approach. In *European Philosophy of Science 2007*. Springer, 2009c.

　　杜能著作开篇便引导读者设想这样一个系统，它不可能被观察到，且除了想象之外似乎不可能存在。他并未使用"模型"这一语词，但基于他确实在描述一个符合现今我们对于模型概念的理解的模型，他实际上暗指模型即想象的系统。他的书是这样开篇的：

　　　　设想一个巨大的城镇，它坐落在沃野平原的中央，那里没有可以通航的河流或运河。这一平原的土地肥力均等，各处都适宜于耕作。远离城市的平原四周，是未经开垦的荒野，那里与外界完全隔绝。平原上没有其他城镇。①

　　在开篇的这一段话中，杜能列出了一些用以刻画其孤立国土地使用模型的假设。之后的研究参与者增列了几条假设。以下这一列表仍然不够完整（我自己作的划分），但已经能让我们了解需要什么样的假设。

　　（1）该地区是一个完美的平原：没有山脉和山谷。

　　（2）平原没有可以通航的河流或运河。

　　（3）该地区的土壤各处都适宜耕种。

　　（4）该地区的土壤肥力均等。

　　（5）该地区气候统一。

　　（6）该地区与外部世界之间的所有交流都被未开垦的荒野切断。

　　（7）在平原的中心有一个没有空间尺寸的城镇。

　　（8）该地区没有其他城镇。

　　（9）所有工业活动都在城镇上进行。

　　（10）所有市场以及生产者之间的所有互动都在城镇之内。

　　（11）生产者之间的互动仅限于最终产品的销售和购买：生产者之间没有中间产品和非市场关系。

　　（12）运输成本与距离和货物的重量以及易损性成正比。

　　（13）所有价格和运输费用都是固定的。

　　（14）生产成本在空间上是恒定的。

　　（15）行动者是其收入的最大化者。

　　（16）行动者拥有全部相关信息。

---

　　① von Thünen, J. H. *Von Thünen's Isolated State*. (P. Hall, ed., C. M. Wartenberg, trans.). Pergamon, 1966, p.7.

假设（1）到（16）描述了最简单的杜能土地使用模型。显而易见，如果将这些假设视为关于世界的断言，那么它们显然是错的，许多假设与典型的实际情况相去甚远。它们从一开始便显然为假，因而识别其虚假性并非事后经验检验的结果。确实，它们并不是被视为真实性候选者而接受检验的假设或猜想。[①]相反，其虚假性是出于策略性的考虑而被有意设定的。它们是建模中所运用的理想化假设的实例，其特征便在于故意为之的策略性的虚假性。问题在于：意义何在？它们具有什么功能？

回答是：这些虚假断言的功能在于通过理想化实现孤立化。[②]理想化假设（1）到（16）的功能在于，通过将这些在因果关系上相关的诸多因素或其效力排除在外从而使其中立化。假设（1）排除了高山和峡谷对于土地使用的影响。假设（2）排除了河流和运河对于土地使用的影响。假设（4）排除了土地肥力变化的影响，而假设（5）则排除了气候变化的影响。假设（6）将该地区与这个世界的其他部分相孤立，从而排除了贸易的影响（因而构成了"孤立国"）。假设（12）排除了道路、铁路以及任何保鲜技术的影响（杜能设想该城镇以牛车来运输货物）。诸如此类。

与实验过程相类似，这样的理想化假设在许多语境下都服务于理论性的孤立化这一策略性目的。通过将其他次要原因和条件中立化，它们帮助我们将一种主要原因及其特有的作用方式孤立出来。杜能的案例也是如此。他的简单模型所孤立出来的影响土地使用分布的主要原因是距离（或者运输成本）。这一见解将在我的论证中发挥核心作用。

应当注意的是，杜能在其阐述中也使用了"孤立化"这一术语：他所分析的是"孤立国"的土地使用。这一国家或地区被假定与世界的其他部分相孤立，从而排除了其他地区对于土地使用的影响。我所主张的观点是，杜能的模型将一种因素与所有其他内外部因素都孤立起来。因而，相比于杜能，我在一种更一般的意义上使用"孤立化"这一术语。值得注意的是，

① 冯·杜能著作（1966）的英译本可能会造成一些误解："Voraussetzungen"被译作"假设"（Hypothesis），这一语词可能意味着其真值是一个悬而未决的问题。相反，我称之为"假定"（Assumption）。

② Mäki, U. On the Method of Isolation in Economics. In *Poznan Studies in the Philosophy of the Sciences and the Humanities*, 1992, Vol.26, pp.319-354. Mäki, U. Isolation, Idealization and Truth in Economics. In *Poznan Studies in the Philosophy of the Sciences and the Humanities*, 1994, Vol.38, pp.147-168. 我使用的术语与其他学者有所不同。例如，相比于诺瓦克（Nowak，1980）和卡特赖特（Cartwright，1989），我使用的"抽象化"和"具体化"更为受限。在这两篇文章中，我对自己的"（去）孤立化""（去）理想化""抽象化"以及"具体化"的用法进行了解释和辩护。

杜能的这本书的暂定名称曾是 Der ideale Staat（理想国），这一书名在某种程度上比 Der isolierte Staat（孤立国）传递了更多的信息。理想国充分捕捉到了其模型在描述一个相当理想化的系统这一层面的本质。它同样强调了这一事实，即我们的思维能力设想了该系统，因而这一系统是"理想化的"。

确实，我们在杜能的引导下设想了一个高度理想化的以一系列理想化假设为特征的系统。在概述了其中的一些假设之后，他随即问道，在这种设想的情境即模型中会发生什么。什么样的土地使用模式将会呈现出来？

> 在这些条件下，耕作的模式将会是什么样的？而不同地区与城镇的距离又会怎么影响其农作制度？①

他随即回答了这一问题，换言之，他描述了该模型中会呈现的结果。这正是在特殊情形下以模型的理想化为特征的土地使用模式。

> ……距离城镇较近的地方应该种植这样的产品：这些产品相对于其价值而言较为笨重或体积较大，因而运输费用高昂，从远地供应这些产品不合算。在这里我们也将发现极易腐烂、必须尽快使用的产品。随着与城镇的距离越来越远，这些土地将会逐渐被那些相对于其自身的价值而言运输成本较低的产品所占据。由于这一原因，城市四周将形成一些界限相当分明的同心环或带，每个同心环都有各自的主要产品。②

因此，呈现出来的模式将是一些同心环，它们围绕着市场所在的点状的城镇。在内环上的是乳制品业和蔬菜水果集约农业，这是因为牛奶、西红柿等产品必须被快速运送到市场；同样还有木料与柴火的生产，这是因为它们较为笨重且体积较大，因而相对于其自身价值而言运输成本高昂。在最远的外环上的是畜牧业或牧场经营，这是由于动物可以自我运输，它们可以走到城镇从而被售卖或屠宰。在中间的一些同心环上的是集约型的农作物种植业，比如谷物，它们比水果更易存放，比木材更轻。图1的上

---

① von Thünen, J. H. Von Thünen's Isolated State. (P. Hall, ed., C. M. Wartenberg, trans.). Pergamon, 1966, p.8.

② von Thünen, J. H. Von Thünen's Isolated State. (P. Hall, ed., C. M. Wartenberg, trans.). Pergamon, 1966, p.8.

半部分描述了著名的杜能环模式。

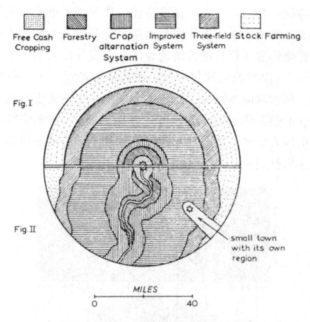

图 1　杜能环：模型世界的土地使用[①]

资料来源：von Thünen, J. H. Von Thünen's isolated state (P. Hall, Ed., C. M. Wartenberg, Trans.). Oxford: Pergamon, (1966). p.216.

　　在该图的下半部分，杜能设想了模型中出现的一种情形，这一模型最简单的版本遗漏了两个特征：一条穿过中心城市的河以及一个较小的附属城镇。描述这一最简单模型的假设（2）和（8）在这里被放宽了。

　　重要的一点是，杜能的阐述表明，模型与其描述是不同的。该模型是设想的世界，它具有一系列理想化假设所规定的特征，同时也忽略了许多真实世界的特征。那些假设以及同心环图形描述了这一模型。它同样也可以用各种数学工具来描述。因而，我们可以拥有口头的、几何的以及代数的等各种对于该模型的特征的描述。

　　将模型与其描述区分开所隐含的第一种意义是，强调了推理在建模中的定位。通过从模型的一些特征推理出其他特征——例如从假设（1）到

　　① von Thünen, J. H. Von Thünen's Isolated State. (P. Hall, ed., C. M. Wartenberg, trans.). Pergamon, 1966, p.216.

（16）规定的特征推理出同心环形状分区的可视化的特征——模型的性质和特性得到了检验。在这一点上，模型描述的作用至关重要。模型的性质是通过在模型的各种描述之间进行推理而得到检验的。土地使用模式是从土地价值或者租金梯度（后杜能传统的说法）中推导出来的。图2展示了这一推导过程。[①]与模型的推理相一致，距离城市越近，土地租金越高，距离城市越远，则运输成本越高；在土地市场上，土地使用者相互竞争从而实现其净利润的最大化，同时他们也受这两个成本因素的影响，最终选定一个能使这些因素实现平衡的地点，最终导致了同心环的模式。我将称这一系列的事实为杜能机制。

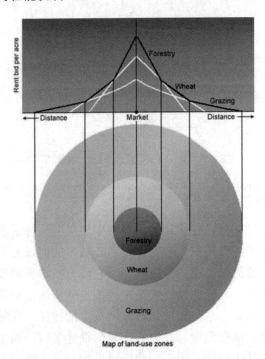

图2 基于租金梯度推断土地使用区段

资料来源：Hoover, E. M., & Giarratani, F. An introduction to regional economics. In S. Loveridge. (Ed.), The Web Book of regional science (http://www.rri.wvu.edu/regscweb. htm). Morgantown, WV: Regional Research Institute, West Virginia University. (1999).

---

① 这一观点与侧重于推理功能的模型解释（例如 Suarez, 2004）相关。在我的解释中，表征观与推理观是相辅相成的。

现在从真实性的角度来考虑杜能的假设和杜能环，我们便会有一个惊人的发现，它们似乎完全不具有任何可能的真实性。虚假内容大行其道。我们所看到的是一系列完全错误的假设和一个完全错误的预测。这些假设似乎错误地理解了世界，而且真实世界中的土地使用不存在同心环。这个模型似乎是错误的。我们将会在后文中看到，杜能自己完全意识到了这一点。

对于这一问题的一个标准的回应在于，认为杜能所提供的只是简单的"一级近似"或诸如此类，并且只有通过使这一模型更加复杂和全面才能接近土地使用的真实情况。我们必须逐个放宽模型的理想化假设，使之前被排除在外的因素施加其对结果的影响，从而更加靠近真实的表征。也就是说，我们必须继续执行在图 1 下半部分开始的程序。因此，通过去理想化来去孤立化是通向真实性的唯一路径，或者说，引言中提及的流行观点是成立的。[①]图 3 说明了这一点。

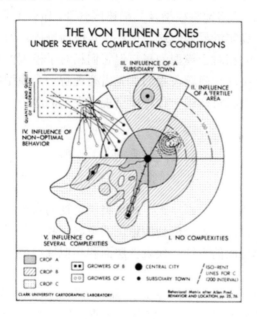

图 3　通过去理想化而去孤立化

来源：Peet, J. R. The spatial expansion of commercial agriculture in the nineteenth century: A von Thünen interpretation. Economic Geography, (1969). Vol.45, p.287.

---

① 参见 Nowak, L. *The Structure of Idealization.* Reidel, 1980.

在这里，我们可以从同心环的简单情形（阶段 1）开始，它只受杜能机制的支配。接着加入土壤肥力的变化（阶段 2），加入另一个城镇（阶段 3），然后放宽完全理性假设（阶段 4）。继续此操作，最终将这些相关的"复杂事物"结合在一起，我们便有可能绘制出接近真实表征的土地使用的图像（阶段 5）。

不可否认的是，获取一些关于世界的有意义的真实断言，需要这样的去孤立化过程。但是对于这一流行观点，即通过去理想化来去孤立化是通向所有可能真实性断言的唯一路径，我持怀疑态度。相反，我将会论证，杜能最简单的模型原则上在不去孤立化的条件下能够传达重要且真实的关于世界的知识。①

但是，我首先需要指出上述推理的一个令人烦恼的特征。这也正是将模型与其描述区分开所隐含的第二种意义，它与模型的表征功能——而非推理功能——相关。模型描述的含义正如其名：它们描述的是模型而非真实世界。如果我们严格地将模型及其描述区分开，那么主张理想化假设（1）到（16）相对于真实世界为假这一说法便是成问题的。对于同心环图像来说也是如此。它们相对于模型为真，但它们相对于模型的对象来说即非真亦非假。为了解决这一问题，我们首先需要理解一个模型所要表征的是什么。因此，接下来我将概述一种将模型视为表征的解释。

3. 作为表征的模型

与大多数当代的哲学家一致，我也将模型视为表征。但是我的解释有一些特殊的特征，出于剩余部分的论证的考虑，我需要对之进行说明。我将模型视为两个层面的表征：代表性层面和相似性层面。模型是一些目标

---

① Mäki, U. On the Method of Isolation in Economics. In *Poznan Studies in the Philosophy of the Sciences and the Humanities*, 1992, Vol.26, pp.319-354. Mäki, U. Isolation, Idealization and Truth in Economics. In *Poznan Studies in the Philosophy of the Sciences and the Humanities*, 1994, Vol.38, pp.147-168. Mäki, U. Realism and the Nature of Theory: A Lesson from J. H. von Thünen for Economists and Geographers. In *Environment and Planning A*, 2004a, Vol.36, pp.1719-1736. Mäki, U. Some Truths about Truth for Economists, Their Critics and Clients. In P. Mooslechner, H. Schuberth, M. Schurtz eds.: *Economic Policy-making Under Uncertainty: The Role of Truth and Accountability in Policy Advice*. Edward Elgar, 2004b, pp.9-39.

系统的代表：它们是代表其目标的代理系统，代替其目标接受检验。相似性则是代理系统和目标系统之间更进一步的关系，它决定了模型在多大程度上代表了目标系统。

代表性层面强调了模型的意向性和主动性特征，强调了模型的特性取决于我们，这些由我们设定的模型服务于我们的兴趣（习语"任何事物皆可充当模型"刻画了这一特征）。模型使用者的目的和语境为塑造模型设置了语用学约束，因此，这一解释有着强烈的语用学色彩。同时，相似性层面强调了表征的不自主性，强调了模型受到或应当受其目标的特征的约束。这一点为建模设置了本体论层面的约束，因而这一概念也隐含着一种实在论色彩。我对于作为表征的模型的解释可以概括如下：

> 行动者 A 出于目的 P 以对象 M（模型）为目标系统 R 的一个代表，并向受众 E 进行表述，促使 M 和 R 之间真正的相似性问题的出现；并且以论述 C 识别上述因素并协调它们之间的关系。

这一解释有一些独特的特点。它包含了受众概念，这一概念是表征的语用学的一部分。基于科学工作的集体性本质，我认为这是对之前的模型解释所作的一个毫无争议的修正。模型不是为某个人的私人兴趣而构建和检验的，而主要是为了迎合并塑造受众的期望。模型使交流得以可能，模型能够帮助传递信息、增强一致性以及说服别人修正其信念强度。受众依赖性可能确实是公共性的，而且实际上可能是预期的受众回应塑造了个人的建模活动。受众在塑造模型描述方面的作用也很明显：在描述一个模型时所运用的媒介部分地取决于听取表述的受众。引入受众完美地展现了吉尔的解释的精神。受众与目的 P 一起构成了语用学语境，进而塑造了吉尔所言的"视角"[①]。

第二个新颖之处在于，这一解释要求促使真正的相似性问题的出现——而不是成功的相似性或者完全不涉及相似性。我通过"真正的问题"想要表达两点。第一，表征预设了 M 能够模拟 R。成功的相似性不应该是空想得出的，它不应当是一个无法企及的目标，以至于关于这一目标是否已实现，任何合理的问题都不可能或不应该出现。为了使真正的相似性问题得以呈现，成功的相似性应当能够为我们所能企及，应当在我们认知的

---

① Giere, R. *Scientific Perspectivism*. University of Chicago press, 2006.

可能性范围之内。第二，真正的相似性问题不涉及 M 和 R 以任何一种任意方式确实（不）以及可能（不）彼此相似。我们所讨论的是相似性的具体层面与程度，它们应当在足够的抽象水平上满足语用学约束。

对于表征而言，仅有相似性是不充分的。可以考虑孤立国模型世界中的同心环模式。这一模式与现实世界中在静止水面投掷一颗鹅卵石所产生的图形模式是极其相似的。然而，杜能模式并不是对水面的这种或其他真实的模式的表征——因为它与杜能模型并无适当关联，杜能的本意是以这个模型表征农业土地使用的机制。为了使相似性问题得以呈现，各个被选作代表的事物必须和想要讨论的问题或者相关的领域相关联。相关领域可以部分地由语用学约束来确定，也可部分地由可能发挥作用的因果机制来确定。就模拟其模式从而对之进行阐明这一点来说，孤立国中的土地使用模式和水面的模式各自的因果机制是相当不同的。这一点值得我们的注意，因为同心环模式和水面的模式的相似性程度很有可能远高于其与真实世界的土地使用模式的相似度。

上文的讨论似乎在主张相似性对于表征而言也不是必要的。但另一方面，我已经作出了断言，表征确实需要相似性层面，因而仅代表性层面不足以构成表征。这一矛盾可以通过两步来解决。第一，表征所需的并非已实现的相似性，而仅仅是使相似性问题得以呈现。第二，表征并不要求在目标的所有层面的所有部分都呈现出相似性问题。接下来我将说明我的解释何以能帮助第二步的实现；然后我将指出一个隐含的含义和一个替代说法用以说明第一步。

表征并不要求模型的所有部分都与目标的所有或者任意方面都相似，或者说相似性问题对于所有部分都应呈现。模型相关的部分、相关的方面和相似程度都必须是限定的。重要的一点在于，模型本身难以将各部分（m1，m2，m3，……）按照其不同的功能区分开。正是在这一点上，其语用学成分发挥了积极的作用。语用学约束确定了模型 M 与目标 R 之间所需的相似性的方面与程度——而不是完全的和精确的相似性。在这一过程中，对于相关目的 P 和受众 E 的确定帮助将不同的功能分配给模型的不同部分。因此，我们可以认为，所需的相似性的方面和程度为{M, R, P, E}的函数，其中 M 由 m1、m2、m3 等部分构成。

但是这一函数不具备识别自身的能力，因而它不能够论及自身。其中的挑战在于，识别并协调各种组成部分，将它们匹配在一切，且能够满足本体论层面的和语用学层面的约束。正是在这里，论述 C 进入了我们的视野。它为各组成部分提供了联系的桥梁，从而明确了我们应当寻求哪些方面的和多大程度的相似性，以及模型的各部分在实现这一目标的过程中是如何发挥其作用的。论述的功能将在下一节得到阐明。

对于近来关于模型的讨论偶有提及的"错误表征"问题，上述的第一步隐含了一些论点。这些讨论中的部分对此问题困惑不解，其原因在于它们没能将表征的代表性层面与相似性层面完全区分开。我的解释隐含的直接论点在于，就相似性而言，"表征"并非一个要求高度相似性的术语。在面对相似性问题时出于某种目的使用某个目标的一个代表便是在进行表征。因而，在这种意义上，表征的失败并不是我们通常理解的"错误表征"的含义。我认为，它应当被用于讨论模拟的失败。但这依然是含糊不清的，因为代表性与相似性层面没有被明确地区分开来。

理所当然，对于科学表征的解释必须容纳失败。"促使真正的相似性问题的呈现"这一观点已经开始考虑这一点。不能够促使这些问题出现便是表征中的一次重大失败（正是在这里"错误表征"可能较为适用），而不能够实现模拟则是较次要的失败。相应地，促使相似性问题出现是一种较弱的成功，而成功实现模拟则是一种较强的成功。

另外一种通过模型刻画成功表征的方式在于，通过探寻并在一定可能性上实现模型和目标之间正确类型的相似性，对于模型的性质的直接检验可能间接地提供关于目标性质的信息。我们通过研究模型来了解目标。正是基于这一原因，我们将模型称为代理系统，它提供了潜在的超出其自身的通向目标系统的认知路径。相反，如果对于模型的研究最多也只提供了关于模型性质的信息，那么其原因可能在于我们对于模型之外的东西不感兴趣，或者模型不具备模拟目标的能力，它只能作为一个替代系统发挥作用。一个代理系统能够充当通往目标的桥梁，但一个替代系统只是一座与世隔绝的小岛，与真实世界毫无联系。①

当然，我们可能想要通过排除目标 R 而仅仅关注 M-P-E 间的联系，从而放宽对于成功表征的限制。例如，我们可能认为，M 满足了一个有用的目的，即教会学生受众凭借城市经济学来运用租金梯度。毫无疑问，杜

---

① Mäki, U. Realistic Realism about Unrealistic Models. In H. Kincaid, D. Ross eds.: *Oxford Handbook of the Philosophy of Economics*. Oxford University Press. 2009a, pp.68-98. Mäki, U. MISSing the World: Models as Isolations and Credible Surrogate Systems. In *Erkenntnis*, 2009b, Vol.70, pp.29-43.

能的模型提供了一种简单的情境来帮助学生学习这一技能——这正是当代的标准教科书都包含了这一模型的原因之一。但是模型的这一功能并不会排除其所具有的其他功能，例如强调关于世界的真实断言，或者启发我们构建其他具备此功能的模型。

4. 模型与真实性

从真实性角度来使我们的挑战更加明确，我们将会问：如果一个模型为真或者包含真实断言，那么它会是什么样的？与模型相关的真实性的定位是什么？我们应当在哪里找到它？我对于模型提出的解释提供了一些可能的路径，可以沿着这些路径来思考如何赋予模型以真实性。我认为我已经表明了我自己的倾向，即将关注点转移到相似性概念上来，但这并非唯一的一种可能性。其他选项依然存在，即孤立和利用作为表征的模型概念中的语用学成分：目的和受众。

诚然，通过采纳一个合适的真实性的语用学概念并将其语用学特性归于模型，我们可以将真实性融入模型。前文对模型的解释提供了两个语用学特性：对于目的而言的有用性，以及对于受众而言的说服力。真实性的概念可以分别以这两个术语来界定：就满足某一目的而言，真实性即有用性，而就塑造或符合受众的信念而言，真实性即说服力。因此，一个模型可能被认为为真，如果该模型成功地实现了某一目的，如帮助实现了一项政策目标；或者是当受众认为该模型具有说服力，吸引其接受这一模型。[①]值得注意的是，这两个选项——真实性的有用性概念和修辞学概念——都倾向于以一种无差别的方式来处理模型。模型的整体而不是其中有限的部分被赋予了真实性。

这并不是我将真实性融入模型的策略，但是在这里，除了指出我不准

---

① 哲学家们对真理的有用性解释传统熟稔于心，但对于真理性的说服性解释可能知之不多，这种解释在最近的探究修辞学运动中颇为流行。参见 McCloskey, D. N. The Rhetoric of Economics. In *Journal of Economic Literature*, 1983, Vol.31, pp.434-461. Gross, A. *The Rhetoric of Science*. Harvard University Press, 1990. 对之的批评可参见 Mäki, U. Diagnosing McCloskey. In *Journal of Economic Literature*, 1995, Vol.33, pp.1300-1318.

备放弃的一些直觉之外，我不会讨论这些概念。①行动者 A 可以成功地使用一个假模型 M 给受众 E 留下深刻的印象。A 也可以成功地用一个假模型 M 来实现某些其他目的 P。这些直觉表明，真实性独立于有用性和说服力。

因此，在尝试对与模型相关的真实性进行定位时，我们不应当优先考虑 M-P 之间以及 M-E 之间的关系。相反，我们在一开始就应该将 M-R 之间的关系从表征的语用学成分中孤立出来。一旦选定了这一焦点，我们就应当给予一种解释，从而能够容纳另一个直觉，即 A 可以成功地使用一个包含了许多明显错误的模型 M 来捕捉关于目标 R 的真实断言。引导我思考的一个关键原则在于，一个模型便是一个结构，其组成部分可能拥有各种不同的功能作用，包括作为主要真实性承载者的作用。语用学成分 P 和 E（由论述 C 确定）部分地决定了这些作用。因此，在第二阶段，P 和 E 重回舞台：它们对于真实性的获得作出了不可或缺的贡献。但 P 和 E 并不构成真实性。它们只是帮助将模型内的相关真实性承载者孤立起来。真实性的获得是追求同时满足建模的语用学约束和本体论约束的共同产物。

让我们来看一看，我们如何能够更加详细地阐述这个粗略的想法。我认为，我们必须解决两个相互关联的问题。一个是定位问题：合适的真实性承载者可能位于模型中的什么位置？另一个是内容问题：对于真实性承载者而言适当的本体论是什么？

从吉尔的解释开始是有益的，因为我所追求的解释可以被视为对于其解释的一种（或多或少有些激进的）修正。基于吉尔的解释，模型是非语言的"抽象对象"，它们通过语言获得描述或通过假设获得定义。由于模型是非语言的，因而它们没有真值。由于模型描述具有语言性，因此它们具有真值，而且因为它们"定义"了自身的含义，所以它们为真但是琐碎而无意义。模型与其目标相关联，不是通过真实性而是通过相似性实现的。模型系统可能在不同方面和不同程度上与其目标系统相类似。我们需要对这些关系进行更进一步的阐述。它们是这样的理论假设，它们与模型与真实系统之间的相似性（相似方面和程度）相关，是负有真值的（语言学的）

① 参见 Mäki, U. Some Truths about Truth for Economists, Their Critics and Clients. In P. Mooslechner, H. Schuberth, M. Schurtz eds.: *Economic Policy-making under Uncertainty: The Role of Truth and Accountability in Policy Advice*. Edward Elgar, 2004b, pp.9-39.

断言。[①]

因此基于这一解释，模型本身无所谓真假，它们也不包含真实性，而只包含关于模型的正确断言。对于定位问题的讨论到此为止。要求真实性承载者为语言性的这一主张表明了在内容问题上的立场。我将通过处理这两个问题并展示我们如何在模型中获得真实性来挑战吉尔解释中的真理怀疑主义立场。我将重新以杜能作为我提出的模型内真实性这一观点的代言人（虽然我承认需要作一些解释；因为他没有明确地使用真实性这一语词）。

那么关于杜能的模型，相关的真实性承载者和现实世界的真实性实现者是什么？一种选择在于，主张模型的假设是其真实性承载者。这些都是语言性的，因此可以满足吉尔的要求。但现实世界中没有任何东西可以使它们为真。正如杜能所认同的那样，理想化假设是错误的，并且在其与现实世界的情况不符的意义上是错误的。但它们是不可或缺的策略性的虚假内容：

> 对于那些愿意花一些时间和精力在我的工作上的读者，我希望他不会对我在开始时作出的虚构的假设提出异议，因为它们与实际情况不符，并且希望他不会反驳这些假设，认为它们是随意的或无意义的。它们是我的论证的一个必要组成部分，使我能够控制某个因素，我们可以在控制中看到这个因素，但在现实中，它与其他类似因素不断冲突，因而我们只能模糊地看到它。[②]

另一种选择在于，将同心环模式视为模型的真实性承载者。这些是几何图像，因此不完全符合吉尔所认可的范畴。而且不管怎样，实际的土地使用模式很难成为真实性实现者。然而，这里通常有一个抽象的相似之处：土地使用经常是以某种粗糙的区域形式而模式化的。但如果其他因果因素足够强大，那么即使这一点也难以成立。在任何情况下，关于区域相似性的进一步细节，从相当接近到几乎难以识别，相似程度因情况不同而大相径庭。

---

① Giere, R. Explaining Science. University of Chicago Press, 1988. Giere, R. Using Models to Represent Reality. In L. Magnani, N. Nersessian, P. Thagard eds.: *Model-based Reasoning in Scientific Discovery*. Kluwer, 1999. Giere, R. *Scientific Perspectivism*. University of Chicago press, 2006.

② von Thünen, J. H. Von Thünen's isolated state. (P. Hall, ed., C. M. Wartenberg, trans.). Pergamon, 1966, pp.3-4.

作为对于真实性承载者定位的这两个候选者——假设和几何模式——的回应，明显的反对意见是，认为他们并不构成模型，而只是对之进行了描述。我们不会在模型中获得真实性。即使他们被接受为真实性承载者，他们的真实性实现者也将是模型本身，而不是现实世界中的任何东西。但是，我认为没有理由不对此持更加灵活的态度。我们也可以考虑将假设和模式视为可能的真实性承载者，它们对于目标而言是错误的（而不是无真值的）。这种说法并没有排除假设和模式在真实地描述模型（以及模型中关于目标的其他主要真实性承载者）这一方面的主要作用。

第三种选择最终在模型中获得了相关的真实性承载者。我将首先关注定位问题，并在稍后讨论内容问题。现在考虑一下杜能的孤立化模型中存在着什么样的东西。这个想象的世界是一个这样的世界，拥有完全最大化信息的农民为地块进行竞争，最终在一片没有河流、道路和对外贸易且土壤肥力均等的平原上耕作。如果存在一个天然的真实性承载者，那它既不是整个模型，也不是模型的任意部分。它是模型的一个特殊组成部分，即驱动这个简单模型世界的因果力量或机制：杜能机制。这个真实性承载者很有可能被其真实性实现者确定为真，这一真实性实现者即真实系统中显著的因果"力量"或机制。正是这一机制通过运输成本和土地价值将距离转变为土地利用模式。至少这似乎是杜能自己的看法：

> 塑造了孤立国形态的原理也存在于现实中，但是现实中出现的现象是以变化的形式表现出来的，因为它们同时受到了其他关系和条件的影响……我们可能会在所有附带条件和一切偶然因素中剥离出一个作用因素[eine wirkende Kraft]，只有通过这种方式我们才能认识到[erkennen]其对于引发我们面前的现象的作用。①

根据我对这段论述的理解，杜能在这里结合了两个观点。该模型将影响土地使用的主要因素，即距离作用因素的影响，与其他所有因素孤立起来。模型在理论上孤立起来的东西也存在于真实的系统中，即使在这里它并没有与其他作用相孤立。简而言之，在想象的模型世界中，这个作用因素是真实性承载者，而现实世界中的作用因素便是其真实性实现者。无论

---

① von Thünen, J. H. *Der Isolierte Staat in Beziehung auf Landwirtschaft und Nationalökonomie*. Verlag von Gustav Fischer, 1910, p.274.

模型包含什么，无论在现实世界中改变作用因素表现形式的其他任何东西是什么，它们都不参与模型的真实性的实现。这是杜能解决定位问题的方法。

在处理定位问题时，模型的论述 C 发挥了关键的作用。表征的其他组成部分难以识别真实性承载者，而且一般来说也难以为模型各部分分派合适的功能。为了在模型的组成部分中将真实性承载者高度孤立化，论述是有必要的。可以换另一种表达方式，论述可以帮助我们确定需要寻找的是模型与目标之间哪一方面的相似性。本文已经提供了例证：我引用的杜能的文本，尤其是后两个段落，正是其模型的论述的重要组成部分。

正如我前文所言，论述的功能在于识别并协调表征的各组成部分。模型中的真实性承载者的孤立化取决于具体的认知目标（控制作用因素从而使土地使用模式得以呈现）和受众的期望（应当注意，杜能明确地表达了其对于"读者"的论述），而且论述的任务便在于在各种不同的语境下处理这些依赖关系。

论述同样可以帮助我们将相似性（或相像性）转化为真实性。这一点是有必要的，因为相似性是对称的，而真实性则是不对称的。为了说明模型为真或包含关于目标的真实断言，我们必须确定模型中相关的真实性承载者与目标中的真实性实现者之间存在相似性，而且真实性确实是在这一方面得以实现的。

现在假定我们已经解决了定位问题。下一步就要问，对于内容问题我们是否可以想出可行的解决方案，同时使我们可以坚持上述针对定位问题的解决方案。在该定位上，是否存在合适且可行的内容？

在尝试将真实性融入模型时，一条路径在于对真实性承载者持激进的多元主义立场：从语句符号到可视图像，从命题到话语，从信念到物质对象等等，任何内容都可以。①这将容许诸如同心环的具体图像或孤立国的抽象实体等事物承担真实性承载者的角色。不论模型的本体论如何，它都是有真值的。

另外一条路径则主张更为克制的观点——至少部分的或者从根本意义上讲所有的——真实性承载者都是思想观念。可以回想一下，杜能的第一

① 例如泰迪熊！用柯克汉姆的一句朗朗上口的话来说："真理对于一只赤裸的熊来说不是太大的负担。" Kirkham, R. *Theories of Truth*. MIT, 1995, p.61.

段文本以"设想"开头，这表明孤立国是一个想象的系统。即使假定设想即思维，孤立国是否是由思想观念构成的或者模型是否可以与思想观念相分离这些问题也依然含糊不清。

一种可能性在于，将思想观念视为思维对象（例如孤立国观念）。可以认为，它包含了一种具有思维逻辑的思想语言，但如今这是一种没有吸引力的选择。或者可以认为，它包含了"在认知上等同于比例模型的事物"[1]，这一观点可能更具吸引力。与吉尔关于模型内容的观点相类似，我们可以将模型和思想视为可分离的。我们可以关注被认为是抽象对象的东西，而不是作为思维对象的思想。这样的抽象对象可能具有类似于实物的结构（例如包含了作用因素的孤立国），或者它也可能具有类似于事实的结构（例如这一作用因素——基于土地价值和运输成本机制的距离因素——极大地影响了土地使用的分布）。与吉尔的观点相反，这些抽象对象可以作为真实性承载者而发挥作用。一个更进一步的可能路径在于，向吉尔的观点妥协，以语句形式（"这一作用因素极大地影响了土地使用的分布"）来表达上述类似于事实结构的命题内容，并且将之视为语言性的真实性承载者，其真实性实现者则存在于真实世界的目标中。其命题内容将等同于模型中的抽象对象。为了通过指出模型存在真实性承载者来表明内容问题可能是可以解决的，我们并不需要在这些不同的选项中进行抉择。

就杜能的模型包含了一个关于作用因素的真实断言来说，我们可能会称之为一个局部真实性。基于两方面原因，这似乎是正确的。首先，这个作用因素仅仅是那些实际塑造了土地使用模式的诸多因果要素中的一个。作用因素的真实性即整个因果结构的部分真实性。其次，论述仅仅将模型的一部分——而且不是其他部分——确定为相关的真实性承载者，它反映了模型在哪些相关的方面与其目标相联系。但在另一方面，一旦这一部分被孤立起来，我们所能拥有的是关于这一部分——例如这一作用因素——的在特定抽象层次上的整体真实性。这一点弱化了第二方面的原因。

无论如何，不管是部分的还是整体的，它都不会是近似真实性。如果我们认为局部真实性反映了模型与其目标之间在哪些方面具有相似性或相像性，那么我们可以将近似真实性视为在相关的方面得到确定之后对于相似程度的反映。换言之，我们可以利用吉尔对方面和程度的区分来丰富我

---

[1] Waskan, J. *Models and Cognition*. MIT, 2006, p.123.

们关于模型的真实性的讨论：模型能够包含局部真实性和近似真实性。但这些是模型之中的真实性，而不是模型的真实性——而且它们不仅仅是相似性的种类，而且是真实性的种类。

最后的问题依然在于，我们现在是否有资格谈论模型的真实性，或者按照更谦虚的说法，仅仅谈论模型中的真实性。后者显然不那么成问题。我们已经在孤立化中定位了一个组成部分，即杜能机制，因此我们确实可能已经在杜能的模型中发现了一个真实断言。现在存在一种方法，可以使我们推断出我们可能也发现了杜能模型的真实性。杜能模型中的真实性意味着关于其组成部分的真实性。如果组成部分 m_n——杜能机制——已经作为模型 M 中唯一的相关真实性承载者而被孤立化（基于表征的语用学规则），那么这也就意味着 m_n 的真实性既是 M 中的真实性也是 M 的真实性。所以我们可能仅仅因为其他部分都不被视为相关的真实性候选者而认为 M 为真。其他的这些部分并不是闲置的：在许多情形中，为了满足更高的目标，使特殊的组成部分为真，它们（如果认为它们有真值）必须是假的。基于语用学的约束，我们需要保证特殊组成部分为真，除此之外再无其他真实愿景。因此，主张 m_n 为真等同于主张 M 为真。我所主张的并不是我们被迫以这种方式谈论模型中的真实性和模型的真实性，而只是说我们可能不会被迫不这样做。

参考文献

[1] Cartwright, N. Nature's capacities and their measurement. Oxford: Clarendon. (1989).

[2] Giere, R. Explaining science. Chicago: University of Chicago Press. (1988).

[3] Giere, R. Using models to represent reality. In L. Magnani, N. Nersessian, & P. Thagard (Eds.), Model-based reasoning in scientific discovery. New York: Kluwer. (1999).

[4] Giere, R. Scientific perspectivism. Chicago: University of Chicago press. (2006).

[5] Gross, A. The rhetoric of science. Cambridge MA: Harvard University Press. (1990).

［6］Hoover, E. M., & Giarratani, F. An introduction to regional economics. In S. Loveridge. (Ed.), The Web Book of regional science (http://www.rri.wvu.edu/regscweb.htm). Morgantown, WV: Regional Research Institute, West Virginia University. (1999).

［7］Kirkham, R. Theories of truth. Cambridge MA: MIT. (1995).

［8］McCloskey, D. N. The rhetoric of economics. Journal of Economic Literature, (1983). Vol.31, pp.434-461.

［9］Mäki, U. On the method of isolation in economics. Poznan Studies in the Philosophy of the Sciences and the Humanities, (1992). Vol.26, pp.319-354.

［10］Mäki, U. Isolation, idealization and truth in economics. Poznan Studies in the Philosophy of the Sciences and the Humanities, (1994). Vol.38, pp.147-168.

［11］Mäki, U. Diagnosing McCloskey. Journal of Economic Literature, (1995). Vol.33, pp.1300-1318.

［12］Mäki, U. Models. In: International encyclopedia of the social and behavioral sciences. Amsterdam: Elsevier. (2001). Vol.15, pp.9931-9937.

［13］Mäki, U. Realism and the nature of theory: A lesson from J. H. von Thünen for economists and geographers. Environment and Planning A, (2004a). Vol.36, pp.1719-1736.

［14］Mäki, U. Some truths about truth for economists, their critics and clients. In P. Mooslechner, H. Schuberth, & M. Schurtz (Eds.), Economic policy-making under uncertainty: The role of truth and accountability in policy advice. Cheltenham: Edward Elgar. (2004b). pp.9-39.

［15］Mäki, U. Models are experiments, experiments are models. Journal of Economic Methodology, (2005). Vol.12, pp.303-315.

［16］Mäki, U. Realistic realism about unrealistic models. In H. Kincaid & D. Ross (Eds.), Oxford handbook of the philosophy of economics. Oxford: Oxford University Press. (2009a). pp.68-98.

［17］Mäki, U. MISSing the world:Models as isolations and credible surrogate systems. Erkenntnis, (2009b). Vol.70, pp.29-43.

［18］Mäki, U. Models and truth. The functional decomposition approach. In European Philosophy of Science 2007. Berlin: Springer. (2009c).

［19］Nowak, L. The structure of idealization. Dordrecht: Reidel. (1980).

［20］Peet, J. R. The spatial expansion of commercial agriculture in the nineteenth century: A von Thünen interpretation. Economic Geography, (1969). Vol.45, pp.283-301.

［21］Suarez, M. An inferential conception of scientific representation. Philosophy of Science, (2004). Vol.71(5), pp.767-779.

［22］von Thünen, J. H. Der isolierte Staat in Beziehung auf Landwirtschaft und Nationalökonomie. Jena: Verlag von Gustav Fischer. (1910).

［23］von Thünen, J. H. Von Thünen's isolated state (P. Hall, Ed., C. M. Wartenberg, Trans.). Oxford: Pergamon. (1966).

［24］Waskan, J. Models and cognition. Cambridge, MA: MIT. (2006).

（本文原载于《综合》2011 年第 180 卷第 1 期）

Models and the locus of their truth

Uskali Mäki

Abstract: If models can be true, where is their truth located? Giere (Explaining science, University of Chicago Press, Chicago, 1988) has suggested an account of theoretical models on which models themselves are not truth-valued. The paper suggests modifying Giere's account without going all the way to purely pragmatic conceptions of truth—while giving pragmatics a prominent role in modeling and truth-acquisition. The strategy of the paper is to ask: if I want to relocate truth inside models, how do I get it, what else do I need to accept and reject? In particular, what ideas about model and truth do I need? The case used as an illustration is the world's first economic model, that of von Thünen (1826/1842) on agricultural land use in the highly idealized Isolated State.

Keywords: Representation · Isolation · Idealization · Truth · von Thünen

1. Introduction

Can scientific models be true? If not, why not, and in such a case does the vocabulary of truth find any use in connection to models? If yes, where exactly is the truth in models located and how is this locus determined? These are questions that can be motivated by their relative neglect in the recent boom in the philosophical inquiry into the nature and functions of models in science. My answers to these questions constitute an attempt to spell out the intuition that, after all, models can be true.

Part of my own motivation has originally derived from a chronic irritation by a feature of economists' disciplinary culture: in response to frequent criticisms of building false theoretical models that employ false assumptions, economists often evasively (and undecidedly) say that it is in the nature of models that they are either necessarily false, or that they are neither true nor false.

Rather than constituting a peculiar special case, typical theoretical models in economics have characteristics that make them particularly suitable representatives for an examination of the issue of truth. Those models and their component parts typically appear false, even utterly so. And they are often heavily criticized, sometimes ridiculed, for their shameless falsity. Yet, economists employing such apparently false models often believe them to provide access to important insights into economic reality. At the same time, those economists are generally unable to articulate this belief in terms of truth. While the primary goal of this paper is to contribute to current philosophical literature on a relatively neglected issue about models, its secondary goal is to show how economists and other practicing scientists could be helped to articulate their metatheoretical beliefs about theoretical models (for earlier attempts, see Mäki 1992, 1994, 2004a,b).

Practicing scientists and philosophers hold two views that I argue should be avoided. Both views hold that a model is "just a model" and not intended as anything as serious as a candidate for truth. But the two views infer to this conclusion differently.

The first idea is that models cannot be true because they contain so much falsehood. Models violate "the whole truth" in that they leave much out and cover so little: *models isolate*. They also violate "nothing but the truth" due to containing assumptions that distort the properties of things in the world: *models idealize*. Both of these ideas are joined in the intuitive thought that the world is much richer and more complex than any such thin streamlined models. Therefore, the intuition (and its philosophical articulations) suggests that getting to truth(s), or closer to them, requires that the models be made thicker and richer by relaxing the idealizing assumptions and thereby adding to their complexity: models must be de-isolated and de-idealized. This is the first popular idea that I want to reject in any general form.

My alternative thought is that there is no necessary conflict between a model being true and that model violating the whole truth and nothing but the truth in the way described above. I accept the weaker idea that a model may be true *despite* false assumptions. I also accept—and argue for in this paper—the stronger idea that a model may help capture truths *thanks to* false assumptions. Thus, many truths are attainable without de-isolation by de-idealization—and indeed are attainable in virtue of isolation by idealization.

Note that the first idea—as well as its rejection—is based on the presumption that a model may be truth-valued. This is denied by the second idea that I argue we should consider avoiding. This second view holds that models cannot be true because they are not the sorts of entity that are truth-valued. An example is Giere's (1988) view that models are not truth-valued because they are not linguistic entities (but are rather "abstract objects"). On this view, truth at most resides in linguistic statements about models' properties (on Giere's account, such statements are "theoretical hypotheses" about similarity relations, and these are truth-valued).

My alternative to this second idea is to focus on (the nature and locus of) truth bearers *inside* models—as well as the truth makers that make them true. So I am not only interested in truths *about* models, but want to see how models themselves could be true. What will be attempted is a modification and elaboration of Giere's account so as to relocate truth with respect to models (which gives us a somewhat more radical revision of Giere's account insofar as the issue of truth is concerned). In order to relocate truth *in* models, we mainly need to rethink the bearers and conditions of truth, but we also suggest some rethinking about the concept of model.

The argument presented in this paper exemplifies what I call the *functional decomposition* approach to the study of modelling (Mäki 1992, 2004a,b, 2009c). Models and the respective representations have numerous components with various functions. The argument proceeds through the identification of these components and their functions. Considering the location of the present paper in current philosophy, I take it to address issues that have suffered from a relative neglect. First, the growing body of literature on scientific models and representations has given relatively little systematic attention to issues and concepts of truth. Second, the debates around scientific realism have made strong claims about truth in science, but the specific units of science that might or might not bear those truths have been left obscure. Third, the recent literature on theories of truth has paid relatively little critical and systematic attention to the issues of truth bearers. What follows can be read as an attempt to start putting these issues on the agenda in connection to one another.

So what I want is to give truth a chance, to take a fresh look at the possibility of truth *in* models, or even the truth *of* models (I say more about these two things at the end). The strategic question is: If this is what I want, how do I get it—what else do I need to accept, and what to reject? How do I need to conceive of models and truth to get them into a more intimate connection with one another?

I take models to be isolative representations (see also Mäki 1992, 2001, 2004a, 2005, 2009a,b,c). It is by way of examining this notion that I seek to relocate truth in models. Throughout, von Thünen's famous 1826/1842 model of agricultural land use will be examined as an illustration. The investigation proceeds in three acts. First, *models as isolations*. I discuss the functions of falsehood in von Thünen's model and elaborate on the notions of idealization and isolation. Second, *models as representations*. I outline my account of the very concept of model as pragmatically enabled and constrained representation with representative and resemblance aspects. Third, *models as truth containers*. I ask what moves are required to accommodate the intuition that a highly unrealistic model—such as Thünen's—captures some truths about the world.

2. Models: isolation by idealization

The simple model of agricultural land use distribution given in Johann Heinrich von Thünen's famous classic *Der isolierte Staat in Beziehung auf Landwirtschaft und Nationalökonomie* (1826/1842) is sometimes called the world's first economic model. Moreover, it has turned out to have a lasting significance. The model remains standard textbook material, and its variations are still widely used in economic geography and geographical economics, in subfields such as location theory, urban economics, and regional science. Given that the model has a geographical dimension, many of its features can be represented visually, which is an advantage for illustrating my argument. Most importantly for our purposes, von Thünen's model employs numerous unrealistic assumptions in envisaging an extremely simple situation that appears to have next to nothing to do with real world situations. It is thus *a most unlikely candidate for truth*, therefore providing a powerful test of my ideas.

The first sentences of von Thünen's book invite the reader to imagine a system that cannot be observed and that does not seem to exist other than in imagination. He does not use the vocabulary of "model", but given that he is clearly describing a model as we nowadays understand this notion, he is implying that a model is an imagined system. This is how his book begins:

> Imagine a very large town, at the centre of a fertile plain which is crossed by no navigable river or canal. Throughout the plain the soil is capable of cultivation and of the same fertility. Far from the town, the plain turns into an uncultivated wilderness which cuts off all communication between this State and the outside world. There are no other towns on the plain. (1966, p.7)

In this opening passage, von Thünen starts listing some of the assumptions that characterize his model of land use in the isolated state. Later contributors have amended the list. The following list is still incomplete (the dissection is mine), but gives a flavour of the sorts of assumption that are needed.

1. The area is a perfect plain: there are no mountains and valleys.

2. The plain is crossed by no navigable river or canal.

3. The soil in the area is throughout capable of cultivation.

4. The soil in the area is homogenous in fertility.

5. The climate is uniform across the state.

6. All communication between the area and the outside world is cut off by an uncultivated wilderness.

7. At the center of the plain there is a town with no spatial dimensions.

8. There are no other towns in the area.

9. All industrial activity takes place in the town.

10. All markets and hence all interactions between the producers are located in the town.

11. The interaction between producers is restricted to the selling and buying of final products: there are no intermediate products and no non-market relationships between producers.

12. Transportation costs are directly proportional to distance and to the weight and perishability of the good.

13. All prices and transportation costs are fixed.

14. Production costs are constant over space.

15. The agents are rational maximizers of their revenues.

16. The agents possess complete relevant information.

Assumptions 1-16 provide von Thünen's simplest model of land use. The striking observation is that if considered as statements about the world, the assumptions are clearly false, many of them being very far from the truth about typical actual situations. Their falsehood is evident from the start, thus their recognition as false does not emerge as an outcome of some *expost* empirical testing, for example. Indeed, they are not hypotheses or conjectures that are examined as candidates for truth.[①] Instead, they are purposeful falsehoods that are strategically mobilized and manipulated. They are instances of *idealizing assumptions* employed in modelling, deliberate and strategic falsehood being their characteristic feature. The question to ask then is: what's the point? What function can they possibly serve?

The answer is: the function of such falsehoods is isolation by idealization (Mäki 1992, 1994).[②] Idealizing assumptions 1-16 serve the function of neutralizing a number of causally relevant factors by eliminating them or their efficacy. Assumption 1 eliminates the impact of mountains and valleys on land use. Assumption 2 eliminates the impact of rivers and canals on land use. Assumption 4 eliminates the impact of variation in soil fertility while assumption 5 eliminates the impact of variation in climate. Assumption 6 isolates the area from the rest of the world, eliminating the impact of trade (hence "the Isolated State"). Assumption 12 eliminates the impact of roads and railways and any sort of preservation technology (von Thünen envisaged that delivery to the town takes place by oxcart). And so on.

In analogy to the experimental procedure, such idealizing assumptions in many contexts serve the further strategic purpose of *theoretical isolation*. By neutralizing other subsidiary causes and conditions, they help isolate a major cause and its characteristic way of operation. This is also what happens in von Thünen's case. What is isolated by his simple model is *distance (or transportation costs) as a major cause of land use distribution*. This insight will play a core role in my argument.

Note that the term "isolation" appears also in von Thünen's own exposition: he is analyzing land use in the "Isolated State". The state, or the

---

① The English translation of von Thünen's book (1966) may mislead: "'Voraussetzungen' has been translated as "Hypotheses" which may suggest that their truth-value is an open question. I am calling them "assumptions" instead.

② My terminology deviates somewhat from that used by some others. For example, my use of "abstraction" and "concretization" is more restricted than that of Nowak (1980) or Cartwright (1989). I explain and defend my use of "(de-)isolation", "(de-)idealization", "abstraction", and "concretization" in Mäki (1992, 1994).

area, is assumed to be isolated from the rest of the world so as to eliminate any influences on land use from outside the area itself. What I have suggested is the idea that von Thünen's model isolates one causal factor from all others, whether inside or outside of the area. So I am using "isolation" in a more general sense than did von Thünen himself. It is noteworthy that von Thünen's working title for his book was *Der ideale Staat* (The Ideal State), which is in some ways more informative than *Der isolierte Staat* (The Isolated State). *Der ideale Staat* aptly captures the nature of his model in depicting a very idealized system. It also highlights the fact that the system is "ideal" in the sense of being imagined by our ideational powers.

Indeed, we were invited by von Thünen to imagine a highly idealized system characterized by a set of idealizing assumptions. Right after having outlined a few of those assumptions, he asks what happens in the imagined situation, that is, in the model. What sort of land use pattern will emerge?

> What pattern of cultivation will take shape in these conditions?; and how will the farming system of different districts be affected by their distance from the Town? (1966, p.8)

He then immediately answers the question, that is, he describes the outcome that emerges within the model. It is the land use pattern under the peculiar circumstances characterized by the idealizations of the model.

> ...near the town will be grown those products which are heavy or bulky in relation to their value and hence so expensive to transport that the remoter districts are unable to supply them. Here too we shall find the highly perishable products, which must be used very quickly. With increasing distance from the Town, the land will progressively be given up to products cheap to transport in relation to their value. For this reason alone, fairly sharply differentiated concentric rings or belts will form around the Town, each with its own particular staple product. (1966, p.8)

So what emerges is a pattern of concentric rings around the point-like town where the market lies. On the inner rings, we find dairying and intensive farming of vegetables and fruit because products such as milk and tomatoes must be transported to the market quickly; and the production of timber and firewood because they are heavy and bulky, hence expensive to transport in relation to their value. On the outermost ring, we find stock farming or ranching because animals are self-transporting, they can walk to the town to be sold or butchered. In between, there are rings for extensive farming of crops such as grains that are more durable than fruit and less heavy than wood. The upper half of Fig. 1 describes the pattern of the famous *Thünen rings*.

In the lower half of the image, von Thünen envisages a situation that emerges in a model that has two characteristics that are missing in the simplest version: a river flowing through the central city and a smaller subsidiary town. Assumptions 2 and 8 that describe the simplest model are here relaxed.

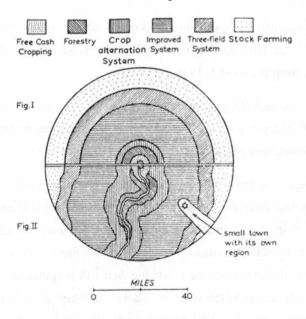

Fig. 1　Thünen rings: land use in the model world. *Source*: von Thünen (1966, p.216)

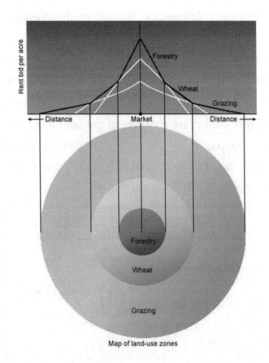

Fig. 2　Inferring land use zones from rent gradients. *Source*: Hoover and Giarratani (1999)

It is important to see that von Thünen's exposition suggests that the model is distinct from its descriptions. The model here is the imagined world, possessing the characteristics provided by the set of idealizing assumptions and missing many characteristics of real world situations. The model is being described by those assumptions and by the figure of concentric rings. It can also be described in terms of various mathematical instruments. So we can have various verbal, geometric, and algebraic descriptions of features of the model.

The first implication of the separation between model and its descriptions highlights the *locus of inference in modelling*. The properties and behaviour of the model are examined by inferring from some of its features to some others—such as from those given by assumptions 1-16 to those that can be visualized in terms of zones that have the form of concentric rings. Here the role of model descriptions becomes essential. The properties of the model are examined by performing inferences among model descriptions. Land-use patterns are derived through land values, or rent gradients (as they became to be called in the later Thünenian tradition). This derivation is shown in Fig. 2. [①] The facts that correspond to this inference in the model itself are that land rents are higher closer to the city and transportation costs are higher further away from the city; and that land users compete in the land market maximizing their net revenues, and are pulled by the two cost factors, finally settling on a location that balances them so as to give rise to the pattern of concentric rings. I will call this set of facts *the Thünen mechanism*.

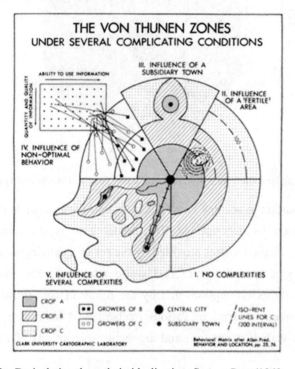

Fig. 3 De-isolation through de-idealization. *Source*: Peet (1969, p.287)

Now thinking of von Thünen's assumptions and the Thünen's rings from the point of view of truth, the striking observation is that there seems to be

---

① This perspective connects with accounts of models that focus on their inferential functions (e.g. Suarez 2004). In my account, the representational and inferential perspectives complement one another.

nothing close to the truth in the offing. Falsehood rules. What we see is a set of utterly false assumptions and an utterly false prediction. The assumptions appear to get the facts wrong about the world, and there are no concentric rings to be observed in real-world land use. The model seems just false. As we will see in a later section, von Thünen himself is fully aware of this.

The standard response is to say that what von Thünen has provided is just the simple "first approximation" or some such, and it is only by way of making the model more complex and comprehensive that truth about land use can be approached. We must relax the model's idealizing assumptions one by one, thereby letting previously excluded causal factors work out their impact on the outcome, to get closer to the true representation. This is to say we must continue the process started in the lower half of Fig. 1. So de-isolation through de-idealization offers the only route to truth, or so the popular doctrine mentioned in the introduction goes (see, e.g., Nowak 1980). Figure 3 illustrates this.

Here one begins with the simple case of concentric rings (Sect. 1), governed merely by the Thünen mechanism. One then adds some variation in fertility (Sect. 2) and another town (Sect. 3), then relaxes the perfect rationality assumption (Sect. 4). By proceeding like this, and finally combining many such relevant "complexities", one hopes to create an image of land use that is close to the true representation (Sect. V). It is undeniable that such a procedure of de-isolation is needed for acquiring some interesting truths about the world. But I dispute the popular doctrine that de-isolation through de-idealization provides the only route to all possible truths. I will argue instead that von Thünen's simplest model is in principle capable of conveying importantly true information about the world without de-isolation (Mäki 1992, 1994, 2004a,b).

But first I point out a troubling feature of the above reasoning. This is the second implication of the separation between models and their descriptions, dealing with the representational—rather than inferential—functions of models. Model descriptions are what their name suggests: they describe models rather than the real world. If one takes the separation between models and their descriptions strictly, it becomes problematic to say that the idealizing assumptions 1-16 are false of the real world. The same applies to the image of concentric rings. They are true about the model, and they are neither true nor false about the target of the model. To deal with this issue, we first need to understand what it is for a model to represent. So I next outline an account of models as representations.

3. Models as representations

Like most contemporary philosophers, I treat models as representations. But my account has some special features that need to be spelled out for the purposes of the rest of the argument. I take models as representations to have two aspects: the representative aspect and the resemblance aspect. Models are *representatives* of some target systems: they are surrogate systems that stand for their targets and are examined in place of their targets. *Resemblance* is a further relationship between the surrogate system and the target system dealing with how adequately the model functions as a representative.

The representative aspect highlights the intentionality and voluntary character of models, the fact that model properties are up to us, that models are made by us to serve our interests (captured by the phrase, "anything can serve as model"). The model users' goals and contexts provide the *pragmatic constraints* that shape models, thus there is a strong pragmatic flavour in this account. On the other hand, the resemblance aspect stresses the involuntariness of representation, the fact that models are, or should be, constrained by the characteristics of their targets. This provides an *ontological constraint* on modelling, thus there is also an underlying realist spirit in this conception. My account of models as representations can be nutshelled like this:

> Agent A uses object M (the model) as a representative of target system R for purpose P, addressing audience E, prompting genuine issues of resemblance between M and R to arise; and applies commentary C to identify the above elements and to coordinate their relationships.

This account has some distinct features. It incorporates the idea of *audience* as part of the pragmatics of representation. I find this an uncontroversial amendment to previous accounts of models given the collective nature of scientific work. Models are not built and examined for one's own private pleasures, but largely to meet and shape audience expectations. Models enable communication, models help convey information, models enhance agreement, and models are used to persuade others to revise their belief intensities. Audience-dependence may be explicitly public, and it may be a matter of anticipated audience responses shaping private modelling activities. The role of the audience is also obvious in shaping model descriptions: the media that are employed for describing a model partly depend on the audience that is addressed. Bringing in the audience should be perfectly in the spirit of Giere's account. Together with other purposes P, audiences constitute the pragmatic context that shapes the "perspectives" that Giere (2006) talks about.

The second novelty is that the account requires *prompting genuine issues of resemblance to arise*—rather than successful resemblance or no reference to resemblance at all. By "genuine issue" I mean to express two ideas. First, representation presupposes that M has the capacity to resemble R. Successful resemblance should not come out as utopian, as an unattainable goal regarding which no sensible issue can or should arise as to whether it has or has not been attained. For a genuine issue of resemblance to arise, successful resemblance should lie within our reach, within the horizon of our cognitive possibilities. Second, genuine issues of resemblance do not deal with just any of the numerous arbitrary ways in which M and R do (not) and might (not) resemble one another. At issue are specific respects and degrees of resemblance that meet the pragmatic constraints at desired levels of abstraction.

Mere resemblance is not sufficient for representation. Think of the pattern of concentric rings in the model world of the Isolated State. This pattern may resemble very closely the real-world pattern I create by dropping a pebble in a still water. Yet, the Thünen pattern is not a representation of this or any other real pattern on the surface of water—simply because it is not properly related to the model that von Thünen intended to construct as a representative of agricultural land use dynamics. For the issue of resemblance to arise, the respective representative must be about the intended or otherwise relevant domain. The relevant domain can be partly identified by the pragmatic constraints, and partly by the kinds of causal mechanism presum-ably in operation. The causal mechanisms responsible for the patterns of land use in the Isolated State and for the patterns on the surface of water are too different for the resemblance of these patterns to be at all illuminating. This is a remarkable point given that the pattern of concentric rings may have a far greater resemblance with a pattern on the surface of water than with any real-world land use patterns.

This last observation may seem like saying that resemblance is not necessary for representation either. But on the other hand I have claimed that representation does require the resemblance aspect, so the representative aspect alone is not sufficient for representation. The tension resolves in two steps. First, representation does not require achieved resemblance but just the issue of resemblance to arise. Second, representation does not require that the issue of resemblance would legitimately arise in regard to all parts of the target in all possible respects. I will next explain how my account helps take the second step; I will then point out an implication and an alternative phrasing of the first.

Representation does not require that all parts of the model resemble the target in all or just any arbitrary respects, or that the issue of resemblance legitimately arises in regard to all parts. The relevant model parts and the relevant respects and degrees of resemblance must be delimited. The important observation is that the model itself is unable to discriminate between its various parts (m_1, m_2, m_3,...) as serving different functions. This is where the pragmatic components take on active roles. The pragmatic constraints determine the required respects and degrees of resemblance—instead of complete and precise resemblance—between model M and target R. In accomplishing this, the recognition of the relevant purposes P and audiences E helps assign different functions to different model parts. So we may say that the required respects and degrees of resemblance are a function of M, R, P, E where M consists of m_1, m_2, m_3,...

But this function lacks the capacity to identify itself, so it cannot speak on its own behalf. The challenge is to identify and coordinate the various components so as to align them with one another in such a way that both the

ontological and pragmatic constraints will be met. This is where Commentary
C enters the picture. It supplies connecting links between the components such
that it becomes clear what aspects and degrees of resemblance are to be sought,
and how various model parts play their roles in pursuing the goals. The role of
Commentary will be illustrated in the next section. The first step mentioned
above has implications for the issue of "misrepresentation" occasionally
addressed in recent discussion on models. Part of this discussion seems
confused due to a failure to keep the representative and resemblance aspects of
representation sufficiently separate. The immediate implication of my account
is that "representation" is not a success term with any high degree of ambition
in terms of resemblance. Using a representative of some target for some
purpose while facing the issue of resemblance is to represent. Now failure to
represent in this sense is not what "misrepresentation" is usually taken to
denote. I think it is rather supposed to be used when talking about failure to
resemble. But this tends to be obscured because the representative and
resemblance aspects are not clearly distinguished.

Naturally, an account of scientific representation must accommodate
failures. The notion of "prompting issues of resemblance to arise" starts taking
care of this. Failing to prompt those issues is a major failure in representation
(and it is here that "misrepresentation" may be appropriately applied), while
failing to resemble is a lesser failure. Respectively, prompting issues of
resemblance gives us weak success, while succeeding to resemble is a matter of
stronger success.

Another way of characterizing successful representation by a model is to
say that in virtue of pursuing and possibly achieving the right kind of
resemblance between the model and the target, the direct examination of the
model's properties may indirectly provide information about the properties of
the target. One learns about the target by studying the model. This is what
justifies calling the model a *surrogate system* that potentially provides
epistemic access beyond itself, to the target system. By contrast, if the study of
a model at most yields information about the model's properties, perhaps
because there is no interest in anything beyond the model, or because the

model lacks the capacity to resemble the target, the model only functions as a *substitute system*. While a surrogate system functions as a bridge to the target, a substitute system is a disconnected island with no links to the real world (Mäki 2009a,b).

Of course, we may want to be more relaxed about successful representation by bracketing target *R* and focusing just on *M-P-E* relations. For example, we may be able to say that an *M* serves a useful purpose in educating the audience of students of urban economics to operate with rent gradients. No doubt von Thünen's model provides a simple set-up that facilitates learning a craft—this is one reason why the model is included in standard contemporary textbooks. But such functions of a model do not rule out its capacity to serve other functions, such as highlighting truths about the world, or inspiring the construction of further models that have this capacity.

4. Models and truth

Putting now our challenge explicitly in terms of truth, we ask: What would it be for a model to be true or to contain truths? What is the locus of truth in relation to models? Where should we look to find it? The account of models that I have suggested offers a few possible lines along which to think of how to ascribe truth to models. I think I have already revealed my preferences that direct the attention towards the notion of resemblance, but this is not the only possibility. There are other options that isolate and exploit the *pragmatic* components in the notion of model as representation: purpose and audience.

Indeed, we can *get truth into models* by adopting a suitable pragmatic concept of truth and then ascribing the respective pragmatic property to models. The account of models in the previous section makes two such pragmatic properties available: usefulness in regard to a purpose, and persuasiveness in regard to an audience. Respectively, concepts of truth can be put in these terms: *truth as usefulness* in serving a purpose, and *truth as persuasiveness* in shaping or conforming to the beliefs of an audience. A given model may thus be said to be true if it successfully serves a purpose such as helping attain a policy goal; or if it is found persuasive by an audience, enticing the audience to accept the model. [①]Note that both of these options—the usefulness notion of truth and the rhetorical notion of truth—are inclined towards treating models in an indiscriminate manner. Truth is ascribed to models as wholes, not to some limited parts of them.

This is not my strategy of getting truth into models, but I will not discuss these conceptions here (but see, for example, Mäki 2004b) other than pointing out a couple of intuitions that I am not prepared to sacrifice. An agent *A* can successfully use a false model *M* to impress an audience *E*. And *A* can successfully use a false model *M* to serve some other purpose *P*. These intuitions suggest that truth is independent of usefulness and persuasiveness.

So when attempting to locate truth in relation to models, one should not have one's primary focus on the *M-P* and *M-E* relations. One should instead start first with isolating the *M-R* relation from the pragmatic components in representation. Once this focus is chosen, an account is needed that is able to pay respect for another intuition, namely that *A* can successfully use a model *M* that involves a lot of apparent falsehood to capture truths about target *R*. A key principle that guides my thinking is that *a model is a structure with component parts that may have different and varying functional roles, including the role of primary truth bearer*. These roles are partly determined by pragmatic components *P* and *E* (and identified by Commentary *C)*. So at this second stage *P* and *E* are brought back to the stage: they make indispensable contributions to truth acquisition. But *P* and *E* do not constitute truth. They rather help isolate relevant truth bearers within models. Truth acquisition is a joint product of a pursuit that meets the pragmatic and ontological constraints of modelling simultaneously.

Let us see how we can spell out this rough idea in somewhat more detail. As I see it, there are two interrelated issues that we must resolve. One is the locus issue: where in models might the appropriate truth bearers be located? The other is the stuff issue: what is the appropriate ontology of truth bearers?

---

① Philosophers are familiar with the tradition of usefulness accounts of truth, but perhaps less knowledgeable about persuasiveness accounts of truth, popular in the recent rhetoric of inquiry movement (see, e.g. McCloskey 1983; Gross 1990; for criticisms, see Mäki 1995).

It is useful to start with Giere's account since the account I am pursuing can be viewed as a (more or less radical) modification of his. On Giere's account, models are non-linguistic "abstract objects" that are linguistically described or defined by assumptions. Since models are not linguistic, they are devoid of truth-value. Since model descriptions are linguistic, they are truth-valued, and because they "define" what they are about, they are trivially true. Models are connected to their targets, not by truth but by similarity. Model systems may be similar to their target systems in varying respects and degrees. Further statements are needed about these relationships. These are the theoretical hypotheses that are truth-valued (linguistic) claims about (respects and degrees of) similarity between the model and the real system (Giere 1988, 1999, 2006).

So on this account, models themselves are not true or false, nor do they contain truths, but true claims can be made *about* models. So much for the locus issue. The requirement that truth bearers be linguistic suggests a stance on the stuff issue. I will challenge the truth-scepticism in Giere's account by dealing with these two issues and showing how we might get truth inside models. I will remobilize von Thünen as my spokesman for the idea of truth-in-models (while I admit that some interpretation is needed since he does not explicitly invoke the vocabulary of truth).

So what are the relevant truth bearers and real-world truth makers in regard to von Thünen's model? One option would be to say that the assumptions of the model are its truth bearers. These are linguistic, so would satisfy Giere's requirement. But there is nothing in the real world that would make them true. As von Thünen agrees, the idealizing assumptions are false, and they are false in the sense that they do not correspond to real-world conditions. But they are indispensable strategic falsehoods:

> I hope the reader who is willing to spend some time and attention on my work will not take exception to the *imaginary assumptions* I make at the beginning because they *do not correspond to conditions in reality*, and that he will not reject these assumptions as arbitrary or pointless. They *are*

a necessary part of my argument, allowing me to establish the operation of a certain factor, a factor whose operation we see but dimly in reality, where it is in incessant conflict with others of its kind. (1966, pp.3-4; italics added)

Another option is to view the pattern of concentric rings as the truth bearer of the model. These are geometric images, thus not quite in Giere's approved category. And actual land-use patterns would seem to do a poor job as truth makers anyway. However, there is often an abstract resemblance in place: land-use is frequently patterned in some rough zone-like manner. But even this can be defeated if other causal factors are strong enough. In any case, in regard to further details on top of zone-likeness, the degree of resemblance varies from case to case, from fairly close to hardly recognizable.

In response to both of these candidates for truth bearer status—the assumptions and the geometric pattern—the obvious objection is that they do not constitute the model, they rather describe it. We would not get truth inside the model. And even if they were accepted as truth bearers, their truth maker would be the model itself, not anything in the real world. However, I see no reason not to be more flexible about this. We can as well consider the assumptions and the pattern also as possible truth bearers that are false (rather than truth-valueless) about that target. This manner of speaking does not rule out the primary role of the assumptions and the pattern to truly describe the model (and the primary truth bearers within the model regarding the target to lie elsewhere).

A third option finally gets the relevant truth bearer inside the model. I first focus on the locus issue and will take up the stuff issue in a moment. Now think of what sorts of thing inhabit von Thünen's model, the Isolated State. This imagined world is one with perfectly informed maximizing farmers competing for parcels of land and ending up with cultivating a flat and evenly fertile soil with no rivers or roads or external trade. If there is a natural truth bearer here, it is neither this model as a whole nor just any arbitrary parts of it. It is rather a special component of the model, namely the causal power or mechanism that drives this simple model world: the Thünen mechanism. This truth bearer has a fair chance of being made true by its truth maker, the respective prominent causal "force" or mechanism in the real system. It is the mechanism that contributes to the transformation of distance into land use patterns through transportation costs and land values. At any rate this appears to be von Thünen's own view:

> The principle that gave the isolated state its shape *is also present in reality*, but the phenomena which here bring it out manifest themselves in changed forms, since they are also influenced at the same time by several other relations and conditions. …we may divest an acting force [eine wirkende Kraft] of all incidental conditions and everything accidental, and *only in this way can we recognize [erkennen] its role in producing the phenomena before us*. (1910, p.274; my translation, italics added)

As I read this comment, Thünen here combines two ideas. The model isolates the major cause of land use, the functioning of the *wirkende Kraft* of distance, from all its other causes. And what the model isolates theoretically is also present in the real system even though here it is not isolated from other influences. In short, the *wirkende Kraft* in the imagined model world is the truth bearer and the respective *wirkende Kraft* in the real world is its truth maker. Whatever else the model contains, and whatever else modifies the manifestation of the *Kraft* in the real world do not participate in the truth making of the model. This is von Thünen's solution to the locus issue.

In dealing with the locus issue, the model Commentary plays a crucial role. The other components of the representation are unable to identify the relevant truth bearers, and in general to assign suitable functions to various model parts. A Commentary is needed to perform a higher-order isolation of the truth bearers amongst the ingredients of a model. Another way of putting this is to say that the Commentary helps determine the respects in which resemblance between the model and the target is to be sought. Illustrations have been provided already: the passages I have quoted from von Thünen, especially the last two, are important parts of his Commentary of his model.

As I said earlier, the task of the Commentary is to identify and coordinate the various components in a representation. The isolation of truth bearers in the model is dependent on specific cognitive goals (to establish the operation of the *Kraft* in contributing to land use patterns) and audience expectations (note that Thünen explicitly addresses his comments to the "reader"), and it is the task of the Commentary to help manage these dependencies in varying contexts.

The Commentary also helps turn mere resemblance (or similarity) into truth. This is needed because resemblance is symmetric, while truth is asymmetric. In order to say that the model is true or contains truth about the target, we must establish that there is resemblance between the relevant truth bearer in the model and its truth maker in the target, and that indeed truth-making runs in this direction.

Now suppose we have settled the locus issue. The next step is to ask whether we can envisage tolerable solutions to the stuff issue such that we can stick to the above solution of the locus issue. Is there suitable stuff available in that location?

In attempting to get truth in models, one line to be pursued would be a radical pluralism about the ontology of truth bearers: any kind of stuff goes, from sentence tokens to visual images, from propositions to utterances, from beliefs to physical objects, and so on. [1] This would allow things such as a concrete image of concentric rings or an abstract object of the Isolated State to serve as truth bearers. Whatever the ontology of models, truth-values can be ascribed.

Another line would be to take the more restrained view that—at least some, or ultimately all—truth bearers are thoughts. Recall that von Thünen's first passage begins with "Imagine ..." suggesting that the Isolated State is an imagined system. Supposing that to imagine is to think, this is still ambiguous as to whether thoughts are the stuff of which the Isolated State is made, or whether the model is separable from the respective thoughts.

---

[1] Such as teddy bears! In Kirkham's catchy phrase, "truth is not too big a burden for a bare bear to bear" (Kirkham 1995, p. 61).

One possibility is to view thoughts as mental objects (such as *the thought of the Iso-lated State*). This could be taken to involve a language of thought with a mental logic, which would nowadays be viewed as an unattractive option. Alternatively, it could be taken to involve "cognitive equivalents of scale models" (Waskan 2006), which might be a more attractive idea. Closer to Giere's view of the stuff of models, we may take a model and the respective thought separable. Instead of thought as a mental object, we could focus on *what is thought* as an abstract object. Such an abstract object could have a thing-like structure (such as *the Isolated State containing the Kraft*), or it could have a fact-like structure (such as *that the Kraft—distance through the land-value plus transportation-cost mechanism—strongly contributes to land use distributions*). Such abstract objects could function as truth bearers, in contrast to Giere's view. A possible further line to take would be to offer a compromise to Giere by expressing the propositional contents of the last mentioned fact-like structure in sentential terms ("the *Kraft* strongly contributes to land use distributions") and taking this as a linguistic truth bearer whose truth makers lie in the real world target. Its propositional contents would be equivalent with the respective abstract object in the model. We do not need to choose between these different options in order to suggest that the stuff issue might be resolvable in such a way that we can have truth bearers inside models.

Insofar as von Thünen's model contains a truth about the *Kraft*, we may be tempted to call it a partial truth. This would seem right for two reasons. First, the *Kraft* is only one among many causal factors actually shaping land use. A truth about the *Kraft* is a partial truth of the whole causal structure. Second, only one part of the model— and not other parts—is identified by the Commentary as the relevant truth bearer that reflects the relevant respects in which the model is supposed to be connected to its target. But on the other hand, once the part has been isolated, what we have may be the whole truth about that part—such as the *Kraft*—at a certain level of abstraction. This weakens the second reason.

In any event, whether partial or whole, it is not as such approximate truth. If we take partial truth to reflect the respects of resemblance or similarity between the model and its target, approximate truth can be viewed as reflecting degrees of resemblance, once the relevant respects have been fixed. In other words, Giere's distinction between respects and degrees can be utilized to enrich our talk about truth in relation to models: models have the capacity of containing partial truths and approximate truths. But these are truths in models, not truths about models—and they are species of truth, not just of similarity.

The final issue remains whether we might now be entitled to talk about truth *of* models or more modestly just about truth *in* models. The latter is clearly less problematic. We have located a component in the Isolated State, the Thünen mechanism, and it is right here that we may have a truth *in* Thünen's model. Now there is a way of seeing things that would permit us to infer that we may also have truth *of* Thünen's model. Having the above truth *in* Thünen's model means having the truth *of* its component. If component m_n—the Thünen mechanism—has been isolated (under the guidance of the pragmatics of this representation) as *the only* relevant truth bearer in model M, then this means that the truth of m_n is both truth *in* M and truth *of* M. So we may say M is true simply because none of its other parts are supposed to be relevant candidates for truth. These other parts are not idle parts: in many cases they (if interpreted as truth valued) must be false in order to serve the higher goal of getting the privileged component true. Given the pragmatic constraints, there are no other veristic aspirations but to ensure the truth of that privileged component part. So saying that m_n is true and saying that M is true amount to the same thing. I am not claiming that one is compelled to talk in this way about truth in models and truth of models, just that one might not be compelled not to.

References

Cartwright, N. (1989). *Nature's capacities and their measurement.* Oxford: Clarendon. Giere, R. (1988). *Explaining science.* Chicago: University of Chicago Press.

Giere, R. (1999). Using models to represent reality. In L. Magnani, N. Nersessian, & P. Thagard (Eds.),

Model-based reasoning in scientific discovery. New York: Kluwer.

Giere, R. (2006). *Scientific perspectivism*. Chicago: University of Chicago press. Gross, A. (1990). *The rhetoric of science*. Cambridge MA: Harvard University Press.

Hoover, E. M., & Giarratani, F. (1999). An introduction to regional economics. In S. Loveridge. (Ed.), *The Web Book of regional science* (http://www.rri.wvu.edu/regscweb.htm). Morgantown, WV: Regional Research Institute, West Virginia University.

Kirkham, R. (1995). *Theories of truth*. Cambridge MA: MIT.

McCloskey, D. N. (1983). The rhetoric of economics. *Journal of Economic Literature, 31*, 434-461.

Mäki, U. (1992). On the method of isolation in economics. *Poznan Studies in the Philosophy of the Sciences and the Humanities, 26*, 319-354.

Mäki, U. (1994). Isolation, idealization and truth in economics. *Poznan Studies in the Philosophy of the Sciences and the Humanities, 38*, 147-168.

Mäki, U. (1995). Diagnosing McCloskey. *Journal of Economic Literature, 33*, 1300-1318.

Mäki, U. (2001). Models. In: *International encyclopedia of the social and behavioral sciences* (Vol.15, pp.9931-9937). Amsterdam: Elsevier.

Mäki, U. (2004a). Realism and the nature of theory: A lesson from J. H. von Thünen for economists and geographers. *Environment and Planning A, 36*, 1719-1736.

Mäki, U. (2004b). Some truths about truth for economists, their critics and clients. In P. Mooslechner,

H. Schuberth, & M. Schurtz (Eds.), *Economic policy-making under uncertainty: The role of truth and accountability in policy advice* (pp.9-39). Cheltenham: Edward Elgar.

Mäki, U. (2005). Models are experiments, experiments are models. *Journal of Economic Methodology, 12*, 303-315.

Mäki, U. (2009a). Realistic realism about unrealistic models. In H. Kincaid & D. Ross (Eds.), *Oxford handbook of the philosophy of economics* (pp.68-98). Oxford: Oxford University Press.

Mäki, U. (2009b). MISSing the world: Models as isolations and credible surrogate systems. *Erkenntnis, 70*, 29-43.

Mäki, U. (2009c). Models and truth. The functional decomposition approach. In *European Philosophy of Science 2007*. Berlin: Springer.

Nowak, L. (1980). *The structure of idealization*. Dordrecht: Reidel.

Peet, J. R. (1969). The spatial expansion of commercial agriculture in the nineteenth century: A von Thünen interpretation. *Economic Geography, 45*, 283-301.

Suarez, M. (2004). An inferential conception of scientific representation. *Philosophy of Science, 71*(5), 767-779.

von Thünen, J. H. (1910). *Der isolierte Staat in Beziehung auf Landwirtschaft und Nationalökonomie*. Jena: Verlag von Gustav Fischer.

von Thünen, J. H. (1966). *Von Thünen's isolated state* (P. Hall, Ed., C. M. Wartenberg, Trans.). Oxford: Pergamon.

Waskan, J. (2006). *Models and cognition*. Cambridge, MA: MIT.

后　记

　　本书收录了南开大学哲学院（系）科技哲学教研室教师们近几十年来撰写发表的部分学术论文，由于时间仓促，加之处于疫情期间，没有能够在短期内收集到所有在教研室工作过的老师们的文章，敬请谅解！所收录的这些论文的作者都（曾）在科技哲学教研室从事过教学和科研工作，值此南开哲学学科创建 103 年及哲学（系）复建 60 周年之际，谨结集出版本文集，向所有（曾）在南开科技哲学工作的老师们致以敬意，感谢他们为南开、为南开哲学所作的奉献。

　　尽管这些论文的选题跨度很大，涉及领域众多，但我们还是可以从中找到一系列共性和主线，而科学、技术与哲学构成文集最基本的三个关键词，这就是对科学（技术）认识以及其属性的哲学反思。从内容来看，这些论文所研究和关注的主题方向非常宽泛，涉及了科技哲学的诸多领域，具体包括了科学认识论、科学哲学与科学史、社会科学哲学、科学社会学等各层面的内容，均为我国当代科技哲学研究的重要议题。从研究的视野或方法论等来看，这些论文也集中反映了自 20 世纪 80 年代以来我国科学哲学典型的研究进路，其中所运用的方法论具有一定的时代特色，从中也能够见证国内科学哲学脉络演变的一些规律。为了能够在这本论文集中立体地展现南开科学技术哲学近几十年的发展轨迹和特色，以及不同时期论文写作和取材等方面的原本面貌，我们在选择论文方向、议题甚至行文格式等方面都尽量保持了原来的样态，只是为了论文集形式的统一性才作了一些必要的变动。同时值得欣喜的是，近几年我们的科学技术哲学研究又增加了数位国际学者的加盟，这样一来，论文集就有了一定的国际化色彩。

　　还需要特别指出的是，自 20 世纪特别是 70 年代末 80 年代初哲学系在全国范围很早就建立起自然辩证法教研室开始，在哲学系科技哲学领域耕耘的老师们出版和发表过许多重要而有影响的著作和论文，例如本学科的创始人刘珺珺教授在科学哲学、科学史和科学社会学等诸多领域都取得了很大成绩，并被 *Dictionary of International Biography* 专门收录。之后李建珊教授、任晓明教授、Aki 教授等也在科学哲学研究领域产生了很大影响。但限于篇幅和各种条件的要求，我们只能对大部分文章割爱，而根据几个有限的主题来选择少数论文结集成册，论文集只涉及 20 世纪 80 年代以来各个时期本教研室老师们的文章，也请广大读者和专业同仁们见谅和理解。

在论文集的整理和结集过程中，我们得到了哲学院的大力支持，李建珊教授虽远在美国仍实时关注论文集的进展，提供了各种建议和修改意见，翟锦程教授在论文集的内容和取材等方面都给出了详细的建议，管晓柯主任也专门提供了科技哲学教研室的一些历史资料以方便我们整理文集……感谢在我们这一工作中出力的每个人，这里不再一一列举。在文章文字等技术处理过程中，我们专业，特别是 2020 和 2021 级的研究生们做了许多的技术工作，一并感谢！最后，由于编者阅历与学识有限，又需要在特殊时期匆忙完成，其中肯定还存在诸多的疏漏、不足和问题，也请方家多多批评指正。

编　者